Russia and the Right to Self-Determination in the Post-Soviet Space

Russia and the Right to Self-Determination in the Post-Soviet Space

JOHANNES SOCHER

OXFORD
UNIVERSITY PRESS

OXFORD
UNIVERSITY PRESS

Great Clarendon Street, Oxford, OX2 6DP,
United Kingdom

Oxford University Press is a department of the University of Oxford.
It furthers the University's objective of excellence in research, scholarship,
and education by publishing worldwide. Oxford is a registered trade mark of
Oxford University Press in the UK and in certain other countries

Dissertation, Speyer 2019

First Edition published in 2021

Impression: 2

Published in the United States of America by Oxford University Press
198 Madison Avenue, New York, NY 10016, United States of America

British Library Cataloguing in Publication Data

Data available

Library of Congress Control Number: 2020953016

ISBN 978–0–19–289717–6

DOI: 10.1093/oso/9780192897176.001.0001

Printed and bound by
CPI Group (UK) Ltd, Croydon, CR0 4YY

Contents

Table of International Instruments

Table of Court Cases, Rulings, Advisory Opinions, Fact-Finding Reports

Republic of Tatarstan'] (Tatarstan Decision), 13 March 1992, Vedomosti S'ezda Narodnÿkh Deputatov RF i Verkhovnogo Soveta RF 1992, no. 13, item 671 . . . . 71–76, 85

International Court of Justice, *East Timor (Portugal v Australia)*, 30 June 1995, ICJ Reports 1995, 90. . . . . 100–1, 102, 165n.117

Constitutional Court of Russia, *По делу о проверке конституционности Указа Президента Российской Федерации от 30 ноября 1994 года № 2137 «О мероприятиях по восстановлению конституционной законности и правопорядка на территории Чеченской Республики», Указа Президента Российской Федерации от 9 декабря 1994 года № 2166 «О мерах по пресечению деятельности незаконных вооружённых формирований на территории Чеченской Республики и в зоне осетино-ингушского конфликта», постановления Правительства Российской Федерации от 9 декабря 1994 года № 1360 «Об обеспечении государственной безопасности и территориальной целостности Российской Федерации, законности, прав и свобод граждан, разоружения незаконных вооружённых формирований на территории Чеченской Республики и прилегающих к ней регионов Северного Кавказа», Указа Президента Российской Федерации от 2 ноября 1993 года № 1833 «Об Основных положениях военной доктрины Российской Федерации»* [In the Case on the Verification of the Constitutionality of Decree of the President of the Russian Federation no. 2137 of 30 November 1994 'On Measures to Restore the Constitutional Legality and Law and Order on the Territory of the Chechen Republic', the Decree of the President of the Russian Federation no. 2166 of 9 December 1994 'On Measures to Repress the Activity of the Illegal Armed Formation on the Territory of the Chechen Republic and in the Area of the Ingush-Ossetian Conflict', the Decree of the Government of the Russian Federation no. 1360 of 9 December 1994 'On Ensuring State Security and Territorial Integrity of the Russian Federation, the Rule of Law, the Rights and Freedoms of Citizens, the Disarmament of Illegal Armed Groups on the Territory of the Chechen Republic and Adjacent Regions of the North Caucasus', and the Decree of the President of the Russian Federation no. 1833 of 2 November 1993 'On the Fundamental Provisions of the Military Doctrine of the Russian Federation'] (Chechnya Decision), Decision No. 10-P/1995, 31 July 1995, *Rossiĭskaya gazeta*, 11 August 1995 84–86

Supreme Court of Russia, Decree of the Plenum No. 8/1995, 31 October 1995, BVS RF 1996, no. 1, 3 61–63

Supreme Court of Canada, *Reference Re Secession of Québec*, 20 August 1998, 1998 DLR 161, 4th Series, 386 . . . . 90–91, 101n.32, 103, 165–66

International Court of Justice, *Difference Relating to Immunity from Legal Process of a Special Rapporteur of the Commission on Human Rights*, Advisory Opinion, 29 April 1999, ICJ Reports 1999, 62 159–60

Supreme Court of Arbitration of Russia, *О действии международных договоров Российской Федерации применительно к вопросом арбитражного процесса* [On the Effect of International Treaties of the Russian Federation with Regard to the Issue of Arbitration Proceedings], Decision of the Plenum No. 8, 11 June 1999, *Rossiĭskaya yustitsiya* 1999, no. 10, 59 61–62

International Court of Justice, *Kasikili/Sedudu Island (Botswana v Namibia)*, 13 December 1999, ICJ Reports 1999, 1045 201–2

Constitutional Court of Russia, *По делу о проверке конституционности отдельных положений Конституции Республики Алтай и Федерального закона «Об общих принципах организации законодательных (представительных) и исполнительных органов государственной власти*

Table of National Laws and Decrees, Policy Documents, Declarations

Abbreviations

ARC	Autonomous Republic of Crimea
ASSR	Autonomous Soviet Socialist Republic
BMD	Bulletin of International Treaties of Russia
BVS RF	Bulletin of the Supreme Court of Russia
CERD	International Convention on the Elimination of All Forms of Racial Discrimination
CIS	Commonwealth of Independent States
CoE	Council of Europe
CSCE	Conference on Security and Co-operation in Europe
CSTO	Collective Security Treaty Organization
CTS	Consolidated Treaty Series
DLR	Dominion Law Reports
EAEC	Eurasian Economic Community
EAEU	Eurasian Economic Union
ECtHR	European Court of Human Rights
EU	European Union
FSB	Federal Security Service of the Russian Federation
GA	United Nations General Assembly
GAOR	General Assembly Official Records
GUAM	Organization for Democracy and Economic Development—GUAM
HRW	Human Rights Watch
ICC	International Criminal Court
ICCPR	International Covenant on Civil and Political Rights
ICESCR	International Covenant on Economic, Social and Cultural Rights
ICG	International Crisis Group
ICJ	International Court of Justice
ICSFT	International Convention for the Suppression of the Financing of Terrorism
IGP RAN	Institute of State and Law of the Russian Academy of Sciences
IIFFMCG	Independent International Fact-Finding Mission on the Conflict in Georgia
ILC	International Law Commission
ILM	International Legal Materials
ITLOS	International Tribunal for the Law of the Sea
LNOJ	League of Nations Official Journal
LNTS	League of Nations Treaty Series
MFA	Ministry of Foreign Affairs
MGIMO	Moscow State Institute of International Relations
MN	marginal number
MPECCoL	Max Planck Encyclopedia of Comparative Constitutional Law

MPEPIL	Max Planck Encyclopedia of Public International Law
NATO	North Atlantic Treaty Organization
NKAO	Nagorno-Karabakh Autonomous Oblast
NKR	Nagorno-Karabakh Republic
OJ	Official Journal of the European Union
OSCE	Organization for Security and Co-operation in Europe
PACE	Parliamentary Assembly of the Council of Europe
PCA	Permanent Court of Arbitration
PCIJ	Permanent Court of International Justice
PMR	Pridnestrovian Moldavian Republic
RAMP	Russian Association of International Law
RC	Russian Constitution
RIAA	Reports of International Arbitral Awards
SAPP RF	Collected Acts of the President and the Government of Russia
SC	United Nations Security Council
SCO	Shanghai Cooperation Organisation
SFSR	Soviet Federative Socialist Republic
SSR	Soviet Socialist Republic
SZRF	Collected Legislation of Russia
UN	United Nations
UNCIO	United Nations Conference on International Organization
UNCLOS	United Nations Convention on the Law of the Sea
UNESCO	United Nations Educational, Scientific and Cultural Organization
UNOMIG	United Nations Observer Mission in Georgia
UNTS	United Nations Treaty Series
USSR	Union of Soviet Socialist Republics
VCLT	Vienna Convention on the Law of Treaties
Venice Commission	European Commission for Democracy through Law
VVS SSSR	Bulletin of the Supreme Soviet of the Soviet Union
YBUN	Yearbook of the United Nations

Before I started on my way here, I was warned in Petersburg, and was myself aware, that I should find here a talented opponent whose psychological insight and subtlety had gained him peculiar renown in legal circles of recent years. But profound as psychology is, it's a knife that cuts both ways. (Laughter among the public.)

The Brothers Karamazov, Book XII, Ch. 10

Introduction

With the Russian Revolution's centenary in 2017 approaching, the Russian government was faced with the challenge to provide an official interpretation of the historic events that had dismantled the Russian Empire and had led to the rise of the Soviet Union. Unlike the Second World War, which is connected with the victory over fascism and as such an almost undisputed source of pride, the Russian Revolution occupies an ambiguous place in the collective memory of Russians.[1] In the first decade following the Soviet Union's collapse, no-one apart from the Communist Party of the Russian Federation continued to celebrate the 'Great Socialist October Revolution' (as it was called in Soviet historiography), and its remembrance was otherwise not a topic of Russian politics of memory. Under the presidency of Vladimir Putin, this gradually changed[2] and ultimately led to the renaming of the events of the 'Great Russian Revolution' in all Russian schoolbooks to denote their 'tragic greatness', as Alexander Tchoubarian, the director of the Institute of World History of the Russian Academy of Sciences, explained the new formula.[3]

Earlier, Putin had famously called the dissolution of the Soviet Union 'the largest geopolitical catastrophe of the century' that had become 'a real drama' for the Russian people, following which '[t]ens of millions of our fellow citizens and compatriots found themselves outside Russian territory'.[4] According to Putin, this drama was also the fault of the revolutionary Vladimir Lenin, who had placed a 'time bomb' under the structure of the Soviet Union. Speaking in front of the All-Russia People's Front on 25 January 2016, Putin stated:

> Lenin said the state, the Soviet Union should be formed on the basis of full equality with the possibility of seceding from the union … That was the time bomb that was planted under the structure of our statehood. Not only did they

[1] See Ekaterina Makhotina, 'Keine Experimente. Russlands Geschichtspolitik und die Revolution', *Osteuropa* 67 (2017), nos 6–8, 211–30.

[2] Ibid., 219–25.

[3] See 'Важно только не политизировать историю, и тогда место в ней найдётся всему' [It is Only Important Not to Politicise History, and Then There Will Be a Place for Everything in It], *Kommersant*, 31 October 2013.

[4] Послание Федеральному Собранию Российской Федерации [Speech to the Federal Assembly of the Russian Federation], 25 April 2005, http://kremlin.ru/events/president/transcripts/22931.

Russia and the Right to Self-Determination in the Post-Soviet Space. Johannes Socher, Oxford University Press.
 DOI: 10.1093/oso/9780192897176.003.0001

set the borders for ethnic groups of a multinational, essentially unitarian state; the borders were also established arbitrarily, without much reason.[5]

The 'time bomb' Putin referred to is, of course, the principle of self-determination. It is therefore interesting to contrast the Russian president's statement with one of his many references to the same principle in the aftermath of Russia's annexation of Crimea almost two years earlier. Referring to article 2(1) of the UN Charter, Putin stated at the 2014 meeting of the Valdai Discussion Club:

> I have spoken about this on numerous occasions, but if necessary, I can repeat it.... It has all been written down [in the UN Charter], and not simply as the right to self-determination, but as the goal of the United Nations. Read the article carefully. I do not understand why people living in Crimea do not have this right, just like the people living in, say, Kosovo.[6]

1. The Unclear Standard of Self-Determination in International Law

The Russian president is not the only person struggling with the right to self-determination's historical origins and contemporary significance; as a concept of international law, it is widely renowned for its unclarity, with almost every monograph on the topic starting with sort of a disclaimer about its inconsistency.[7] The problem starts already with the difficulty in defining the bearer of the right: nations are, to use Benedict Anderson's famous phrase, 'imagined communities' of common language, culture, and tradition.[8] As such, images of nations are reflections of different social constructions of reality. Different imaginations of groups perceiving themselves as 'peoples' will therefore lead to divergent narratives and

[5] See Meeting of the Russian Popular Front's (ONF) Interregional Forum, 25 January 2016, http://en.kremlin.ru/events/president/news/51206.

[6] Meeting of the Valdai International Discussion Club, 24 October 2014, http://en.kremlin.ru/events/president/news/46860.

[7] See e.g. Michla Pomerance, *Self-determination in Law and Practice: The New Doctrine of the United Nations* (The Hague: Martinus Nijhoff, 1982), 14; Christian Tomuschat, 'Self-determination in a Post-Colonial World', in Christian Tomuschat (ed.), *Modern Law of Self-determination* (Dordrecht: Nijhoff, 1993), 1–20, 15–16; Antonio Cassese, *Self-determination of Peoples: A Legal Reappraisal* (Cambridge: Cambridge University Press, 1995), 1; James Summers, *Peoples and International Law* (Leiden: Brill Nijhoff, 2nd edn, 2014), 32–4, with more references cited therein.

[8] Benedict Anderson, *Imagined Communities: Reflections on the Origin and Spread of Nationalism* (London: Verso, 2nd edn, 1991). On the history and conceptualization of political nationalism see e.g. Eric J. Hobsbawm, *Nations and Nationalism since 1780: Programme, Myth, Reality* (Cambridge: Cambridge University Press, 2nd edn, 1992); Ernest Gellner, *Nations and Nationalism* (Ithaca, NY: Cornell University Press, 2nd edn, 2008); Anthony D. Smith, *Nationalism: Theory, Ideology, History* (Cambridge: Polity Press, 2nd edn, 2010).

justifications for claims over a shared territory. Attempts to define 'peoples' as a meaningful category on an international level seem therefore almost destined to fail.[9] To complicate things further, 'peoples' need to be differentiated from 'indigenous peoples' and 'minorities' as separate categories of international law.[10]

Similar difficulties arise with regard to the scope and content of the right. Broadly speaking, one can differentiate between two opposing traditions: the 'classic' (liberal) and the 'romantic' (nationalist) conception of self-determination. A good summary of these two traditions was provided by Martti Koskenniemi in a widely quoted article in the *International and Comparative Law Quarterly*.[11] In the first, 'classic' or liberal tradition (Koskenniemi calls it *Hobbesean*), self-determination is identical with the state, and nations appear as artificial communities that should be channelled through state functions: '[i]t starts from the assumption that the authentic expression of human nature in primitive communities is something essentially negative', Koskenniemi writes, adding: 'unless it can be channelled into formally organised States, whatever natural bonds exist will not prevent a *bellum omnium*'.[12] Consequently, the classic conception has a strong preference for statehood, and it attempts to reconcile claims for self-determination within an existing state. In other words, from the liberal perspective, self-determination works as a justification of a state-centred order, and serves as a legitimizing principle for states.

The second conception, by contrast, is 'romantic' and potentially revolutionary (or, in Koskenniemi's terminology: *Rousseauesque*). He states:

> [f]or this view, the crucial question is less *how* popular will is exercised, more to what end it is exercised, whether it participates in the natural life-form appropriate for each nation as an authentic (and not artificial) community. For it, the primitive is good, something that was tragically lost in the political struggle that organised themselves into the State.[13]

From the nationalist perspective, therefore, self-determination is not a justification of a state-centred order but becomes a potential challenge to it.

In modern international law, the balance between these two opposing traditions is sought in an attempt to contain or 'domesticate' the nationalist conception

[9] But see UNESCO, International Meeting of Experts on Further Study of the Concept of the Rights of Peoples, 27–30 November 1989, Final Report and Recommendations, SHS-89/CONF.602/7.

[10] See e.g. Joshua Castellino, 'Peoples, Indigenous Peoples, and Minorities', in Christian Walter, Antje von Ungern-Sternberg, and Kavus Abushov (eds), *Self-determination and Secession in International Law* (Oxford: Oxford University Press, 2014), 27–44.

[11] Martti Koskenniemi, 'National Self-determination Today: Problems of Legal Theory and Practice', *International and Comparative Law Quarterly* 43 (1994), 241–69, 249–57.

[12] Ibid., 249.

[13] Ibid., 250.

of self-determination by limiting it to 'abnormal' cases,[14] that is to colonialism in the sense of 'alien subjugation, domination and exploitation'.[15] By extension of that argument, in 'normal' cases self-determination is reduced and limited to minority rights, at least as long as an ethnic group can express its self-determination 'internally', with the possible exception in extreme cases of abuse (the idea of a right of 'remedial' secession).[16] Essentially, this distinction between 'normal' and 'abnormal' situations has since been the heart of the matter in the legal discourse on the right to self-determination,[17] with the important qualification regarding the need to preserve existing borders to maintain regional stability (the principle of *uti possidetis*).[18]

2. The Revived Discourse on Russian Approaches to International Law

This study situates Russia's post-Soviet approach to the right of peoples to self-determination in that legal discourse. In doing so, the general hypothesis is that (1) there is such a thing as a distinct 'Russian' approach to self-determination, possible inconsistencies and hypocrisies notwithstanding, and (2) that this approach diverges significantly from the consensus view in international law doctrine, at least partly due to a lasting legacy of the former Soviet doctrine of international law.

Traditionally, regional-specific narratives of international law have usually been told from within that region itself.[19] Russia is an important exception in that

[14] Ibid., 253 et seq. The term 'domestication' seems to have been coined by James Mayall in *Nationalism and International Society* (Cambridge: Cambridge University Press, 1990), 50, 55–7. It also served as the subtitle of one of the most recent books on the history of self-determination: Jörg Fisch, *A History of the Self-determination of Peoples: The Domestication of an Illusion* (Cambridge: Cambridge University Press, 2015).

[15] See e.g. GA Res 1514(XV) (Declaration on the Granting of Independence to Colonial Countries and Peoples), 14 December 1960, UN Doc. A/4684, para. 1. It should be noted, however, that this definition is not limited to the process of dismantlement of the colonial empires established prior to the First World War, but has been extended in the past to other situations where a foreign minority imposed rules on the majority, see GA Res 42/23 A (International Solidarity with the Liberation Struggle in South Africa), 20 November 1987, UN Doc. A/RES/42/23; GA Res 46/18 (The Situation in Cambodia), 20 November 1991, UN Doc. A/RES/46/18; and GA Res 72/160 (The Right of the Palestinian People to Self-determination), 19 December 2017, UN Doc. A/RES/72/160.

[16] Seminal Lee C. Buchheit, *Secession: The Legitimacy of Self-determination* (New Haven, CT: Yale University Press, 1978), 220–3.

[17] The literature on the right of peoples to self-determination is overwhelming. For an overview see the entry 'Self-determination in International Law' by James Summers in *Oxford Bibliographies* (last modified: 27 June 2017), available at: http://www.oxfordbibliographies.com/view/document/obo-9780199796953/obo-9780199796953-0033.xml. For some of the reference works see n. 7 above; for a good overview see Christian Tomuschat, 'International Law: Ensuring the Survival of Mankind on the Eve of a New Century', *Recueil des Cours de l'Académie de la Haye en ligne* 281 (1999), 9–438, 239–61.

[18] On the historical precedent for the application of this principle, the decolonization of Latin America in the second half of the nineteenth century, see Anderson, *Imagined Communities* (1991) (n. 8), 52–65.

[19] See Carl Landauer, 'Regionalism, Geography, and the International Legal Imagination', *Chicago Journal of International Law* 11 (2010–2011), 557–95, 562–9, referring to Alejandro Álvarez in Latin America, Taslim Olawale Elias in Africa, and Nagendra Singh in India.

regard, and it is even possible to distinguish three different 'schools' or traditions. A first, fairly recent tradition developed in some of the former union republics following the dissolution of the Soviet Union, in particular in Georgia and Ukraine.[20] Although offering invaluable insights on Russian materials and sources, the assessments offered by these scholars, however, tend to oversimplify the discussion and jump to conclusions, not least probably due to the direct involvement of 'their' states in conflicts to which Russia is also a party.

A second tradition dealing with Russian approaches to international law originates in the policy-oriented New Haven School of international law, pioneered by Myres McDougal and Harold Lasswell in the United States.[21] During the Cold War period, scholars like John Hazard were concerned with the question whether international law was understood differently behind the Iron Curtain,[22] and some international law scholars from the younger generation in the United States have recently promoted the notion of 'Cold War II' as a useful category for assessing the post-Soviet Russian approach to international law.[23]

A third tradition or 'school' is the discipline of *Ostrecht*, developed primarily in pre- and post-Second World War Germany.[24] With the fall of the Berlin Wall, German scholarship dealing with a distinct Russian approach to international law faded away somewhat.[25] Against the background that two of the founding fathers of that tradition (Boris Meissner in Germany and Henn-Jüri Uibopuu in Austria) were originally from Estonia, it is however interesting to note that the discourse has recently been revived by another scholar from Estonia, Lauri Mälksoo, professor of international law at the University of Tartu.[26] In his principal work on the

[20] With regard to Russia's approach to self-determination see e.g. Levan Alexidze, 'Kosovo and South Ossetia: Similar or Different? Consequences for International Law', *Baltic Yearbook of International Law* 12 (2012), 75–102; Oleksandr Zadorozhnii, 'To Justify Against All Odds: The Annexation of Crimea in 2014 and the Russian Legal Scholarship', *Polish Yearbook of International Law* 35 (2015), 139–69; Oleksandr Merezhko, 'Crimea's Annexation in the Light of International Law: A Critique of Russia's Legal Argumentation', *Kyiv-Mohyla Law and Politics Journal* 2 (2016), 37–89.

[21] See e.g. Myres S. McDougal and Harold D. Lasswell, 'The Identification and Appraisal of Diverse Systems of Public Order', *American Journal of International Law* 53 (1959), 1–29.

[22] For an overview see William E. Butler, 'Anglo-American Research on Soviet Approaches to Public International Law', in William E. Butler (ed.), *International Law in Comparative Perspective* (Alphen aan den Rijn: Sijthoff & Noordhoff, 1980), 169–90.

[23] See Boris N. Mamlyuk, 'The Ukraine Crisis, Cold War II, and International Law', *German Law Journal* 16 (2015), 479–522. For a similar approach see Christopher J. Borgen, 'Whose Public, Whose Order? Imperium, Region, and Normative Friction', *Yale Journal of International Law* 32 (2007), 331–74.

[24] See Boris Meissner, 'Entwicklungen und Stand der deutschen Ostrechtsforschung und ihre Stellung in der internationalen Ostwissenschaft', in Boris Meissner, Herwig Roggemann, Friedrich-Christian Schroeder, and Klaus Westen (eds), *Grundsatzfragen der Ostrechtsforschung* (Tübingen: Erdmann, 1980), 103–6.

[25] For the few notable exceptions see Sebastian Pritzkow, 'Kontinuität and Diskontinuität: Sowjetisches und modernes Völkerrechtsdenken im Vergleich', *Osteuropa-Recht* 54 (2008), 397–406; Angelika Nußberger, 'Völkerrechtliche Bezüge', in Angelika Nußberger (ed.), *Einführung in das russische Recht* (Munich: Beck, 2010), 60–5; Wolfgang Graf Vitzthum, 'Russland und das Völkerrecht', *Archiv des Völkerrechts* 65 (2016), 239–60; Angelika Nußberger, 'Russia', in the MPEPIL (online edn).

[26] Mälksoo himself embeds his work in a distinct tradition which he calls the 'Estonian School of International Law', see Lauri Mälksoo, 'The Science of International Law and the Concept of Politics.

topic, *Russian Approaches to International Law*, Mälksoo argues for a 'civilizational' perspective: 'because of their different history, culture and "civilization", different Great Powers tend to perceive and use international law differently, and even if they violate it, they may violate it differently or for different reasons'.[27] Mälksoo's main argument is therefore that 'a crucial key to understanding the post-Soviet Russian approach to international law is the powerful idea of Russia's civilizational distinctness from the West'.[28]

One argument in favour of this perspective is certainly that an increasing number of Russian scholars look at international law from precisely that angle. Stanislav Chernichenko for example, one of the most influential international law scholars in Russia, describes international law as 'a product of interaction of different civilizations', and maintains that 'its social nature inevitably includes civilizational components'.[29] Other Russian scholars argue in a similar vein, speaking of 'Western' and 'non-Western' civilizations, or even of Russia as a unique civilization in its own right.[30] On the other hand, one has hardly to be reminded that 'civilization' is a notoriously ambiguous concept which has historically been prone to abuse.[31] It is therefore maybe not surprising that Mälksoo's civilizational perspective has been described as 'border[ing] on the polemical'.[32] At the same time, his study was praised by the same critic as a 'treasure house of engaged argumentation and extraordinary erudition',[33] and others found it to be a 'well-written

The Arguments and Lives of the International Law Professors at the University of Dorpat/Yur'ev/Tartu 1855–1985', *British Yearbook of International Law* 75 (2005), 383–501.

[27] Lauri Mälksoo, *Russian Approaches to International Law* (Oxford: Oxford University Press, 2015), 9. Earlier works with this theme include 'The History of International Theory in Russia: A Civilizational Dialogue with Europe', *European Journal of International Law* 19 (2008), 211–32, and 'Russia-Europe', in Anne Peters and Bardo Fassbender (eds), *The Oxford Handbook of the History of International Law* (Oxford: Oxford University Press, 2012), 764–86.

[28] Mälksoo, *Russian Approaches to International Law* (2015) (n. 27), 190.

[29] S.V. Chernichenko, *Очерки по философии и международному праву* [Essays on Philosophy and International Law] (Moscow: Nauchnaya kniga, 2009), 676–7.

[30] See S.L. Rogozhin, 'Международное право как диалог и столкновение цивилизаций' [International Law as a Dialogue and a Clash of Civilizations], *Moskovskiĭ zhurnal mezhdunarodnogo prava* 47 (2002), no. 3, 16–30; V.M. Shumilov, 'Взгляд на историю международных отношений и международного права в контексте цивилизационного подхода' [A Look at the History of International Relations and International Law in the Context of the Civilizational Approach], *Moskovskiĭ zhurnal mezhdunarodnogo prava* 95 (2014), no. 3, 46–64. For an extended argument by a Russian political scientist see E.L. Sadykova, *Межцивилизационный диалог в современных международных отношениях: теоретические и практические аспекты* [Intercivilizational Dialogue in Contemporary International Relations: Theoretical and Practical Aspects] (Moscow: Diplomatic Academy of the Russian Ministry of Foreign Affairs, 2014).

[31] See Martti Koskenniemi, *The Gentle Civilizer of Nations: The Rise and Fall of International Law 1870–1960* (Cambridge: Cambridge University Press, 2001); Antony Anghie, *Imperialism, Sovereignty and the Making of International Law* (Cambridge: Cambridge University Press, 2005).

[32] Bill Bowring, 'Russian Approaches to International Law', *British Yearbook of International Law* 85 (2015), 189–93, 191.

[33] Ibid., 189.

book [that] fills an important lacuna in the meta-analysis of present-day international law doctrine'.[34]

3. Situating Russia's Approach to Self-Determination and the Continuity Question

When situating Russia's approach to the right of peoples to self-determination in the discourse of international law, two meaningful points of comparison come to mind: a temporal comparison with the former Soviet doctrine of international law, and a regional comparison vis-à-vis a Western or European perspective on the right to self-determination. At first sight, the latter point of comparison may appear unusual, since it is contrary to the fundamental claim of international law to have universal validity.[35] Due to its controversial origins as a normative order applicable only between 'civilized nations', structured around and shaped by European values,[36] the claim of international law to be universal however always appeared somewhat presumptuous. Many scholars have therefore started openly to question the Eurocentrism of international law,[37] and research on divergent views or distinct 'regional' or even 'national' approaches has become a recent trend in academia.[38]

A useful technique for ascertaining distinct regional or national approaches to international law was introduced by Anthea Roberts in her monograph *Is International Law International?*.[39] Drawing on theories about social fields by Pierre Bourdieu and others, Roberts argues that international law can be understood as a

[34] Angelika Nußberger, 'Lauri Mälksoo. Russian Approaches to International Law', *European Journal of International Law* 26 (2015), 790–3, 793. For a review of Mälksoo's book by a Russian scholar see Gleb Bogush, 'Book Review Notes: The Illusive Nature of "Russian International Law"', *Russian Law Journal* 3 (2015), no. 4, 165–9.

[35] The question here is not thematic universality of international law, i.e. the widely discussed problem arising from its diversification and expansion. On this problem see only ILC, Fragmentation of International Law: Difficulties Arising from the Diversification and Expansion of International Law, 13 April 2006, UN Doc. A/CN.4/L-682.

[36] See Koskenniemi, *The Gentle Civilizer of Nations* (2001) (n. 31).

[37] Anghie, *Imperialism, Sovereignty and the Making of International Law* (2005) (n. 31); Onuma Yasuaki, *A Transcivilizational Perspective on International Law: Questioning Prevalent Cognitive Frameworks in the Emerging Multi-polar and Multi-civilizational World of the Twenty-first Century* (Leiden: Nijhoff, 2010).

[38] See e.g. Emmanuelle Jouannet, 'French and American Perspectives on International Law: Legal Cultures and International Law', *Maine Law Review* 58 (2006), 291–336; Arnulf Becker Lorca, 'International Law in Latin America or Latin American International Law? Rise, Fall, and Retrieval of a Tradition of Legal Thinking and Political Imagination', *Harvard International Law Journal* 47 (2006), 283–305; Xue Hanqin, 'Chinese Contemporary Perspectives on International Law: History, Culture and International Law', *Recueil des Cours de l'Académie de la Haye en ligne* 355 (2012), 41–234; Anthea Roberts, Paul B. Stephan, Pierre-Hugues Verdier, and Mila Versteeg (eds), *Comparative International Law* (New York, NY: Oxford University Press, 2018).

[39] Anthea Roberts, *Is International Law International?* (New York, NY: Oxford University Press, 2017), 23–7.

transnational legal field, in other words as 'a social sphere made up of objective relations between different agents who interact and compete'.[40] According to Roberts, Bourdieu's concepts of *doxa* and *opinion* denote 'a society's or field's taken for granted, unquestioned truths, on the one hand, and the sphere of what may be openly contested and discussed, on the other hand'.[41] What counts as doxa and opinion may, however, vary between the national and international levels. Moreover, considering the right of self-determination's unclear nature outlined above, it is reasonable to assume that the sphere of doxa in this particular subject area of international law is relatively small, leaving a lot of room for manoeuvre for national-specific opinion. However, it should also be clear that not everything in the discourse of international law is relative. Certain arguments may simply make no sense, because they are badly reasoned, are not founded on established facts, contradict other arguments of the same actor, have no basis in international custom or treaties, etc.

The second point of comparison for situating Russia's approach to the right of peoples to self-determination deals with the question of continuity between Soviet and post-Soviet approaches to international law in one particular subject area.[42] Generally, the Soviets argued the existence of a distinct 'Soviet' or 'socialist' regional international law on the basis of Marxism-Leninism.[43] However, the Soviet doctrine of international law was arguably never very Marxist,[44] and could probably be better understood through the concept of hegemony.[45] The claim of a distinct regional international law applicable in the Soviet sphere of influence had in any case to be taken seriously, and arguably led to the regional

[40] Ibid., 23–4, referring to Pierre Bourdieu, 'The Force of Law: Toward a Sociology of the Juridical Field', *Hastings Law Journal* 38 (1987), 805–53; Pierre Bourdieu and Loïc J.D. Wacquant, *An Invitation to Reflexive Sociology* (Chicago, IL: University of Chicago Press, 1992); Neil Fligstein and Doug McAdam, *A Theory of Fields* (Oxford: Oxford University Press, 2012).

[41] Roberts, *Is International Law International?* (2017) (n. 39), 24, referring to Pierre Bourdieu, *Outline of a Theory of Practice* (Cambridge: Cambridge University Press, 1977), 72–87.

[42] On this question more generally see George Ginsburgs, *From Soviet Russian to Russian International Law: Studies in Continuity and Change* (Leiden: Nijhoff, 1998); Pritzkow, 'Kontinuität and Diskontinuität' (2008) (n. 25); Mälksoo, *Russian Approaches to International Law* (2015) (n. 27), 3–11.

[43] From the numerous works that have been written on that topic during the Cold War period see only Ivo Lapenna, *Conceptions soviétiques de droit international public* (Paris: Pedone, 1954); Edward McWhinney, *'Peaceful Coexistence' and Soviet-Western International Law* (Leiden: Sythoff, 1964); Kazimierz Grzybowski, *Soviet Public International Law. Doctrines and Diplomatic Practice* (Leiden: Sythoff, 1970); Theodor Schweisfurth, *Sozialistisches Völkerrecht? Darstellung–Analyse–Wertung der sowjetmarxistischen Theorie vom Völkerrecht 'neuen Typs'* (Berlin: Springer, 1979).

[44] On Marxism and international law see e.g. Bhupinder Chimni, 'An Outline of a Marxist Course on Public International Law', *Leiden Journal of International Law* 17 (2004), 1–30.

[45] See e.g. Boris Meissner, 'Das Wesen und der Geltungsbereich des Völkerrechts' in Reinhart Maurach and Boris Meissner (eds), *Völkerrecht in Ost und West* (Stuttgart: Kohlhammer, 1967), 9–38, 36 (describing the Soviet concept of proletarian internationalism as nothing but 'the ideological description of the concept of hegemony we have known since ancient times'). On hegemony and international law see e.g. Detlev Vagts, 'Hegemonic International Law', *American Journal of International Law* 95 (2001), 843–8. For a contribution by a Russian scholar see A.Kh. Abashidze, 'Концепция «гегемония» в современном международном праве' [The Concept of 'Hegemony' in International Law], *Vestnik Diplomaticheskiĭ Akademii MID Rossii. Mezhdunarodnoe pravo* 2013, 166–79.

fragmentation of international law after the Russian Revolution in 1917, not only but also with regard to the theory and practice of the right of peoples to self-determination.

4. Russia as a Regional Power of Continuous Hegemonic Ambitions

When looking for functional equivalents of Soviet hegemony in the Soviet Union's sphere of influence during the Cold War period, some *Ostrecht* scholars were reminded of Carl Schmitt's theory of *Großraum*.[46] Interestingly, this parallel is also one of the central themes in Mälksoo's reading of Russian approaches to international law.[47] At the outset of his book, Mälksoo maintains:

> [a]lthough Soviet legal theory denied any proximity to Schmitt's ideas, the 'socialist international law' propagated by the USSR was in practice very much a 'concrete legal order' (in Schmitt's terms: *konkrete Ordnung*) that challenged the abstract universal logic of the principles of the UN Charter in its realm. In today's Russia, things have changed to the extent that the conservatives set the ideological tone and reference to Schmitt's ideas have become fashionable in Russia.[48]

To what degree Eurasianist and Neo-Eurasianist ideas of Russia as a *Reich* (or, in the Russian terminology: *derzhava*) shape Russia's post-Soviet approach to international law remains an open question. What can be said for certain, however, is that Russia has consistently assumed primacy in its 'Near Abroad' since the dissolution of the Soviet Union in December 1991.[49] As early as 1993, Russian president Boris Yeltsin announced that the moment had come 'when responsible

[46] Schweisfurth, *Sozialistisches Völkerrecht?* (1979) (n. 43), 568–9. See also Dieter Schröder, 'Die Idee der kollektiven Regionalintervention. Rechtsvergleichende Betrachtungen zur Breschnew-Doktrin', *Recht in Ost und West* 13 (1969), 203–10, 206–7. On Schmitt's theory of *Großraum* see Carl Schmitt, *Völkerrechtliche Großraumordnung mit Interventionsverbot für raumfremde Mächte. Ein Beitrag zum Reichsbegriff* (Berlin: Rechtsverlag, 1941). See also Mathias Schmöckel, *Die Großraumtheorie: ein Beitrag zur Geschichte der Völkerrechtswissenschaft im Dritten Reich, insbesondere der Kriegszeit* (Berlin: Duncker & Humblot, 1994).

[47] Mälksoo, *Russian Approaches to International Law* (2015) (n. 27), 4–5, 144, 167, 175, 178, 184, 195.

[48] Ibid., 4–5, referring to Alexander Dugin, *Геополитика постмодерна* [Postmodern Geopolitics] (Saint Petersburg: Amfora, 2007), 7 et seq; A. Filippov, 'Суверенитет как политический выбор' [Sovereignty as Political Choice], in N. Garadzha (ed.), *Суверенитет. Сборник* [Sovereignty. Compilation] (Moscow: Evropa, 2006), 173–200; N.I. Grachev, *Происхождение суверенитета. Верховная власть в мировоззрении и практике государственного строительства традиционного общества* [The Origin of Sovereignty. The Supreme Power in the Worldview and Practice of State Building] (Moscow: Zertsalo, 2009), 57, 65, 110, 296. On Dugin's influence see e.g. Dmitry Shlapentokh, 'Dugin Eurasianism: A Window on the Minds of the Russian Elite or an Intellectual Ploy?', *Studies in East European Thought* 59 (2007), 215–36.

[49] On the origins of this phrase see William Safire, 'On Language: The Near Abroad', *The New York Times*, 22 May 1994.

international organisations, including the United Nations, should grant Russia special powers as a guarantor of peace and stability in the region of the former [Soviet] Union'.[50] For Andrey Kozyrev, Russia's foreign minister at the time, Russia's special role in the post-Soviet space resulted from the geographic location of the former Soviet republics in a 'zone of interest and special responsibility'. It would be an 'unwarranted loss' for Russia, Kozyrev argued, 'to pull out completely from the zones of traditional influence which evolved or ... were won over centuries'.[51] Similar views were repeatedly expressed by senior Russian officials and in Russian policy documents over the course of the following years. In 2006, for example, Russian defence minister Sergei Ivanov wrote in a guest article for the *Wall Street Journal* that Russia's primary concern was the internal situation in some of the post-Soviet states, and that Russia needed to be prepared to respond to 'a political or military-political conflict or process that has a potential to pose a direct threat to Russia's security, or to change the geopolitical reality in a region of Russia's strategic interest'.[52] Similarly, the Foreign Policy Concept of the Russian Federation of 2008 called to acknowledge Russia's 'legitimate interests' in the post-Soviet space.[53]

Apart from the various integration efforts in the fields of the economy and trade which ultimately led to the creation of the Eurasian Economic Union as a counter model to the European Union,[54] Russia's 'legitimate interests' also translated into a number of multilateral security agreements: although there was no direct follow-up institution to the Warsaw Treaty Organization,[55] Russia concluded a Treaty on Collective Security in 1992 with the five former union republics of Armenia, Kazakhstan, Kyrgyzstan, Tajikistan, and Uzbekistan.[56] Azerbaijan, Belarus, and Georgia also signed the following year, and in 2002, all signatory states except Azerbaijan, Georgia, and Uzbekistan agreed to create the

[50] Russia TV, 28 February 1993, quoted in Roy Allison, *Russia, the West, and Military Intervention* (Oxford: Oxford University Press, 2013), 123.

[51] RIA News Agency, 20 November 1993, quoted in ibid.

[52] Sergei Ivanov, 'Russia Must be Strong', *The Wall Street Journal*, 11 January 2006.

[53] Foreign Policy Concept of the Russian Federation, 12 July 2008, http://en.kremlin.ru/supplement/4116.

[54] Russian economic integration efforts in the post-Soviet space were initiated as early as 1992. In 2000, Russia, Belarus, Kazakhstan, Kyrgyzstan, and Tajikistan formed the Eurasian Economic Community (EAEC), renamed the Eurasian Customs Union in 2010. On 10 October 2014, an agreement on the termination of the EAEC was signed, and the Eurasian Economic Union (EAEU) simultaneously launched. On the economic integration process see Zhenis Kembayev, *Legal Aspects of the Regional Integration Processes in the Post-Soviet Area* (Berlin: Springer, 2009); Angelika Nußberger, 'Supranationales Recht jenseits des Ural—Zur Diskussion über die Übertragung von Hoheitsrechten im Rahmen der Zollunion zwischen Russland, Kasachstan und Weißrussland', *Osteuropa-Recht* 56 (2010), 113–21; Burkhard Breig and Caroline von Gall, 'Der Vertrag über die Eurasische Wirtschaftsunion', *Jahrbuch für Ostrecht* 56 (2015), 49–63.

[55] The Warsaw Treaty Organization (the 'Warsaw Pact') existed from 1955 until 1991 as a counterpart to the North Atlantic Treaty Organization (NATO), with the Soviet Union as its leading member. See Pál Sonnevend, 'Warsaw Treaty Organization', in MPEPIL (online edn).

[56] Treaty on Collective Security, 15 May 1992, 1894 UNTS 313.

Collective Security Treaty Organization (CSTO).[57] According to article 3 of the CSTO Charter, the organization's aim is 'to strengthen peace and international and regional security and stability and to ensure the collective defence of the independence, territorial integrity and sovereignty of the member States'.[58] The CSTO furthermore envisages the coordination of 'foreign policy positions regarding international and regional security problems' and a collective security system.[59] In 2007, the creation of a CSTO peacekeeping force was declared,[60] and in 2009, the six CSTO member states Armenia, Belarus, Kazakhstan, Kyrgyzstan, Russia, and Tajikistan established the Collective Rapid Reaction Force, a joint combined arms task force with the purpose to counter a limited military aggression against CSTO member states, to fight terrorism, and drug trafficking.[61] (As of February 2021, CSTO mandated forces have been active only in the form of military exercises,[62] although CSTO peacekeepers were almost deployed during the 2010 Kyrgyz Revolution.[63])

5. Outline of Study

In *Russian Approaches to International Law*, Lauri Mälksoo focuses on theory, whereas Russia's post-Soviet state practice is only dealt with in 'patterns', with the part dealing with the secessionist conflicts that arose in the break-up of the Soviet Union covering as few as ten pages.[64] At the same time, these secessionist conflicts usually play an important part in general studies on the practice on the right to self-determination. However, since these works are normally not written with the aim to understanding a specific Russian approach to the field, they usually limit themselves to judge Russia's involvement in these conflicts.

In order to fill this gap, this book provides a detailed assessment of Russia's state practice in the post-Soviet space with the aim to ascertain a distinct Russian approach to self-determination. As such, it may serve as a detailed documentation of

[57] Azerbaijan, Georgia, and Uzbekistan withdrew their membership in 1999. Uzbekistan rejoined in 2006, but withdrew again in 2012. On the CSTO in more detail see Nikolai Bordyuzha, 'The Collective Security Treaty Organization: A Brief Overview', in Institute for Peace Research and Security Policy at the University of Hamburg (ed.), *OSCE Yearbook 2010: Yearbook on the Organization for Security and Co-operation in Europe (OSCE)* (Baden-Baden: Nomos, 2011), 339–50; Alena Douhan, 'CIS, CSTO and the United Nations: Could an Active Regional System of Collective Security Be Established?', *Baltic Yearbook of International Law* 12 (2012), 131–55.

[58] Charter of the Collective Security Treaty Organization, 6 October 2002, 2235 UNTS 79.

[59] Ibid., arts 7 and 9.

[60] Соглашение о миротворческой деятельности ОДКБ [Agreement on the Peacekeeping Activity of the CSTO], 6 October 2007, BMD 2009, no. 6, 23.

[61] See Douhan, 'CIS, CSTO and the United Nations' (2012) (n. 57), 149–52.

[62] See CSTO, 'CSTO Collective Force Trainings', https://en.odkb-csto.org/training.

[63] See Allison, *Russia, the West, and Military Intervention* (2013) (n. 50), 143–4.

[64] Mälksoo, *Russian Approaches to International Law* (2015) (n. 27), 172–82.

the raw material necessary to form and identify rules of customary international law, produced by one particular state. Beyond that, it seeks to test the accuracy of and give substance to Mälksoo's general assessment that the

> evolution of Moscow's legal argumentation and views in these complex cases … has not followed some overarching legal principle but reflected changing power politics. Until 2014, Russia claimed that sovereignty trumped self-determination but in 2014 partly destroyed its own earlier argumentation by its own actions in Ukraine.[65]

Finally, this study is a contribution to what Mälksoo calls the 'debatable nexus' between legal scholarship and state practice of international law in Russia, the open question of to what extent international law as an academic discipline continues to be subjugated to the *raison d'état* in Russia.[66]

The book starts with an illustration of the history of self-determination by stressing the Soviet Union's contribution to its evolution from a political principle to an international legal right (Chapter 1). In doing so, it argues that the history of the right to self-determination as a concept of international law starts with the Russian Revolution, and not with Woodrow Wilson's Fourteen Points (as is sometimes suggested in the standard literature of international law). Moreover, Chapter 1 highlights that the Soviet Union was *the* decisive force behind the codification of the right to self-determination in international legal instruments following the Second World War, while at the same time it modified or even perverted its meaning and content in its own sphere of influence. A review of the Soviet scholarship on the right to self-determination completes the first part.

Against this historical background, the bulk of the book then portrays Russia's post-Soviet state practice with regard to the right to self-determination in the territory of the former Soviet Union through the prisms of sovereignty (Chapter 2), secession (Chapter 3), and annexation (Chapter 4). Each chapter starts with a short introduction and a general overview of these connected concepts, followed by a total of seven case studies, unevenly distributed over the respective parts: Russia's restoration of sovereignty in Chechnya and Tatarstan (*Case Studies 1* and *2*) in Chapter 2, Russia's involvement in the secessionist conflicts over Nagorno-Karabakh, Transnistria, South Ossetia, and Abkhazia (*Case Studies 3–6*) in Chapter 3, and Russia's annexation of Crimea (*Case Study 7*) in Chapter 4. The term 'state practice' is understood here to encompass the broad range of materials of what Russia as a state says, what it does, and what it says about what it does, while having regard to all the relevant circumstances to determine their true

[65] Ibid., 179–80.
[66] Ibid., 77–85.

significance.[67] Compared to a narrow approach to state practice, which has regard only to what states actually do, this more flexible understanding is justified by the consideration that if a state acts unlawfully, it usually nevertheless seeks to justify what it has done (or omitted to do) with legal argument, and the justification then becomes in itself an element of state practice, and may even have more legal significance than the action itself (although one has of course to be cautious to distinguish between legal and political justifications).[68] Furthermore, actions of all branches of Russia's government, be they executive, legislative, or judicial, are considered state practice, as long as they might be seen as attributable to Russia as a state.[69] Consequently, Russia's state practice is understood to embrace not only its external conduct with other states but is also evidenced by such internal matters as Russia's domestic legislation, judicial and parliamentary decisions, presidential speeches and decrees, and ministerial statements.

The book's final part then discusses to what extent international law scholarship in Russia continues to correlate with Russia's state practice by taking the Russian discourse on the right to self-determination as an example (Chapter 5). During the Cold War period, *Ostrecht* scholars like Theodor Schweisfurth assumed that state views and scholarly doctrine in the Soviet Union were more or less identical, and that Soviet scholarship merely explained and legitimized the Soviet Union's official view.[70] As Mälksoo has shown, contemporary Russian international law scholarship is no longer a 'monolithic bloc' as it used to be during Soviet times, but shows signs of doctrinal pluralism.[71] With regard to the right to self-determination, Mälksoo maintains that prior to Russia's annexation of Crimea, most prominent representatives of the Russian scholarship of international law have 'argued that, in international law, the principle of state sovereignty clearly trumps the right to self-determination',[72] whereas afterwards 'no Russian international lawyer to my knowledge publicly declared the invasion and annexation of Crimea to be illegal under international law'.[73] Chapter 5 shows how this apparent inconsistency was accommodated, partly by construing an idiosyncratic approach to the right to self-determination, partly by drawing on 'old' arguments of the former Soviet doctrine of international law.

[67] Cf. Michael Wood and Omri Sender, 'State Practice', in MPEPIL (online edn), MN 6.

[68] See e.g. ICJ, *Military and Paramilitary Activities in and Against Nicaragua* (*Nicaragua v USA*), 27 June 1986, ICJ Reports 1986, 14, para. 207.

[69] Wood and Sender, 'State Practice' (n. 67), MN 9.

[70] Schweisfurth, *Sozialistisches Völkerrecht?* (1979) (n. 43), 556 et seq.

[71] Lauri Mälksoo, 'International Law in Russian Textbook: What's in the Doctrinal Pluralism?', *Göttingen Journal of International Law* 1 (2009), 279–90. For example, the status of individuals in international law is widely discussed in Russian international law textbooks, ibid., 284–9. On this question see also Lauri Mälksoo, 'International Legal Theory in Russia: A Civilizational Perspective, or Can Individuals be Subjects of International Law?', in Anne Orford and Florian Hoffmann (eds), *The Oxford Handbook of the Theory of International Law* (Oxford: Oxford University Press, 2016), 257–75.

[72] Lauri Mälksoo, 'Crimea and (the Lack of) Continuity in Russian Approaches to International Law', *EJIL: Talk!*, 28 March 2014.

[73] Mälksoo, *Russian Approaches to International Law* (2015) (n. 27), 192.

1
The Soviet Doctrine on the Right to Self-Determination Revisited

In the standard literature of international law, the former Soviet doctrine on self-determination is usually portrayed as hypocritical and contradictory. The *Max Planck Encyclopedia of Public International Law*, for instance, maintains that according to Soviet doctrine, self-determination existed 'only for cases where it served the cause of class struggle and so-called socialist justice; it was only a tactical means to serve the aims of world communism and not an end in itself'.[1] A similar assessment is made in *The Charter of the United Nations: A Commentary* (2012). Here, Vladimir Lenin's support for self-determination is reduced to the means of a 'political weapon', whereas Woodrow Wilson, with his famous Fourteen Points on the reorganization of Europe after the First World War, reputedly takes the role of a progressive precursor, who enabled the transformation of self-determination from the realm of politics into the discourse of international law.[2] However, to accredit this achievement to Wilson rather than Lenin is a historical distortion, as Jörg Fisch highlighted in *A History of the Self-determination of Peoples: The Domestication of an Illusion* (2015, first published in German in 2010):

> Wilson spoke increasingly of self-government and the fight against despotism and autocracy. If he wished to have a sustained influence, he had to formulate his ideas in potent watchwords. The right of self-determination, however, did not belong to his repertoire.... The public shared Lenin's understanding of the right of self-determination, not Wilson's, but wanted to hear it from Wilson and not from Lenin. This is understandable, if one takes the global political and ideological situation of the year 1918 into account. Wilson was the most powerful man in the

[1] Daniel Thürer and Thomas Burri, 'Self-determination', in MPEPIL (online edn), MN 3.

[2] Stefan Oeter, 'Self-determination', in Bruno Simma, Daniel Erasmus-Khan, Georg Nolte, and Andreas Paulus (eds), *The Charter of the United Nations: A Commentary*, vol. 1 (Oxford: Oxford University Press, 3rd edn, 2012), MN 5. On the Wilsonian concept of which one should speak of self-government rather than self-determination see Michla Pomerance, 'The United States and Self-determination: Perspectives on the Wilsonian Concept', *American Journal of International Law* 70 (1976), 1–27, 16–20; Anthony Whelan, 'Wilsonian Self-determination and Versailles Settlement', *International & Comparative Law Quarterly* 43 (1994), 99–115.

Russia and the Right to Self-Determination in the Post-Soviet Space. Johannes Socher, Oxford University Press.
 DOI: 10.1093/oso/9780192897176.003.0002

> world, with extraordinarily great hopes riding on him. Lenin, on the other hand, appeared to be a gambler.[3]

Consequently, some international law scholars like Bill Bowring reject purely negative assessments of the Soviet contribution to the evolution of self-determination as a concept of international law, arguing that 'the early Soviet government was entirely consistent in implementing self-determination', and that later 'the USSR had done everything to ensure that the right became one of the fundamental principles of international law'.[4]

The most balanced analysis was arguably provided by Lauri Mälksoo in his contribution to a special issue of the *Journal of the History of International Law* dedicated to the centenary of the Russian Revolution in 2017. Mälksoo calls it 'misleading to pick and choose certain pro self-determination moves by the Bolsheviks in 1917 and 1920, and then conclude that the Soviets advanced this right in international law'.[5] On the other hand, it would be similarly misleading to reduce Soviet claims and practices on self-determination to its tactical and propaganda purposes, Mälksoo concedes, since they were above all manifestations of a regional fragmentation of international law:

> Instead, I argue that the real contribution of the Russian Bolsheviks to the history of international law has been overlooked. They brought 'old international law', *jus publicum europaeum*, to an end in its classical form and at least separated Soviet Russia from this historical legal family. Instead of being one of the European colonial states, as imperial Russia was, Soviet Russia became the main external critic of European colonialism and its remnants. The price for this was that two legal spaces with different legal understandings of international legal standards emerged. Throughout the 20th century, what became known as the West and the USSR with its Soviet bloc followed different standards and usages of the right of peoples to self-determination, thus presenting a persistent challenge to the idea of the universality of international law.[6]

Proceeding from Mälksoo's general line of argument, this chapter revisits the Soviet doctrine on self-determination in more detail. In order to provide a nuanced and

[3] Jörg Fisch (Anita Mage transl.), *A History of the Self-determination of Peoples: The Domestication of an Illusion* (Cambridge: Cambridge University Press, 2015), 133–6. German original: Jörg Fisch, *Das Selbstbestimmungsrecht der Völker: Die Domestizierung einer Illusion* (Munich: C.H. Beck, 2010).

[4] Bill Bowring, *Law, Rights and Ideology in Russia: Landmarks in the Destiny of a Great Power* (Abingdon: Routledge, 2013), 85. See also Bill Bowring, 'Positivism versus Self-determination: The Contradictions of Soviet International Law', in Susan Marks (ed.), *International Law on the Left: Re-examining Marxist Legacies* (Cambridge: Cambridge University Press, 2008), 133–68.

[5] Lauri Mälksoo, 'The Soviet Approach to the Right of Peoples to Self-determination: Russia's Farewell to *jus publicum europaeum*', *Journal of the History of International Law* 19 (2017), 200–18, 214.

[6] Ibid., 204.

de-ideologized picture of the Soviet contribution to the development of the principle from a political idea to a legally binding norm of international law, it highlights the Soviet Union's achievements and contributions, without leaving out existing hypocrisies and contradictions. In this spirit, Section 1 revisits the political and ideological foundations of the Soviet doctrine on self-determination around the time of the Russian Revolution. Section 2 analyses the Soviet Union's subsequent state practice in the drafting processes of the most important international legal materials that led to the juridification of the concept, that is the Charter of the United Nations (UN), the two Human Rights Covenants, and two seminal resolutions of the UN General Assembly, the so-called Colonial Independence Declaration and the Friendly Relations Declaration. Section 3 follows with a portrayal of the purported modifications of self-determination within the Soviet sphere of influence, and Section 4 completes the picture with a discussion on how self-determination was theorized and debated in Soviet international law scholarship up until the collapse of the Soviet Union in 1991.

1. Political and Ideological Foundations

The roots of self-determination in the history of ideas can be traced back at least to the eighteenth century, in which the French Revolution and the wars of independence in the two Americas play a particularly important role. In particular, the rationales in the American declarations of independence of the settlers from their colonial masters can be regarded as the antecedents to the evolution of self-determination on the European continent, although the term 'self-determination' itself is not yet mentioned in the respective documents.[7] In the United States Declaration of Independence of 4 July 1776, for example, the thirteen British colonies ascribe to themselves a right to freedom as well as a right in participating in the exercise of state power. The preamble states:

> We hold these truths to be self-evident, that all men are created equal, that they are endowed by their Creator with certain unalienable Rights, that among these are Life, Liberty and the pursuit of Happiness. That to secure these rights, Governments are instituted among Men, deriving their just powers from the consent of the governed, That whenever any Form of Government becomes destructive of these ends, it is the Right of the People to alter or to abolish it, and to institute new Government, laying its foundation on such principles and

[7] See Fisch, *Das Selbstbestimmungsrecht der Völker* (2010) (n. 3), 79–93. Other authors regard the French Revolution as the decisive primordial event, see e.g. Antonio Cassese, *Self-determination of Peoples: A Legal Reappraisal* (Cambridge: Cambridge University Press, 1995), 11–13.

> organizing its powers in such form, as to them shall seem most likely to effect their Safety and Happiness.[8]

From this passage it becomes clear that the proclaimed right to state independence is said to follow from the misconduct of the British king towards the settlers. Moreover, the declaration doesn't condemn colonial rule per se but focuses on the unlawful conduct of the ruler towards the ruled. Arguably, its legal reasoning was therefore not new but can be traced back to the much older idea of a right of resistance and revolution of those who suffered under an unjust ruler.[9]

Over the course of the Hispanic wars of independence (1809–1825) this reasoning changed, and first declarations emerged that didn't limit themselves to the right of resistance for the secession from the Spanish crown but invoked a natural right to independence which was not conditional anymore, that is it was claimed in absolute terms.[10] For example, the Declaration of Independence of the Mexican Empire of 28 September 1821 states: 'The Mexican people, that for three centuries has had neither its own will nor the free use of its voice, leaves today the repression under which it has lived ... and so this part of the North has been restituted the exercise of all the rights, which the creator of Nature has granted.'[11]

1.1 The Roots of Self-Determination and the International Labour Movement

The emergence of the notions 'self-determination', 'right to self-determination', 'self-determination of nations', and their equivalents in other languages has to be viewed against this background. The terms were first discussed in the bourgeois-nationalist circles of Europe,[12] and after 1871 the debate increasingly shifted towards the international labour movement.[13] According to Fisch, the reason for this concentration of the debate can be seen in the specific interests of the socialist and Marxist parties which were active at the time, especially in the great multi-ethnic

[8] A Declaration by the Representatives of the United States of America (Declaration of Independence), 4 July 1776, available in the digital collection of the Library of Congress at: https://www.loc.gov/rr/program/bib/ourdocs/declarind.html.

[9] Fisch, *Das Selbstbestimmungsrecht der Völker* (2010) (n. 3), 79–93. On the right of resistance in legal philosophy more generally see e.g. Karl-Peter Sommermann (Jeremy Gaines transl.), 'The Right of Resistance: Approaches in Legal Philosophy', in Peter Weibel (ed.), *Global Activism: Art and Conflict in the 21st Century* (Cambridge, MA: MIT Press, 2014), 119–28.

[10] Fisch, *Das Selbstbestimmungsrecht der Völker* (2010) (n. 3), 82–8.

[11] Acta de Independencia del Imperio Mexicano, 28 September 1821. Quotation from the English translation in Fisch, *A History of the Self-determination of Peoples* (2015) (n. 3), 75.

[12] The most prominent representatives of this movement are Pasquale Mancini and Johann Caspar Bluntschli, of which the latter had famously called for '[j]ede Nation ein Staat, jeder Staat ein nationales Wesen', Johann Caspar Bluntschli, *Allgemeine Staatslehre* (Stuttgart: Cotta, 5th edn, 1875), 107.

[13] See Fisch, *Das Selbstbestimmungsrecht der Völker* (2010) (n. 3), 134.

empires of Russia and Austria-Hungary and in the states with multiple nationalities like Germany, France, and Spain: in order not to threaten the unity of the labouring classes and the victory of the revolutions, Fisch argues, socialist and Marxist thinkers 'were concerned with the reconciliation between different nationalities. As long as the nationalities fought each other, there was no realistic chance that they would join in the class struggle.'[14]

Competing concepts of self-determination were developed only at the turn of the twentieth century.[15] In Austria, the so-called Austromarxists were convinced that the national question in the Habsburg Empire could be solved with the help of self-determination, conceptualized not as a group right but on an individual level to retain someone's cultural identity. Leading thinkers of the Austromarxist group like Otto Bauer or Karl Renner believed that the political aspects of nationalism were best expressed in a non-territorial ('national-cultural' or 'personal-cultural') autonomy where each nation is treated 'not as a territorial corporation, but as a union of individuals'.[16]

The opposite position to the Austromarxists' understanding of self-determination was developed under the Bolsheviks in the Russian Empire, where the term self-determination (*samoopredelenie*) was increasingly conceptualized in a territorial rather than a national-cultural sense and as a group right rather than an individual right that ultimately also included a right to state independence.[17] Understood that way, the claim for self-determination soon became a central theme for a future revolution in Tsarist Russia: as early as 1903, Lenin successfully initiated the inclusion of the 'right of self-determination for all nations' of the Russian Empire in the party programme of the Russian Social Democratic Labour Party in order to achieve as 'its most immediate political task the overthrow of the Tsarist autocracy'.[18]

[14] Ibid., 133 et seq. Quotation from the English translation (n. 3), 117.

[15] For a discussion of the 'perplexing legacy' of Marx and Engels for the concept see Ephraim Nimni, *Marxism and Nationalism: Theoretical Origins of a Political Crisis* (London: Pluto Press, 1991), 17–43. See also Bill Bowring, 'Marx, Lenin and Pashukanis on Self-determination: Response to Robert Knox', *Historical Materialism* 19 (2011), no. 2, 113–27, 123–5.

[16] See Karl Renner [Synopticus], *Nation und Staat: Staatsrechtliche Untersuchungen über die möglichen Principien einer Lösung und die juristischen Voraussetzungen eines Nationalitäten-Gesetzes* (Vienna: Dietl, 1899); Otto Bauer, *Die Nationalitätenfrage und die Sozialdemokratie* (Vienna: Brand, 1907); Karl Renner, 'Das Personalitätsprinzip', in Karl Renner (ed.), *Österreichs Erneuerung: Politisch-programmatische Aufsätze*, vol. 2 (Vienna: Brand, 1916), 160–4. Recent works on this particular conception of self-determination include Ephraim Nimni, *National Cultural Autonomy and its Contemporary Critics* (London: Routledge, 2005) and Mark E. Blum (ed.), *Austro-Marxism: The Ideology of Unity* (Leiden: Brill, 2016), 2 vols.

[17] See Samad Shaheen, *The Communist (Bolshevik) Theory of National Self-determination: Its Historical Evolution up to the October Revolution* (The Hague: van Hoeve, 1956). On the competing positions in Russia at the turn of the twentieth century see Richard Pipes, *The Formation of the Soviet Union* (Cambridge, MA: Harvard University Press, 6th edn, 1997), 27–34.

[18] Programme of the Russian Social Democratic Labour Party, 1903. Quotation from the English translation available at: https://www.marxists.org/history/international/social-democracy/rsdlp/1903/program.htm.

1.2 Lenin's Concept of Self-Determination

Lenin was a strong opponent of the Austromarxist approach of national-cultural autonomy and denounced it as a 'bourgeois falsity'.[19] To him, self-determination was a *collective* right of a territorial defined nation to choose freely over the withdrawal from or the remaining in an existing state, that is, the right to state independence. The substantial work in which he sets out his theory of self-determination is 'The Right of Nations to Self-determination', originally published in a series of articles in the Bolshevik magazine *Prosveshchenie* in 1914.[20] Here, Lenin leaves no doubt about his understanding of the concept: 'it would be wrong to interpret the right to self-determination as meaning anything but the right to existence as a separate state', he states, adding:

> The epoch of bourgeois-democratic revolutions in Western, continental Europe embraces a fairly definite period, approximately between 1789 and 1871. This was precisely the period of national movements and the creation of national states. When this period drew to a close, Western Europe had been transformed into a settled system of bourgeois states, which, as a general rule, were nationally uniform states.... In Eastern Europe and Asia the period of bourgeois-democratic revolutions did not begin until 1905. The revolutions in Russia, Persia, Turkey and China, the Balkan wars—such is the chain of world events of *our* period in our 'Orient'. And only a blind man could fail to see in this chain of events the awakening of a *whole series* of bourgeois-democratic national movements which strive to create nationally independent and nationally uniform states. It is precisely and solely because Russia and the neighbouring countries are passing through this period that we must have a clause in our programme on the right of nations to self-determination.[21]

In Lenin's view, the right of all nations to self-determination was a necessary precondition for a future international union of socialist states. He was convinced that only on a voluntary basis could nationalism be overcome and eventually lead to a

[19] V.I. Lenin, 'Draft Platform of the 4th Congress of the Social Democrats of the Latvian Area' (1913), in *Lenin Collected Works*, vol. 19 (Moscow: Progress Publishers, 1977), 110–18, 17.

[20] V.I. Lenin, 'The Right of Nations to Self-determination' (1914), in *Lenin Collected Works*, vol. 20 (Moscow: Progress Publishers, 1972), 393–454. Lenin had already written about self-determination earlier in two shorter texts, see Lenin, 'The Cadets and "The Right of Nations to Self-determination"' (1913), in *Lenin Collected Works*, vol. 19 (Moscow: Progress Publishers, 1977), 525–7, and Lenin, 'National-Liberalism and the Right of Nations to Self-determination' (1913), in *Lenin Collected Works*, vol. 20 (Moscow: Progress Publishers, 1972), 56–8. On Lenin's concept of self-determination see Boris Meissner, 'Lenin und das Selbstbestimmungsrecht der Völker', *Osteuropa* 20 (1970), 245–61 and Hélène Carrère d'Encausse, 'Unité prolétarienne et diversité nationale: Lénine et la théorie de l'autodétermination', *Revue française de science politique* 21 (1971), 221–55. For a more recent appreciation of Lenin's concept see Bowring, 'Positivism versus Self-determination' (2008) (n. 4), 138–43.

[21] Lenin, 'The Right of Nations to Self-determination' (1914) (n. 20), 397, 405–6.

lasting interregional and widespread commonwealth.[22] A passage from a letter to Karl Radek illustrates that view:

> We demand freedom of self-determination, i.e. independence, i.e. freedom of secession for the oppressed nations, not because we have dreamt of splitting up the country economically, or of the ideal of small states, but, on the contrary, because we want large states and the closer unity and even fusion of nations, only on a truly democratic, truly internationalist basis, which is inconceivable without the freedom to secede.[23]

While Lenin's understanding of the scope of self-determination was never really questioned, the issue of who was to be regarded as the bearer of the concept was subject of harsh criticism. In the 1913 pamphlet *Marxism and the National Question*, Joseph Stalin[24] provided the following definition of a nation: 'A nation is a historically constituted, stable community of people, formed on the basis of a common language, territory, economic life, and psychological make-up manifested in a common culture.'[25] Only if all these four criteria are met, Stalin asserted, one could speak of a nation. By defining the term as a closed territorial unit, the 'nation' has to be distinguished from the 'nationality' in the sense of a people living in a scattered region. The ethnical-cultural component is however not abandoned entirely in the definition by including the criterion of a 'psychological make-up manifested in a common culture'.[26]

Proceeding from this definition in *Marxism and the National Question*, Nikolai Bukharin and Lenin argued fiercely over the question whether the term encompasses the entire nation independent of its class structure or is limited to the workers in the respective territory.[27] While Bukharin (in line with Stalin) asserted in *The ABC of Communism* (1920) that the term embodies only 'the working majority of the nation and not the bourgeoisie',[28] Lenin strongly contested such a limitation to the proletariat as the sole bearer of the right. Already a year earlier, at

[22] See Fisch, *Das Selbstbestimmungsrecht der Völker* (2010) (n. 3), 55 et seq.

[23] V.I. Lenin, 'The Revolutionary Proletariat and the Right of Nations to Self-determination' (1915), in *Lenin Collected Works*, vol. 21 (Moscow: Progress Publishers, 1974), 407–14, 413–14.

[24] Stalin's authorship is debated, see Pipes, *The Formation of the Soviet Union* (1997) (n. 17), 38 et seq.

[25] I.V. Stalin, 'Marxism and the National Question' (1913), in *Stalin Collected Works*, vol. 2 (Moscow: Foreign Languages Publishing House, 1953), 300–81, 307.

[26] Cf. Boris Meissner, 'Der sowjetische Nationsbegriff und seine politische und rechtliche Bedeutung', in Boris Meissner and Jens Hacker (eds), *Die Nation in östlicher Sicht* (Berlin: Duncker & Humblot, 1977), 7–39, 9–10.

[27] On this debate in more detail see ibid., 33–4, and Boris Meissner, *Sowjetunion und Selbstbestimmungsrecht* (Cologne: Verlag Wissenschaft und Politik, 1962), 24 et seq.

[28] N. Buharin and E. Preobrazhensky (Eden and Cedar Paul transl.), *The ABC of Communism: A Popular Explanation of the Program of the Communist Party of Russia* (Ann Arbor, MI: University of Michigan Press, 1966), 200.

the 8th Congress of the Russian Communist Party (Bolsheviks) on 19 April 1919, Lenin argued:

> Our programme must not speak of the self-determination of the working people, because that would be wrong.... A nation means the bourgeoisie together with the proletariat. And are we, the proletarians, to recognise the right to self-determination of the despised bourgeoisie? That is absolutely incompatible! Pardon me, it is compatible with what actually exists. If you eliminate this, the result will be sheer fantasy. You refer to the process of differentiation which is taking place within the nations, the process of separation of the proletariat from the bourgeoisie.... Every nation must obtain the right to self-determination, and that will make the self-determination of the working people easier.[29]

After Bukharin had to withdraw his position four years later at the 12th Congress of the Russian Communist Party (Bolsheviks), Lenin's insistence of the entire nation being the bearer of the right to self-determination took hold and was never challenged thereafter.[30]

1.3 The Decree on Peace and the Declaration of the Rights of the Peoples of Russia

Following the success of the Russian Revolution on 26 October (8 November) 1917, Lenin's promotion of self-determination translated also in a number of important documents of the new Bolshevik government. The first was the Decree on Peace, written by Lenin and passed by the Second All-Russian Congress of Soviets of Workers' and Soldiers' Deputies, published in *Izvestiya* on 9 November 1917. Although the suggestions in the decree could not prevail in the peace negotiations with the Central Powers that ended Russia's participation in the First World War (the Treaty of Brest-Litovsk),[31] the Decree on Peace is an important document in the development of the concept since it asked, for the first time, for self-determination of *all* nations as a binding international obligation.[32] The decisive passage reads as follows:

[29] V.I. Lenin, 'Report on the Party Programme (19 March 1919)', in *Lenin Collected Works*, vol. 29 (Moscow: Progress Publishers, 1974), 141–225, 174.

[30] See Meissner, 'Der sowjetische Nationsbegriff und seine politische und rechtliche Bedeutung' (1977) (n. 26), 30.

[31] On the relevance of self-determination in this treaty see Borislav Chernev, 'The Brest-Litovsk Moment: Self-determination Discourse in Eastern Europe before Wilsonianism', *Diplomacy & Statecraft* 22 (2011), 369–87.

[32] See Fisch, *Das Selbstbestimmungsrecht der Völker* (2010) (n. 3), 150 et seq.

> In accordance with the sense of justice of democrats in general, and of the working classes in particular, the government conceives the annexation of seizure of foreign lands to mean every incorporation of a small or weak nation into a large or powerful state without the precisely, clearly, and voluntarily expressed consent and wish of that nation, irrespective of the time when such forcible incorporation took place, irrespective also of the degree of development or backwardness of the nation forcibly annexed to the given state, or forcibly retained within its borders, and irrespective, finally, of whether this nation is in Europe or in distant, overseas countries. If any nation whatsoever is forcibly retained within the borders of a given state, if, in spite of its expressed desire—no matter whether expressed in the press, at public meetings, in the decisions of parties, or in protests and uprisings against national oppression—is not accorded the right to decide the forms of its state existence by a free vote, taken after the complete evacuation of the troops of the incorporating or, generally, of the stronger nation and without the least pressure being brought to bear, such incorporation is annexation, i.e., seizure and violence.[33]

A second important document was the Declaration of the Rights of the Peoples of Russia, promulgated by the Bolshevik government on 2 November (15 November) 1917, proclaiming not only the equality and sovereignty of all peoples of Russia, free development of national minorities and ethnic groups residing in the territory of Russia, and the abolition of all national and religious privileges and restrictions, but also expressly providing for a right to self-determination, including secession and formation of a separate state.[34] Subsequently, more than forty territories of the collapsing Russian Empire declared their independence. The newly created Russian Soviet Federative Socialist Republic (SFSR) recognized some of them as independent states, based on the Declaration of the Rights of the Peoples of Russia, by explicitly referring to self-determination in the respective peace treaties. The first such document was the Treaty of Tartu, concluded on 2 February 1920 between the Russian SFSR and Estonia. Article 2 reads as follows:

> On the basis of the right of all peoples freely to decide their own destinies, and even to separate themselves completely from the State of which they form part, a right proclaimed by the Federal Socialist Republic of Soviet Russia, Russia unreservedly recognises the independence and autonomy of the State of Esthonia, and renounces voluntarily and for ever all right of sovereignty formerly held by Russia over the Esthonian people and territory by virtue of the former legal

[33] V.I. Lenin, 'Decree on Peace' (1917), in *Lenin Collected Works*, vol. 26 (Moscow: Progress Publishers, 1964), 249–53, 250 (line breaks omitted).

[34] Декларация прав народов России [Declaration of the Rights of the Peoples of Russia], 15 November 1917. English translation: https://www.marxists.org/history/ussr/government/1917/11/02.htm. The document is signed by Lenin and Stalin.

> situation, and by virtue of international treaties, which, in respect of such rights, shall henceforth lose their force. No obligation towards Esthonia develops upon the Esthonian people and territory from the fact that Esthonia was formerly part of Russia.[35]

Similar treaties emphasizing the principle of self-determination were concluded with Georgia (Treaty of Moscow, 7 May 1920),[36] Lithuania (Soviet–Lithuanian Peace Treaty, 12 July 1920),[37] Latvia (Soviet–Latvian Peace Treaty, 11 August 1920),[38] and Poland (Peace of Riga, 18 March 1921).[39] In this context it is interesting to note that in the case of Finland, which gained its independence via a similar peace treaty with the Russian SFSR on 14 October 1920, a reference to self-determination was not included.[40] As Lauri Mälksoo has pointed out in the earlier mentioned article for the *Journal of the History of International Law*, there lies a certain irony of history in this omission,[41] since Finland was one of only two countries in the mentioned group (together with Poland) that managed to preserve its statehood after the Second World War: Georgia was occupied and annexed in February 1921, less than a year after the conclusion of the Treaty of Moscow,[42] and the Molotov–Ribbentrop Pact of 23 August 1939 and its secret protocol enabled the Soviet Union to do the same with Estonia, Latvia, and Lithuania in 1940.[43]

These later developments notwithstanding, the Declaration of the Rights of the Peoples of Russia arguably marks an important step in the evolution of the principle

[35] Esthonia and Soviet Republic of Russia Peace Treaty (Treaty of Tartu), 2 February 1920, 11 LNTS 29, 51, 53.

[36] Московский договор [Treaty of Moscow] (Soviet–Georgian Peace Treaty), 7 May 1920. English translation reprinted in Walter Russell Batsell, *Soviet Rule in Russia* (New York, NY: The Macmillan Company, 1929), 247 (art. 1: 'Recognizing the principles proclaimed by the RSFSR concerning the right of all peoples to self-determination, including complete secession from the state to which they belong...').

[37] Lithuania and Soviet Government of Russia Peace Treaty and Protocol (Soviet–Lithuanian Peace Treaty), 12 July 1920, 3 LNTS 105 (art. 1: 'Proceeding from the right, proclaimed by the Russian Socialist Federated Soviet Republic, of all nations to self-determination up to their complete separation from the State into the composition of which they enter...').

[38] Latvia and Russia Treaty of Peace (Soviet–Latvian Peace Treaty), 11 August 1920, 2 LNTS 195 (art. 11: 'By virtue of the principle proclaimed by the Federal Socialist Republic of the Russian Soviets, which establishes the right of self-determination for all nations, even to the point of total separation from the States which they have been incorporated...').

[39] Treaty of Peace Between Poland, Russia, and the Ukraine (Peace of Riga), 18 March 1921, 6 LNTS 51 (art. 2: 'The two Contracting Parties, in accordance with the principle of national self-determination...').

[40] Peace Treaty between the Republic of Finland and the Russian Socialist Federal Soviet Republic (Moscow Peace Treaty), 14 October 1920, 3 LNTS 91.

[41] Mälksoo, 'The Soviet Approach to the Right of Peoples to Self-determination' (2017) (n. 5), 209 (however overlooking that the Peace of Riga actually has a reference to self-determination, see n. 39 above).

[42] On the political conflict within the Soviet leadership (the so-called Georgian affair) that preceded this decision see Moshe Lewin (A.M. Sheridan Smith transl.), *Lenin's Last Struggle* (Ann Arbor, MI: University of Michigan Press, 2005).

[43] See Section 3 below.

of self-determination since here, for the first time, a former imperial power explicitly recognized independence based on the principle of self-determination. Or, in the words of Mälksoo: 'The right of peoples to self-determination as part of bilateral and regional international treaty law starts here.'[44]

2. The Soviet Contribution to the Codification of Self-Determination

Histories on the manifestation of the principle of self-determination in international legal materials usually don't start with Lenin's Decree on Peace, the Declaration of the Rights of the Peoples of Russia, or the Russian peace treaties of 1920–1921, but with the Atlantic Charter,[45] a policy statement issued on 14 August 1941 during the Second World War in which US President Franklin Roosevelt and UK Prime Minister Winston Churchill documented their desire to see 'no territorial changes that do not accord with the freely expressed wishes of the peoples' after the end of the war, granted 'the right to all peoples to choose the form of government under which they will live', and expressed their wish that all oppressed peoples regain their 'sovereign rights and self-government'.[46] Although hinting at the principle, self-determination is not explicitly mentioned. (The reason for that is simple: the United Kingdom in particular was reluctant to acknowledge that the war was being fought to ensure self-determination due to fears of calls for independence in its colonies. Churchill, for instance, stressed in a speech in front of the House of Lords that the principles mentioned in the Atlantic Charter were meant to apply to the countries under German occupation, but not to states that formed part of the British Empire).[47] Explicit reference to the principle of self-determination was, however, made by the representative of the Soviet Union, Ambassador to the United Kingdom Ivan Maisky, in his statement before the adoption of the resolution of the Inter-Allied Meeting in London on 24 September 1941,[48] in which the governments of the Soviet Union, Belgium, Czechoslovakia, Greece, Luxemburg,

44 Mälksoo, 'The Soviet Approach to the Right of Peoples to Self-determination' (2017) (n. 5), 207. Cf. Report of the International Commission of Jurists, *Legal Aspects of the Aaland Islands Question*, Advisory Opinion, October 1920, LNOJ Special Supplement 3, in which the Commission of Jurists found that the principle of self-determination had not (yet) been firmly established in international law and did not automatically allow for secession. See also The Aaland Islands Question: Report Submitted to the Council of the League of Nations by the Commission of Rapporteurs, League of Nations Doc. B7 [C] 21/68/106 (April 1921).

45 See e.g. Thürer and Burri, 'Self-determination' (n. 1), MN 5.

46 Joint Declaration by the President of the United States of America and Mr. Winston Churchill representing His Majesty's Government in the United Kingdom, known as the Atlantic Charter, 14 August 1941, 1946–47 YBUN 2.

47 *The Times*, 10 August 1941, 9, reprinted in *Zeitschrift für ausländisches öffentliches Recht und Völkerrecht* 11 (1942), 91–2, 92.

48 Inter-Allied Meeting Held in London at St James's Palace on 24 September 1941. Report of Proceedings, Misc. 3 (1941), Cmd. 6315, 6–7, reprinted in ibid., 93.

the Netherlands, Norway, Poland, and Yugoslavia adjoined and referred to the principles of the Atlantic Charter. Maisky claimed:

> The Soviet Union was, and is, guided in its foreign policy by the principle of self-determination of nations.... Accordingly, the Soviet Union defends the right of every nation to independence and territorial integrity of its country, and its right to establish such a social order and to choose such a form of government as it deems opportune and necessary for the better promotion of its economic and cultural prosperity.[49]

Moreover, it is interesting to note the expressed reservation that followed this general statement: in applying the principle of self-determination, Maisky added, one would have to consider that it would 'necessarily adapt itself to the circumstances, needs and historic peculiarities of particular countries',[50] arguably a hint to the Soviet Union's own (double) standards with regard to the application of the principle of self-determination in the Baltic states a year earlier.

2.1 The United Nations Charter

When the Soviet Union, together with the other main allies China, the United Kingdom, and the United States worked out the core features of the UN Charter at Dumbarton Oaks in Washington, D.C. in 1944, an explicit reference to self-determination was not yet included.[51] This changed only at the urge of the Soviet Union during the UN Conference on International Organization in San Francisco in 1945, where it proposed to include as one of the principles of the organization 'to develop friendly relations among nations based on respect for the principle of equal rights and self-determination of peoples, and to take other appropriate measures to strengthen universal peace'.[52] It was due to this Soviet initiative that a

[49] Ibid., 93–5, 94 (fn. 1).
[50] Ibid.
[51] On the history of the creation of the United Nations Charter more generally see Ruth B. Russell and Jeanette E. Muther, *A History of the United Nations Charter, The Role of the United States, 1940–1945* (Washington, D.C.: Brookings Institution, 1958); S.B. Krylov, *История создания Организации Объединённых Наций: разработка текста устава Организации Объединённых Наций (1944–1945)* [History of the Creation of the United Nations: The Development of the Text of the Charter of the United Nations] (Moscow: IMO, 1960).
[52] See ibid., 94; Cassese, *Self-determination of Peoples* (1995) (n. 7), 38; James Summers, *Peoples and International Law* (Leiden: Brill Nijhoff, 2nd edn, 2014), 194. On the role of the Soviet Union in insisting on the inclusion of self-determination in the UN Charter in more detail see G.B. Starushenko, *Принцип самоопределения народов и наций во внешней политике советского государства* [The Principle of Self-determination of Peoples and Nations in the Foreign Policy of the Soviet States] (Moscow: Izdatel'stvo Instituta mezhdunarodnȳkh otnoshenii̮, 1960), 120 et seq (English translation: Gleb Starushenko, *The Principle of National Self-determination in Soviet Foreign Policy* (Moscow: Foreign Languages Publishing House, 1964), 142 et seq); L.V. Speranskaya, *Принцип самоопределения наций в международном*

corresponding article was finally inserted in the proposed amendment.[53] The successful introduction of the formula of self-determination as one of the principles of the United Nations in the Charter may therefore rightly be called a distinctive Soviet contribution.

In the final version of the UN Charter, the principle of self-determination is mentioned two times:[54] according to article 1(2), one of the purposes of the United Nations is to 'develop friendly relations among nations based on respect for the principle of equal rights and self-determination of peoples, and to take other appropriate measures to strengthen universal peace'; article 55 proclaims that the organization shall promote 'universal respect for, and observance of human rights and fundamental freedoms' in order to create 'conditions of stability and well-being which are necessary for peaceful and friendly relations among nations based on respect for the principle of equal rights and self-determination of peoples'.[55] What the incorporation of the principle of self-determination into the UN Charter meant varied, however, greatly: whereas Western scholarship at the time regarded it as having no binding force,[56] the Soviet doctrine considered it the elevation to a legally binding principle.[57]

The division about the nature and scope of the principle of self-determination could already be observed during the debates on the provisions regarding an international trusteeship system, the later Chapter XII of the UN Charter.[58] For the

праве [The Principle of Self-determination of Nations in International Law] (Moscow: Gos. Izd. yurid. lit., 1961), 35–44; Meissner, *Sowjetunion und Selbstbestimmungsrecht* (1962) (n. 27), 100–1.

[53] On the massive criticism towards the introduction of self-determination into the Charter, in particular by Belgium, see Cassese, *Self-determination of Peoples* (1995) (n. 7), 39 et seq.

[54] Charter of the United Nations, 24 October 1945, 1 UNTS XVI.

[55] Whether the proclamation of self-determination in the UN Charter as a 'principle' and not as a 'right' is the outcome of a compromise between the Soviet Union (and, to some degree, China) on the one hand and the colonial powers France and the United Kingdom (together with the United States) on the other hand appears plausible at first sight, but ultimately remains unclear: the (also authoritative) French version of the text speaks of 'le principe de l'égalité des droits des peuples et de leur *droit* à disposer d'eux mêmes' (emphasis added). In light of this obvious discrepancy, one could therefore also argue the exact opposite: maybe the authors of the Charter were simply unconcerned about the different connotations. In this vein Fisch, *Das Selbstbestimmungsrecht der Völker* (2010) (n. 3), 220–1.

[56] See e.g. Alfred Verdross, *Völkerrecht* (Vienna: Springer, 4th edn, 1959), 428–9; Friedrich Berber, *Lehrbuch des Völkerrechts*, vol. 1 (Munich: Beck, 1960), 75. In the 1955 edition of the most authoritative international law textbook in English language at the time, self-determination does not even appear in the index, and is mentioned only in passing when outlining the various purposes of the United Nations, with no discussion on the legal significance of the principle, see Hersch Lauterpacht (ed.), *Oppenheim's International Law: A Treatise*, vol. 1 (London: Longmans, Green and Co., 8th edn, 1955), 404.

[57] See e.g. Yu.G. Barseghov, *Территория в международном праве* [Territory in International Law] (Moscow: Gos. izd. yurid. lit., 1958), 74; D.B. Levin and G.P. Kalyuzhnaya (eds), *Международное право* [International Law] (Moscow: Yurid. literatura, 1960), 91–2. For an overview of this view in Soviet doctrine see Hans Werner Bracht, 'Rechtscharakter und Rang des Selbstbestimmungsrechts nach sowjetischer Völkerrechtslehre', in Heinz Kloss (ed.), *Beiträge zu einem System des Selbstbestimmungsrechts* (Vienna: Braumüller, 1970), 29–34, 29–32, with more Soviet sources cited therein.

[58] See Meissner, *Sowjetunion und Selbstbestimmungsrecht* (1962) (n. 27), 100–1; Starushenko, *The Principle of National Self-determination in Soviet Foreign Policy* (1964) (n. 52), 145–7.

Soviet delegation, the purpose of the trusteeship system was not only 'to promote the advancement of the trust territories and their inhabitants and their progressive development toward self-government', as the United States had proposed. The Soviet Union also wanted to add a reference to self-determination, which would have included 'active participation of peoples of these territories having the aim to expedite the achievement by them of the full national independence'.[59] In the end, the colonial powers were successful in softening the Soviet proposal,[60] and an explicit reference to self-determination is missing in the final wording of article 76(b) of the UN Charter. Thus, one of the basic objectives of the trusteeship system is 'to promote the political, economic, social, and educational advancement of the inhabitants of the trust territories, and their progressive development towards self-government or independence', but only as far as it 'may be appropriate to the particular circumstances of each territory and its peoples'.

For the later Chapter XI of the UN Charter, the Soviet delegation could not even achieve a similar reference to independence.[61] Final article 73(b) only aims at the development of self-government, taking into account 'the political aspirations of the peoples' and assisting them in 'the progressive development of their free political institutions, according to the particular circumstances of each territory and its peoples and their varying stages of advancement'.

2.2 The Human Rights Covenants

The Soviet efforts in further incorporating self-determination in international treaties could be observed during the elaboration of the two Human Rights Covenants, the International Covenant on Civil and Political Rights (ICCPR), and the International Covenant on Economic, Social and Cultural Rights (ICESCR), jointly adopted by General Assembly Resolution 2200 (XVI) on 16 December 1966 and in force since 23 March 1976.[62] The Soviet Union's call for including the right of peoples to self-determination into the catalogue of human rights goes back to the debates on the draft of the Universal Declaration of Human Rights, another resolution adopted by the UN General Assembly almost two decades earlier, in 1948.[63]

[59] Soviet Union, Doc. 2 (English), G/26 (f), 11 May 1945, UNCIO 618.

[60] For their arguments see e.g. France, Doc. 2 (English), G/26 (a), 5 May 1945, UNCIO 604–6, 605; United Kingdom, Doc. 2 (English), G/26 (d), 6 May 1945, UNCIO 609–14, 609.

[61] See Meissner, *Sowjetunion und Selbstbestimmungsrecht* (1962) (n. 27), 100; Starushenko, *The Principle of National Self-determination in Soviet Foreign Policy* (1964) (n. 52), 146–7.

[62] International Covenant on Economic, Social and Cultural Rights (ICCPR), 16 December 1966, 1967 ILM 368; International Covenant on Civil and Political Rights (ICESCR), 16 December 1966, 1967 ILM 360. On the role of UN Secretary General Dag Hammarskjöld in the debates to the effect that the covenants were not opened for signature for another ten years see Jeff King and A.J. Hobbins, 'Hammarskjöld and Human Rights: The Deflation of the UN Human Rights Programme 1953–1961', *Journal of the History of International Law* (2003), 337–86, 351–2.

[63] GA Res 217 A (III) (Universal Declaration of Human Rights), 10 December 1948, UN Doc. A/RES/3/217 A. On the drafting process of the Declaration generally see Johannes Morsink, *The*

During the considerations on the resolution, the Soviet representatives proposed amendments stipulating that 'every people and every nation has the right to national self-determination. States responsible for the administration of Non-Self-Governing Territories, including colonies, shall facilitate the implementation of the right', and 'the human and civic rights and fundamental freedoms set out in the present Declaration shall be extended to the population of Non-Self-Governing Territories, including colonies'.[64] The proposal could however not convince the General Assembly, and a reference to self-determination in the final resolution is missing.

The Universal Declaration of Human Rights was however only a first step on the way to an international Bill of Human Rights, as its Part E provided for the drafting of a legally binding agreement which ultimately came into existence in the form of the ICCPR and ICESCR after a long drafting process.[65] In 1950, shortly after the Third Committee of the UN General Assembly started working on it, the Soviet Union renewed its criticism that the right to self-determination should be part of a future agreement, and proposed a corresponding provision.[66] Although the Third Committee initially rejected the proposal, the Soviet Union's stance subsequently gradually fell on fertile soil against the background of the yearly growing number of new UN members:[67] in addition to the socialist states, some African and Asian states embraced the Soviet position in the Third Committee, and in November 1950, the General Assembly commissioned it to conduct a study on

Universal Declaration of Human Rights: Origin, Drafting and Intent (Philadelphia, PA: University of Philadelphia Press, 1999), and, focusing on the Soviet Union's efforts, Meissner, *Sowjetunion und Selbstbestimmungsrecht* (1962) (n. 27), 101–2Bill Bowring, 'The Soviets and the Right to Self-determination of the Colonized: Contradictions of Soviet Diplomacy and Foreign Policy in the Era of Decolonization', in Jochen von Bernstorff and Philipp Dann (eds), *The Battle for International Law in the Decolonization Era* (Oxford: Oxford University Press, 2019), 404–25, 414–15.

64 Soviet Union, 1948 GAOR, Annexes, Part I, agenda item 58, UN Doc. A/748, 545.

65 See Antonio Cassese, 'The Self-determination of Peoples', in Louis Henkin (ed.), *The International Bill of Rights: The Covenant on Civil and Political Rights* (New York, NY: Columbia University Press, 1981), 92–113; Cassese, *Self-determination of Peoples* (1995) (n. 7), 47–66; Summers, *Peoples and International Law* (2014) (n. 52), 286–365. With a focus on the Soviet Union's efforts Meissner, *Sowjetunion und Selbstbestimmungsrecht* (1962) (n. 27), 102–4; A.P. Movchan, 'The Human Rights Problem in Present-Day International Law', in Grigory Tunkin (ed.), *Contemporary International Law* (Moscow: Progress Publishers, 1969), 233–50, 241–8; Bowring, 'The Soviets and the Right to Self-determination of the Colonized' (2019) (n. 63), 415–19.

66 Soviet Union, 1950 GAOR, 3rd Committee, 289th Meeting, UN Doc. A/C.3/SR.289, para. 34; Soviet Union, UN Doc. A/C.3/L.96, 17: 'Every people and every nation shall have the right to national self-determination. States which have responsibilities for the administration of Non-Self-Governing Territories shall promote the fulfilment of this right, guided by the aims and principles of the United Nations in relation to the peoples of such Territories. The State shall ensure to national minorities the right to use their native tongue and to possess their national school, museums and other cultural and educational institutions.'

67 In 1950, sixty members existed, and five years later the number went up to seventy-six, cf. the listing in 1955 YBUN 452–3.

self-determination.[68] After the study failed to materialize, some Asian and African states, with the support of the Soviet Union (and against the expressed will of Belgium, France, the Netherlands, the United Kingdom, and the United States), took the initiative, and prepared and successfully introduced a draft in the committee, subsequently adopted by the UN General Assembly.[69] The relevant provision in General Assembly Resolution 545 (VI) included, for the first time, that all people are not only *entitled* but have a *right* to self-determination.[70] In 1954, the draft agreement was split into two parts, in which one should deal with civil and political rights, whereas the other should cover social, economic, and cultural rights. The decision left the relevant provision on self-determination however untouched, which would remain as a common article 1 with identical wording. In November 1955, the Third Committee eventually agreed on the final wording of the provision, guaranteeing that '[a]ll peoples have the right of self-determination. By virtue of that right they freely determine their political status and freely pursue their economic, social and cultural development.'[71] The voting record on the resolution of article 1 is telling: while the Soviet Union voted in favour, it was in particular the colonial powers like Belgium, France, the Netherlands, and the United Kingdom which were among the eleven states that voted against it.[72]

The preceding debates on the meaning of self-determination in the Third Committee of the General Assembly are probably the most coherent evidence of *opinio juris* in international state practice up until today.[73] Particular disagreement existed with regard to the question whether self-determination should be prescribed as a binding norm, and, if so, how this right should be designed. Critics argued that the future treaties regulate individual rights, while self-determination refers to groups. Including self-determination into the Human Rights Covenants would therefore be misplaced. Moreover, the concept of self-determination would be too vague to be designed as a right, not least because a clear-cut definition of the bearer of the right, the 'peoples' or 'nations', was lacking. The Soviet Union, on

[68] GA Res 421 (V) (Draft International Covenant on Human Rights and Measures of Implementation: Future Work of the Commission of Human Rights), 4 December 1950, UN Doc. A/1775, Section D.

[69] GA Res 545 (VI) (Inclusion in the International Covenant on Human Rights of an Article Relating to the Right of Peoples to Self-determination), 5 February 1952, UN Doc. A/PV.375.

[70] Ibid., para. 83.

[71] ICCPR and ICESCR (n. 62), common art. 1(1). Moreover, '2. All peoples may, for their own ends, freely dispose of their natural wealth and resources without prejudice to any obligations arising out of international economic co-operation, based upon the principle of mutual benefit, and international law. In no case may a people be deprived of its own means of subsistence. 3. The States Parties to the present Covenant, including those having responsibility for the administration of Non-Self-Governing and Trust Territories, shall promote the realization of the right of self-determination, and shall respect that right, in conformity with the provisions of the Charter of the United Nations.'

[72] For the full voting record see 1955 GAOR, 3rd Committee, 676th Meeting, UN Doc. A/C.3/SR.676, para. 27.

[73] See Cassese, 'The Self-determination of Peoples' (1981) (n. 65), 92–107; Cassese, *Self-determination of Peoples* (1995) (n. 7), 50–2; Summers, *Peoples and International Law* (2014) (n. 52), 291–3; Bowring, 'The Soviets and the Right to Self-determination of the Colonized' (2019) (n. 63), 415–19.

the other hand, took the view that self-determination was a precondition for the respect of human rights and insisted on including the right to self-determination in the covenants.[74] Evidently, the Soviet position ultimately prevailed, giving the concept the character of a fundamental human right or, more accurately, that of an essential prerequisite for the existence of individual human rights.[75]

2.3 The Colonial Independence Declaration

By 1960, the decolonization process had gained momentum and, with the inclusion of seventeen new members in the General Assembly, the United Nations' approach to self-determination reached a turning point, reflected in the adoption of Resolution 1514 (XV) on 14 December 1960 (the so-called Colonial Independence Declaration).[76] According to the International Court of Justice's advisory opinion in *Legal Consequences of the Separation of the Chagos Archipelago*, the resolution's adoption 'represents a defining moment in the consolidation of State practice on decolonization',[77] and Héctor Gros Espiell even called the resolution the 'Magna Carta of decolonisation' in his 1980 report for the United Nations Commission on Human Rights on the implementation of UN resolutions dealing with the right to self-determination.[78]

Although the finally adopted resolution was based on a common draft by forty-three African and Asian states, it was again the Soviet Union which originally initiated the process and presented a first draft to the General Assembly.[79] Later, the

[74] See e.g. Soviet Union, 1954 GAOR, 3rd Committee, 565th meeting, UN Doc. A/C.3/SR.565, para. 24.

[75] On the right to self-determination as a prerequisite for human rights see Movchan, 'The Human Rights Problem in Present-Day International Law' (1969) (n. 65), 233–6, 248; Lung-Chu Chen, 'Self-determination as a Human Right', in W. Michael Reisman and Burns H. Weston (eds), *Toward World Order and Human Dignity* (New York, NY: Free Press, 1976), 198–261; Robert McCorquodale, 'Self-determination: A Human Rights Approach', *International Law and Comparative Law Quarterly* 43 (1994), 857–85.

[76] GA Res 1514 (XV) (Declaration on the Granting of Independence to Colonial Countries and Peoples), 14 December 1960, UN Doc. A/4684. See V.I. Lisovsky, *Международное право и XV сессия Генеральной Ассамблеи ООН* [International Law and the XVth Session of the General Assembly] (Moscow: Gosyurizdat, 1961), 8–16; Meissner, *Sowjetunion und Selbstbestimmungsrecht* (1962) (n. 27), 105–8; Samuel Blay, 'Self-determination Versus Territorial Integrity in Decolonization', *New York University Journal of International Law and Politics* 18 (1985–1986), 441–72, 442–9; Anthony Whelan, 'Self-determination and Decolonization: Foundations for the Future', *Irish Studies in International Affairs* 3, no. 4 (1992), 25–52, 30–6; Cassese, *Self-determination of Peoples* (1995) (n. 7), 71–4; Summers, *Peoples and International Law* (2014) (n. 52), 201–12. With a focus on the Soviet Union's role see also Bowring, 'The Soviets and the Right to Self-determination of the Colonized' (2019) (n. 63), 419–22.

[77] ICJ, Legal Consequences of the Separation of the Chagos Archipelago from Mauritius in 1965, Advisory Opinion, 25 February 2019, ICJ Reports 2019, 95, para. 150. See also ICJ, Western Sahara, Advisory Opinion, 16 October 1975, ICJ Reports 1975, 12, para. 57 ('provided the basis for the process of decolonization').

[78] Héctor Gros Espiell, The Right to Self-determination: Implementation of United Nations Resolutions, UN Doc. E/CN.4/Sub.2/405/Rev.1, 8.

[79] Soviet Union, 1960 GAOR, Plenary Meetings, 869th meeting, UN Doc. A/PV.869, para. 183: 'All colonial countries and Trust and Non-Self-Governing Territories must be granted forthwith complete

Soviet Union went even further and demanded a binding date (the end of the year 1961) to be fixed for the abolishment of colonialism.[80] This championing of the termination of colonial rule based on self-determination was, of course, based on an extreme hypocrisy: the Soviet Union could only support the calls for 'national liberation' in Africa and Asia without risking its own territorial integrity because it presented itself as a commonwealth of free and equal nations, united by shared economic, social, and political ambitions. In 1960, Nikita Khrushchev, for example, maintained in the UN General Assembly:

> It may be said that it is easy for the Soviet Union to advocate the liquidation of the colonial system, since the Soviet Union has no colonies. Yes, that is so. We have no colonies and no capital in other countries. But there was a time when many of the nationalities inhabiting our country suffered the bitter oppression of Tsarism, of the landlord bourgeois system. Conditions in remote areas of the Tsarist Empire hardly differed from those of colonies because their populations were cruelly exploited by the autocracy, by capitalism. Whereas the autocracy looked upon the peoples of Central Asia and Transcaucasia, and other nationalities inhabiting the Russian Empire, as a source of profit, after the October Revolution, when these peoples obtained complete freedom, they quickly improved their economic, cultural and social condition.... The Tsarist Government pursued in the borderlands of Russia an essentially colonialist policy which differed little from what can be observed today in colonial countries. Uzbeks, Kazakhs, Tadzhiks, and other non-Russian nationalities were scornfully called 'aliens'. They were not considered human beings and were ruthlessly exploited. National differences, hatred and dissension were fomented between these nationalities, and the Tsarist Empire was held together only by bayonets and oppression. When the peoples of Central Asia and Transcaucasia were given their national freedom and equal rights with the other peoples of Russia, they showed their capabilities in the development of their national economy and culture. Did the development of our country suffer by the granting to the peoples of the right of independence and self-determination? Is there strife and enmity between nationalities in our multi-national country or a disintegration of the State? No, there is nothing of the sort, nor can there be.[81]

independence and freedom to build their own national States in accordance with the freely-expressed will and desire of their peoples. The colonial system and colonial administration in all these forms must be completely abolished in order to afford the peoples of the territories concerned an opportunity to determine their own destiny and form of government.' See Cassese, *Self-determination of Peoples* (1995) (n. 7), 71; Summers, *Peoples and International Law* (2014) (n. 52), 203.

[80] Soviet Union, 1960 GAOR, Plenary Meetings, 945th meeting, UN Doc. A/PV.945, paras 119–23.
[81] Soviet Union, UN Doc. A/PV.869 (n. 79), paras 192–208.

Such crude assessments in front of the international public were possible because 'colonialism' as a term was ambiguous, and although many states identified the Soviet Union as a colonial power,[82] references to geographical separation dominated as an objective prerequisite (the so-called saltwater test).[83] It was also due to this ambiguity that the word 'colonialism' was ultimately used only in the preamble of the final text of the declaration, stating that 'the continued existence of colonialism prevents the development of international economic co-operation, impedes the social, cultural and economic development of dependent peoples and militates against the United Nations ideal of universal peace'. Therefore, 'an end must be put to colonialism and all practices of segregation and discrimination associated therewith'. According to paragraph 5 of the Colonial Independence Declaration,

> immediate steps shall be taken, in Trust and Non-Self-Governing Territories or all other territories which have not yet attained independence, to transfer all powers to the peoples of those territories, without any conditions or reservations, in accordance with their freely expressed will and desire, without any distinction as to race, creed or colour, in order to enable them to enjoy complete independence and freedom.

The right to self-determination itself was defined in paragraph 2 of the resolution, in the same wording that was already used in the Human Rights Covenants: 'All peoples have the right to self-determination; by virtue of that right they freely determine their political status and freely pursue their economic, social and cultural development.'[84]

2.4 The Friendly Relations Declaration

Another important step in the evolution of the right to self-determination was the adoption of UN General Assembly Resolution 2625 (XXV) of 25 October 1970.[85] Adopted by consensus,[86] this so-called Friendly Relations Declaration is the result

[82] See the references quoted in Summers, *Peoples and International Law* (2014) (n. 52), 207 (fn. 80).

[83] Geographical separation was then also the first out of three elements in the test to determine which territories qualify as 'non-self-governing' in principle IV of subsequent General Assembly Resolution 1541(XV) of 15 December 1960, which defined the basic colonial unit and the means by which those territories could attain self-government, see Summers, *Peoples and International Law* (2014) (n. 52), 212–21.

[84] It is sometimes maintained in international law scholarship that it was the other way around, i.e. that the definition in the Human Rights Covenants was based on that in the Colonial Independence Declaration. Since the final wording of article 1 of the Covenants was agreed on already in November 1955 (see previous subsection), such an assumption is obviously incorrect.

[85] GA Res 2625 (XXV) (Friendly Relations Declaration), 25 October 1970, UN Doc. A/RES/25/2625.

[86] On this decision-making procedure see Rüdiger Wolfrum and Jakob Pichon, 'Consensus', in MPEPIL (online edn).

of the Soviet Union's long-pursued efforts in the codification of the principles of 'peaceful coexistence', a concept of Soviet foreign policy coined at the 20th Congress of the Communist Party of the Soviet Union in October 1956 and according to which two fundamentally different systems of international law existed between which harmonizing rules needed to be established.[87] After initial resistance, the General Assembly decided in December 1963 to set up a Special Committee to work on the formulation of the 'principles of international law concerning friendly relations and co-operation among states in accordance with the UN Charter'.[88] (The cumbersome formulation is the outcome of a compromise avoiding the term 'peaceful coexistence', which Western states dismissed and considered to be socialist propaganda.)[89] As the fifth principle, it was agreed to include the 'principle of equal rights and self-determination of peoples', of which the final formulation was agreed only in 1970 after a long negotiating process.[90] Final paragraph 1 defines the principle as the right of all peoples 'freely to determine, without external interference, their political status and to pursue their economic, social and cultural development, and every State has the duty to respect this right in accordance with the provisions of the Charter'. Modes of implementation of the right of peoples to self-determination are '[t]he establishment of a sovereign and independent State, the free association or integration with an independent State or the emergence into any other political status freely determined by the people' (paragraph 4). Moreover, every state has the duty 'to refrain from any forcible action which deprives peoples

[87] See Nikita S. Khrushchev, 'On Peaceful Coexistence', *Foreign Affairs* 38 (1959), no. 1, 1–18. The term was however much older and can be traced back to the early 1920s, see Ivo Lapenna, *Conceptions soviétiques de droit international public* (Paris: Pedone, 1954), 66. In 1927, Stalin adopted the term and from there it gradually found its way into the Soviet political vocabulary. Of the numerous analyses of the concept in Western scholarship at the time see only Edward McWhinney, *'Peaceful Coexistence' and Soviet-western International Law* (Leiden: Sythoff, 1964). On the importance of the concept in Soviet scholarship see Section 4 below. On the Soviet endeavours in the 'codification' of international law see A.P. Movchan, *Кодификация и прогрессивное развитие международного права* [Codification and Progressive Development of International Law] (Moscow: Yuridicheskaya literatura, 1972). German translation: Anatol Petrowitsch Mowtschan (J. Kirsten and K. Wolf transl.), *Kodifizierung und Weiterentwicklung des Völkerrechts* (Berlin: Staatsverlag der DDR, 1974).

[88] GA Res 1966 (XVIII) (Consideration of Principles of International Law Concerning Friendly Relations and Co-operation among States in Accordance with the UN Charter of the United Nations), 16 December 1963, UN Doc. A/RES/18/1966.

[89] See Robert Rosenstock, 'The Declaration of Principles of International Law Concerning Friendly Relations: A Survey', *American Journal of International Law* 65 (1971), 713–35, 713 (fn. 1).

[90] See, in particular, Felix Ermacora, 'Die Selbstbestimmung im Lichte der UN-Deklaration betreffend die völkerrechtlichen Grundsätze über die freundschaftlichen Beziehungen und die Zusammenarbeit zwischen den Staaten entsprechend der Charta', *Internationales Recht und Diplomatie* (1972), 55–67. From the vast amount of scholarship on the Friendly Relations Declaration with a focus on the principle of equal rights and self-determination of peoples see only Olga Šuković, 'Principle of Equal Rights and Self-determination of Peoples', in Milan Šahović (ed.), *Principles of International Law concerning Friendly Relations and Co-operation* (Belgrade: Institute for International Politics and Economics, 1972), 323–73; Bernt Graf zu Dohna, *Die Grundprinzipien des Völkerrechts über die freundschaftlichen Beziehungen und die Zusammenarbeit zwischen den Staaten* (Berlin: Duncker & Humblot, 1973), 192–222; Cassese, *Self-determination of Peoples* (1995) (n. 7), 109–25; Summers, *Peoples and International Law* (2014) (n. 52), 221–50.

referred to above in the elaboration of the present principle of their right to self-determination and freedom and independence', and, correspondingly, these peoples have a right to resistance and are 'entitled to seek and to receive support in accordance with the purposes and principles of the Charter' (paragraph 5).

The formulations in paragraphs 4 and 5 of the fifth principle are a compromise on one of the most controversial issues regarding the implementation of self-determination that arose during the debates of the Special Committee: whether the use of force in pursuit of self-determination is allowed. While the Western states were strictly opposed to the idea, the Soviet Union, together with African and Asian states, argued that people engaged in an armed struggle for self-determination were acting in self-defence, that they could receive assistance from third states, and that such assistance was not a violation of the UN Charter or the territorial integrity of states.[91] Accordingly, the Soviet Union proposed the following provision in a joint draft with Czechoslovakia, Poland, and Romania: 'Peoples who are under colonial domination have the right to carry on the struggle, by whatever means, including armed struggle, for their liberation from colonialism and may receive in their armed struggle assistance from other States.'[92] The softer wording of final paragraph 5—'in pursuit of their right to self-determination' (instead of being merely 'deprived' of it), allowing for 'actions against' and resistance (instead of 'whatever means, including armed struggle')—thereby conceals a sharp disagreement between the Soviet Union and the African and Asian states on the one hand and the Western states, mostly (former) colonial powers, on the other hand.[93]

The penultimate paragraph (paragraph 7) of the Friendly Relations Declaration's fifth principle is the so-called savings clause, which reads:

> Nothing in the foregoing paragraphs shall be construed as authorizing or encouraging any action which would dismember or impair, totally or in part, the territorial integrity, or political unity of sovereign and independent States conducting themselves in compliance with the principle of equal rights and

[91] See e.g. Soviet Union, UN Doc. A/AC.125/SR.89, 93. On the origins of that theory and its trajectory in Soviet doctrine see Johannes Socher, 'Lenin, (Just) Wars of National Liberation, and the Soviet Doctrine on the Use of Force', *Journal of the History of International Law* 19 (2017), 219–45.

[92] Czechoslovakia, Poland, Romania, and Soviet Union, UN Doc. A/AC.125/L.74.

[93] The question whether forcible action is allowed in pursuit of self-determination was further discussed and developed in the drafting process of General Assembly Resolution 3314 (XXIX) of 13 December 1974, defining aggression in international law. The result, article 7 of the definition, reads as follows: 'Nothing in this Definition, and in particular article 3, could in any way prejudice the right to self-determination, freedom and independence, as derived from the Charter, of peoples forcibly deprived of that right and referred to in the Declaration on Principles of International Law concerning Friendly Relations and Cooperation among States in accordance with the Charter of the United Nations, particular peoples under colonial and racist regimes or other forms of alien domination nor the right of these peoples to struggle to that end and to seek and receive support, in accordance with the principles of the Charter and in conformity with the above-mentioned Declaration.' On the drafting history of this article and the Soviet Union's position during the process see Socher, 'Lenin, (Just) Wars of National Liberation, and the Soviet Doctrine on the Use of Force' (2017) (n. 91), 230–3.

> self-determination of peoples as described above and thus possessed of a government representing the whole people belonging to the territory without distinction as to race, creed or colour.

The savings clause originates in two proposals by the United States and the United Kingdom designed to further the concept of political democracy,[94] and were interestingly also supported at one point by the Soviet Union.[95] In response to strong criticism by many other socialist and developing countries which realized that the language of the text could be invoked to legitimize secession under certain circumstances, Italy tabled a revised draft, amended by Lebanon, which essentially reproduced the US and UK drafts, but added the decisive qualification 'without distinction as to race, creed or colour'.[96] The potential impact of the savings clause was initially largely overlooked or played down in international law scholarship,[97] although some authors soon noticed its great importance.[98]

3. The Modifications in the Soviet Sphere of Influence

While the Soviet Union may therefore rightly be called one of the strongest and most aggressive supporters of self-determination *outside* its own sphere of influence in the context of decolonization specifically but also in the evolution of the concept as a right under international law more generally, the Soviet doctrine on self-determination played a second, very contradictory and one might say perverted role *inside* the Eastern Bloc. Three historical events shed light on

[94] For the US proposal see UN Doc. A/AC.125/L.32; for the UK proposal see UN Doc. A/AC.125/SR.69, 18.

[95] See UN Doc. A/AC.125/SR.106, para. 62. On the drafting history of the savings clause and the preceding discussions see Report of the Special Committee on Principles of International Concerning Friendly Relations and Co-operation among States, 1968, UN Doc. A/7326; Special Committee on Principles of International Concerning Friendly Relations and Co-operation among States, 1969, UN Doc. A/7619; Special Committee on Principles of International Concerning Friendly Relations and Co-operation among States, 1970, UN Doc. A/8018; Ermacora, 'Die Selbstbestimmung im Lichte der UN-Deklaration betreffend die völkerrechtlichen Grundsätze über die freundschaftlichen Beziehungen' (1972) (n. 90), 64–5; Cassese, *Self-determination of Peoples* (1995) (n. 7), 116–17.

[96] Curiously, the wording of this qualification was taken from the joint amendment submitted in 1969 by Czechoslovakia, Poland, Romania, and the Soviet Union (n. 92), which in turn was taken from para. 5 of the Colonial Independence Declaration (for the wording see previous section above). For a discussion on the implications of this qualification specifically and the savings clause more generally see Cassese, *Self-determination of Peoples* (1995) (n. 7), 112–18.

[97] See the numerous examples provided in ibid., 111 (fn. 17).

[98] See, in particular, Lee C. Buchheit, *Secession: The Legitimacy of Self-determination* (New Haven, CT: Yale University Press, 1978), 92. See also Jimenéz de Aréchaga, 'International Law in the Past Third of a Century', *Recueil des Cours de l'Académie de la Haye en ligne* 159 (1978), 1–344, 109–10; George Abi-Saab, 'Wars of National Liberation in the Geneva Convention and Protocols', *Recueil des Cours de l'Académie de la Haye en ligne* 165 (1979), 353–445, 396–7; Daniel Turp, *Le droit de sécession en droit international public et son application au cas du Québec* (Montreal: Mémoire de Maîtrise en Droit, 1979), 261–78.

this development: the Soviet Union's annexation of the Baltic republics in 1940, and the Soviet interventions in Hungary and Czechoslovakia in 1956 and 1968, respectively.

3.1 The Soviet Annexation of the Baltic States

The starting point for the Soviet Union's annexation of the Baltic states was the secret protocol attached to the Molotov–Ribbentrop Pact of 23 August 1939 which divided the area in between Nazi Germany and the Soviet Union into German and Soviet spheres of influence.[99] Accordingly, Estonia and Latvia were allocated to the Soviet sphere, whereas Lithuania was originally intended to fall under German influence.[100] A second secret protocol transferred Lithuania from the German to the Soviet sphere of influence in exchange for the renunciation of Soviet claims to the Polish provinces of Lublin and Warsaw.[101] After the outbreak of the Second World War, the Soviet Union compelled the Baltic states to conclude mutual assistance treaties which allowed the establishment of Soviet military bases on their territories.[102] (After Finland had rejected similar demands, the Soviet Union attacked Finland, which led to the expulsion of the Soviet Union from the League of Nations on 14 December 1939.)[103] On 14 and 16 June 1940, the Soviet Union delivered an ultimatum to the Baltic states demanding the total occupation and the formation of new cabinets. Any resistance would be suppressed; the Baltic states accepted under the condition that their independence would be guaranteed within the framework of the treaty provisions. Subsequent to the occupation of the three Baltic republics, Stalin dispatched three emissaries to the Baltic capitals to direct the Soviet takeover. The newly established governments ordered new parliamentary elections which took place on 15–16 July 1940 and were fundamentally rigged. On 21–22 July 1940, the new parliaments applied for membership to the Soviet Union, and

[99] On the annexation of the Baltic states see Krystyna Marek, *Identity and Continuity of States in Public International Law* (Geneva: Droz, 1954); Boris Meissner, *Die Sowjetunion, die baltischen Staaten und das Völkerrecht* (Cologne: Verlag für Politik und Wirtschaft, 1956); Lauri Mälksoo, *Illegal Annexation and State Continuity: The Case of the Incorporation of the Baltic States by the USSR: A Study of the Tension Between Normativity and Power in International Law* (Leiden: Martinus Nijhoff, 2003).

[100] Treaty of Non-Aggression between Germany and the Union of Soviet Socialist Republics, 23 August 1939. English translation reprinted in J.A.S. Grenville (ed.), *The Major International Treaties 1914–1945: A History and Guide with Texts* (London: Methuen, 1987), 195–6, Secret Additional Protocol, art. 3.

[101] German-Soviet Frontier Treaty, 28 September 1939. English translation reprinted in Jane Degras (ed.), *Soviet Documents on Foreign Policy*, vol. 3 (London: Oxford University Press, 1953), 377.

[102] Pact of Mutual Assistance between the Republic of Estonia and the Union of Soviet Socialist Republics, 28 September 1939, 198 LNTS 223; Pact of Mutual Assistance between the Republic of Latvia and the Union of Soviet Socialist Republics, 5 October 1939, 198 LNTS 381; Treaty on the Transfer of Vilnius and Soviet–Lithuanian Mutual Assistance, 10 October 1939, English translation reprinted in Bronis J. Kaslas (ed.), *The USSR–German Aggression against Lithuania* (New York, NY: Speller & Sons, 1973), 149 et seq.

[103] Decision of the Council of the League of Nations, 14 December 1939, LNOJ 1939, 505.

three weeks later, the Soviet Union's Supreme Soviet formally accepted the Baltic states' 'request' for incorporation into the Soviet Union.[104]

While there is broad consensus in Western international law scholarship that the Soviet Union's incorporation of the Baltic states qualifies as annexation illegal under international law in force at the time,[105] the Soviets argued for its legality, maintaining that the Baltic peoples had exercised their right to self-determination by having 'voluntarily' asked to join the Soviet Union. Soviet foreign minister Vyacheslav Molotov stated in his speech to the Supreme Soviet of the Soviet Union on 1 August 1940:

> The most important measure carried out by the governments friendly to the Soviet Union that were set up in Estonia, Latvia and Lithuania was the holding of free parliamentary elections. In July, democratic elections were held for the Lithuanian Diet, the Latvian Diet and the Estonian State Duma. The elections proved that the ruling bourgeois cliques of Lithuania, Latvia and Estonia did not express the will of their peoples, but represented only a small group of exploiters. The Diets of Lithuania and Latvia and the State Duma of Estonia were elected on the basis of universal direct and equal suffrage and secret ballot, and have already expressed their unanimous opinion on fundamental political questions. We can note with satisfaction that the peoples of Estonia, Latvia and Lithuania voted solidly for their representatives who unanimously pronounced in favour of introducing the Soviet system and the incorporation of Lithuania, Latvia and Estonia into the Union of Soviet Socialist Republics.[106]

3.2 The Soviet Interventions in Hungary and Czechoslovakia: The Brezhnev Doctrine

On 23 October 1956, Hungarian students went into the streets of Budapest and demanded the withdrawal of Soviet troops, the formation of a new government, and the introduction of free elections, broadcast, and press. The demonstrations quickly expanded to a popular uprising.[107] Imre Nagy, the leader of the revolution, declared that Hungary was neutral, renounced the Warsaw Treaty,[108] and in

[104] Mälksoo, *Illegal Annexation and State Continuity* (2003) (n. 99), 83–7.

[105] See e.g. Meissner, *Die Sowjetunion, die baltischen Staaten und das Völkerrecht* (1956) (n. 99), 256 et seq. For the most comprehensive argument see Mälksoo, *Illegal Annexation and State Continuity* (2003) (n. 99), 80–105, with further sources cited therein.

[106] Vyacheslav Molotov, Speech Delivered on 1 August 1940, *Pravda*, 2 August 1940. Quotation from the English translation available at: https://www.marxists.org/archive/molotov/1940/peace.htm.

[107] For detailed accounts of the historical events see Johanna Granville, *The First Domino: International Decision Making During the Hungarian Crisis of 1956* (College Station, TX: A&M University Press, 2004); Charles Gati, *Failed Illusions: Moscow, Washington, Budapest, and the 1956 Hungarian Revolt* (Stanford, CA: Stanford University Press, 2006).

[108] Treaty of Friendship, Co-operation and Mutual Assistance between the People's Republic of Albania, the People's Republic of Bulgaria, the Hungarian People's Republic, the German Democratic

a telegram to UN General Secretary Dag Hammarskjöld asked the international community for support.[109] Two days later, a Hungarian delegation was arrested during negotiations with representatives of the Soviet Union about a possible withdrawal of Soviet troops, and on 4 November 1956, the Soviet Army attacked Budapest. By 11 November 1956, the resistance was broken, and the Soviet Union installed a pro-Soviet government under the leadership of János Kádár, who would eventually shape an entire era and rule the country until the late 1980s. (Nagy was sentenced to death in a secret trial and hanged on 16 June 1958.)[110]

The international community as well as Western commentators at the time assessed the Soviet intervention as illegal under international law.[111] It was argued that the Soviet intervention violated the prohibition on the use of force, the principle of intervention, and the right to self-determination as guaranteed in the 1947 Treaty of Peace with Hungary.[112] The Soviet Union, on the other hand, justified its actions by portraying the Hungarian uprising as a 'counter-revolutionary turmoil', and Nagy as an ally of these forces who, by terminating the Warsaw Treaty, had undermined the solidarity between the socialist states. The ideological reasoning, which in retrospect can be seen as a precursor to the later so-called Brezhnev Doctrine, was provided in the Declaration of the Government of the USSR on the Principles of Development and further Strengthening of Friendship and Cooperation between the Soviet Union and other Socialist States, published in *Pravda* on 31 October 1956:

> This policy finds its deepest and most consistent expression in the mutual relations among the socialist countries. United by the common ideals of building a socialist society and by the principles of proletarian internationalism, the countries of the great commonwealth of socialist nations can build their mutual relations only on the principles of complete equality, of respect for territorial integrity, state independence and sovereignty, and of non-interference in one another's internal affairs. Not only does this not exclude close fraternal cooperation and mutual aid

Republic, the Polish People's Republic, the Romanian People's Republic, the Union of Soviet Socialist Republics and the Czechoslovak Republic (Warsaw Treaty), 14 May 1955, 219 UNTS 3. The Warsaw Treaty Organization (the 'Warsaw Pact') existed from 1955 until 1991 as a counterpart to NATO, with the Soviet Union as its leading member, see Pál Sonnevend, 'Warsaw Treaty Organization', in MPEPIL (online edn).

[109] Letter dated 2 November 1956, to the Secretary-General from the President of the Council of Ministers and Acting Foreign Minister of the Hungarian People's Republic, UN Doc. S/3726, 119–20.

[110] See Granville, *The First Domino* (1956) (n. 107), 94–124.

[111] See e.g. Quincy Wright, 'Intervention, 1956', *American Journal of International Law* 51 (1957), 257–76. For a recent re-evaluation see Eliav Lieblich, 'The Soviet Intervention in Hungary—1956', in Tom Ruys and Olivier Corten (eds), *The Use of Force in International Law: A Case-based Approach* (Oxford: Oxford University Press, 2018), 48–66, 51–7.

[112] Treaty of Peace with Hungary, 10 February 1947, 41 UNTS 135.

> among the countries of the socialist commonwealth in the economic, political and cultural spheres; on the contrary, it presupposes these things.[113]

Therefore, in the Soviet Union's view, core principles of international law such as the sovereign equality of states, territorial integrity, and non-intervention did not prevent 'fraternal cooperation' and 'mutual aid', but 'presupposed' them. Moreover, Lenin's and Stalin's concept of proletarian internationalism was officially re-established as an instrument of foreign policy among socialist countries.[114] How this rhetoric also affected the Soviet Union's approach to self-determination became evident during the Soviet intervention in Czechoslovakia in 1968 to suppress the Prague Spring.[115] As with the Soviet intervention in Hungary twelve years earlier, the international community as well as Western commentators at the time widely agreed on the illegality of the Soviet actions.[116] The Soviet Union, on the other hand, resorted to various grounds for justification, in particular consent by the Czechoslovakian government and self-defence in the sense of article 4 of the Warsaw Treaty.[117] But above all, the actions were justified with 'the struggle for socialist self-determination'. The official reasoning was again provided in a

[113] Declaration of the Government of the Soviet Union, *Pravda*, 31 October 1956. Quotation from the English translation in Paul E. Zinner (ed.), *Documents on American Foreign Relations 1956* (New York, NY: Harper & Brothers, 1957), 252–5, 252.

[114] According to Lenin, proletarian internationalism demanded 'first, that the interests of the proletarian struggle in any one country should be subordinated to the interests of that struggle on a world-wide scale, and, second, that a nation which is achieving victory over the bourgeoisie should be able and willing to make the greatest national sacrifices for the overthrow of international capital', V.I. Lenin, 'Preliminary Draft Theses on the National and the Colonial Questions for the Second Congress of the Communist International' (1920), in *Lenin Collected Works*, vol. 31 (Moscow: Progress Publishers, 1966), 144–51, 148. Building on this definition, Stalin refined and further developed the concept. In a speech on 1 August 1927, Stalin stated: 'A *revolutionary* is one who is ready to protect, to defend the U.S.S.R. without reservation, without qualification, openly and honestly, without secret military conferences; for the U.S.S.R. is the first proletarian, revolutionary state in the world, a state which is building socialism. An *internationalist* is one who is ready to defend the U.S.S.R. without reservation, without wavering, unconditionally; for the U.S.S.R. is the base of the world revolutionary movement, and this revolutionary movement cannot be defended and promoted unless the U.S.S.R. is defended. For whoever thinks of defending the world revolutionary movement apart from, or against, the U.S.S.R., goes against the revolution and must inevitably slide into the camp of the enemies of the revolution', Joseph Stalin, 'Joint Plenum of the Central Committee and Central Control Commission of the C.P.S.U.(B.): The International Situation and the Defence of the U.S.S.R' (1927), in *Stalin Collected Works*, vol. 10 (Moscow: Foreign Language Publishing House, 1954), 1–62, 53–4. On the significance of the principle of proletarian internationalism as an instrument of foreign policy among socialist states more broadly see Boris Meissner, 'Die interparteilichen Beziehungen im Ostblock und das Prinzip des "proletarisch-sozialistischen Internationalismus"', *Internationales Recht und Diplomatie* (1961), 147–64.

[115] On the historical background see Mark Kramer, 'The Prague Spring and the Soviet Invasion in Historical Perspective', in Günter Bischof, Stefan Karner, and Peter Ruggenthaler (eds), *The Prague Spring and the Warsaw Pact Invasion of Czechoslovakia in 1968* (Lanham, MD: Lexington Books, 2010), 35–58.

[116] See e.g. Bernard A. Ramundo, 'Czechoslovakia and the Law of Peaceful Coexistence: Legal Characterization in the Soviet National Interest', *Stanford Law Review* 22 (1970), 963–78. For a recent re-evaluation see Gerhard Hafner, 'The Intervention in Czechoslovakia–1968', in Ruys and Corten, *The Use of Force in International Law* (2018) (n. 111), 143–57, 147–51.

[117] On these justifications see ibid., 153–5.

Pravda article, entitled 'Sovereignty and the International Obligations of Socialist Countries'.[118] The text starts by calling the socialist commonwealth 'the main achievement of the international working class', which the Soviet Union had to defend in Czechoslovakia. Allegations that the Soviet Union's intervention was contrary to 'the Marxist-Leninist principle of sovereignty and the right of the nations to self-determination' were false because these principles 'are based on an abstract, non-class approach'. All socialist countries would be sovereign, albeit only to the degree that 'any decision of theirs must damage neither socialism in their own country, nor the fundamental interests of the other socialist countries, nor the worldwide workers' movement'. The decisive passage of the article reads as follows:

> The weakening of any link in the world socialist system has a direct effect on all the socialist countries, which cannot be indifferent. Thus, the anti-socialist forces in Czechoslovakia were in essence using talk about the right to self-determination to cover up demands for so-called neutrality and the withdrawal of the CSSR from the socialist commonwealth. But implementation of such 'self-determination', i.e., Czechoslovakia's separation from the socialist commonwealth, would run counter to Czechoslovakia's fundamental interests and would harm the other socialist countries. Such 'self-determination', as a result of which NATO troops might approach Soviet borders and the commonwealth of European socialist countries could be dismembered, in fact infringes on the vital interest of these countries' peoples, and fundamentally contradicts the right of these peoples to socialist self-determination.[119]

Other socialist countries protested against this understanding of 'socialist self-determination' and the implicit assertion that a Soviet intervention to preserve socialist governments would be justified. Romanian leader Nicolae Ceauşescu, for example, stated that 'under no circumstances' military action against other socialist countries was allowed, and Albania even left the Warsaw Treaty system under protest on 13 September 1968.

The arguments raised in the context of the two Soviet interventions in Hungary and Czechoslovakia resulted in the formation of the so-called Brezhnev Doctrine, according to which any deviation in the Eastern Bloc from the socialist system

[118] Sergei Kovalev, 'Суверенитет и интернациональные обязанности социалистических стран' [Sovereignty and the International Obligations of Socialist Countries], *Pravda*, 26 September 1968. See also Speech by L.I. Brezhnev at the 5th Congress of the Polish United Workers' Party on 12 November 1968 (Moscow: Novosti Press Agency Publishing House, 1968): 'When forces that are hostile to socialism try to turn the development of some socialist country towards capitalism, it becomes not only a problem of the country concerned, but a common problem and concern of all socialist countries.'

[119] Kovalev, 'Sovereignty and the International Obligations of Socialist Countries' (1968) (n. 118). Quotation from the English translation in Letfen Stavros Stavrianos, *The Epic of Man* (Englewood Cliffs, NJ: Prentice-Hall, 1971), 465–6.

among its allies needed to be prevented.[120] During the Soviet–Afghan War (1979–1989) the socialist-internationalist argument was once more invoked as a justification for Soviet military intervention.[121] Thereafter, the Brezhnev Doctrine was never officially revoked, but when the spokesperson of the last Soviet foreign minister Eduard Shevardnadze was asked in October 1989 by reporters about its continuing relevance, he only replied jokingly: 'You know the Frank Sinatra song, "I Did It My Way?" Hungary and Poland are doing it their way. I think the Brezhnev doctrine is dead.'[122]

4. The Right to Self-Determination in Soviet Scholarship

The Soviet Union's strong support for self-determination in the colonial context, thwarted by a perverted understanding and state practice in its own sphere of influence, was also reflected in the Soviet scholarship of international law that gradually emerged following the Russian Revolution in 1917.[123] While many renowned scholars like Mikhail Taube, Boris Nolde, and André Mandelstam emigrated,[124] a 'socialist' theory of international law was developed in the Soviet Union, thereby making its international law scholarship part of the struggle between two antagonistic world views.[125] In particular, the universality, and also, at the beginning, the binding character of international law was questioned.

[120] The most recent detailed account on the political importance of the Brezhnev Doctrine is Matthew J. Ouimet, *The Rise and Fall of the Brezhnev Doctrine in Soviet Foreign Policy* (Chapel Hill, NC: The University of North Carolina Press, 2003). The normative implications of the Brezhnev Doctrine are discussed in more detail in Boris Meissner, *Die 'Breschnew-Doktrin'. Das Prinzip des proletarisch-sozialistischen Internationalismus und die Theorie von den 'verschiedenen Wegen zum Sozialismus'* (Cologne: Verlag Wissenschaft und Politik, 1969); Stephen G. Glazer, 'The Brezhnev Doctrine', *International Lawyer* 5 (1971), 169–79; Stephen M. Schwebel, 'The Brezhnev Doctrine Repealed and Peaceful Co-Existence Enacted', *American Journal of International Law* 66 (1971), 816–19; and Nicholas Rostow, 'Law and the Use of Force by States: The Brezhnev Doctrine', *Yale Journal of International Law* 7 (1981), 209–43.

[121] See David Ross, 'Beyond the Soviet Invasion: Afghanistan and the Concept of Self-determination', *University of Toronto Faculty of Law Review* 48 (1990), 92–116. For a legal assessment of the Soviet use of force in Afghanistan see Georg Nolte and Janina Barkholdt, 'The Soviet Intervention in Afghanistan—1970–80', in Ruys and Corten, *The Use of Force in International Law* (2018) (n. 111), 297–305, 300–3.

[122] Bill Keller, 'Gorbachev, in Finland, Disavows Any Right of Regional Intervention', *The New York Times*, 26 October 1989.

[123] On the scholarship of international law in Russia before 1917 see in particular Boris Meissner, 'Die Völkerrechtswissenschaft im zaristischen und bolschewistischen Russland', *Internationales Recht und Diplomatie* (1963), 63–9, 63–7; V.E. Grabar (William E. Butler transl.), *The History of International Law in Russia, 1647–1917: A Bio-Bibliographical Study* (Oxford: Clarendon Press, 1990); Tarja Långström, *Transformation in Russia and International Law* (Leiden: Martinus Nijhoff Publishers, 2003), 36–50; Lauri Mälksoo, 'F.F. Martens and His Time. When Russia Was an Integral Part of the European Tradition of International Law', *European Journal of International Law* 25 (2014), 811–29; and Lauri Mälksoo, *Russian Approaches to International Law* (Oxford: Oxford University Press, 2015), 36–51.

[124] See William E. Butler, 'Russian International Lawyers in Emigration', *Journal of the History of International Law* 3 (2001), 235–41.

[125] For the most coherent study of the claim that a distinct 'socialist' international law based on Marxism-Leninism existed see Theodor Schweisfurth, *Sozialistisches Völkerrecht? Darstellung-Analyse-Wertung der sowjet marxistischen Theorie vom Völkerrecht 'neuen Typs'* (Berlin: Springer, 1979).

4.1 Protagonists and Core Themes of the Soviet Scholarship of International Law

Broadly speaking, four periods in the development of Soviet scholarship of international law can be distinguished, of which each had a specific *leitmotif* and one or two scholars that coined that period.[126] Evgeny Korovin (1892–1964) of Moscow State University is usually regarded as the founding father of a distinct concept of international law based on Marxism-Leninism. Korovin denied the existence of a universal, for all states binding international law, and instead established the thesis of a 'compromise law' existing between two antagonistic class systems which consists of only a few shared principles and norms. In his seminal work, *International Law of the Transitional Period* (1923), Korovin maintained:

> In reality, there is currently no 'general' international law. Since long ago and also today, international law is divided in a number of legal circles.... Today too the theory of 'universal' and 'global' international law is nothing more than a myth and at that unfortunately not a very beautiful one. What in our times is called international law, encompasses in reality only a circle of a group of European powers and in particular Great Powers. In parallel there exists a separate system of American international law that solves a number of problems not only differently from Europe but in contradiction to it.... When we give up the old legend of universal international law as not-corresponding to international legal realities, and put ourselves on the position of legal pluralism, the notion of Soviet international law or international law of the transitionary period as one of the special systems of international law does not present any further theoretical difficulties.[127]

The central thesis of Korovin's book is that the emergence of socialist states brought about a new era of international law which is fundamentally different from the old 'bourgeois' international law.[128] Thus bourgeois international law will gradually

[126] The following periodization follows Rima Tkatova, 'Russian Spirits, Soviet Heritage and Western Temptation: "Un-'Peaceful-Coexistence'" in Russia's International Doctrine and Practice', *Baltic Yearbook of International Law* 12 (2012), 1–28. For earlier, slightly different periodizations see Boris Meissner, 'Das Wesen und der Geltungsbereich des Völkerrechts', in Reinhart Maurach and Boris Meissner (eds), *Völkerrecht in Ost und West* (Stuttgart: Kohlhammer, 1967), 9–38, 17–20; Kasimierz Grzybowski, *Soviet Public International Law, Doctrines and Diplomatic Practice* (Leiden: Sijthoff, 1970), 3; Långström, *Transformation in Russia and International Law* (2003) (n. 123), 35 (fn. 6).

[127] E.A. Korovin, *Международное право переходного времени* [International Law of the Transitional Period] (Moscow: Gosyurizdat, 1st edn, 1923), vii, 7–8, 13. Quotation from the English translation in Lauri Mälksoo, 'The History of International Legal Theory in Russia: A Civilizational Dialogue with Europe', *European Journal of International Law* 19 (2008), 211–32, 226. Complete German translation of the second (revised) edition: E.A. Korowin (J. Robinson-Kaunas transl.), *Das Völkerrecht der Übergangszeit: Grundlagen der völkerrechtlichen Beziehungen der Union der Sowjetrepubliken* (Berlin: Rothschild, 1929). For a reproduction of Korovin's ideas in English language see Eugene Korovin, 'Soviet Treaties in International Law', *American Journal of International Law* 22 (1928), 753–63.

[128] Korovin, *International Law of the Transitional Period* (1923) (n. 127), 10.

vanish together with the capitalist state system, Korovin asserted, and will be replaced by an 'inter-Soviet' international law.[129] Until this goal was achieved, Korovin conceded the need for a transitional law governing the relations between the two hostile camps facing each other. Due to a lack of a common sociological base and thus an ideological agreement, this 'international law of the transitional period' was, however, limited to technical-economic cooperation and extended only to areas unaffected by political considerations such as cooperation in the fight against epidemics.[130]

A definition of international law is still missing in Korovin's 1923 study but according to the first comprehensive Soviet international law textbook published by Korovin three years later international law was defined as 'the entirety of the current legal norms that determine the rights and duties of the ... ruling classes as participants in international relations'.[131] Another, quite different definition of international law was provided in the same year in the *Encyclopedia of State and Law* by Evgeny Pashukanis (1891–1937), in which he defined international law as 'the totality of forms which the capitalist, bourgeois states apply in their relations with each other, while the remainder of the world is considered as a simple object of their completed transactions'.[132] Pashukanis' writings are characterized by a certain legal nihilism in which international law appears as an instrument of struggle of Soviet foreign policy and is accepted only in its form, whereas the content of international law is shaped entirely by the specific requirements of politics. According to Pashukanis, the Soviet Union was therefore in particular entitled to terminate obligations under international law at any time, if a change of interests so required. Works like *General Theory of Law and Marxism* (1927)[133] or *Essays on International Law* (1935)[134] are sophisticated Marxist reflections on international law but could never gain lasting significance for the further development of the Soviet doctrine due to Pashukanis' execution in 1937 during Stalin's Great Purge.[135]

[129] Ibid., 36.

[130] Ibid., 15–16.

[131] E.A. Korovin, *Современное международное публичное право* [Modern Public International Law] (Moscow: Gosudarstvennoe Izdatel'stvo, 1926), 5.

[132] E.B. Pashukanis, 'Международное право' [International Law], in *Энциклопедия государства и права* [Encyclopedia of State and Law], vol. 2 (Moscow: Izd. Kommunisticheskoĭ Akademii, 1926), 858–74. Quotation from the English translation in Piers Beirne and Robert Sharlet (eds), *Pashukanis: Selected Writings on Marxism and Law* (London: Academic Press, 1980), 168–83, 172.

[133] E.B. Pashukanis, *Общая теория права и марксизм* [General Theory of Law and Marxism] (Moscow: Izdatel'stvo Kommunisticheskoĭ Akademii 1927). English translation: E.B. Pashukanis (Peter B. Maggs transl.), *The General Theory of Law & Marxism* (New Brunswick, NJ: Transaction Publishers, 2002).

[134] E.B. Pashukanis, *Очерки по международному праву* [Essays on International Law] (Moscow: Gosudarstvennoe izdatel'stvo 'Sovetskoe zakonodatel'stvo', 1935).

[135] Pashukanis worked as a legal advisor in the Soviet Ministry of Foreign Affairs until 1924, when he became a member of the Communist Academy. In 1931, after having revised his theory of state, he was rewarded by being made director of the Institute of Soviet Construction and Law, the predecessor of the Institute of State and Law of the Soviet Academy of Sciences. In 1937, Pashukanis was denounced as a 'Trotskyist saboteur' and executed. See Michael Head, 'Rise and Fall of a Soviet Jurist: Evgeny Pashukanis and Stalinism', *Canadian Journal of Law and Jurisprudence* 17 (2004), 269–94. On the

The second period in the development of the Soviet doctrine of international law was coined by Andrey Vyshinsky and Fyodor Kozhevnikov. Vyshinsky (1883–1954) is mostly known in the West for his role as state prosecutor of the show trials during Stalin's purges and later at the Nuremberg trials as well as deputy and then Soviet foreign minister from 1940 to 1953. But Vyshinsky was also an active academic, first at Moscow State University and later as the director of the Institute of Law of the Soviet Academy of Sciences.[136] Between 1947 and 1957, a series of international law textbooks was published under the Institute of Law's auspices. Editor of the third (and last) edition in this line of collectively prepared treatises was Fyodor Kozhevnikov (1903–1998),[137] judge at the International Court of Justice from 1953 until 1961 and author of *The Russian State and International Law* (1947) and *The Soviet State and International Law* (1948).[138] According to Lauri Mälksoo, these two books offered 'a Messianic concept of Russia as the most progressive civilizational force in the history of humankind and international law': whereas Korovin emphasized the Marxist-Leninist aspect of Russia's specialness, for Kozhevnikov it was rather the Russian nationalist aspect that made Soviet Russia unique.[139]

De-Stalinization following Stalin's death in 1953 had also an effect on Soviet international law scholarship and led to a clear (re-)turning to the European-American legal community, evidenced, for example, by the translations of the international law textbooks of Alfred Verdross and Dionisio Anzilotti in 1959 and 1961, respectively.[140] In 1957, the Soviet Association of International Law was founded, with Grigory Tunkin (1906–1993) as its first president, who was

enormous influence of Pashukanis' writings for contemporary Marxist approaches to international law see e.g. China Miéville, *Between Equal Rights: A Marxist Theory of International Law* (Leiden: Brill, 2005); Michael Head, *Evgeny Pashukanis: A Critical Reappraisal* (Abingdon: Routledge-Cavendish, 2008); Bowring, *Law, Rights and Ideology in Russia* (2013) (n. 4), 48–76.

[136] Vyshinsky's main contribution to the Soviet doctrine of international law are his twelve *Theses on International Law*, which he drafted and were adopted by the international law section at the First Conference on the Questions of the Soviet Science of the State and Law in 1938, see A.Y. Vyshinsky, 'Тезисы по международному праву' [Theses on International Law], *Sovetskoe gosudarstvo* 7 (1938), no. 5, 119–22. For a discussion of Vyshinsky's theses see Långström, *Transformation in Russia and International Law* (2003) (n. 123), 74–7. On Vyshinsky's life in more detail see Arkady Vaksberg, *Stalin's Prosecutor: The Life of Andrei Vyshinsky* (New York, NY: Grove Weidenfeld, 1991).

[137] F.I. Kozhevnikov (ed.), *Международное право* [International Law] (Moscow: Gosyurizdat, 1957). German translation: F.I. Koschewnikow (Lothar Schultz transl.), *Völkerrecht* (Hamburg: Hansischer Gildenverlag, 1960).

[138] F.I. Kozhevnikov, *Русское государство и международное право* [The Russian State and International Law] (Moscow: Yurizdat, 1947); F.I. Kozhevnikov, *Советское государство и международное право. 1917–1947 гг. (Опыт историко-правового исследования)* [The Soviet State and International Law. 1947–1947 (Experience of Historical and Legal Research)] (Moscow: Yuridicheskoe izdatel'stvo, 1948).

[139] Mälksoo, 'The History of International Legal Theory in Russia' (2008) (n. 127), 226.

[140] See Alfred Verdross [А. Фердросс] (F.A. Kublitskii and R.L. Narŷshkina transl.), *Международное право* [International Law] (Moscow: Izdatel'stvoinostrannoĭ literaturŷ, 1959); Dionisio Anzilotti [Д. Анцилотти] (A.L. Saketti and É.M. Fabrikova transl.), *Курс международного права* [Course of International Law], vol. 1 (Moscow: Izdatel'stvo inostrannoĭ literaturŷ, 1961).

the head of the legal department of the Soviet Ministry of Foreign Affairs from 1957 until 1966, successor of Korovin as chair of international law at Moscow State University, and *the* single most influential Soviet international law scholar in the post-War period. Tunkin's seminal work is *Theory of International Law* (1970), a revised version of *Questions on the Theory of International Law*, published in 1962.[141] The core element of Tunkin's approach was the 'peaceful coexistence' of two different systems.[142] In his first *Cours* at The Hague Academy of International Law, Tunkin introduced the concept into Soviet doctrine. Although the socialist and the capitalist systems differ in their social values which had to be protected by law, a common understanding—and therefore also a common legal system—was possible, Tunkin argued.[143]

The fourth and last period of the Soviet doctrine of international law coincided with Mikhail Gorbachev's time as General Secretary of the Communist Party of the Soviet Union starting from 1985, when a 'new thinking' in Soviet foreign policy was proclaimed.[144] This new thinking during the time of *perestroĭka* ('restructuring') entailed the proclamation that the principle of peaceful coexistence applies not only in the relationship between 'bourgeois' states on the one hand and socialist states on the other hand but in the relationship between *all* states, and influenced the post-Tunkin era of Soviet international law scholarship accordingly. Now, not the peaceful coexistence of two different systems was central any more but the interdependence of the world.[145] Two articles in the journal *Soviet State and Law* illustrate that view, in which Rein Müllerson (1944–) and Vladlen Vereshchetin (1932–) of the Institute of State and Law of the Soviet Academy of Sciences jointly discussed the impact of Gorbachev's proclaimed new thinking on international law. In the first article, published in 1988, Müllerson and Vereshchetin argued that peaceful coexistence entails not only the absence of armed conflicts but includes

[141] G.I. Tunkin, *Теория международного права* [Theory of International Law] (Moscow: Mezhdunarodnye otnosheniya, 1970). English translation: G.I. Tunkin (William E. Butler transl.), *Theory of International Law* (London: Wildy, Simmonds and Hill Publishing, 2nd edn, 2003); G.I. Tunkin, *Вопросы теории международного права* [Questions on the Theory of International Law] (Moscow: Gosyurizdat, 1962), which has been translated into French, German, Hungarian and Polish. For the French translation see Grigoriei I. Tunkin (Centre de Recherches sur l'U.R.S.S. et les Pays de l'est transl.), *Droit international public: problèmes théoriques* (Paris: Pedone, 1965); for the German translation see Grigorij Ivanovič Tunkin (Klaus Wolf transl.), *Das Völkerrecht der Gegenwart: Theorie und Praxis* [The International Law of the Present: Theory and Practice] (Berlin: Staatsverlag der DDR, 1963).

[142] On 'peaceful coexistence' as a concept of Soviet foreign policy see Section 2 above.

[143] G.I. Tunkin, 'Co-existence and International Law', *Recueil des Cours de l'Académie de la Haye en ligne* 95 (1958), 1–81. On Tunkin's approach to international law in more detail see William E. Butler, 'The Learned Writings of Professor G. I. Tunkin', *Journal of the History of International Law* 4 (2002), 394–424.

[144] Mikhail Gorbachev, *Перестройка и новое мышление для нашей страны и для всего мира* [Restructuring and New Thinking for Our Country and the Whole World] (Moscow: Politizdat, 1987). English translation: Mikhail Gorbachev, *Perestroika: New Thinking for Our Country and the World* (New York, NY: Harper & Row Publishers, 1988).

[145] See Edward McWhinney, 'The "New Thinking" in Soviet International Law: Soviet Doctrines and Practice in the Post-Tunkin Era', *Canadian Yearbook of International Law* (1990), 309–37.

active cooperation in all areas.[146] Now, the aspect of class struggle in peaceful co-existence plays a subordinate role, and has to be understood as a 'peaceful competition' between different social systems, Müllerson and Vereshchetin argued.[147] In the second article, 'The Primacy of International Law in World Politics' (1989), Müllerson and Vereshchetin maintained that an increasing global interdependence does not tolerate unilateral actions by individual states that violate the interests of other states and peoples.[148] All states should therefore recognize the primacy of international law over politics. Contemporary international law is neither 'bourgeois' nor socialist in character but rather a general human-democratic normative system, Müllerson and Vereshchetin claimed.[149]

4.2 Sovereignty in Soviet Scholarship of International Law

The starting point for the Soviet doctrine's deviation from old 'bourgeois' international law with regard to the right of peoples to self-determination was a different conceptualization of sovereignty. According to the Soviet doctrine, sovereignty existed not only in the form of state sovereignty but also as national and people's sovereignty.[150] Nikolai Ushakov (1918–2001), head of the Institute of State and Law of the Soviet Academy of Sciences from 1965 to 1987, member of the International Law Commission from 1967 to 1986, and the leading Soviet scholar on sovereignty in his time, explained the distinction between the three dimensions in *Sovereignty in Contemporary International Law* (1963) the following way: people's sovereignty in the Soviet understanding exists only in socialist countries, since only there 'state power is directly organized by the working masses'.[151] National sovereignty, on the other hand, is a sort of an inchoate right, realized through self-determination. When a nation becomes an independent state, national sovereignty becomes a

[146] R.A. Müllerson and V.S. Vereshchetin, 'Новое мышление и международное право' [New Thinking in International Law], *Sovetskoe gosudarstvo i pravo* 50 (1988), no. 3, 3–9. See Henn-Jüri Uibopuu, 'Kopernikanische Wende in der sowjetischen Völkerrechtstheorie', *Recht in Ost und West* 32 (1988), 242–5.

[147] Müllerson and Vereshchetin, 'New Thinking in International Law' (1988) (n. 146), 4–5.

[148] R.A. Müllerson and V.S. Vereshchetin, 'Примат международного права в мировой политике' [Primacy of International Law in World Politics], *Sovetskoe gosudarstvo i pravo* 51 (1989), no. 7, 3–11. English translation: R.A. Müllerson and V.S. Vereshchetin, 'The Primacy of International Law in World Politics', in Anthony Carty and Gennady Danilenko (eds), *Perestroika and International Law: Current Anglo-Soviet Approaches to International Law* (Edinburgh: Edinburgh University Press, 1990), 6–14.

[149] Müllerson and Vereshchetin, 'Primacy of International Law in World Politics' (1989) (n. 148), 4.

[150] For more details on this conceptualization see Boris Meissner, 'Der Souveränitätsgedanke in der sowjetischen Völkerrechtslehre', in Eduard Kröker and Theodor Veiter (eds), *Rechtspositivismus, Menschenrechte und Souveränitätslehre in verschiedenen Rechtskreisen* (Vienna: Braumüller, 1976), 110–29; Henn-Jüri Uibopuu, 'Art. 76', in Martin Fincke (ed.), *Handbuch der Sowjetverfassung*, vol. 2 (Berlin: Duncker & Humblot, 1983), MN 3 et seq.

[151] N.A. Ushakov, *Суверенитет в современном международном праве* [Sovereignty in Contemporary International Law] (Moscow: Mezhdunarodnÿe otnosheniya, 1963), 6.

perfect right, and the sovereignty of the nation then merges with state sovereignty, Ushakov explained.[152]

What state sovereignty meant varied over the various periods of the Soviet doctrine. In the first phase, state sovereignty was understood in an almost absolute sense. Korovin for example believed that any restriction of (Soviet) state sovereignty would be a victory of capitalism over the socialist system. In the typical tone of the time, Korovin declared in *International Law of the Transitional Period* that the Soviet Union was called to emerge as 'the world champion of the doctrine of "classical" sovereignty, as far as its formal seclusion serves as a legal armour against the effects of those factors, under whose pressure the present borders of the capitalist states are shifted and their legal form transformed'.[153]

After the Second World War, Vyshinsky's definition dominated. He had defined state sovereignty as 'the external and internal independence of the state from any other force'.[154] A very similar definition was still used up until the 1957 edition of the international law textbook published under the auspices of the Institute of State and Law of the Soviet Academy of Sciences, although state sovereignty was now explicitly limited, at least insofar as a state was not allowed to 'act arbitrarily in its foreign affairs' and must 'not ignore the generally recognized principles of international law and its voluntary obligations under international law'.[155] Any breach of such obligations or arbitrary unilateral withdrawal from a treaty could not be justified with reference to sovereignty, the textbook maintained.[156] The most explicit departure from Vyshinsky's absolute vision of sovereignty was formulated by Tunkin already a year earlier. In *Fundamentals of Modern International Law* (1956), Tunkin maintained that 'freedom of action of the state is subject to legal restrictions', because '[w]hen we speak of sovereignty of the state in terms of international relations, then we do not mean any kind of "absolute sovereignty" or "unlimited freedom of action"'. State sovereignty in international relations is the actual independence of states,

[152] Ibid.
[153] Korowin, *Das Völkerrecht der Übergangszeit* (1929) (n. 127), 42–3.
[154] A.Y. Vyshinsky, 'О некоторых вопросах теории государства и права' [On Some Questions of the Theory of State and Law], *Sovetskoe gosudarstvo i pravo* 10 (1948), no. 6, 1–17, 8. See also A.Y. Vyshinsky, 'Международное право и международная организация' [International Law and International Organisation], *Sovetskoe gosudarstvo i pravo* 10 (1948), no. 1, 1–24. This definition, which had both a legal and a political-economic aspect, was preceded by a heated debate between Joseph Levin, Korovin, and Vyshinsky, but was ultimately able to assert itself. Levin's theory of sovereignty is laid down in I.D. Levin, *Принцип суверенитета в советском и международном праве* [The Principle of Sovereignty in Soviet and International Law] (Moscow: Pravda, 1947), and *Суверенитет* [Sovereignty] (Moscow: Yurid. izd-vo, 1948). On the reasons and content of the debate see Meissner, 'Der Souveränitätsgedanke in der sowjetischen Völkerrechtslehre' (1976) (n. 150), 111–14.
[155] Koschewnikow, *Völkerrecht* (1960) (n. 137), 91–3.
[156] Ibid.

Tunkin argued, which however is not unlimited.[157] In line and proceeding from Tunkin's definition, Ushakov later argued:

> The supremacy of the state means subordination to it of all persons and organisations within the bounds of state territory. The state has supreme power over all the organisations and persons on its territory.... The state's supremacy and sovereignty are not rooted in any outer forces but in the material living conditions of society at a certain stage of its historical development which engender the need for establishing a state with all the attributes of its public power.[158]

Thus, the state's territorial supremacy ('internal independence') is not absolute but 'is restricted by its obligations to respect the sovereignty of other states', whereas the state's independence in international affairs ('external independence') has to be understood as 'independence in foreign policy within the framework of international law', Ushakov maintained.

4.3 The Soviet Doctrine on Self-Determination

'National' sovereignty, on the other hand, was expressed through self-determination according to the Soviet doctrine. At the beginning and in line with Stalin's definition, the bearer of the right to self-determination were 'nations' (*natsii*), not 'peoples' (*narodov*). Following the signing of the UN Charter in 1945, the formulation was gradually blended into 'right of peoples and nations to self-determination' (*pravo narodov i natsii na samoopredelenie*).[159] Apart from that, Stalin's definition was kept almost untouched throughout the various periods. Writing in 1960, Gleb Starushenko (1922–2007), for example, evidently borrowed from it when stating in his influential monograph *The Principle of Self-determination of Peoples and Nations in the Foreign Policy of the Soviet States* (1960) that

> subjects of the right to self-determination ... are usually nations and national groups, as well as peoples consisting of several nations, nationalities and national

[157] G.I. Tunkin, *Основы современного международного права* [Fundamentals of Modern International Law] (Moscow: Vŷsshaya partiĭnaya shkola, 1956). German translation: G.I. Tunkin (Peter Rossbacher and Dietrich Frenzke transl.), 'Grundlagen des modernen Völkerrechts', in Institut für Internationales Recht an der Universität Kiel (ed.), *Drei sowjetische Beiträge zur Völkerrechtslehre* (Hamburg: Hansischer Gildenverlag, 1969), 1–57.

[158] N.I. Ushakov, 'International Law and Sovereignty', in Tunkin, *Contemporary International Law* (1969) (n. 65), 97–117, 99–100.

[159] See Meissner, *Sowjetunion und Selbstbestimmungsrecht* (1962) (n. 27), 35.

> groups which have a common territory, possess one or more common traits (historic, cultural, linguistic, religious, social, etc.), and strive to achieve a common aim through self-determination.[160]

Although the bearer of the right to self-determination were therefore both nations and peoples, the latter notion was understood more comprehensively. To qualify as a people, the respective group did not demand the degree of organization that the concept of nation presupposed. 'Peoples', on the other hand, included 'nations', and both groups were united by a common goal: independence with the help of the right to self-determination.[161]

With regard to the scope of the right to self-determination, the Soviet doctrine of international law was very consistent over the various periods. In particular, it was claimed that self-determination also entailed a right to secede. The third edition of the Soviet Academy of Science's international law textbook claimed, for example, that 'under contemporary international law, both the secession of a nation from one state and the creation of a new, independent state, as well as the reverse, the incorporation of one nation on the basis of a clear and free will of a nation into another state, is lawful'.[162] Similarly, V.V. Evgenev stated in an often quoted article in the journal *Soviet State and Law*:

> Each nation has the right to determine freely all questions relating to its national fate without violating the rights of other nations. A nation has the right to choose its form of statehood, either in the form of autonomy, by way of entering into federative relations with other nations, or, finally, by seceding completely, because each nation is sovereign and all nations are equal.[163]

But the Soviet reading of the right to self-determination went even further. Based on Lenin's definition of annexations in the Decree on Peace of 1917,[164] it was argued that the principle of self-determination was the sole basis for assessing the legality of territorial acquisitions.[165] Consequently, the decisive criterion for the

[160] Starushenko, *The Principle of National Self-determination in Soviet Foreign Policy* (1964) (n. 52), 197.

[161] See Hans Werner Bracht, 'Das Selbstbestimmungsrecht der Völker in der sowjetischen Völkerrechtslehre', in Boris Meissner (ed.), *Das Selbstbestimmungsrecht der Völker in Osteuropa und China* (Cologne: Verlag Wissenschaft und Politik, 1968), 9–20, 14, with numerous Soviet sources cited therein.

[162] Koschewnikow, *Völkerrecht* (1960) (n. 137), 252.

[163] V.V. Evgenev, 'Правосубъектность, суверенитет и невмешательство в международном праве' [Legal Personality, Sovereignty and Non-interference in International Law], *Sovetskoe gosudarstvo i pravo* 17 (1955), no. 2, 75–84. Quotation from the German translation: W.W. Jewgenjew (I. Leuschner transl.), 'Rechtssubjektivität, Souveränität, und Nichteinmischung im Völkerrecht', *Rechtswissenschaftlicher Informationsdienst* 4 (1955), MN 567–77, 570.

[164] See Section 1 above.

[165] See Peter Morré, *Die Änderung der staatlichen Gebietshoheit nach sowjetischer Völkerrechtslehre und Völkerrechtspraxis mit besonderer Berücksichtigung des Annexionsverbots* (Münster: PhD thesis 1967), 156, 165, 176.

legality of territorial alignments was not the agreement of the affected *state* but that of the *people* residing in that territory. Fyodor Kozhevnikov wrote, for example, in *The Soviet State and International Law* (1948):

> Soviet international law doctrine broadly allows the possibility of territorial changes on the ground of law and justice ... The enlargement of the USSR territory is primarily possible by means of plebiscite that is held on the question of the territorial accession of a transferred region or on the incorporated state ... According to the Soviet state's stance on international law, a plebiscite may, for example, be held as a method of reunification that is an accession of former Soviet territories *which were taken by force.*[166]

Although such explicit affirmations of the irrelevance of the use of force for the legality of territorial acquisitions were later abandoned, the Soviet doctrine remained consistent with regard to the will of the people as the decisive criterion for their assessment. Representative for this view is Yuri Barseghov (1925–2008), whose *Territory in International Law* (1958) was probably the most influential work on the subject written during the Soviet era. Starting from the Soviet understanding outlined above that state sovereignty is the realization of national sovereignty, Barseghov claimed that the state territory ideally reaches as far as it is approved by a nation living on its national territory.[167] Any change in the state's sovereignty, and hence also its state territory, will affect the right to self-determination of the population concerned, and therefore requires its consent, Barseghov argued.[168] Although the doctrine was later softened by Boris Klimenko and others,[169] this general assumption prevailed throughout the various periods of the Soviet doctrine. A contemporary critic in the West noted on this remarkable Soviet understanding:

> the use of consent or disagreement of the will of the people as the sole criterion for the legality and illegality of a territorial alignment makes it possible to regard as lawful any territorial change made against the will of the state concerned, which in the traditional view is nothing but an annexation, provided that consent is given by the affected population.[170]

[166] Kozhevnikov, *The Soviet State and International Law* (1948) (n. 138), 181 (emphasis added).

[167] Barseghov, *Territory in International Law* (1958) (n. 57), 79. For core passages of the monograph in German translation see Meissner, *Sowjetunion und Selbstbestimmungsrecht* (1962) (n. 27), Docs 507, 517, 537, 543, 555, 582, 603, 616.

[168] Barseghov, *Territory in International Law* (1958) (n. 57), 56–79.

[169] See B.M. Klimenko, *Государственная территория* [State Territory] (Moscow: Mezhdunarodnўe otnosheniya, 1974); B.M. Klimenko, *Мирное решение территориальных споров* [Peaceful Resolution of Territorial Disputes] (Moscow: Mezhdunarodnўe otnosheniya, 1982).

[170] Morré, *Die Änderung der staatlichen Gebietshoheit* (1967) (n. 165), 156.

4.4 Self-Determination and the Right of Assistance in Wars of National Liberation

Interest in the theorization of self-determination diminished from around 1960 onwards.[171] Instead, self-determination was more and more discussed with regard to its practical application in the process of decolonization and the struggle of dependant peoples in so-called wars of national liberation.[172] Whereas post-Second World War Soviet international law scholarship promoted a strict prohibition of the use of force, it simultaneously maintained—in line with and support of the Soviet policy expressed in international fora like the UN General Assembly[173]—that wars of national liberation by peoples under colonial regimes or other forms of alien domination were lawful as well as the support, including the use of force, given to those peoples by third states.[174]

Although the arguments in favour of this view varied over time depending on the Soviet doctrine's development, the predominant position seemed to be that colonialism was considered a permanent armed attack, against which self-defence outside the scope of article 51 of the UN Charter and independently from other legal rights was allowed.[175] As late as 1983, Grigory Tunkin explicitly reaffirmed

[171] See the bibliography of the Soviet literature on self-determination published between 1962 and 1973 in Boris Meissner, Dietrich Frenzke, and Erika Chilecki (eds), *Sowjetunion und Völkerrecht 1962–1973. Bibliographie und Analyse* (Cologne: Verlag Wissenschaft und Politik, 1977), 235–43. Key texts on self-determination after 1960 include: D.B. Levin, 'Принцип самоопределения наций в международном праве' [The Principle of Self-determination of Nations in International Law], *Sovetskiĭ ezhegodnik mezhdunarodnogo prava* 1962/1963, 25–45; N.M. Minasyan, 'Ленинское учение самоопределении наций и международное право' [Lenin's Doctrine of Self-determination of Nations and International Law], *Sovetskiĭ ezhegodnik mezhdunarodnogo prava* 1970, 29–42; and G.I. Tunkin, 'Ленинские принципы равноправия и самоопределения народов и современное международное право' [Lenin's Principles of Equal Rights and Self-determination of Peoples and Contemporary International Law], *Vestnik Moskovskogo universiteta. Pravo* 2 (1970), 62–71.

[172] See e.g. Gleb Starushenko, 'Abolition of Colonialism and International Law', in Tunkin, *Contemporary International Law* (1969) (n. 65), 77–96; Gleb Starushenko, *Africa Makes a Choice. The Development of Socialist-Oriented States* (Moscow: Novosti Press Agency Publishing House, 1975). On the Soviet Union's engagement in this process more broadly see Galia Golan, *The Soviet Union and National Liberation Movements in the Third World* (Boston, MA: Unwin Hyman, 1988).

[173] See Section 2 above.

[174] For two good surveys of that view see Friedrich-Christian Schroeder, 'Die Rechtmäßigkeit des Krieges nach westlicher und sowjetischer Völkerrechtsauffassung', in Maurach and Meissner (eds), *Völkerrecht in Ost und West* (1967) (n. 126), 178–218, 216–17, and Jiri Toman, 'La conception soviétique des guerres de libération nationale', in Antonio Cassese (ed.), *Current Problems of International Law* (Milan: Giuffrè, 1975), 355–75, with numerous Soviet accounts cited therein. Other Western accounts dealing with the Soviet perspective on national wars of liberation written during the Cold War period include George Ginsburgs, '"Wars of National Liberation" and the Modern Law of Nations—The Soviet Thesis', *Law and Contemporary Problems* 29 (1964), 910–42; Eckart Klein, 'Nationale Befreiungskämpfe und Dekolonialisierungspolitik der Vereinten Nationen: Zu einigen völkerrechtlichen Tendenzen', *Zeitschrift für ausländisches öffentliches Recht und Völkerrecht* 36 (1976), 618–53, 647–50; Daniel Papp, 'National Liberation during Détente: the Soviet Outlook', *International Journal* 32 (1976–1977), 82–99. For a recent review of this doctrine see Socher, 'Lenin, (Just) Wars of National Liberation, and the Soviet Doctrine on the Use of Force' (2017) (n. 91), 219–45.

[175] For a description of the doctrine's evolution see Schroeder, 'Die Rechtmäßigkeit des Krieges' (1967) (n. 174), 216–17.

in *Law and Force in the International System* that 'modern international law also includes the right of peoples of colonial and dependent countries to proceed to armed force against the metropolitan states, which prevent the respective countries or territories from exercising their right to self-determination'.[176] Such a recourse to armed force would be legitimate self-defence, following 'in general form' from the UN Charter, Tunkin maintained. Moreover, the right to use force in wars of national liberation was not restricted to colonial situations, Tunkin asserted towards the end of the book: external support to wars of national liberation would be necessary in order to fight 'imperialistic politics', in particular of the United States, which left 'the peoples of these states no free choice in the path of their economic and social development', and which 'bind them to the chains of neocolonialism to the capitalist world and to prevent their development on the path of socialist orientation'. 'As a counterweight to this policy', Tunkin concluded, 'the Soviet Union and the other countries of the socialist camp follow a policy of defence of the new states against imperialist attacks in accordance with the norms of international law and assist them in the consolidation of their political independence.'[177]

4.5 The Theory of 'Limited Sovereignty' or 'Limited Self-Determination' in the Eastern Bloc

Within the Soviet sphere of influence, the rhetoric of 'socialist self-determination' articulated in the Brezhnev Doctrine also affected the legal literature. Soon after the Soviet intervention in Hungary in 1956, Korovin, Tunkin, and others started to argue that within the Eastern Bloc, the principle of peaceful coexistence had to be replaced by the principle of proletarian internationalism.[178] The relationship between these two principles was best summarized in a book chapter entitled 'International Law in Relations among Socialist Countries' as part of a collection of articles published under the editorship of Tunkin in 1969. According to the author, V.M. Shurshalov,

[176] G.I. Tunkin, *Право и сила в международной системе* [Law and Force in the International System] (Moscow: Mezhdunarodnȳe otnosheniya, 1983). Quotation from the German translation: Grigorij Ivanovič Tunkin (Elmar Rauch transl.), *Recht und Gewalt im internationalen System* (Berlin: Duncker & Humblot, 1986), 64.

[177] Ibid.

[178] E.A. Korovin, 'Пролетарский интернационализм и международное право' [Proletarian Internationalism and International Law], *Sovetskiĭ ezhegodnik mezhdunarodnogo prava* (1958), 50–69; G.I. Tunkin, 'Новый тип международных отношений и международное право' [New Type of International Relations and International Law], *Sovetskoe gosudarstvo i pravo* 21 (1959), no. 1, 81–94, 83–5, 93. See also Sh. Sanakoev, 'Пролетарский интернационализм—основа взаимоотношений стран социализма' [Proletarian Internationalism—The Basis for the Relations between Socialist States], *Mezhdunarodnaya zhizn'* (1958), no. 7, 30–43. On the concept of proletarian internationalism see Section 3 above.

> [t]he principle of peaceful coexistence and the principle of socialist internationalism operate in two different spheres: the former in relations between states with different socio-economic systems, the latter within the socialist community of nations. Consequently, in the relations between socialist states the principle of peaceful coexistence is replaced by the higher, more profound and qualitatively new principle of socialist internationalism.[179]

From 1970 onwards, similar assertions could be found in almost every Soviet international law textbook.[180]

The consequence of this theory was that within the Eastern Bloc, core principles of international law such as sovereignty and equality of states, non-intervention and self-determination continued to exist but were filled with a new 'socialist' content. Most prominently, this claimed different standard in the Soviet sphere of influence included a right of 'brotherly assistance', which, according to Tunkin, was 'the right of each state of the socialist world system to receive help from other socialist states, and the duty of each socialist state to assist other socialist states. This obligation of mutual assistance regards equally political, economic, military and other relations.'[181] This claim of the existence of a socialist right to 'brotherly assistance' under international law was raised in Soviet international law textbooks as late as 1987.[182] Explicit affirmations of the Soviet interventions in Hungary and Czechoslovakia were rare, but existed. For Evgeny Usenko (1918–2010), for example, the Soviet intervention in Hungary in 1956 was a prime example of brotherly assistance,[183] and Tunkin argued in *Theory of International Law* that the 'events' in Czechoslovakia in 1968 were a 'logical extension' of the concept already applied in Hungary.[184] The provided 'aid' had preserved the country's sovereignty and national independence, Tunkin maintained.[185]

[179] V.M. Shurshalov, 'International Law in Relations among Socialist Countries', in Tunkin, *Contemporary International Law* (1969) (n. 65), 59–76, 71.

[180] See e.g. V.I. Lisovskii, *Международное право* [International Law] (Moscow: Vўsshaya shkola, 3rd edn, 1970), where a new chapter on 'International Principles and Norms in Effect in the World System of Socialism' was added in the third edition, in which it was claimed that the socialist states in their mutual relations 'apply generally accepted norms of international law and also new norms which are being assembled in the process of conducting these relationships' (at 50).

[181] Tunkin, *Questions on the Theory of International Law* (1962) (n. 141), 321.

[182] See E.T. Usenko, 'Международное право в отношениях между социалистическими государствами' [International Law in Relations Between Socialist States], in Natalia Blatova (ed.), *Международное право* [International Law] (Moscow: Yuridicheskaya literatura, 1987), 184–215, 196–7.

[183] E.T. Usenko, 'Основные международно-правовые принципы сотрудничества социалистических государств' [Basic International Legal Principles of Co-operation of Socialist States], *Sovetskoe gosudarstvo i pravo* 23 (1961), no. 3, 16–29, 28. German translation: E.T. Usenko (I. Brehme transl.), 'Die völkerrechtlichen Grundprinzipien der Zusammenarbeit der sozialistischen Staaten', *Sowjetwissenschaft. Gesellschaftswissenschaftliche Beiträge* 14 (1961), no. 7, 749–65.

[184] Tunkin, *Theory of International Law* (1970) (n. 141), 498–9.

[185] Ibid.

5. Conclusions

For Lenin, the originator arguably not only of the Soviet approach to self-determination but also of self-determination as a concept of international law more broadly, self-determination was above all a means to destroy Tsarist autocracy. Following the Russian Revolution and the ensuing Russian Civil War, the Declaration of the Rights of the Peoples of Russia and the subsequent peace treaties with Estonia, Georgia, Latvia, Lithuania, and Poland granted the peoples on the territory of the collapsed Russian Empire the right to self-determination and even state independence. These documents constitute the first formulations of a former imperial power recognizing the principle of self-determination. Subsequent Soviet state practice under Stalin however degraded these early proclamations, and apart from Poland, none of these republics were able to sustain their newly gained independence but were shortly thereafter annexed by and incorporated into the newly formed Soviet Union.

In the first decades after the Second World War, the Soviet Union acted as a strong supporter of self-determination in the drafting processes of all important international legal instruments that led to the juridification of the principle. Self-determination was introduced as one of the principles of the United Nations only at the urge of the Soviet Union at the San Francisco Conference in 1945, and the same might be said of the Human Rights Covenants, in which the right of self-determination would arguably not have been included without the insistence on the part of the Soviet delegates in the UN General Assembly. On the other hand, the strong support for self-determination in the Colonial Independence Declaration appeared hypocritical, since the call for the termination of colonialism implied no practical risks for the Soviet Union due to the ambiguity of colonialism as defined by the General Assembly and the dominant prerequisite of geographical separation from the parent state (the 'saltwater test').

It is therefore interesting to note how the Soviet Union's approach to self-determination changed after the adoption of the Friendly Relations Declaration in 1970, when the focus gradually shifted to situations outside the colonial context. During the Conference on Security and Co-operation in Europe (CSCE), the Soviet Union was initially very reluctant about the idea of including the right to self-determination among the principles guiding relations between participating states.[186] Although it did later propose one of the four drafts on self-determination,[187] the Soviet Union simultaneously stressed the principle of

[186] See Boris Meissner, 'Die Grundsätze der "friedlichen Koexistenz" als Elemente eines gesamteuropäischen Sicherheitssystems', in Boris Meissner and Alexander Uschakow (eds), *Probleme der Konferenz über Sicherheit und Zusammenarbeit in Europa* (Berlin: Berlin Verlag, 1975), 45–66, 62–5.

[187] See Soviet Union, CSCE, Provisional Verbatim Records I/3, 3, according to which one of the 'principles of primary significance' to be respected and observed by states was that of equal rights and self-determination of peoples 'in accordance with which all peoples possess the right to establish the social regime and to choose the form of government which they consider expedient and necessary to secure

'inviolability of borders' with which self-determination had to be balanced. That the inviolability of borders was included as a separate principle in the concluding document, the 1975 Helsinki Final Act,[188] and not only as a subsidiary corollary of the principle of sovereign equality of states (as previously in the Friendly Relations Declaration) was quite striking and followed from the Soviet goal of achieving recognition of the existing *de facto* borders of Europe at the time.[189]

During the debates on the Charter of Paris for a New Europe in 1990,[190] the Soviet Union ultimately called the application of self-determination on the European continent into question: on the eve of its collapse, the Soviet Union raised the spectre that territorial changes could have 'destructive snowball effects that would throw Europe back into the kind of situation, which it knows only too well from its own history'.[191] The result was a compromise: compared to the Helsinki Final Act, in which the universal significance of the right to self-determination and its basis for friendly relations was once more stressed, the Charter of Paris only 're-affirmed' the right in conformity with the UN Charter and their relevant norms in international law, including the territorial integrity of states.[192]

the economic, social and cultural development of their country'. Quotation from Antonio Cassese, 'The Helsinki Declaration and Self-determination', in Thomas Buergenthal (ed.), *Human Rights, International Law and the Helsinki Accord* (Allanheld: Osmun & Co., 1977), 83–119, 95.

[188] Helsinki Final Act, 1 August 1975, 1975 ILM 1292. See Cassese, 'The Helsinki Declaration and Self-determination' (1977) (n. 187), 93–105; Juha Salo, 'Self-determination: An Overview of History and Present State with Emphasis on the CSCE Process', *Finnish Yearbook of International Law* 2 (1991), 268–342, 310–19; Cassese, *Self-determination of Peoples* (1995) (n. 7), 278–92; Summers, *Peoples and International Law* (2014) (n. 52), 275–80.

[189] Sir Michael Wood and Daniel Purisch, 'Helsinki Final Act (1975)', in MPEPIL (online edn), MN 9. On the principle of inviolability of borders see Boris Meissner, 'Die Entwicklungstendenzen in der sowjetischen außenpolitischen Theorie und Völkerrechtslehre 1962 bis 1973', in Boris Meissner, Dietrich Frenzke, and Erika Chilecki (eds), *Sowjetunion und Völkerrecht 1962–1973* (1977) (n. 171), 9–58, 35. According to Meissner, the principle was first introduced in the 1972 edition of the international law textbook published under the auspices of the Moscow State Institute of International Relations (MGIMO): F.I. Kozhevnikov (ed.), *Курс международного права* (Moscow: Mezhdunarodnye otnosheniya, 3rd edn, 1972), 44.

[190] Charter of Paris for a New Europe, 21 November 1990, 1990 ILM 193. See Cassese, *Self-determination of Peoples* (1995) (n. 7), 292–6; Summers, *Peoples and International Law* (2014) (n. 52), 280–3.

[191] Soviet Union, CSCE, Provisional Verbatim Records II/2, 37, quoted from Summers, *Peoples and International Law* (2014) (n. 52), 282.

[192] Cf. Helsinki Final Act (1975) (n. 188), Principle VIII ('1. The participating States will respect the equal rights of peoples and their right to self-determination, acting at all times in conformity with the purposes and principles of the Charter of the United Nations and with the relevant norms of international law, including those relating to the territorial integrity of States. 2. By virtue of the principle of equal rights and self-determination of peoples, all peoples always have the right, in full freedom, to determine, when and as they wish, their internal and external political status, without external interference, and to pursue as they wish their political, economic, social and cultural development. 3. The participating States reaffirm the universal significance of respect for and effective exercise of equal rights and self-determination of peoples for the development of friendly relations among themselves as among States: they also recall the importance of the elimination of any form of violation of this principle') with the wording of the relevant passage in the Charter of Paris ('We reaffirm the equal rights of peoples and their right to self-determination in conformity with the Charter of the United Nations and with the relevant norms of international law, including those relating to territorial integrity of States'), Charter of Paris for a New Europe (1990) (n. 190), 197.

On a theoretical level, the Soviet scholarship of international law was part of the struggle of two antagonistic world views, and its doctrine on self-determination served not only as an apology of Soviet foreign policy but was also a reflection of a more general regional fragmentation of international law that was first postulated by Korovin in *International Law of the Transitional Period* in the 1920s, and later refined and updated by Vyshinsky, Kozhevnikov, Tunkin, and others. The promotion of 'peaceful coexistence' as a legal principle in the relations between states of different systems on the one hand and the principle of 'proletarian internationalism' among socialist states on the other hand meant above all the assertion of the existence of two different legal standards, depending on the region or sphere of influence where international law was applied. This was also true for the 'right of peoples and nations to self-determination', which the Soviet doctrine generally promoted in its most romantic (or, in Koskenniemi's terminology: *Rousseauesque*) conception, including a right of secession, and even up to the point of arguing for an exception to the prohibition of the use of force for third states in support of so-called wars of national liberation. For situations inside the Soviet Union's claimed sphere of influence, on the other hand, self-determination was said to exist in a perverted 'socialist' variant, which meant above all that it was conditional upon the continuous 'fraternal cooperation' between the socialist states in the Eastern Bloc. Understood that way, the rhetoric of 'socialist' self-determination served as a pretext for Soviet military interventions in Hungary, Czechoslovakia, and Afghanistan, and a faked 'will of the peoples' of Estonia, Latvia, and Lithuania was used already earlier as a justification for the Soviet Union's annexation of the Baltic states in 1940.

2
Russia, the Right to Self-Determination and Sovereignty

On 12 June 1990, the Congress of People's Deputies of the Russian Soviet Federative Socialist Republic (SFSR)—the largest, most populous, and most economically developed union republic of the Soviet Union—adopted a declaration on the republic's state sovereignty.[1] It was the seventh such declaration in a 'parade of sovereignties' in the territory of the Soviet Union which had started with Estonia's declaration of sovereignty in November 1988 and had continued with similar declarations in Lithuania, Latvia, and Azerbaijan over the course of 1989.[2] Following the Russian SFSR's declaration of sovereignty, the development almost instantly spilled over into the union republic's territory, and within the next six months, fourteen of the then sixteen autonomous republics inside the Russian SFSR followed with similar sovereignty declarations of their own.[3]

Unlike the Soviet Union as a whole, the disintegration of the Russian SFSR could however be averted with the conclusion of three separate agreements between the (now renamed) Russian Federation and its sub-units on the different administrative levels.[4] On 31 March 1992, the three agreements—commonly jointly referred

[1] Декларация о государственном суверенитете РСФСР [Declaration on the State Sovereignty of the RSFSR], 12 June 1990, *Argumenty i Fakty* 1990, no. 24, 1. English translation reprinted in William E. Butler, *Collected Legislation of Russia*, Supp 1993-1 (Dobbs Ferry, NY: Oceana Publications), 65–7.

[2] See Jeffrey Kahn, 'The Parade of Sovereignties: Establishing the Vocabulary of the New Russian Federalism', *Post-Soviet Affairs* 16 (2000), no. 1, 58–89; Theodor Schweisfurth, 'Vom Einheitsstaat (UdSSR) zum Staatenbund (GUS)', *Zeitschrift für ausländisches öffentliches Recht und Völkerrecht* 52 (1992), 541–702, 586–93.

[3] See Jeffrey Kahn, *Federalism, Democratization, and the Rule of Law in Russia* (Oxford: Oxford University Press, 2002), 106.

[4] Договор о разграничении предметов ведения и полномочий между федеральными органами государственной власти РФ и органами власти суверенных республик в составе РФ [Treaty on the Delimitation of the Subjects of Jurisdiction and Powers between the Federal Bodies of State Power of the Russian Federation and the Authorities of Sovereign Republics within the Russian Federation], 31 March 1992; Договор о разграничении предметов ведения и полномочий между федеральными органами государственной власти Российской Федерации и органами власти краев, областей, городов Москвы и Санкт-петербурга Российской Федерации [Treaty on the Delimitation of the Subjects of Jurisdiction and Powers between the Federal Bodies of State Power of the Russian Federation and the Authorities of the Territories, Regions, and the Cities of Moscow and Saint Petersburg of the Russian Federation], 31 March 1992; Договор о разграничении предметов ведения и полномочий между федеральными органами государственной власти Российской Федерации и органами власти автономной области, автономных округов в составе Российской Федерации [Treaty on the Delimitation of the Subjects of Jurisdiction and Powers between the Federal Bodies of State Power of the Russian Federation and the Authorities of the Autonomous Regions and Autonomous National Areas of the Russian Federation], 31 March 1992. English translations of all three

Russia and the Right to Self-Determination in the Post-Soviet Space. Johannes Socher, Oxford University Press.
 DOI: 10.1093/oso/9780192897176.003.0003

to as the Treaty of Federation—were concluded, just before a heavy constitutional crisis broke out, reaching its tipping point in September 1993 when Russian president Boris Yeltsin sought to dissolve the Congress of People's Deputies and its Supreme Soviet without the constitution giving him the power to do so. Mass protests and the storming of the White House (then the Russian parliament building) followed. Notwithstanding that the parliament declared Yeltsin's decision null and void, impeached him, and proclaimed vice-president Alexander Rutskoy acting president, Yeltsin was able to consolidate his power.[5] On 12 December 1993, a new Russian constitution was adopted, approved in a national referendum by a majority of 58 per cent, on a 55 per cent turnout.[6]

According to article 65(1) of the Russian Constitution (RC), the Russian Federation consists of twenty-two republics,[7] nine territories (*krais*), and forty-six regions (*oblasts*),[8] three cities of federal importance,[9] one autonomous region, and four autonomous national areas (*okrugs*), constituting together the eighty-five subjects of the Russian Federation.[10] Formally, all constituent entities have equal rights (article 5 RC), although republics have certain privileges compared to other subjects, for example the right to establish their own state language (article 68(2) RC) or the right to enact their own constitution (article 66(1) RC). Following the conclusion of the Treaty of Federation, an asymmetrical federal system was gradually established, and by 2003, nearly all constituent entities had defined their relationship to the federal government individually on the basis of treaties.[11] Since the

treaties reprinted in William E. Butler and Jane Henderson (eds), *Russian Legal Texts: The Foundations of a Rule-of-Law State and a Market Economy* (London: Simmonds & Hill, 1998), 51–72.

[5] For a recent re-telling of the events see Masha Gessen, *The Future is History: How Totalitarianism Reclaimed Russia* (New York, NY: Riverhead Books, 2017), 96–117.

[6] Конституция Российской Федерации [Constitution of the Russian Federation], *Rossiĭskaya gazeta*, 25 December 1993. All quotations from the Russian Constitution follow the English translation available on the Russian Constitutional Court's website: http://www.ksrf.ru/en/info/legalbases/constitutionrf/documents/constitution-eng.pdf. On the constitution's drafting history see Rainer Grote, 'The Russian Federation: Introductory Note', in Rüdiger Wolfrum, Rainer Grote, and Erika de Wet (eds), *Constitutions of the Countries of the World*, vol. 15, Supp 2014-6 (Oxford: Oxford University Press), 4–12. Since adoption in 1993, the Russian Constitution has been amended five times. For the most recent reforms see Johannes Socher, 'Farewell to the European Constitutional Tradition: The 2020 Russian Constitutional Amendments', *Zeitschrift für ausländisches öffentliches Recht und Völkerrecht* 80 (2020), 615–48.

[7] Adygeia, Altai, Bashkortostan, Buryatia, Dagestan, Ingushetia, Kabardino-Balkaria, Kalmykia, Karachay-Cherkessia, Karelia, Komi, Mari El, Mordovia, Sakha, North Ossetia–Alania, Tatarstan, Tuva, Udmurtia, Khakassia, Chechnya, Chuvashia, and, since March 2014, Crimea.

[8] Territories and regions are legally identical and the different denotation is purely traditional.

[9] Moscow, Saint Petersburg, and, since March 2014, Sevastopol.

[10] Originally, the Russian Federation comprised eighty-nine federal subjects. By 2008, the number had decreased to eighty-three due to several administrative reforms. On 18 March 2014, the city of Sevastopol and the Republic of Crimea became the eighty-fourth and eighty-fifth federal subjects of Russia. On the legality of their incorporation into the Russian Federation see Chapter 4 Section 2 below.

[11] A process which Jeffrey Kahn later called, with reference to the earlier 'parade of sovereignties', the 'parade of treaties', see Kahn, *Federalism, Democratization, and the Rule of Law in Russia* (2002) (n. 3), 150–73.

substance of these individual agreements differed from one another, the shared jurisdiction between the federation and the respective federal subjects varied sometimes considerably. In 1999, however, the Russian federal government adopted a law to streamline the treaty-making process[12] and eventually decided to stop the process entirely by requesting that any agreement in force had to be confirmed by a federal law, or, in the case of agreements concerning the transfer of the effectuation of powers, by a decree of the federal government, within two years. All agreements not confirmed in this manner would be terminated after the two-year period had expired, that is as from 8 July 2005.[13]

Only two federal subjects refused to sign the Treaty of Federation in 1992: Tatarstan and Chechnya.[14] Among the various independence movements inside the Russian Federation, Tatarstan and Chechnya stand out for at least two more reasons: both have long histories of resistance to Russian rule, originating in events long before the collapse of the Soviet Union and even that of the Russian Empire, and both were subject to Russian Constitutional Court cases in the 1990s in which the right of peoples to self-determination under international law was discussed.

This chapter analyses Russia's state practice inside the Russian Federation with regard to the right of peoples to self-determination and state sovereignty through the prism of these two conflicts. Following an assessment of the interplay of international law and domestic law in the Russian Constitution more generally, the constitutional balance between state sovereignty and self-determination is scrutinized in more detail (Section 1). Subsequently, the first two case studies in this book on Tatarstan (Section 2) and Chechnya (Section 3) illustrate how Russia dealt with claims for self-determination within its international borders of 1991 in practice.

1. The Balance in the Russian Constitution

A first reference to self-determination and international law more generally can be found already in the preamble of the Russian Constitution. It reads:

> We, the multinational people of the Russian Federation, united by a common fate on our land, establishing human rights and freedoms, civil peace and accord,

[12] Federal Law of Russia No. 119-FZ, О принципах и порядке разграничения предметов ведения и полномочий между органами государственной власти Российской Федерации и органами государственной власти субъектов Российской Федерации [On the Principles and Procedure for Delimitation of Subjects of Jurisdiction and Powers between Bodies of State Power of the Russian Federation and Bodies of State Power of the Subjects of the Russian Federation], 24 June 1999, SZRF 1999, no. 26, item 3176.

[13] William E. Butler, *Russian Law* (Oxford: Oxford University Press, 3rd edn, 2009), MN 4.42; Angelika Nußberger, 'Russia', in MPEPIL (online edn), MN 63.

[14] Tatarstan did however sign separate treaties in 1994 and 2007, see Section 2 below.

> preserving the historically established State unity, proceeding from universally acknowledged principles of equality and self-determination of peoples, ... reviving the sovereign statehood of Russia and asserting the firmness of its democratic basis, striving to ensure the well-being and prosperity of Russia, proceeding from the responsibility for our Fatherland before present and future generations, reconizing ourselves to be part of the world community....

The preamble can be seen as a reflection of a general openness of the Russian Constitution towards international law,[15] an assessment which is confirmed by several references to international law in the text of the constitution itself. Apart from articles 15 and 17 RC (which will be discussed in more detail below), international law is mentioned in articles 46 and 55 RC[16] and also in articles 62–63, 67, 69, and 125 RC.

1.1 The General Relationship between Domestic Law and International Law in Russia

The Russian Constitution regulates the relationship between domestic law and international law in article 15 RC. Paragraph 1 declares that the Russian Constitution has 'supreme legal force, direct effect and shall be applicable on the entire territory of the Russian Federation', and according to paragraph 4 of the same article,

> [u]niversally recognized principles and norms of international law as well as international agreements of the Russian Federation should be an integral part of its legal system. If an international agreement of the Russian Federation establishes rules, which differ from those stipulated by law, then the rules of the international agreement shall be applied.

William Butler has called this formal recognition of international law as an integral part of the Russian Constitution 'one of the most momentous changes of the twentieth century in the development of Russian law'.[17] And indeed, compared to its Soviet predecessors, this formal recognition may be described as revolutionary,

[15] See Angelika Nußberger and Yuri Safoklov, 'Präambel', in Bernd Wieser (ed.), *Handbuch der russischen Verfassung* (Vienna: Verlag Österreich, 2014), MN 15.

[16] Article 46(3) RC states that '[e]veryone shall have the right in accordance with international treaties of the Russian Federation to appeal to interstate bodies for the protection of human rights and freedoms if all available internal means of legal protection have been exhausted', and according to article 55(1) RC, '[t]he enumeration in the Constitution of the Russian Federation of the basic rights and freedoms should not be interpreted as a denial or diminution of other universally recognized human and civil rights and freedoms'.

[17] Butler, *Russian Law* (2009) (n. 13), MN 18.68.

since it is in stark contrast to the former Soviet constitutional doctrine according to which international law applied only if specifically enacted into domestic law.[18]

Article 15(4) RC differentiates between two sources of international law: international treaties and 'universally recognized principles and norms of international law'. According to article 2 of the Law on International Treaties of the Russian Federation, international treaties are all 'international agreements concluded by the Russian Federation with a foreign state or with an international organization in written form and regulated by international law, irrespective of whether such agreement is contained in one or several related documents, and also irrespective of its specific name'.[19] Different Russian courts further concretized this definition. The Russian Supreme Court of Arbitration has defined international treaties with reference to article 2 of the 1969 Vienna Convention on the Law of Treaties (VCLT),[20] according to which a treaty is 'an international agreement concluded between States in written form and governed by international law, whether embodied in a single instrument or in two or more related instruments and whatever its particular designation'.[21] By contrast, a decree by the Russian Supreme Court from 1995 limits the stated supremacy of international treaties in the second sentence of article 15(4) RC to agreements which were not only signed but also ratified by the Russian Federation.[22] And in another decree from 2003, the same court ruled that if federal or regional executive bodies conclude an international treaty within the scope of their competencies, then this treaty takes precedence over the sub-legislative acts of the signing organ.[23] Lastly, the Russian Constitutional

[18] Soviet scholars usually rejected both dualist and monist theories. From a Marxist-Leninist perspective, dualism was ideologically problematic, since its underlying rationale is the separation of powers (which was perceived as 'bourgeois'). Monism, on the other hand, represented a cosmopolitan world view threatening the Soviet Union's sovereignty. Nevertheless, Soviet post-Second World War doctrine resembled Western dualist doctrines, since there was general agreement that domestic law and international law were two separate legal systems, see Tarja Långström, *Transformation in Russia and International Law* (Leiden: Martinus Nijhoff, 2003), 348–61, esp. at 349–52. Following this approach, the Soviet Union was able to sign numerous international treaties, including treaties on human rights, and at the same time could avoid implementing some or all of their provisions in the domestic legal order, see Grote, 'The Russian Federation' (2014) (n. 6), 16; Gennady M. Danilenko, 'The New Russian Constitution and International Law', *American Journal of International Law* 88 (1994), 451–70, 458. This approach changed only with the Declaration of the Rights and Freedoms of Man and Citizen, adopted by the Supreme Soviet of the Russian SFSR on 22 November 1991, by which, for the first time in Russian history, generally recognized international norms on human rights were given priority over domestic Russian laws in an amended article of the Russian SFSR Constitution of 1978, see ibid., 461.

[19] Federal Law of Russia No. 101-FZ, О международных договорах Российской Федерации [On International Treaties of the Russian Federation], 15 July 1995, SZRF 1995, no. 29, item 2757.

[20] Supreme Court of Arbitration of Russia, *О действии международных договоров Российской Федерации применительно к вопросом арбитражного процесса* [On the Effect of International Treaties of the Russian Federation with Regard to the Issue of Arbitration Proceedings], Decision of the Plenum No. 8, 11 June 1999, *Rossiĭskaya yustitsiya* 1999, no. 10, 59. (The Russian Supreme Court of Arbitration was dissolved and merged with the Russian Supreme Court in 2014.)

[21] Vienna Convention on the Law of Treaties, 23 May 1969, 1155 UNTS 331.

[22] Supreme Court of Russia, Decree of the Plenum No. 8/1995, 31 October 1995, BVS RF 1996, no. 1, 3.

[23] Supreme Court of Russia, Decree of the Plenum No. 5/2003, 10 October 2003, BVS RF 2003, no. 12, 3.

Court ruled in 2012 that temporarily applied, but not yet ratified treaties have to be treated equally with ratified treaties if they concern individual legal positions.[24]

With regard the second category of sources mentioned in article 15(4) RC, it is important to note that the Russian Constitution doesn't refer to international custom, but uses instead the term 'universally recognized principles and norms of international law'. Although this expression is not entirely foreign to the language of international legal instruments,[25] the wording deviates from the standard terminology used by international tribunals such as the International Court of Justice, whose statutes usually differentiate between the categories 'custom', 'treaty', and 'general principles' as the three sources of international law.[26]

This terminological difference notwithstanding, it is sometimes maintained in Western scholarship that Russian constitutional doctrine equates 'universally recognized principles and norms of international law' with customary international law.[27] On closer inspection, however, this assertion turns out to be inaccurate, and some clarification seems therefore appropriate:[28] a certain blending of categories of the different sources of international law in Russian doctrine already becomes evident in the aforementioned two decrees by the Russian Supreme Court. According to the 2003 decree, universally recognized principles and norms are all 'basic imperative norms of international law adopted and recognized by the international community of states as a whole, from which deviation is inadmissible'.[29] According to the 1995 decree, these imperative norms are 'laid down in international covenants, conventions and other documents';[30] as examples, the latter decree explicitly

[24] Constitutional Court of Russia, *По делу о проверке конституционности пункта 1 статьи 23 Федерального закона «О международных договорах Российской Федерации» в связи с жалобой гражданина И.Д. Ушакова* [In the Case on the Verification of the Constitutionality of Paragraph 1 of Article 23 of the Federal Law 'On International Treaties of the Russian Federation' in Connection with the Complaint of Citizen I.D. Ushakov], Decision No. 8-P/2012, 27 March 2012, *Rossiĭskaya gazeta*, 13 April 2012.

[25] See e.g. the wording in the second and third paragraphs of the seventh principle of the 1970 Friendly Relations Declaration: 'Every State has the duty to fulfil in good faith its obligations under the generally recognized principles and rules of international law. Every State has the duty to fulfil in good faith its obligations under international agreements valid under the generally recognized principles and rules of international law', GA Res 26/25 (XXV) (Friendly Relations Declaration), 24 October 1970, UN Doc. A/RES/25/2625.

[26] Cf. Statute of the International Court of Justice, art. 38(1): 'the Court, whose function is to decide in accordance with international law such disputes as are submitted to it, shall apply: a. international conventions, whether general or particular, establishing rules expressly recognized by the contesting states; b. international custom, as evidence of a general practice accepted as law; c. the general principles of law recognized by civilized nations'.

[27] See e.g. Butler, *Russian Law* (2009) (n. 13), MN 18.68 ('The formal recognition of generally-recognized principles and norms of international law, that is, customary norms of international law . . .').

[28] For a detailed discussion of this issue by a Russian scholar see B.L. Zimnenko, *International Law and the Russian Legal System* (Utrecht: Eleven International Publishing, 2007), 170–92.

[29] Supreme Court of Russia, Decree of the Plenum No. 5/2003 (n. 23).

[30] Supreme Court of Russia, Decree of the Plenum No. 8/1995 (n. 22).

lists the International Covenant on Civil and Political Rights and the International Covenant on Economic, Social and Cultural Rights, that is, also international treaties.

Russian constitutional law scholarship is similarly ambivalent.[31] Commentaries on the Russian Constitution usually refer to *opinio juris* and consensus among states when defining how 'universally recognized principles and norms of international law' are generated, thereby suggesting a close resemblance between these principles and norms and customary international law.[32] At the same time, the term 'custom' is usually avoided, and reference to article 38(1) of the Statute of the International Court of Justice is sometimes explicitly regarded as misplaced.[33] On the other hand, the same Russian commentaries usually provide lists of principles and norms which include the UN Charter, the Vienna Convention on the Law of Treaties, and other international treaties with universal binding effect. As with the definitions in the two decrees by the Russian Supreme Court, this is confusing since these documents already fall under the first category of 'international treaties' mentioned in article 15(4) RC. To complicate things further, the provided lists usually include not only binding treaties but also non-binding international instruments, in particular UN General Assembly resolutions such as the Friendly Relations Declaration.[34] This mixing of binding and non-binding documents under one category is problematic (to say the least), since it bypasses the usual requirement for customary international law to be demonstrated by state practice.[35]

1.2 International Law in the Hierarchy of the Russian Legal System

As has been noted earlier, the Russian Constitution 'shall have supreme legal force' in the Russian legal system (article 15(1) RC). The exact meaning of this

[31] For an overview of the discussion among Russian international law scholars see Zimnenko, *International Law and the Russian Legal System* (2007) (n. 28), 170–92.

[32] See Nußberger and Safoklov, 'Art 15', in Wieser, *Handbuch der russischen Verfassung* (2014) (n. 15), MN 28.

[33] Ibid., MN 24, referring to e.g. V.D. Zorkin (ed.), *Комментарий к Конституции Российской Федерации* [Commentary on the Constitution of the Russian Federation] (Moscow: Eksmo, 3rd edn, 2013), 161–2.

[34] See e.g. L.V. Lazarev (ed.), *Комментарий к Конституция Российской Федерации* [Commentary on the Constitution of the Russian Federation] (Moscow: Prospekt, 3rd edn, 2010), 101–2; Zorkin, *Commentary on the Constitution of the Russian Federation* (2013) (n. 33), 162.

[35] Jane Henderson, *The Constitution of the Russian Federation: A Contextual Analysis* (Oxford: Hart Publishing, 2011), 93.

claim with regard to international law is debated among Russian constitutional lawyers. Most prominently, Valery Zorkin (1943–), the first and current Chairman of the Russian Constitutional Court, has indicated in a contribution to the Russian governmental newspaper *Rossiĭskaya gazeta* that the Russian Constitution rests on top of *all* other laws, in other words not only of domestic but also of international law.[36]

With regard to international agreements, this assessment is undisputed in Russian scholarship and was also confirmed by the Russian Constitutional Court.[37] Three arguments are generally raised in favour of this view: (1) the high democratic legitimacy of the Russian Constitution, having been adopted by referendum in 1993; (2) the wording of article 125(6) RC, according to which unconstitutional international treaties cannot be enforced and applied; and (3) article 22 of the Law on International Treaties of the Russian Federation, which allows for the ratification of an international treaty that requires a constitutional amendment only after the constitution has been changed.[38]

With regard to the second category of sources of international law mentioned in article 15(4) RC, the 'universally recognized principles and norms of international law', in the official commentary published under the auspices of the Russian Constitutional Court former judge of the Russian Constitutional Court Boris Ebzeev (1950–) maintains that only those norms of international law can be an integral part of domestic law to which the Russian Federation has explicitly agreed.[39] The inviolability of Russia's state sovereignty and the peculiarities of Russia's legal culture would make this necessary, Ebzeev maintains. This view is also widely shared among Russian international law scholars.[40] As Angelika Nußberger and Yuri Safoklov rightly observe in the Austro-German *Handbook of the Russian Constitution*, this view 'questions the importance of customary international law and even jus cogens', and interestingly corresponds to the former Soviet doctrine which was critical towards custom.[41]

[36] V.D. Zorkin, 'Предел уступчивости' [The Limit of Compromise], *Rossiĭskaya gazeta*, 29 October 2010. See also Ebzeev, in Zorkin, *Commentary on the Constitution of the Russian Federation* (2013) (n. 33), 158–9.

[37] See e.g. Constitutional Court of Russia, *По делу о проверке конституционности не вступившего в силу международного договора Российской Федерации—Протокола о присоединении Российской Федерации к Марракешскому соглашению об учреждении Всемирной торговой организации* [In the Case on the Verification of the Constitutionality of the International Treaty of the Russian Federation Which Did not Enter Into Force—The Protocol on the Accession of the Russian Federation to the Marrakesh Agreement Establishing the World Trade Organization], Decision No. 17-P/2012, 9 July 2012, SZRF 2012, no. 29, item 4169.

[38] Federal Law of Russia No. 101-FZ 1995 (n. 19).

[39] Zorkin, *Commentary on the Constitution of the Russian Federation* (2013) (n. 33), 159.

[40] See Zimnenko, *International Law and the Russian Legal System* (2007) (n. 28), 183–4.

[41] Nußberger and Safoklov, 'Art 15' in Wieser, *Handbuch der russischen Verfassung* (2014) (n. 15), MN 33.

1.3 State Sovereignty in the Russian Constitution and International Law Aspects

In another continuity with the former Soviet doctrine, Russian constitutional theory conceptualizes sovereignty as a three-dimensional phenomenon appearing in the forms of 'state', 'national', and 'people's' sovereignty.[42] Suren Avakyan (1940–) of Moscow State University, one of the most influential constitutional lawyers in Russia, explains the different modes of sovereignty in the latest edition of his textbook on Russian constitutional law the following way:

> State sovereignty is expressed in the supremacy of state power, its unity, self-sufficiency, and independence.... National sovereignty is expressed in the right of the nation to determine the nature of its being, to decide essential questions, both internally (language, writing, customs, traditions, etc.) as well as regarding the relations with other nations [and] nationalities, the creation of its own state, national-state (autonomous) units or the refusal of its formation, becoming a part of a state or the existence as an independent state ... In turn, people's sovereignty, as the realization of the power of the whole people, unites all citizens living on the corresponding territory, regardless of their national identity.[43]

Avakyan adds that all three forms of sovereignty are interrelated and at the same time independent. In principle, however, people's sovereignty can be considered a prerequisite to the other two forms of sovereignty, whereas state sovereignty and national sovereignty do not necessarily correspond with each other.[44] Moreover, contrary to the former Soviet doctrine and notwithstanding the apparent similarities in the descriptions, national sovereignty and self-determination are claimed to be two different concepts: '[i]n the Constitution of the Russian Federation, one of the foundations of its federal system is not national sovereignty, but equal rights and self-determination of peoples in the Russian Federation', Avakyan writes, 'and peoples here are understood to be a group of citizens living in different parts of the country regardless of their nationality, and related to the interests of the organization of general life'.[45]

Russia's sovereignty is mentioned in the constitution's preamble, and several times in the text of the constitution itself. In particular, article 3(1) RC provides that '[t]he bearer of sovereignty and the sole source of power in the Russian Federation shall be its multinational people', and '[t]he sovereignty of the Russian Federation shall extend to the entirety of its territory' (article 4(1) RC). In its *Altai*

[42] See Chapter 1 Section 4 above.
[43] S.A. Avakyan, *Конституционное право России* [Constitutional Law of Russia], vol. 1 (Moscow: Norma, 5th edn, 2014), 362–4.
[44] Ibid., 364.
[45] Ibid., 365.

decision of 7 June 2000, the Russian Constitutional Court has defined sovereignty within the meaning of the Russian Constitution as the 'supremacy, independence, and self-sufficiency of state power, completeness of the legislative, executive and judicial powers of the state on its territory, and independence in international relations', and as 'a necessary qualitative feature of the Russian Federation as a state, characterizing its constitutional and legal status'. Furthermore, with regard to the Altai Republic's claimed status in its constitution to be 'sovereign', the court ruled:

> the Russian Federation does not allow any other bearer of sovereignty and no other source of power than the multinational people of the Russian Federation, and, therefore, does not imply any other state sovereignty in addition to the sovereignty of the Russian Federation. The sovereignty of the Russian Federation, by virtue of the Constitution of the Russian Federation, excludes the existence of two levels of sovereign powers in a single system of state power, which would have supremacy and independence, i.e. it does not allow the sovereignty of republics or of other subjects of the Russian Federation.[46]

Interestingly, sovereignty in the sense of article 4 RC is not only interpreted as a constitutional norm but also in terms of international law according to Russian doctrine.[47] Internally, the provision serves as the basis for the Russian Federation as the only subject of international law on its territory. Externally, article 4 RC establishes Russia's independence in its international relations.[48] As such, sovereignty includes the right to have diplomatic relations, to conclude international agreements, and to participate in the activities of international organizations.[49]

1.4 Self-determination of the 'Multinational People of the Russian Federation'

Corresponding to the pivotal importance of the concept of self-determination in the former Soviet doctrine of international law, the right of peoples to

[46] Constitutional Court of Russia, *По делу о проверке конституционности отдельных положений Конституции Республики Алтай и Федерального закона «Об общих принципах организации законодательных (представительных) и исполнительных органов государственной власти субъектов Российской Федерации»* [In the Case on the Verification of the Constitutionality of Certain Provisions of the Constitution of the Republic of Altai and the Federal Law 'On General Principles of the Organisation of Legislative (Representative) and Executive Bodies of State Power of the Subjects of the Russian Federation'], Decision No. 10-P/2000, 7 June 2000, SZRF 2000, no. 25, item 2728, para. 2.1.

[47] See Michael Geistlinger, 'Art 4', in Wieser, *Handbuch der russischen Verfassung* (2014) (n. 15), MN 9.

[48] Ibid.

[49] In 2012 for example, the Russian Constitutional Court ruled that Russia's accession to the World Trade Organization and its dispute settlement mechanism did not constitute a violation of the sovereignty of the Russian Federation, Constitutional Court of Russia, Decision No. 17-P/2012 (n. 37).

self-determination has always had a central position in Soviet constitutions. The first constitution of the Russian SFSR of 1918 already referred to the 'free determination of the peoples' of Russia in its article 4.[50] The so-called Brezhnev Constitution of 1977 endorsed self-determination by declaring the 'principle of socialist federalism' as the basis for the Soviet Union 'as a result of the free self-determination of nations and the voluntary association of equal Soviet Socialist Republics'.[51] And in the Constitution of the Russian SFSR of 1978, self-determination was mentioned already in the preamble, stating that 'Soviet power has guaranteed equality and free-self-determination to all the peoples of Russia' which, by formation of the Russian SFSR, are provided with 'favourable conditions for all-round economic, social, and cultural development', taking into account their national peculiarities in the 'fraternal family of Soviet peoples'.[52]

The Russian Constitution of 1993 refers to self-determination in two instances. As has already been mentioned at the beginning of this chapter, the first reference can be found in the preamble, in which 'the multinational people of the Russian Federation' invokes the 'universally acknowledged principles of equality and self-determination of peoples'. A second reference to self-determination is made in article 5(3) RC, which states:

> The federal structure of the Russian Federation shall be based on its State integrity, the unity of the system of State power, the division of matters of authority and powers between State government bodies of the Russian Federation and State government bodies of constituent entities of the Russian Federation, [and] the equality and self-determination of peoples in the Russian Federation.

If one is comparing the two provisions it becomes evident that the wording with regard to the bearer of the right to self-determination is not congruent: whereas the preamble speaks of 'the multinational people of the Russian Federation', article 5(3) RC refers to 'self-determination of peoples in the Russian Federation'. In particular, the second wording is potentially dangerous, since the usage of the plural form could be interpreted as an acknowledgement that more than one 'people' may

[50] Конституция Российской Социалистической Федеративной Советской Республики [Constitution of the Russian Socialist Federative Soviet Republic], 10 July 1918, *Izvestiya*, 19 July 1918. English translation reprinted in *The Nation*, 4 January 1919, 3–20.

[51] Конституция (Основной Закон) Союза Советских Социалистических Республик [Constitution (Fundamental Law) of the Union of Soviet Socialist Republics], 7 October 1977, VVS SSSR 1977, no. 41, item 616. English translation: William E. Butler (ed.), *Collected Legislation of the Union of Soviet Socialist Republics and the Constituent Union Republics*, vol. 1, Supp 1985-2 (Dobbs Ferry, NY: Oceana Publications), 2–46.

[52] Конституция (Основной Закон) Российской Советской Федеративной Социалистической Республики [Constitution (Basic Law) of the Russian Soviet Federative Socialist Republic], 12 April 1978, VVS SSSR 1978, no. 15, item 407. Quotation English translation: Butler, *Collected Legislation of the Union of Soviet Socialist Republics and the Constituent Union Republics* (n. 51), vol. 2, Supp 1980 2, 3–49, 3.

claim the right to self-determination in the territory of the Russian Federation.[53] This is an impression which Avakyan, for instance, is careful to avoid by asserting that there is only one bearer of the right to self-determination in the Russian Federation, and that is 'the multinational people of the Russian Federation'.[54]

The term 'multinational people' is a Soviet remnant,[55] and is defined by Avakyan as 'all *citizens* of the Russian Federation regardless of age and nationality'.[56] Consequently, according to the last Russian census of 2010, the multinational people of the Russian Federation consists of more than 190 ethnic groups.[57] Its unity (in the words of the preamble) 'by a common fate on our land' is regarded as the basis for peaceful life and political unity amongst the different ethnic groups within the Russian Federation.[58]

Unlike the Brezhnev Constitution of 1977, which famously stated in its article 72 that '[t]he right of free secession from the USSR shall be preserved for each union republic', the Russian Constitution does not provide for such a constitutional right of secession. Compared to other modern state constitutions, this approach is in line with the overwhelming majority, and modern constitutions that explicitly recognize a right of secession are highly exceptional.[59] The reasons put forward for this position in Russian constitutional law literature are however special. Ebzeev for instance argues that the similar wording in the preambles of the UN Charter ('We, the peoples of the United Nations ...') and the Russian Constitution ('We, the multinational people of the Russian Federation ...') proves the existence of 'a general principle of international law' according to which peoples may exercise their right to self-determination by merging into a unified whole.[60] Self-determination and territorial integrity are therefore no contradictions, Ebzeev maintains. To the contrary: in Ebzeev's view, a people relates to the state like an individual to society. Just like an individual cannot exist without society, peoples depend on

[53] Since the 2020 constitutional amendments, article 68(1) RC similarly speaks of 'peoples' [*narodov*] in the plural form, see Socher, 'Farewell to the European Constitutional Tradition' (2020) (n. 6), 633–4. (Apparantly aware of its possible implications, the official English translation tellingly translates the term here as 'nations' rather than 'peoples'.)

[54] Avakyan, *Constitutional Law of Russia*, vol. 2 (2014) (n. 43), 98 (basing his argument on the preposition '*in* the Russian Federation' in article 5 RC instead of '*of* the Russian Federation' in the preamble).

[55] Article 70 of the Brezhnev Constitution of 1977 spoke of the Soviet Union as an 'integral, federal, multinational state' which embodies 'the state unity of the Soviet people'.

[56] Avakyan, *Constitutional Law of Russia*, vol. 2 (2014) (n. 43), 97 (emphasis in the original).

[57] Russian Federal State Statistics Service, 'Всероссийская перепись населения 2010 года' [2010 All-Russian Population Census], http://www.gks.ru/free_doc/new_site/perepis2010/croc/perepis_itogi1612.htm.

[58] See e.g. V.V. Lazarev (ed.), *Научно-практический комментарий к Конституции Российской Федерации* [Scientific-practical Commentary on the Constitution of the Russian Federation] (Moscow: Yuraït, 4rd edn, 2009), 50.

[59] Elisa Novic and Priya Urs, 'Secession', in MPECCoL (online edn), MN 5.

[60] Boris Ebzeev, Sergey Krasnoburytsev, and Igor Levakin, *Государственное единство и целостность Российской федерации, Конституционно-правовые проблемы* [State Unity and Integrity of the Russian Federation, Constitutional Problems] (Moscow: Ekonomika, 2005), 150.

organizations based on the rule of law, Ebzeev claims.[61] Commenting on this remarkable comparison, Caroline von Gall states:

> In connection with the discussion about the relationship of the self-determination of peoples to the maintenance of the Russian Federation's sovereignty over the territory of its peoples, this comparison is crushing for the right to self-determination. The statement contains the assumption that peoples within the Russian Federation could not exist without the Russian state. In this light, the statement has to be seen as a reference to the Great Russian idea according to which only the centrally organized Russian state lays the foundation for the life of humans living in this area.[62]

Other Russian constitutional and international lawyers have expressed similar views, stressing the absolute character of Russia's territorial unity.[63] In sum, one can therefore conclude that for situations inside the Russian Federation, Russian constitutional doctrine understands self-determination in its 'classic' or Hobbesean conception as outlined by Koskenniemi:[64] the right to self-determination is acknowledged, albeit of only one unified people in its state territory (the 'multinational people of the Russian Federation'), and as long as it is not in conflict with Russia's state unity and 'indivisible' sovereignty.

2. *Case Study 1*: Tatarstan

Tatarstan is an economically rich region approximately 800 kilometres east of Moscow between the Volga and Kama rivers, extending to the Ural Mountains in the East. According to the 2010 Russian census, the population of Tatarstan reached close to 4 million, of which 53 per cent were Volga Tatars,[65] a Turkic ethnic group with predominantly Sunni Islam religion.

2.1 Origins of the Conflict Over Tatarstan

The origins of the conflict over the territory of what today is the Republic of Tatarstan date back to 1552, when Ivan the Terrible destroyed the Khanate of

[61] Ibid., 159.

[62] Caroline von Gall, *Die Konzepte 'staatliche Einheit' und 'einheitliche Macht' in der russischen Theorie von Staat und Recht. Der Einfluss des Gemeinschaftsideals auf die russische Verfassungsentwicklung* (Berlin: Duncker & Humblot, 2010), 302.

[63] See ibid., 299–302.

[64] See Introduction to this book.

[65] Russian Federal State Statistics Service, '2010 All-Russian Population Census' (n. 57).

Kazan, heir to the Bulgar kingdom and the Golden Horde.[66] Following the military conquest, a systematic policy of colonization was applied.[67] In particular, after an initial period of religious tolerance, various measures were taken to eradicate Islam. The campaign reached its peak at the beginning of the eighteenth century under Peter the Great, whose persecution policy has been compared to the worst period of Stalin's purges.[68] A massive Tatar exodus towards Turkestan, the Kazakh Steppe, and Siberia followed throughout the eighteenth century. The Russian anti-Muslim campaign came only to a halt in 1783 when Catherine the Great established a Central Muslim Spiritual Board in the city of Orenburg. Although Tatars were thereafter able to regain a high level of spiritual and cultural autonomy, a political nationalist movement gradually formed.[69] On 23 March 1918, the People's Commissariat of Nationalities proclaimed the Tatar-Bashkir Soviet Republic of the Russian Soviet Federation on the territory of Southern Ural and Middle Volga,[70] but when the Russian Civil War broke out, the decree became meaningless: after the Bolsheviks ultimately gained power over the territory, they split the Bashkirs again from the Tatars and created two separate Autonomous Soviet Socialist Republics (ASSRs) in 1919/20.[71]

2.2 Tatar Resistance During the Soviet Era

Among the different nationalist movements in the Soviet Union, the Tatar was one of the strongest. As Terry Martin notes in *The Affirmative Action Empire*, '[t]he Tatar nationalist elite lobbied aggressively for and vigorously supported the Soviet policy of *korenizatsiya*: the formation of a Tatar republic, the promotion of Tatars into leadership positions, the use of the Tatar language in government and education, and support for Tatar national culture'.[72] The movement, however, faced strong resistance, also from within: the Communist Party of the Tatar ASSR was divided between a 'right' faction—Tatar nationalists under the leadership of Mirsaid Sultan-Galiev, the highest ranking Muslim in the Communist Party and

[66] See Azade-Ayşe Rorlich, *The Volga Tatars: A Profile in National Resilience* (Stanford, CA: Hoover Institution Press, 1986).

[67] See Marie Bennigsen-Broxup, 'Tatarstan and the Tatars', in Graham Smith (ed.), *The Nationalities Question in the Post-Soviet States* (London: Longman, 2nd edn, 1996), 75–93, 76–7.

[68] Ibid., 76.

[69] On the origins of Tatar nationalism see Uli Schamiloglu, 'The Formation of a Tatar Historical Consciousness: Şihabäddin Märcani and the Image of the Golden Horde', *Central Asian Survey* 9 (1990), 39–49.

[70] Bennigsen-Broxup, 'Tatarstan and the Tatars' (1996) (n. 67), 78.

[71] The borders were drawn arbitrarily: only around one fourth of the ethnic Tatar population was included in the newly established Tatar ASSR, while in the Bashkir ASSR the Tatar ethnic group represented the majority, see ibid., 78.

[72] Terry Martin, *The Affirmative Action Empire: Nations and Nationalism in the Soviet Union, 1923–1939* (Ithaca, NY: Cornell University Press, 2001), 58.

a member of the Central Executive Committee of the Tatar ASSR—and a 'left' faction—almost exclusively ethnic Russian communists living in the republic and favouring a federal solution.[73] In 1923, the situation flipped: Sultan-Galiev was arrested 'for counter-revolutionary nationalist conspiracy against the power of the Soviets', and systematic purges directed towards literally everyone who defended political or cultural autonomy of native Muslims followed. By 1939, the entire Tatar political and intellectual elite was 'liquidated'.[74]

After the Second World War, Tatarstan underwent an intensive industrialization programme and experienced heavy Russian immigration. Tatar nationalism was henceforth more sophisticated and subtle compared to similar movements in Central Asia or in the Caucasus, and direct conflict with the central government in Moscow didn't break out until the time of *perestroïka*.[75] Less than three months after the Russian SFSR's declaration of sovereignty (and as the first autonomous republic within the union republic to do so), the Supreme Soviet of the Tatar ASSR proclaimed itself to be sovereign on 30 August 1990, with no reference of Tatarstan being part of the Russian SFSR.[76]

2.3 The *Tatarstan* Case in Front of the Russian Constitutional Court

Demonstrations and political strikes spread throughout Tatarstan in the year that followed the declaration of sovereignty, and on 21 February 1992, in response to the nationalist movement, the Supreme Soviet of the Tatar ASSR decided to hold a referendum to determine the future status of the republic.[77] The Russian Constitutional Court stepped in, and ruled over the constitutionality of Tatarstan's declaration of sovereignty, the planned amendments to the Tatar Constitution, and the scheduled referendum.

At the outset of its *Tatarstan* decision of 13 March 1992, the Russian Constitutional Court states:

> At the present time, processes of the renewal of the federation are taking place, directed toward the development of the status of constituent republics of the RSFSR.... The Constitutional Court of the RSFSR views . . . with understanding

[73] Bennigsen-Broxup, 'Tatarstan and the Tatars' (1996) (n. 67), 79.
[74] Ibid., 79–80.
[75] Ibid., 81.
[76] Декларация о Государственном Суверенитете Татарской Советской Социалистической Республики [Declaration on the State Sovereignty of the Tatar Soviet Socialist Republic], 30 August 1990, *Sovetskaya Tatariya*, 31 August 1990.
[77] Bennigsen-Broxup, 'Tatarstan and the Tatars' (1996) (n. 67), 83. On the referendum see also Anne Peters, *Das Gebietsreferendum im Völkerrecht: seine Bedeutung im Licht der Staatenpraxis nach 1989* (Baden-Baden: Nomos, 1995), 203–8.

> the aspiration of the multinational People of Tatarstan to develop and reinforce the statehood of the republic, which was expressed in the adoption of the Declaration of State Sovereignty of the Republic of Tatarstan.[78]

However, the court continues, the planned amendments to the Tatar Constitution violate a number of provisions of the (then still valid) 1978 Russian SFSR Constitution. In particular, the planned deletion of the provisions in the Tatar Constitution according to which the republic is part of the Russian SFSR and the rejection of the supremacy of the laws of the Russian SFSR over the laws of Tatarstan would be contrary to the constitutional status of the republics and violate article 71, defining the Russian SFSR as a federation, the Constitutional Court holds.[79] Furthermore, the court finds, the planned change of Tatarstan's status by way of referendum violates article 70 (altering of the territory and state boundaries only by mutual agreement) as well as article 81 (supremacy of federal laws over the laws of autonomous republics) of the 1978 Russian SFSR Constitution. However:

> In assessing the constitutionality of the Decree of the Supreme Soviet of the Republic of Tatarstan under consideration it is essential to take into account that the Republic of Tatarstan has the right to raise the issue of its state and legal status, inasmuch as this right is derivative from the right of the People to self-determination. The Decree of the Third (Extraordinary) Congress of People's Deputies of the RSFSR 'On Fundamental Principles of the National-State Structure of the RSFSR (on the Federation Treaty)' establishes that the right of peoples to self-determination shall be guaranteed in the Russian Federation (Article 3). This right may be exercised in various national-state and national-cultural forms.[80]

[78] Constitutional Court of Russia, *По делу о проверке конституционности Декларации о государственном суверенитете Республики Татарстан от 30 августа 1990 года, Закона Республики Татарстан от 18 апреля 1991 года «Об изменениях и дополнениях Конституции (Основного Закона) Республики Татарстан», Закона Республики Татарстан от 29 ноября 1991 года «О референдуме Республики Татарстан», Постановления Верховного Совета Республики Татарстан от 21 февраля 1992 года «О проведении референдума Республики Татарстан по вопросу о государственном статусе Республики Татарстан»* [In the Case on the Verification of the Constitutionality of the Declaration of State Sovereignty of the Republic of Tatarstan of 30 August 1990, the Law of the Republic of Tatarstan of 18 April 1991 'On Amendments and Additions to the Constitution (Fundamental Law) of the Republic of Tatarstan', the Law of the Republic of Tatarstan of 29 November 1991 'On the Referendum of the Republic of Tatarstan', and the Decree of the Supreme Soviet of the Republic of Tatarstan of 21 February 1992 'On the Conduct of a Referendum of the Republic of Tatarstan on the Question of the State Status of the Republic of Tatarstan'] (*Tatarstan Decision*), 13 March 1992, Vedomosti S'ezda Narodnÿkh Deputatov RF i Verkhovnogo Soveta RF 1992, no. 13, item 671. Quotation from the English translation in *Statutes & Decisions: The Laws of the USSR and its Successor States* 30 (1994), no. 3, 32–48, 34–5.

[79] Ibid., 35.

[80] Ibid., 39.

From here, the Russian Constitutional Court assesses the scope of the right of peoples to self-determination under international law in more detail. 'In the contemporary international law system', the court notes, 'the right to self-determination is included in the group of norms regulating human rights and freedoms', an assessment which emerges from common article 1 of the Human Rights Covenants, which were ratified by the Presidium of the Supreme Soviet of the Soviet Union on 18 September 1973. 'In accordance with these international documents, all peoples have the right to self-determination', the court quotes, and 'on the strength of this right, peoples "shall freely establish their political status and freely provide for their economic, social, and political development," and all states shall be obliged "to promote the exercise of the right of self-determination and to respect this right"'.[81]

With further reference to the General Assembly's Friendly Relations Declaration of 1970,[82] the Russian Constitutional Court stresses that self-determination 'is one of the basic principles of international law'. It quotes paragraph 4 of the declaration's fifth principle, which, in the court's formulation, lists '[t]he establishment of a sovereign and independent State, the free association with or integration into an independent State or the emergence into any other political status' as the various modes of implementation of the right of peoples to self-determination.[83] These provisions have to be viewed in light of article 29 of the Universal Declaration of Human Rights[84] as well as of General Assembly resolution 41/117 of 4 December 1986,[85] the court finds, according to which 'the development and protection of one category of rights can never exempt or excuse States from the development and protection of the other rights'.[86] 'Otherwise', the court states, 'during the exercise of any

[81] Ibid., 40. Note that the original text of article 1 of the Human Rights Covenants speaks of 'economic, social, and *cultural* development', cf. International Covenant on Economic, Social and Cultural Rights, 16 December 1966, 1967 ILM 360, art. 1, and International Covenant on Civil and Political Rights, 16 December 1966, 1967 ILM 368, art. 1. (The mistake is no translation error and appears also in the Russian original.)

[82] Friendly Relations Declaration (1970) (n. 25), fifth principle. See also Chapter 1 Section 2 above.

[83] Constitutional Court of Russia, Tatarstan Decision (1992) (n. 78) (quotation from the Russian original). This time, the translation in *Statutes & Decisions: The Laws of the USSR and its Successor States* (1994) (n. 78) is misleading by translating the Court's 'svobodnoe prisoedinenie k nezavisimomu gosudarstvu' as 'free *annexation* to an independent state' (emphasis added).

[84] GA Res 217 A (III) (Universal Declaration of Human Rights), 10 December 1948, UN Doc. A/RES/3/217. Art. 29 reads: '(1) Everyone has duties to the community in which alone the free and full development of his personality is possible. (2) In the exercise of his rights and freedoms, everyone shall be subject only to such limitations as are determined by law solely for the purpose of securing due recognition and respect for the rights and freedoms of others and of meeting the just requirements of morality, public order and the general welfare in a democratic society. (3) These rights and freedoms may in no case be exercised contrary to the purposes and principles of the United Nations.'

[85] GA Res 41/117 (Indivisibility and Interdependence of Economic, Social, Cultural, Civil and Political Rights), 4 December 1986 UN Doc. A/RES/41/117.

[86] Constitutional Court of Russia, Tatarstan Decision (1992) (n. 78), 40. Quotation from the Russian original, since the translation in *Statutes & Decisions: The Laws of the USSR and its Successor States* (1994) (n. 78) is again not accurate. But note also the slightly different wording in the decision itself, which speaks of 'razvitie i zashchita' (*development* and protection), compared to the official Russian translation of GA Res 41/117, which reads 'pooshchrenie i zashchita' (*promotion* and protection).

right, including that to self-determination, what would occur would be the abuse of the right and not the exercise of the right'.[87]

International documents such as the Friendly Relations Declaration of 1970, the 1975 Helsinki Final Act,[88] the 1986 Concluding Document of the Vienna Meeting,[89] and the 1990 Document of the Copenhagen Meeting of the Conference on the Human Dimension of the Conference on Security and Co-operation in Europe (CSCE)[90] all 'emphasize the impermissibility of making reference to the principle of self-determination in order to jeopardize state and national unity' or embody '[a]nalogous principles'.[91] This becomes particular evident through the savings clause in paragraph 7 of the fifth principle of the Friendly Relations Declaration, the Russian Constitutional Court holds, and quotes it in full length.[92] Thus, the court finds,

> without negating the right of a People to self-determination exercised by means of the lawful expression of will, it is appropriate to proceed from the premise that international law restricts it by the observance of the requirements of the principle of territorial integrity and the principle of the observance of human rights.[93]

Taking these considerations into account, the court concludes:

> The Constitution of the RSFSR does not envision the right of a constituent republic of the RSFSR to secede from the Federation ... The unilateral establishment by the Republic of Tatarstan of such a right would signify the recognition of the lawfulness of the total or partial violation of the territorial integrity of a sovereign federative state and of the national unity of the peoples inhabiting it. Any actions having as their goal the violation of this unity cause harm to the constitutional order of the RSFSR and are incompatible with international norms on human rights and the rights of peoples.[94]

[87] Constitutional Court of Russia, Tatarstan Decision (1992) (n. 78), 40.

[88] Helsinki Final Act, 1 August 1975, 1975 ILM 1292.

[89] Concluding Document of the Vienna Meeting 1986 of Representatives of the Participating States of the Conference on Security and Co-operation in Europe, held on the Basis of the Provision of the Final Act Relating to the Follow-up to the Conference, 17 January 1989, reprinted in Burns Weston and Jonathan Carlson (eds), *International Law & World Order: Weston's & Carlson's Basic Documents* (online edn), III.B.24b.

[90] Document of the Copenhagen Meeting of the Conference on the Human Dimension of the Conference on Security and Co-operation in Europe, 29 June 1990, reprinted in ibid., I.D.10c.

[91] Constitutional Court of Russia, Tatarstan Decision (1992) (n. 78), 41.

[92] Friendly Relations Declaration (1970) (n. 25), para. 7 of the fifth principle: 'Nothing in the foregoing paragraphs shall be construed as authorizing or encouraging any action which would dismember or impair, totally or in part, the territorial integrity or political unity of sovereign and independent States conducting themselves in compliance with the principle of equal rights and self-determination of peoples as described above and thus possessed of a government representing the whole people belonging to the territory without distinction as to race, creed or colour.'

[93] Constitutional Court of Russia, Tatarstan Decision (1992) (n. 78), 41.

[94] Ibid. But note the separate opinion of judge Ametistov, summarized in Långström, *Transformation in Russia and International Law* (2003) (n. 18), 404: 'While agreeing with the majority in all other parts

Although the outcome of the *Tatarstan* decision—no right of secession of the Tatar population or its republic from the Russian Federation under Russian constitutional as well as under international law—is in line with the assessments in the available scholarship on the issue, the way in which the Russian Constitutional Court arrives at this conclusion is problematic for a number of reasons and therefore deserves some further discussion.[95]

First, the Russian Constitutional Court does not differentiate between the different sources of the international documents it refers to nor does it discuss their binding nature or general relevance. This is already noteworthy with regard to the Friendly Relations Declaration, in principle a non-binding UN General Assembly resolution, but is particularly striking with regard to the CSCE documents, since the signatory states of those documents expressively wanted to exclude their binding nature.[96] The *Tatarstan* decision can therefore be seen as an important example where the earlier observed confusion of the different sources of international law in Russian doctrine has a severe practical impact. Moreover, the CSCE documents bind only states, not sub-units of states or peoples, so it is difficult to comprehend how the Republic of Tatarstan or its population may possibly have violated the territorial integrity of Russia.

Second, the Russian Constitutional Court's reasoning that the Universal Declaration of Human Rights limits the right of peoples to self-determination is

of the decree, [Ametsistov] was in disagreement with the majority on the question concerning the unconstitutionality of the Tatarstanian decree on the referendum. He invoked the same international instruments as the majority, reminded that the USSR had ratified the 1966 Human Rights Covenants in 1973, and that the Russian Federation remained bound by these covenants by virtue of state succession. In his reading, the republic of Tatarstan was realising its right of self-determination when it adopted the decree on referendum.... For Ametistov the conflict was not only between the Tatarstanian decree on referendum and the constitution, but also between different constitutional provisions .... The Russian Federation was, after all, bound to "promote the realisation of the right of self-determination, and ... respect this right, in conformity with the provisions of the Charter of the United Nations." Therefore, judge Ametistov was of the opinion that the Tatarstanian decree on referendum was in conformity with the constitution.'

[95] The following analysis is drawn from Wiebke Rückert, *Das Völkerrecht in der Rechtsprechung des russischen Verfassungsgerichts* (Berlin: Berliner Wissenschaftsverlag, 2005), 131–6. The *Tatarstan* decision is also discussed in Långström, *Transformation in Russia and International Law* (2003) (n. 18), 402–4; Angelika Nußberger, 'Entwicklung der Verfassungsrechtsprechung in Russland', in Angelika Nußberger, Carmen Schmidt, and Tamara Morščakova (eds), *Verfassungsrechtsprechung in der Russischen Föderation: Dokumentation und Analyse der Entscheidungen des Russischen Verfassungsgerichts 1991–2007* (Kehl: N.P. Engel Verlag, 2009), 43–82, 46–7; von Gall, *Die Konzepte 'staatliche Einheit' und 'einheitliche Macht'* (2010) (n. 62), 385–8; and James Summers, *Peoples and International Law* (Leiden: Brill Nijhoff, 2nd edn, 2014), 402–3.

[96] With regard to the Helsinki Final Act see Suzanne Bastid, 'The Special Significance of the Helsinki Final Act', in Thomas Buergenthal (ed.), *Human Rights, International Law and the Helsinki Accord* (Montclair: Allanheld, Osmun & Co., 1979), 11–19, 13–14; with regard to the follow-up meeting in Vienna see Hannes Tretter, 'Human Rights in the Concluding Document of the Vienna Follow-up Meeting of the Conference on Security and Co-operation in Europe of January 15, 1989: An Introduction', *Human Rights Law Journal* 10 (1989), 257–69, 260 ('programmatic character').

flawed, as Wiebke Rückert rightly observes in her study *International Law in the Jurisdiction of the Russian Constitutional Court*:

> There is no justification why the recognition and respect for human rights of others according to the Universal Declaration of Human Rights shall amount to a generally limiting norm of the right of peoples to self-determination.... The limitation which is contained in the Universal Declaration of Human Rights is part of a statutory reservation that relates to the exercise of individual freedom. It does *a priori* not relate to the exercise of collective rights of a people. To guarantee the recognition and respect of the rights and freedoms of others is, according to article 29(2) of the declaration, one of the only admissible aims which a law that restricts the exercise of rights and freedoms may pursue. The requirement is thus addressed to the legislator, who infringes citizens' rights and freedoms but not to a people exercising its right to self-determination.[97]

Third, UN General Assembly resolution 47/117 also and explicitly only binds states. Moreover, the mentioned principle in the resolution refers solely to the indivisibility and indeterminacy of economic, social, and cultural rights on the one hand and civil and political rights on the other hand. Therefore, when the Russian Constitutional Court concludes from the resolution that the exercise of the right of peoples to self-determination constitutes an abuse of that right if it is directed towards the territorial integrity of a state, it overlooks that while the right of peoples to self-determination may be attributed to the two categories of human rights, the territorial integrity of states may not.

In sum, one has to agree with Rückert, who concludes her assessment of the *Tatarstan* decision by stating that the Russian Constitutional Court

> assumed that the Republic of Tatarstan can in principle benefit from the international right of peoples to self-determination ... and has assessed the domestic regulations on its compliance with international law. In determining the scope of the right to self-determination, [the court] has however based its conclusion on the limits of the right to self-determination in a legally untenable manner.[98]

Following the court's decision and notwithstanding various attempts by the Russian federal government to intimidate the Tatar separatist movement, Tatarstan refused to sign the Treaty of Federation and held the referendum anyway, putting the following question to the vote: 'Do you agree that the Republic of Tatarstan is a sovereign state, a subject of international law that constructs its relations with the

[97] Rückert, *Das Völkerrecht in der Rechtsprechung des russischen Verfassungsgerichts* (2005) (n. 95), 135

[98] Ibid., 137.

Russian Federation and other republics and states on the basis of treaties between equal parties? Yes or No.'[99] The question was carefully phrased. By asking the electorate if it endorses 'sovereignty', Tatar nationalists could hope for independence, while ethnic Russians (who at the time constituted 43 per cent of the population, compared to 49 per cent ethnic Tatars) could be reassured that it meant nothing more than autonomy.[100] The plan worked out, and in the end 61 per cent voted for Tatarstan as a 'sovereign state', on an 82 per cent turnout.[101]

On 26 October 1992, the Supreme Soviet of Tatarstan met to vote on the amendment of the Tatar Constitution, and, after a ten-day-long session, it was finally amended by a vote of 174 out of 249 deputies, just over the required two-thirds majority. As such, Tatarstan became the first republic in Russia to adopt a new constitution, even before the Russian Federation itself.[102] Already earlier, Tatarstan had furthermore held its own presidential elections on 12 June 1991, parallel to the Russian federal elections. Mintimer Shaimiev, the only candidate, was elected president on a 60 per cent turnout, whereas only 36 per cent of the electorate in Tatarstan took part in the Russian federal elections, of which as little as 14 per cent supported Yeltsin.[103]

2.4 The 1994 Russo-Tatar Treaty and Agreements

The adoption of a new Tatar constitution and the refusal to sign the Treaty of Federation, however, did not develop into the promotion of complete separation from Russia. Instead, Tatar president Shaimiev signed with the Russian federal government the Treaty on the Delimitation of Jurisdiction and Mutual Delegation of Powers between the State Authorities of the Russian Federation and the State Authorities of the Republic of Tatarstan.[104] Together with a series of bilateral agreements, the 1994 Russo-Tatar Treaty granted Tatarstan far-reaching autonomy rights such as the creation of its own national bank, conducting foreign relations on its own, and the independent organization of its foreign and economic

[99] Quotation from the English translation of the Russian Constitutional Court's Tatarstan Decision (1992) (n. 78), 39.

[100] Bennigsen-Broxup, 'Tatarstan and the Tatars' (1996) (n. 67), 83.

[101] Commission on Security and Cooperation in Europe, Presidential Elections and Independence Referendums in the Baltic States, the Soviet Union and Successor States: A Compendium of Results 1991–1992 (Washington, D.C.: Commission on Security and Cooperation in Europe, 1992), 157–63.

[102] Bennigsen-Broxup, 'Tatarstan and the Tatars' (1996) (n. 67), 84.

[103] Ibid., 82–3.

[104] Договор о разграничении предметов ведения и взаимном делегировании полномочий между органами государственной власти Российской Федерации и органами государственной власти Республики Татарстан [Treaty on the Delimitation of Jurisdiction and Mutual Delegation of Powers between the State Authorities of the Russian Federation and the State Authorities of the Republic of Tatarstan], 15 February 1994. English translation reprinted in Butler and Henderson, *Russian Legal Texts* (1998) (n. 4), 73–9.

activities.[105] In the preamble, the 1994 Russo-Tatar Treaty explicitly mentions self-determination, territorial integrity, and the unity of the economic space, stressing at the same time that 'the Republic of Tatarstan as a State is associated with the Russian Federation'.

Although 'some contentious issues' remained, as Shaimiev later reportedly said, the Tatar president viewed the negotiated result as a compromise that worked as 'a safeguard against a possible unitary development on the part of Russia', whose 'imperial mentality, unfortunately, is still prevalent in Russia today'.[106] The apparent political solution notwithstanding, ethnic Tatars within the republic continued however to consider themselves to be predominantly citizens of Tatarstan, and a majority of the population was still of the view that the republic should be a sovereign state.[107]

2.5 The Amended Tatar Constitution and the 2007 Russo-Tatar Treaty

When the new Russian federal government under Vladimir Putin initiated a territorial reform of the Russian Federation in May 2000, the fragile arrangement of the 1994 Russo-Tatar Treaty was contested for a first time.[108] In order to bring Tatar legislation in line with federal laws, a commission was set up, and the Russian Constitutional Court ruled in two decisions that Tatarstan had to amend its constitution.[109]

[105] On the negotiations and the content of the 1994 Russo-Tatar Treaty and agreements in more detail see Malik Hafeez, 'Tatarstan's Treaty with Russia: Autonomy or Independence?', *Journal of South Asian and Middle Eastern Studies* 18 (1994), no. 2, 1–36; Elizabeth Teague, 'Russia and Tatarstan Sign Power-sharing Treaty', *Radio Free Europe/Radio Liberty Research Report* 3 (1994), 19–27; Kahn, *Federalism, Democratization, and the Rule of Law in Russia* (2002) (n. 3), 151–7.

[106] President of the Republic of Tatarstan Mintimer Shaimiev, quoted in Valeri Tishkov, *Ethnicity, Nationalism and Conflict in and after the Soviet Union: The Mind Aflame* (London: Sage, 1997), 243.

[107] See D.M. Ishakov, L.V. Sagitova, and I.L. Izmailov, 'The Tatar National Movement of the 1980s-90s', *Anthropology & Archaeology of Eurasia* 43 (2004), no. 3, 11–44, 15.

[108] The reform was initiated by Putin shortly after becoming Russian president in order to reassert federal authority and brought about the subdivision of Russia into seven (since 2014: eight) federal districts, each administered by an envoy serving as link between the constituent subject and the federal government. Envoys get appointed by the Russian president and are primarily responsible for overseeing the compliance of the federal subjects with federal laws.

[109] Constitutional Court of Russia, *По запросу группы депутатов Государственной Думы о проверке соответствия Конституции Российской Федерации отдельных положений конституций Республики Адыгея, Республики Башкортостан, Республики Ингушетия, Республики Коми, Республики Северная Осетия-Алания и Республики Татарстан* [At the Request of a Group of Deputies of the State Duma on the Verification of Compliance with the Constitution of Certain Provisions of the Constitutions of the Republic of Adygea, the Republic of Bashkortostan, the Republic of Ingushetia, the Republic of Komi, the Republic of North Ossetia-Alania, and the Republic of Tatarstan], Decision No. 92-0/2000, 27 June 2000, SZRF 2000, no. 29, item 3117; Constitutional Court of Russia, *По ходатайству Президента Республики Башкортостан об официальном разъяснении Определения Конституционного Суда Российской Федерации от 19 апреля 2001 года по ходатайству полномочного представителя Президента Российской Федерации в Приволжском федеральном округе об официальном разъяснении Определения Конституционного Суда*

The amended Tatar constitution continues to refer in its preamble to 'the customary right of peoples to self-determination' but stresses at the same time the 'preservation of the historical unity of the nations of the Russian Federation on the basis of the principle of federalism'.[110] New article 1(1) of the amended constitution spells out the relationship between the Republic of Tatarstan and the Russian Federation in more detail:

> The Republic of Tatarstan is a democratic constitutional State associated with the Russian Federation by the Constitution of the Russian Federation, the Constitution of the Republic of Tatarstan and the Treaty between the Russian Federation and the Republic of Tatarstan on Delimitation of Jurisdictional Subjects and Mutual Delegation of Powers between the State Bodies of the Russian Federation and the State Bodies of the Republic of Tatarstan, and is a subject of the Russian Federation. The sovereignty of the Republic of Tatarstan shall consist in the full possession of the State authority (legislative, executive and judicial) outside the jurisdiction of the Russian Federation and the powers of the Russian Federation in the sphere of shared jurisdiction between the Russian Federation and the Republic of Tatarstan and shall be an inalienable qualitative attribute of the Republic of Tatarstan.

Further reference to Tatarstan's sovereignty is made in article 3 ('The sovereignty of the Republic of Tatarstan shall lie on its multinational people, which shall be the only source of power of the Republic of Tatarstan'). New article 1 furthermore states that the republic's status may not be altered without the mutual consent of Tatarstan and the Russian Federation (paragraph 3), and determines that the republic, within its jurisdiction, may independently participate in international and foreign economic relations (paragraph 4).

Российской Федерации от 27 июня 2000 года по запросу группы депутатов Государственной Думы о проверке соответствия Конституции Российской Федерации отдельных положений конституций Республики Адыгея, Республики Башкортостан, Республики Ингушетия, Республики Коми, Республики Северная Осетия-Алания и Республики Татарстан [On the Petition of the President of the Russian Federation of the Republic of Bashkortostan on the Official Explanation of the Definition of the Constitutional Court of the Russian Federation of 19 April 2001; At the Request of the Plenipotentiary Representative of the President of the Russian Federation in the Volga Federal District; On the Official Explanation of the Definition of the Constitutional Court of the Russian Federation of 27 June 2000; At the Request of a Group of Deputies of the State Duma Regarding the Compliance of Certain Provisions of the Republic of Adygea, the Republic of Bashkortostan, the Republic of Ingushetia, Komi Republic, the Republic of North Ossetia-Alania, and the Republic of Tatarstan with the Constitution of the Russian Federation], Decision No. 249-0/2001, 6 December 2001, SZRF 2002, no. 4, item 374.

[110] Quotation from the English translation of the amendedconstitution reprinted in Philip Raworth (ed.), *Constitutions of Dependencies and Territories*, vol. 9, Supp 2007-5 (Dobbs Ferry, NY: Oceana Publications) 5–39.

In addition to the amendments to the Tatar constitution, a new Russo-Tatar Treaty was negotiated and signed on 26 June 2007.[111] While this new Russo-Tatar Treaty still contained certain privileges like the right to issue its own passports with a Tatar emblem and an addendum in Tatar language, other privileges in the areas of foreign relations and economy were now missing.[112] Moreover, the right of the Tatar people to self-determination was not mentioned anymore. On 25 July 2017, ten years after coming into force, the agreement expired, thereby making Tatarstan the last autonomous republic of the Russian Federation to lose its special status.[113]

A last sign of Tatar national resistance was a declaration by the Milli Mejlis (National Assembly) of the Tatar People under the leadership of Vil Mirzayanov following Russia's recognition of Abkhazia and South Ossetia in August 2008. In the declaration of 20 December 2008, the Mejlis declares its 'support for the Declaration of State Sovereignty of 30 August 1990' and stresses the 'illegitimacy of including the Republic of Tatarstan into the Russian Federation without its consent'. The Mejlis furthermore asks the United Nations for recognition, announces a government in exile and calls 'all Tatars around the world to organize a permanent mass campaign in support of the Independence of Tatarstan before their governments and societies'.[114] The document was ignored by both the United Nations and the Russian federal government.

3. *Case Study 2*: Chechnya

Chechnya is a landlocked territory in the North Caucasus, within 100 kilometres of the Caspian Sea. It borders Georgia to the south and is otherwise surrounded by the federal subjects of the Russian Federation Dagestan, Ingushetia, North Ossetia, and the Stavropol Krai. According to the Russian census of 2010, 1.2 million people

[111] Договор о разграничении предметов ведения и полномочий между органами государственной власти Российской Федерации и органами государственной власти Республики Татарстан [Treaty on the Delimitation of the Subjects of Jurisdiction and Powers between the State Authorities of the Russian Federation and the State Authorities of the Republic of Tatarstan], 26 June 2007. English translation available at: http://1997-2011.tatarstan.ru/english/append20.html#.

[112] For example, international agreements concluded by Tatarstan had henceforth to be authorized by the Russian Ministry of Foreign Affairs, and the former right to decide on the exploitation of its natural resources (article 2(6) of the 1994 Russo-Tatar Treaty) was reduced to a right to conclude agreements with the government of the Russian Federation concerning the resolution of questions in this area (article 2(2) of the 2007 Russo-Tatar Treaty).

[113] See Lena Smirnova, 'Tatarstan, the Last Region to Lose Its Special Status Under Putin', *The Moscow Times*, 25 July 2017.

[114] An English translation of the declaration had been published on the *CNN iReport* website on 17 January 2009 but was taken offline again some time thereafter. An archived copy can still be retrieved from https://web.archive.org/web/20140330111914/http://ireport.cnn.com/docs/DOC-183351.

live in the region, of which 95 per cent belong to the Chechen ethnic group.[115] Like the Volga Tatars, the Chechens are of Sunni Islamic religion.

3.1 Origins of the Conflict Over Chechnya

The origins of the conflict over Chechnya date back to the eighteenth century, when Peter the Great first attempted to conquer the Caucasus, and resumed under Catherine the Great, when King Giorgi XII of Georgia requested protection from the Russian Empire.[116] After having largely repulsed the remaining Ottoman and Persian interests in the region by the time of the Napoleonic Wars (1803–1815),[117] Russia tried to consolidate its power over the region in the following years by setting up military bases, including the fort Grozny (Chechnya's today capital), founded in 1818 by Russian general Aleksei Yermolov, the commander-in-chief in Georgia with jurisdiction over the entire Caucasus region.[118] Yermolov advocated and implemented a harsh deportation policy which forced Chechens into the inhospitable Caucasus mountains or led to the deportation into Siberian exile.[119]

In the 1830s, Russian rule in Chechnya was contested under the leadership of three imams from neighbouring Dagestan, of which Shamil was the most successful. By 1847, Shamil managed to organize a full-scale rebellion and was able to take control over the region for roughly a decade.[120] During that period, an independent government and basic administrative structures were established, with taxes being collected, currency minted, justice dispensed, and a standing army maintained. However, although communications were entered into with the Ottoman Empire, Egypt, and Persia, Shamil apparently did not establish continuous relations with any third state, nor a diplomatic corps as such.[121] In the following decades, the Chechens continued to fight against Russian rule but the

[115] Russian Federal State Statistics Service, '2010 All-Russian Population Census' (n. 57). The numbers are debated, see e.g. Liz Fuller, 'Preliminary Chechen Census Findings Unveiled', *Radio Free Europe/Radio Liberty*, 3 November 2010.

[116] John Dunlop, *Russia Confronts Chechnya: Roots of a Separatist Conflict* (Cambridge: Cambridge University Press, 1998), 6–9. For more detailed accounts on the origins of the conflict see John Frederick Baddeley, *The Russian Conquest of the Caucasus* (London: Longmans, Green & Co., 1908) and Moshe Gammer, *Muslim Resistance to the Tsar: Shamil and the Conquest of Chechnia and Dagestan* (London: Cass, 1994).

[117] Cf. the various peace treaties between Russia and the Ottoman Empire (Treaty of Bucharest in 1812, confirmed by the Treaty of Adrianople in 1829) and between Russia and Persia (Treaty of Gulistan in 1813, confirmed by the Treaty of Turkmanchai in 1828).

[118] Dunlop, *Russia Confronts Chechnya* (1998) (n. 116), 13–14.

[119] Ibid., 14–16. On Yermolov and his policy in more detail see Baddeley, *The Russian Conquest of the Caucasus* (1908) (n. 116), 92–163 and Moshe Gammer, '"Proconsul of the Caucasus": A Re-examination of Yermolov', *Social Evolution & History* 2 (2003), 177–94.

[120] Dunlop, *Russia Confronts Chechnya* (1998) (n. 116), 23–9.

[121] Gammer, *Muslim Resistance to the Tsar* (1994) (n. 116), 225–35.

resistance was never as successful or organized as under Shamil and therefore remained sporadic for the remainder of the Tsarist period.[122]

3.2 Chechen Resistance during the Soviet Era

When the Russian Empire collapsed in 1917, Sufi leaders from the region took advantage of the chaotic situation and successfully revolted against the forces of the White Army. On 11 May 1918, the Mountainous Republic of the Northern Caucasus was declared, recognized as an independent state by the Central Powers of the First World War.[123] The statehood of the young republic was however fragile and only short-lived: in 1920, the Red Army moved into the region and by 1925 Russian control was gradually restored.[124]

In June 1920, Chechnya was declared part of the Mountainous Republic of the Northern Caucasus within the Russian SFSR. Shortly thereafter, the republic was however dissolved again and divided into a number of autonomous regions which in the case of Chechnya led to the transformation into the Chechen Autonomous Oblast in November 1922.[125] In 1934, the two oblasts of Chechnya and Ingushetia were merged into the Chechen-Ingush Autonomous Oblast, whose status was elevated to that of an autonomous republic (ASSR) on 5 December 1936.[126] Despite this 'divide and rule' strategy by the Soviet government, Chechen unrest continued. Following the end of the Second World War, Soviet authorities carried out severe reprisals on the pretext of Chechen collaboration with Nazi Germany.[127] (German forces never reached Chechnya.) On 23 February 1944, a large number of troops entered the territory, the entire population was deported to Central Asia,[128] and the Chechen-Ingush ASSR was abolished.[129]

Following the death of Stalin in 1953, the first Chechens and Ingush began to reappear in the region and, after the measures were officially reversed by Khrushchev in 1956 and the Chechens 'rehabilitated', the survivors of the deportation returned in large numbers.[130] On 8 January 1957, the Chechen-Ingush ASSR was reconstituted.

[122] For example, the outbreak of war between Russia and Turkey fuelled a revolt in 1877–1878, see Dunlop, *Russia Confronts Chechnya* (1998) (n. 116), 32.

[123] Ibid., 37.

[124] Ibid., 39–41.

[125] The remaining territory of the republic was partitioned into the North Ossetian Autonomous Oblast and the Ingush Autonomous Oblast.

[126] Thomas Grant, 'Chechnya', in MPEPIL (online edn), MN 10.

[127] Dunlop, *Russia Confronts Chechnya* (1998) (n. 116), 58–9.

[128] Approximately 22–23 per cent of the population died on their way due to bad nutrition, typhus, and inadequate shelter, ibid., 70–1.

[129] See ibid., 61–74.

[130] Ibid., 75–6. In 1956 alone, an estimated 25,000 to 30,000 Chechens and Ingush returned.

The latent conflict broke out again in the wake of *perestroĭka* in the late 1980s. In opposition to the Supreme Soviet of the Chechen-Ingush ASSR, the All-National Congress of the Chechen People was formed which, on 27 November 1990, declared the sovereignty of the Chechen-Ingush ASSR. Parliamentary and presidential elections were held and made Dzhokhar Dudayev president, and on 6 September 1991, the newly elected parliament declared the independence of the former Chechen-Ingush ASSR. (Its Ingush part insisted on remaining part of the Russian SFSR.) On 27 October 1991, Chechnya held an independence referendum which was neither monitored nor ratified by the central government. On 1 November 1991, Dudayev issued a unilateral declaration of independence, and on 12 March 1992 the constitution of the newly proclaimed Chechen Republic of Ichkeria was adopted.[131] In the preamble, Chechnya is proclaimed 'a sovereign state' and 'as an equal member state of the world community'. Moreover, article 1 of the Chechen Constitution states:

> Chechnya is a sovereign, democratic, rule of law state created as a result of the self-determination of the Chechen people. It has supreme power over its territory and national values; it independently determines its internal and foreign policy, adopts the Constitution and laws which are supreme within all its territory. The state sovereignty of Chechnya is indivisible.[132]

3.3 The *Chechnya* Case in Front of the Russian Constitutional Court

When Chechnya refused to sign the Treaty of Federation and neglected the validity of the new Russian Constitution, the situation escalated. The Yeltsin administration first tried to destabilize the Dudayev regime but when a Moscow-supported coup failed, Yeltsin decided to invade, and in December 1994 the First Chechen War broke out. Two decrees issued on 9 December 1994 served as the legal basis for the intervention.[133] Upon request by a number of Russian State Duma deputies, the

[131] An English translation of the Chechen Constitution is reprinted in Philip Raworth (ed.), *Constitutions of Dependencies and Territories*, vol. 5, Supp 2005-5 (Dobbs Ferry, NY: Oceana Publications), 3–28.

[132] Quotation from the English translation in ibid., 3.

[133] Decree of the President of Russia No. 2166, О мерах по пресечению деятельности незаконных вооружённых формирований на территории Чеченской Республики и в зоне осетино-ингушского конфликта [On Measures to Repress the Activity of the Illegal Armed Formation on the Territory of the Chechen Republic and in the Area of the Ingush-Ossetian Conflict], 9 December 1994, SZRF 1994, no. 33, item 3422; Decree of the Government of Russia No. 1360, Об обеспечении государственной безопасности и территориальной целостности Российской Федерации, законности, прав и свобод граждан, разоружения незаконных вооружённых формирований на территории Чеченской Республики и прилегающих к ней регионов Северного Кавказа [On Ensuring State Security and Territorial Integrity of the Russian Federation, the Rule of Law, the Rights and Freedoms

Russian Constitutional Court was asked to assess the constitutionality of these acts, together with the presidential decree 'On Basic Provisions of the Military Doctrine of the Russian Federation' of 2 November 1993,[134] inasmuch as it dealt with the use of military force in order to settle internal conflicts.

In its *Chechnya* decision of 31 July 1995, the Russian Constitutional Court starts its assessment by portraying the situation in Chechnya as a product of historical injustices:

> This extraordinary situation is historically associated with the fact that, during the period of Stalinist repressions, the Chechen [people] was subjected to mass deportation, the rectification of the consequences of which turned out to have been insufficiently effective. The state power, first of the USSR and then of Russia, was not able to assess correctly the justified resentment of the Chechens, the events that were coming to a head in the republic, and the driving forces behind them.[135]

In the view of the court, Russia's main responsibility for the situation in Chechnya seems, however, not to lie in its dealing with these injustices but in its passivity in restoring order. The court adds:

of Citizens, the Disarmament of Illegal Armed Groups on the Territory of the Chechen Republic and Adjacent Regions of the North Caucasus], 9 December 1994, SZRF 1994, no. 33, item 3454.

[134] Decree of the President of Russia, Об Основных положениях военной доктрины Российской Федерации [On Basic Provisions of the Military Doctrine of the Russian Federation], 2 November 1993, SAPP RF 1993, no. 45, item 4329.

[135] Constitutional Court of Russia, *По делу о проверке конституционности Указа Президента Российской Федерации от 30 ноября 1994 года № 2137 «О мероприятиях по восстановлению конституционной законности и правопорядка на территории Чеченской Республики», Указа Президента Российской Федерации от 9 декабря 1994 года № 2166 «О мерах по пресечению деятельности незаконных вооружённых формирований на территории Чеченской Республики и в зоне осетино-ингушского конфликта», постановления Правительства Российской Федерации от 9 декабря 1994 года № 1360 «Об обеспечении государственной безопасности и территориальной целостности Российской Федерации, законности, прав и свобод граждан, разоружения незаконных вооружённых формирований на территории Чеченской Республики и прилегающих к ней регионов Северного Кавказа», Указа Президента Российской Федерации от 2 ноября 1993 года № 1833 «Об Основных положениях военной доктрины Российской Федерации»* [In the Case on the Verification of the Constitutionality of Decree of the President of the Russian Federation no. 2137 of 30 November 1994 'On Measures to Restore the Constitutional Legality and Law and Order on the Territory of the Chechen Republic', the Decree of the President of the Russian Federation no. 2166 of 9 December 1994 'On Measures to Repress the Activity of the Illegal Armed Formation on the Territory of the Chechen Republic and in the Area of the Ingush-Ossetian Conflict', the Decree of the Government of the Russian Federation no. 1360 of 9 December 1994 'On Ensuring State Security and Territorial Integrity of the Russian Federation, the Rule of Law, the Rights and Freedoms of Citizens, the Disarmament of Illegal Armed Groups on the Territory of the Chechen Republic and Adjacent Regions of the North Caucasus', and the Decree of the President of the Russian Federation no. 1833 of 2 November 1993 'On the Fundamental Provisions of the Military Doctrine of the Russian Federation'] (Chechnya Decision), Decision No. 10-P/1995, 31 July 1995, *Rossiĭskaya gazeta*, 11 August 1995. Quotation from the English translation in *Statutes & Decisions: The Laws of the USSR and its Successor States* 31 (1995), no. 5, 48–94, 51.

> The federal bodies of power of the Russian Federation weakened law-enforcement activity in the Chechen Republic, did not provide for the security of state storehouses of weapons on its territory, and, during the course of several years, exhibited passivity in the resolution of the problems of mutual relations with this republic as a subject of the Russian Federation.[136]

Following these considerations, the Russian Constitutional Court starts its legal assessment by holding that the Russian Constitution does not provide for a right to secede for its constituent republics, 'just like the 1978 Constitution previously in effect'. (Although this is correct, the comparison to the 1978 Russian SFSR Constitution appears selective: article 72 of the latest constitution of the Soviet Union, which did provide for a constitutional right of secession, is ignored.) According to the Russian Constitution, any change in the status of a subject is possible only by mutual agreement and in accordance with federal laws, the court adds, stressing that the integrity of the Russian state 'is one of the fundamental principles of the constitutional order of the Russian Federation'.[137]

As in the *Tatarstan* decision, the Russian Constitutional Court then goes on to briefly consider the right of peoples to self-determination under international law.[138] Unlike in the *Tatarstan* case however, the court bases its considerations in the *Chechnya* decision solely on the Friendly Relations Declaration of 1970, whereas references to the UN Charter, the two Human Rights Covenants, or any other international legal instrument dealing with the right of peoples to self-determination and/or the territorial integrity of states under international law are missing.

By way of quoting from the savings clause of the Friendly Relations Declaration, the court holds that

> the exercise of the right to self-determination 'must not be interpreted as sanctioning or encouraging any actions that would lead to the division or the complete violation of the territorial integrity or political unity of sovereign and independent states acting in observance of the principle of the equal rights and self-determination of nations'.

[136] Ibid.

[137] Ibid.

[138] Ibid., 52. The decision's international law aspects are also discussed in Paola Gaeta, 'The Armed Conflict in Chechnya before the Russian Constitutional Court', *European Journal of International Law* 7 (1996), 563–70; Långström, *Transformation in Russia and International Law* (2003) (n. 18), 416–19; Diana Draganova, 'Chechnya's Right of Secession under Russian Constitutional Law', *Chinese Journal of International Law* 3 (2004), 571–89, 581–3; Rückert, *Das Völkerrecht in der Rechtsprechung des russischen Verfassungsgerichts* (2005) (n. 95), 211–19; Angelika Nußberger, 'Rechts- und Verfassungskultur in der Russischen Föderation', *Jahrbuch des öffentlichen Rechts* 54 (2006), 35–55, 45–9; Summers, *Peoples and International Law* (2014) (n. 95), 403–4.

'Taking this into consideration', the court continues, 'federal powers … repeatedly undertook attempts to overcome the crisis that had arisen in the Chechen Republic.' After these attempts failed, 'the application of measures of state compulsion in order to provide for the state security and territorial integrity of the Russian Federation and for the disarmament of illegal armed formations on the territory of the Chechen Republic' had to be prescribed, the court ruled.[139]

Apart from the lacking assessment of the right to self-determination's content and scope under international law in the *Chechnya* decision, it is interesting to note that the Russian Constitutional Court's reference to the savings clause is incomplete,[140] thereby arguably turning its potential meaning into its exact opposite. Paola Gaeta comments on the Constitutional Court's remarkable omission:

> [I]t seems unquestionable that the saving clause has been misconstrued in the judgement under discussion. The Court, rather surprisingly, failed to mention the last part of the saving[s] clause quoted above. In so doing, it avoided the central issue raised by the saving[s] clause, i.e. is the Government of the RF sufficiently representative and not discriminating? … It appears that the Court jumped to a conclusion and simply took it for granted that, under the 1970 Declaration and its saving[s] clause, the Chechen Republic was not entitled to the right to secession on the grounds of the principle of self-determination. Rather paradoxically, the Court would appear to have based its judgment in part on a[n] international instrument providing for the right, under extreme circumstances, to secession of groups living within the territory of sovereign states.[141]

3.4 The Khasavyurt Accord

The first Chechen War ended after Chechen separatist forces recaptured Grozny in August 1996. The Russian federal government agreed to sign a ceasefire, which was followed by the conclusion of the Khasavyurt Accord of 31 August 1996.[142] 'Based on the generally accepted principles of the right of peoples to self-determination, the principles of equal rights … and the security of peoples', the Khasavyurt Accord set forth four principles: (1) the conclusion of an agreement before 31 December

[139] Constitutional Court of Russia, Chechnya Decision (1995) (n. 135), 52.

[140] For the full wording of the savings clause (para. 7 of the fifth principle) of the Friendly Relations Declaration see n. 92 above.

[141] Gaeta, 'The Armed Conflict in Chechnya before the Russian Constitutional Court' (1996) (n. 138), 566 (italics omitted). On the omission of the last part of the savings clause in the decision see also Rückert, *Das Völkerrecht in der Rechtsprechung des russischen Verfassungsgerichts* (2005) (n. 95), 213.

[142] Хасавюртские соглашения [Khasavyurt Accord], 31 August 1996, *Nezavisimaya gazeta*, 3 September 1996. English translation: Richard Sakwa (ed.), *Chechnya: From Past to Future* (London: Anthem Press, 2005), 295–6 (Appendix 1).

2001 on the terms for relations between the Russian Federation and the Chechen Republic, 'to be decided in accordance with generally accepted principles and norms of international law'; (2) the formation of a joint commission by 1 October 1996; (3) the laws of the Chechen Republic 'will be based on respect for human rights and rights of citizens, the right of peoples to self-determination, the principles of equality of peoples, the protection of peace, international harmony, and security of civilians living in the territory of the Chechen Republic, regardless of their national origin, religious denomination or other differences'; and (4) the joint commission will undertake its work in accordance with a mutual agreement.[143]

Due to the Khasavyurt Accord's vague terminology, the meaning of some of its aspects surrounding the status question of Chechnya remained controversial between the signatories.[144] First, establishing international law as the regime which shall regulate Russo-Chechen relations suggests that the Khasavyurt Accord is an international treaty under international law between two independent states. That international law shall govern the mutual relations between the Russian Federation and the Chechen Republic was a concession by Russia for which the Chechens argued fiercely in the negotiation process and to which the federal government eventually gave in only to put an end to the brutal war. For Russia, however, the Khasavyurt Accord was 'more political-psychological in nature than it [was] legal', as the spokesperson to the Russian president Yeltsin, Sergey Yastrzhembsky, later reportedly put it.[145] And even if the Khasavyurt Accord was legally binding, Yastrzhembsky argued, the agreement was subject to Russian national law, not international law, since the mere mentioning of international law in the text would not elevate it to an international treaty between two independent states. International law is also part of the Russian Federation's legal system as evidenced by article 15(4) of the Russian Constitution, Yastrzhembsky claimed.[146]

Second, whereas Chechnya viewed the inclusion of 'the right of peoples to self-determination' and 'principles of equality of peoples' in the Khasavyurt Accord as the basis for Russo-Chechen relations on the way towards eventual recognition as a sovereign and independent state, Russia maintained that it thereby committed itself only to self-determination *within* the territory of the Russian Federation. For Russia, the reference to self-determination meant above all the provision of a framework in which a bilateral agreement between the Chechen Republic and the Russian Federation could be worked out, similar to the other federation agreements with its constituent subjects under the umbrella of the Treaty of Federation.[147]

143 Ibid.

144 See Wendy Turnoff Atrokhov, 'The Khasavyurt Accords: Maintaining the Rule of Law and Legitimacy of Democracy in the Russian Federation Amidst Chechen Crisis', *Cornell International Law Journal* 32 (1999), 367–92, 379–81.

145 *Kommersant*, 13 May 1997. Quotation from the English translation of a condensed text of the newspaper article in *Current Digest of the Soviet Press* 49 (1997), no. 19, 10–11, 10.

146 Ibid.

147 Atrokhov, 'The Khasavyurt Accords' (1999) (n. 144), 380.

Third, the fact that the Khasavyurt Accord failed to mention Russia's territorial integrity but stipulated that the final status of the Russian–Chechen relations 'must be reached before 31 December 2001', could be construed as only a matter of time until Russia will eventually recognize Chechnya as an independent state.[148] 'In sum', as Wendy Turnoff Atrokhov concluded her assessment of the agreement under international law in the *Cornell International Law Journal*, 'the ambiguities in the Khasavyurt accords are numerous and deliberate'. While 'Russia interprets the agreement as providing for Chechen sovereignty within the Russian Federation', the 'Chechens view the terms as a precursor for full recognition as an independent state'.[149]

3.5 Chechen Autonomy after the Second Chechen War

On 1 October 1999, after Russian allegations of sending fighting groups based in Chechnya to carry out attacks in neighbouring Dagestan and a series of bomb attacks destroying apartment blocks in Moscow which Russian authorities had attributed to Chechen rebels, Russian troops entered Chechnya and started the Second Chechen War. This time, Russian forces were successful in re-establishing control over the main centres of population in Chechnya, and on 6 December 1999, an ultimatum was issued to the citizens of Grozny to leave the capital or be subject to a comprehensive bombardment. By early February 2000, Grozny was recaptured by Russian forces, and in March 2000, the war officially came to an end when a Russian security chief declared that 'the military phase of antiterrorist operations in Chechnya is drawing to a close'. The Chechen Republic was reintegrated into the Russian Federation, and the insurgent-led administration dispersed.[150]

On 23 March 2003, a new Chechen Constitution was adopted.[151] It was drawn up under the auspices of the Russian federal authorities and as such differs considerably from its predecessor and also from those of other autonomous republics of the Russian Federation. For example, according to article 66 of the 2003 Chechen Constitution, all citizens of the Russian Federation are eligible for the presidency of the Chechen Republic, whereas the constitutions of other autonomous republics require candidates to have resided in the territory for a minimum of fifteen years and to speak the language of the republic's titular nation.[152] Moreover, unlike the 1992 Chechen Constitution, the new constitution leaves no doubt of Chechnya

[148] Ibid.

[149] Ibid.

[150] On the events in more detail see Mark Kramer, 'The Perils of Counterinsurgency: Russia's War in Chechnya', *International Security* 29 (2004/2005), no. 3, 5–62.

[151] Reprinted in Philip Raworth (ed.), *Constitutions of Dependencies and Territories*, vol. 9 Supp, 2004-4 (Dobbs Ferry, NY: Oceana Publications), 3–47.

[152] See e.g. the Constitution of the Republic of Sakha, art. 66, reprinted in ibid., Supp 2000-1, 3–31, 16.

being an integral part of the Russian Federation. This is made clear already in the preamble, which, although it continues to refer to 'the universally-recognized principles of equal rights and the self-determination of peoples', points to Chechnya's 'historical commonality with Russia and her multinational people'. Chechnya's sovereignty and/or status as a state is not mentioned any more, and article 1(2) explicitly provides for its territory to be 'an inalienable part of the territory of the Russian Federation'. The relationship between Chechnya and the Russian Federation is further spelled out in article 58:

> The relationship of the Chechen Republic with the Russian Federation is determined by the Constitution of the Russian Federation, federal law, the Constitution of the Chechen Republic and agreements between state bodies of the Chechen Republic and those of the Russian Federation with respect to the demarcation of jurisdiction and authority between the executive organs of the Chechen Republic and federal executive bodies as well as to the transfer to each other of part of their authority.

Borders of the Chechen Republic and other parts of the Russian Federation can only be changed by mutual consent, whereas borders of Chechnya with foreign states 'constitute the state border of the Russian Federation' (article 59). According to article 10, the official languages of the Chechen Republic are Chechen and Russian. However, Russian is the language of 'inter-ethnic affairs' and official documentation, article 10(2) as well as the language of the courts, article 99(2).

Following the adoption of the new Chechen Constitution, presidential elections were held and made Akhmad Kadyrov the new president of the Republic of Chechnya. Officially, Kadyrov received 81 per cent of the votes, on an 88 per cent turnout. However, the election was 'so plainly fixed as to be farcical, were the outcome not so tragic for the Chechens', attaining a 'Soviet style absurdity' with turnouts in some regions as high as 98 per cent, *The Economist* commented in an article on the elections.[153] In May 2004, Kadyrov was assassinated in a bomb attack, and his son, Ramzan Kadyrov, succeeded. On 15 April 2009, the retreat of Russian military forces from Chechnya was officially announced.[154] Since then, Chechnya has developed a parallel system within the Russian Federation, created and endorsed by the federal government.[155]

[153] 'Turnout in the deserted capital was 98%. It was the same in the nearby Zavodskoy district, a stronghold of Wahhabites, the Islamic radicals whom Mr Kadyrov has sworn to wipe out. Abdullah Bugayev, one of the remaining opposition candidates, got 6% overall, but barely more than 1% in the north-western Nadterechny district, one of his supposed strongholds. "One would hope", declared an official from Russia's federal election committee, "to see such levels of propriety, lawfulness and *glasnost* in many other regions." He was not being ironic', *The Economist*, 11 October 2003.

[154] 'Russia "ends Chechnya Operation"', *BBC News*, 16 April 2009.

[155] A 2015 report by the International Crisis Group summarizes the situation as follows: 'Ramzan Kadyrov's Chechnya is an absolute exception within the Russian Federation, a parallel polity with informal well-trained, combat-ready security structures inside the official ones, a parallel tax system, its

4. Conclusions

Chapter 2 has shown that the post-Soviet Russian constitutional order acknowledges the right of peoples to self-determination, albeit strictly within its territorial boundaries and with sometimes unusual or even flawed argumentation. In the Russian Constitution, the right of peoples to self-determination appears in two central provisions: first in the preamble and then again in article 5(3) as the basis of the federal structure of the Russian Federation. Unlike its Soviet predecessors, the Russian Constitution of 1993 does not, however, recognize a constitutional right of secession. The right to self-determination of a single ethnic group in the Russian Federation is always trumped by Russia's state sovereignty and territorial unity. Consequently, a right of secession is also dismissed in Russian constitutional doctrine. Most importantly, the right of a unified 'multinational people of the Russian Federation' to self-determination and Russia's sovereignty are usually 'balanced' by an equation of the two concepts, ultimately resulting in the portrayal of a harmonic, indivisible whole.

The subsequent two case studies confirmed this general assessment. First, although the relationship between the right to self-determination and Russia's territorial integrity was discussed by the Russian Constitutional Court in two important decisions, the argumentation that led to the conclusion that international law does not provide for a right of secession was flawed. In the *Chechnya* decision, the discussion was even shortened to a restatement of the first part of the savings clause in the Friendly Relations Declaration, thereby reversing its potential meaning into its exact opposite.[156] Other international instruments dealing with self-determination were not even mentioned, and reflections on self-determination as a customary

own legal regime and, in effect, foreign relations. Despite superficial appearances, this arrangement has not resolved the Chechen conflict. The status quo is based on military defeat of the separatists in an asymmetric war, but in the absence of any positive political dynamic or legal redress, the insurgency continues to recruit. Stability is fragile and overly personalised, based on the bond between Ramzan and Vladimir Putin.... If the political landscape were to change in Moscow, Ramzan's security forces could conceivably prove a problem for the Kremlin. Ramzan's own situation would also be vulnerable. Without Putin's support, he could face serious challenges from a wide spectrum of insurgents, would-be strongman successors and citizens dissatisfied with the oppressive aspects of his rule threatening full-fledged deadly conflict. The prudent response to these multiple risks for all concerned would be for Moscow to initiate measures to bring Chechnya under the Russian constitution and laws, improve its quality of governance, put an end to parallel economic practices, integrate and control the Chechen security forces and end their impunity. It would not be easy, but turning a blind eye to the current situation on the assumption that the conflict is solved stores up worse problems for the future', ICG, Europe Report No. 236, Chechnya: The Inner Abroad, 30 June 2015, 39.

[156] Other national courts have also contemplated the possibility that the formula might provide the basis for a right of secession under international law. Most notably, the Supreme Court of Canada has reflected about this possibility in Re Secession of Quebec, but in the end distanced itself from this theory, see Supreme Court of Canada, Reference Re Secession of Québec, 20 August 1998, Dominion Law Reports 161 (1998), 4th Series, 386, 440–1, paras 133–135. The Canadian Supreme Court's decision is discussed e.g. in Anne Bayefsky, *Self-determination in International Law, Quebec and Lessons Learned* (The Hague: Kluwer Law International, 2000); James Crawford, 'The Right of Self-determination in International Law: Its Development and Future', in Philip Alston (ed.), *Peoples' Rights* (Oxford: Oxford University Press, 2001), 7–67, 47–63; and Allen Buchanan, 'The Quebec Secession Issue: Democracy,

rule, that is a discussion of the relevant state practice and *opinio juris* with regard to a possible right of secession, was also nonexistent.

In line with these observations, Angelika Nußberger has called the use of international law by the Russian Constitutional Court 'carefully formulated—eclectic'.[157] Referring to the omission of the last part of the savings clause in the *Chechnya* decision, she writes: 'This is not an isolated case. In a series of constitutional court decisions, citations of international law norms and court decisions are incorporated in a way that their original meaning is at least alienated, if not turned into their opposite.' According to Nußberger, one possible explanation for this approach could be the authority that is linked to the reference to international law: 'not the plausibility of the legal argument is the objective, but the authoritative safeguarding of the results which are obtained on the basis of the Russian Constitution'.[158]

On a more general level, the case studies on Tatarstan and Chechnya provide examples of how, as a general rule, international law grants states the right to preserve their territorial integrity and to restore constitutional order in secessionist conflicts, irrespective of grave historical injustices in the past. This view could be observed in the case of Tatarstan (a conflict barely noticed by the international community and in international law scholarship),[159] but it is also clearly confirmed by state practice in relation to the Chechen crisis, in which the international community consistently supported Russia's claim of Chechnya being an integral part of the Russian Federation. For example, United States Deputy Secretary of State Strobe Talbott said on 5 February 1995:

> We support the sovereignty and territorial integrity of the Russian Federation. We oppose attempts to alter international boundaries by force, whether in the form of aggression by one state against another or in the form of armed secessionist movements such as the one led by Dzokhar Dudyaev. That is why we have said that we regard Chechnya as a matter which the Russian Government and the people of Chechnya will have to resolve together peacefully by political means.[160]

Minority Rights, and the Rule of Law' in Allen Buchanan and Stephen Macedo (eds), *Secession and Self-determination* (New York, NY: New York University Press, 2003), 238–2=71; Summers, *Peoples and International Law* (2014) (n. 95), 417–424.

[157] Nußberger, 'Rechts- und Verfassungskultur in der Russischen Föderation' (2006) (n. 138), 45–6.

[158] Ibid., 46, 48.

[159] For one of the very few exceptions see Babak Nikravesh, 'Quebec and Tatarstan in International Law', *The Fletcher Forum of World Affairs* 23 (1999), 227–58.

[160] Statement by United States Deputy Secretary of State Strobe Talbott, 'Supporting Democracy and Economic Reform in the New Independent States: Statement before the Subcommittee of Foreign Operations of the Senate Appropriations Committee', Washington, D.C., 9 February 1995, reprinted in *US Department of State Dispatch* 6 (1995), no. 8, 119–24, 120.

Similar statements were issued in the interwar period by other states and intergovernmental and international organizations.[161] The view also prevailed during and after Russia launched the Second Chechen War to regain control over Chechnya at the price of gross violations of human rights. Moreover, Russia was even explicitly conceded the use of military force. For example, although the European Council declared that it condemned 'the intense bombardments of Chechen cities, the threat levelled at the residents of Grozny and the ultimatum set by the Russian military commanders, as well as the treatment of the internally displaced persons as totally unacceptable', it also stressed that it 'does not question the right of Russia to preserve its territorial integrity nor its right to fight against terrorism'.[162] In a similar vein, NATO recognized 'Russia's right to preserve its territorial integrity and to protect all citizens against terrorism and criminality',[163] and the European Court of Human Rights stated in *Isayeva v Russia*, the leading case in front of the court dealing with the human rights violations that occurred during the Chechen Wars:

> The Court accepts that the situation that existed in Chechnya at the relevant time called for exceptional measures on behalf of the State in order to regain control over the Republic and to suppress the illegal armed insurgency. Given the context of the conflict in Chechnya at the relevant time, those measures could presumably include the deployment of army units equipped with combat weapons, including military aviation and artillery.[164]

In April 2000, the Russian delegates' voting rights in the Parliamentary Assembly of the Council of Europe (PACE) were suspended, but were restored again in January 2001.[165]

[161] See e.g. Statement by Government spokesperson in the House of Lords, Lord Inglewood, 18 April 1995, reprinted in Geoffrey Marston (ed.), 'United Kingdom Materials on International Law 1995', *British Yearbook of International Law* 66 (1995), 583–757, 621: 'the exercise of the right [to self-determination] must also take into account questions such as what constitutes a separate people and respect for the principle [of] territorial integrity of the unitary state. In the case of Chechnya no country has recognised President Dudayev's unilateral declaration of independence, but we have repeatedly called on the Russians to work for a political solution which would allow the Chechen people to express their identity within the framework of the Russian Federation', PACE Res 1055 (1995), Russia's Request on Membership in the Light of the Situation in Chechnya, 2 February 1995, para. 1: 'the political conflict between Chechnya and the central authorities of the Russian Federation is an internal matter', OSCE, Permanent Council Decision No. 35, 11 April 1995, according to which the OSCE promotes the 'peaceful resolution of the crisis and the stabilization of the situation in the Chechen Republic in conformity with the principle of the territorial integrity of the Russian Federation'.

[162] European Council, Declaration on Chechnya, 10 December 1999, reprinted in Presidency Conclusions, Helsinki European Council, 10 and 11 December 1999, Annex II.

[163] Ministerial Meeting of the North Atlantic Council Held in Budapest, Final Communiqué, 30 May 2001, para. 61.

[164] ECtHR, Isayeva v Russia, judgment, 24 February 2005, application no. 57950/00, MN 180; for a similar statement see ECtHR, Isayeva, Yusupova and Bazayeva v Russia, judgment, 24 February 2005, application nos 57947, 57948, and 57949/00, MN 178.

[165] PACE Recommendation 1456 (2000), Conflict in the Chechen Republic—Implementation by the Russian Federation of Recommendation 1444 (2000), 6 April 2000; PACE Res 1241 (2001), Credentials of the Delegations of the Russian Federation, 25 January 2001. See Philip Leach, 'Egregious Human

In international law scholarship, Chechnya is sometimes discussed as a possible example of a right of 'remedial' secession, where a people is granted a right to state independence as an exception to the traditional view that self-determination outside the colonial context has to be exercised within a given state territory, and that secession is not regulated under international law.[166] On a general level, Antonio Cassese has argued for a remedial right of secession *de lege ferenda*

> when the central authorities of a sovereign State persistently refuse to grant participatory rights to a religious or racial group, grossly and systematically trample upon their fundamental rights, and deny the possibility of reaching a peaceful settlement within the framework of the State structure. Thus, denial of the basic right of representation does not give rise *per se* to the right of secession. In addition, there must be gross breaches of fundamental human rights, and, what is more, the exclusion of any likelihood for a possible peaceful solution within the existing State structure.[167]

Other prominent advocates of this theory include eminent scholars like Oscar Schachter and Christian Tomuschat,[168] who have also argued for a qualified right of secession under similar conditions like Cassese, based on arguments developed by Lee Buchheit, Allen Buchanan, and others.[169]

Looking at the international law literature that deals with the question of a possible right of Chechnya to secede from the Russian Federation, a number of authors can be found who argued in favour of such a right as a result of the serious and widespread violations of human rights and humanitarian law, in particular *before* Russia regained control over the territory, that is up until 1999.[170] Later however,

Rights Violations in Chechnya: Appraising the Pursuit of Justice', in Lauri Mälksoo (ed.), *Russia and the European Court of Human Rights: the Strasbourg Effect* (Cambridge: Cambridge University Press, 2018), 255–94, 258–60.

[166] For a prominent example of this state-centred, 'classic view' see James Crawford, *The Creation of States in International Law* (Oxford: Oxford University Press, 2nd edn, 2006), 374–448.

[167] Antonio Cassese, *Self-determination of Peoples: A Legal Reappraisal* (Cambridge: Cambridge University Press, 1995), 119–20.

[168] Oscar Schachter, 'Micronationalism and Secession' in Ulrich Beyerlin, Michael Bothe, Rainer Hofmann, and Ernst-Ulrich Petersmann (eds), *Recht zwischen Umbruch und Bewahrung: Völkerrecht, Europarecht, Staatsrecht (Festschrift für Rudolf Bernhardt)* (Berlin: Springer, 1995), 179–86, 185; Christian Tomuschat, 'Secession and Self-determination', in Marcelo Kohen (ed.), *Secession: International Law Perspectives* (Cambridge: Cambridge University Press, 2006), 1–45, 41.

[169] Lee C. Buchheit, *Secession: The Legitimacy of Self-determination* (New Haven, CT: Yale University Press, 1978); Allen Buchanan, *The Morality of Political Divorce from Fort Sumter to Lithuania and Quebec* (Boulder, CO: Westview, 1991); Allen Buchanan, 'Theories of Secession', *Philosophy and Public Affairs* 26 (1997), no. 1, 30–61; Allen Buchanan, 'The International Institutional Dimension of Secession', in Percy B. Lehning (ed.), *Theories of Secession* (London: Routledge, 1998), 227–56.

[170] See e.g. Soili Nystén-Haarala, 'Does the Russian Constitution Justify an Offence against Chechnya?', *Humanitäres Völkerrecht* (1995), no. 2, 104–7, 106; René Lefeber and David Raič, 'Frontiers of International Law, Part One: The Chechen People', *Leiden Journal of International Law* 9 (1996), 1–6, 3; Trent Tappe, 'Chechnya and the State of Self-determination in a Breakaway Region of the former Soviet Union: Evaluating the Legitimacy of Secessionist Claims', *Colombia Journal of Transnational Law*

the majority view became that Chechnya does not have a right to secede from Russia.[171] The main reason for this shift can be seen in the continuous state-centric state practice even during and after the Second Chechen War, but lies probably also in the fact that the Chechen political and military leadership never seriously tried to reach a peaceful solution with the Russian federal government.[172] Thus, instead of providing precedential value for the existence of a right of remedial secession under positive international law, the case of Chechnya is arguably rather a confirmation for the non-existence of such a right *de lege lata*.

34 (1996), 255–95, 295. But see Tarcisio Gazzini, 'Considerations on the Conflict in Chechnya', *Human Rights Law Journal* 17 (1996), 93–105, 96–7.

[171] See e.g. Cherylyn Brandt Ahrens, 'Chechnya and the Right of Self-determination', *Columbia Journal of Transnational Law* 42 (2004), 575–615, 609; Heiko Sauer and Niklas Wagner, 'Der Tschetschenien-Konflikt und das Völkerrecht. Tschetscheniens Sezession, Russlands Militärinterventionen und die Reaktionen der Staatengemeinschaft auf dem Prüfstand des internationalen Rechts', *Archiv des Völkerrechts* 45 (2007), 55–83, 62; Nußberger, 'Russia' (n. 13), MN 72–3.

[172] On the other hand, one could of course also argue that Russian efforts to find a peaceful solution were similarly questionable, see Brandt Ahrens, 'Chechnya and the Right of Self-determination' (2004) (n. 171), 603–9.

3
Russia, the Right to Self-Determination and Secession

On 8 December 1991, the heads of state of the Russian Soviet Federative Socialist Republic (SFSR), the Ukrainian Soviet Socialist Republic (SSR), and the Byelorussian SSR signed the so-called Belavezha Accords, which famously declared that the Soviet Union had 'terminated its existence as a subject of international law and a geopolitical reality'.[1] On the same day, the Commonwealth of Independent States (CIS) was created, and on 21 December 1991, the signatories of the Belavezha Accords together with Armenia, Azerbaijan, Kazakhstan, Kyrgyzstan, Moldova, Tajikistan, Turkmenistan, and Uzbekistan signed the Alma-Ata Declaration, thereby also joining the CIS.[2] On 22 January 1993, the CIS Charter was signed and subsequently ratified by all founding states of the CIS except Turkmenistan and Ukraine, which decided to participate in the CIS without being members.[3] (Ukraine announced it would stop cooperating with the CIS in May 2018, following the organization's 'failure to denounce Russia's aggression' in Ukraine.[4] Georgia also joined the CIS in 1993, but withdrew its membership following the Russo-Georgian War of 2008. The three Baltic states Estonia, Latvia, and Lithuania refused to participate in the entire process.)

The Belavezha Accords, the Alma-Ata Declaration, and the CIS Charter all proclaim that the parties recognize and respect the territorial integrity and the inviolability of their existing borders within the CIS.[5] The recognition of the former union republics' administrative boundaries as the boundaries of the newly established independent states in these documents strongly supports the argument that the dissolution process of the Soviet Union followed the principle of *uti possidetis*. Generally, the application of the *uti possidetis* principle means that former internal

[1] Соглашения о создании Содружества Независимых Государств [Agreement Establishing the Commonwealth of Independent States] (Belavezha Accords), 8 December 1991, *Diplomaticheskiĭ vestnik* 1992, 1. English translation: 31 ILM 138.

[2] Алма-Атинская Декларация [Alma-Ata Declaration], 21 December 1991, *Diplomaticheskiĭ vestnik* 1992, 6. English translation: 31 ILM 148.

[3] Устав Содружества Независимых Государств [Charter of the Commonwealth of Independent States], 22 January 1993. English translation: 34 ILM 1283.

[4] See 'Ukraine Shuts Down Offices in CIS Member States', *Radio Free Europe/Radio Liberty*, 28 August 2018.

[5] See also CIS, Декларация о соблюдении суверенитета, территориальной целостности и неприкосновенности границ государств [Declaration on Respect of Sovereignty, Territorial Integrity, and Inviolability of Boundaries of Member States], 15 April 1994, BMD 1994, no. 7, 9.

Russia and the Right to Self-Determination in the Post-Soviet Space. Johannes Socher, Oxford University Press.
 DOI: 10.1093/oso/9780192897176.003.0004

state boundaries are regarded as boundaries between newly independent states.[6] Outside the colonial context, the principle was first applied in the dissolution process of Yugoslavia by the Arbitration Commission of the Peace Conference on Yugoslavia (commonly known as the Badinter Commission, named after the president of the five-member committee and president of the French Constitutional Council, Robert Badinter) which held:

> Except where otherwise agreed, the former boundaries become frontiers protected by international law. This conclusion follows from the principle of respect for the territorial status quo and, in particular, from the principle of uti possidetis. Uti possidetis, though initially applied in settling decolonization issues in America and Africa, is today recognized as a general principle.[7]

Although the principle of *uti possidetis* 'in and of itself, does not identify which administrative divisions and lines are to be preserved',[8] its application in the dissolution process of the Soviet Union was clearly limited to that of union republics.[9] This becomes evident from the reading of the founding documents of the CIS, and is furthermore supported by article 72 of the last constitution of the Soviet Union, the so-called Brezhnev Constitution of 1977, which stated that (only) the former union republics had a constitutional right to secede.[10]

[6] Giuseppe Nesi, 'Uti Possidetis Doctrine', in MPEPIL (online edn); Steven R. Ratner, 'Drawing a Better Line: Uti Possidetis and the Borders of New States', *American Journal of International Law* 90 (1996), 590–624; Suzanne Lalonde, *Determining Boundaries in a Conflicted World: The Role of Uti Possidetis* (Montreal & Kingston: McGill-Queen's University Press, 2002). For a contribution by a Russian scholar see F.S. Mirzaev, 'Принцип uti possidetis в современном международном праве и его применение на постсоветском пространстве: Теория и практика' [The Principle of Uti Possidetis in Modern International Law and its Application in the Post-Soviet Space], *Pravo i politika* (2004), no. 6, 43–53. See also ICJ, Case Concerning the Frontier Dispute (Burkina Faso v Republic of Mali), 22 December 1986, ICJ Reports 1986, 554, paras 20–23.

[7] Conference on Yugoslavia Arbitration Commission, Opinion No. 3, 11 January 1992, 1992 ILM 1499, 1500. See Peter Radan, 'Post-Secession International Borders: A Critical Analysis of the Opinions of the Badinter Commission', *Melbourne University Law Review* 3 (2000), 50–76.

[8] Lalonde, *Determining Boundaries in a Conflicted World* (2002) (n. 6), 237.

[9] The Russian SFSR, the Ukrainian SSR, the Byelorussian SSR, and the Transcaucasian SFSR constituted the four founding republics of the Soviet Union, created on the basis of the Treaty on the Establishment of the Union of Soviet Socialist Republics of 30 December 1922. Additional union republics were later set up: the Turkmen and the Uzbek SSR in 1924, the Tajik SSR in 1929, and the Kazakh and Kirghiz SSR in 1936. In 1937, the Transcaucasian SFSR was dissolved and divided between the Armenian, the Azerbaijan, and the Georgian SSR. In 1940, the Moldavian, Estonian, Latvian, Lithuanian, and the Karelo-Finnish SSR were established, although the latter was reabsorbed into the Russian SFSR in 1956, leaving a total of fifteen union republics until the dissolution of the Soviet Union in 1991.

[10] Конституция (Основной Закон) Союза Советских Социалистических Республик [Constitution (Fundamental Law) of the Union of Soviet Socialist Republics], 7 October 1977, VVS SSSR 1977, no. 41, item 616. English translation: William E. Butler (ed.), *Collected Legislation of the Union of Soviet Socialist Republics and the Constituent Union Republics*, vol. 1, Supp 1985-2 (Dobbs Ferry, NY: Oceana Publications), 2–46. A Soviet Law on Secession was enacted in 1990, which allowed not only union republics but also their sub-units the right to decide 'whether to remain in the Soviet Union or in the seceding Republic as well as to decide on their state legal status', Law of the Soviet Union О порядке решения вопросов, связанных с выходом союзной республики из СССР [On

Accordingly, only the fifteen former union republics were admitted to the United Nations following the dissolution of the Soviet Union, whereas their respective sub-units were implicitly deemed integral parts of the newly independent states: the three Baltic states Estonia, Latvia, and Lithuania joined on 17 September 1991; Armenia, Azerbaijan, Kazakhstan, Kyrgyzstan, Moldova, Tajikistan, Turkmenistan, and Uzbekistan were admitted on 2 March 1992; Georgia joined the United Nations on 31 July 1992; Belarus and Ukraine retained the memberships of the Byelorussian SSR and the Ukrainian SSR, respectively;[11] and the Russian Federation declared that it would take over the Soviet Union's membership to the United Nations as its 'continuator state'.[12]

On the ground, the situation was however less clear-cut. In some of the union republics, calls for 'national liberation' turned into violent secessionist conflicts at the eve of the Soviet Union's collapse. In four instances, these calls ultimately resulted in the separation of *de facto* independent republics, claiming to be sovereign states: Nagorno-Karabakh in Azerbaijan, Transnistria in Moldova, and Abkhazia and South Ossetia in Georgia. Since 2006, the latter three form the Community for Democracy and Rights of Nations to which Nagorno-Karabakh also joined a year later. In the founding document, the parliaments of the breakaway republics declare:

> The principle of international law on equal rights and self-determination of nations is one of the cornerstones of world justice and the most significant aspect of self-identification of a nation as an international legal entity. Ignoring this puts in peril the stability and security of the international system; ... we call upon the international community to recognise the results of our nations' referendums and build relations with the Republic of Abkhazia, the Pridnestrovian Moldavian Republic, and the Republic of South Ossetia

the Procedure for Resolving Questions Connected with a Union Republic's Secession from the USSR], 3 April 1990, Vedomosti S'ezda narodnўkh deputatov RSFSR i verkhovnogo soveta RSFSR 1990, no. 13, item 252. English translation: Hurst Hannum (ed.), *Documents on Autonomy and Minority Rights* (Dordrecht: Nijhoff, 1993), 753–60. Since the law set out a very disadvantageous, complex, and cumbersome mechanism to enact this right, none of the union republics made however use of it but instead based their claim directly on article 72 of the Constitution of the Soviet Union when declaring independence from the Soviet Union, see Theodor Schweisfurth, 'Vom Einheitsstaat (UdSSR) zum Staatenbund (GUS)', *Zeitschrift für ausländisches öffentliches Recht und Völkerrecht* 52 (1992), 541–702, 603–6.

[11] The Byelorussian SSR and the Ukrainian SSR had been members of the UN since the organization's foundation in 1945.

[12] On the controversy over this claim see Angelika Nußberger, 'Russia', in MPEPIL (online edn), MN 105–108. Since the 2020 constitutional amendments, this position is also codified in article 67(1) [1] of the Russian Constitution, see Johannes Socher, 'Farewell to the European Constitutional Tradition: The 2020 Russian Constitutional Amendments', *Zeitschrift für ausländisches öffentliches Recht und Völkerrecht* 80 (2020), 615–48, 630–1.

> as independent, sovereign nations and equal subjects of international-legal relations.[13]

In all four cases, Russia has supported this call for independence in the name of the right of peoples to self-determination, albeit at various times to different degrees, and often in an ambivalent fashion. By way of examining this involvement, this chapter analyses Russia's state practice with regard to self-determination in the context of these four conflicts in the post-Soviet space. Section 1 provides a general framework of the relevance of secession as a concept of international law by situating Russia's position towards Kosovo's declaration of independence from Serbia in the wider debate on the scope of the right of peoples to self-determination. The subsequent sections portray the conflicts over Nagorno-Karabakh (Section 2), Transnistria (Section 3), South Ossetia (Section 4), and Abkhazia (Section 5) in more detail, with a focus on Russia's role in them.

1. Russia's Position in the *Kosovo* Case

If one looks at the relevant state practice since the end of the Second World War, the international community has been very discouraging towards secession.[14] In a strict sense, the concept of secession in international law denotes (only) the unilateral withdrawal of a constituent part of a state from that state, resulting in the creation of a new state, while the parent state continues to exist.[15] Understood this way, one may identify only a single instance which comes close to a successful secession, the separation of Bangladesh from Pakistan in 1971, but even there the former was admitted to the United Nations only after the latter had recognized it as an independent state.[16]

Since then, Kosovo's withdrawal from Serbia was the first case in which the separation of a part of a state was promoted by a large number of states, even though the existing state, of which the separating entity was a part, expressly opposed the

[13] Соглашения между парламентами Абхазии, Приднестровья и Южной Осетии [Agreement between the Parliaments of Abkhazia, Transnistria, and South Ossetia], 4 July 2006, Russian text available at: https://regnum.ru/news/667681.html.

[14] See James Crawford, 'State Practice and International Law in Relation to Secession', *British Yearbook of International Law* 69 (1999), 85–117; James Crawford, *The Creation of States in International Law* (Oxford: Oxford University Press, 2nd edn, 2006), 374–448.

[15] Daniel Thürer and Thomas Burri, 'Secession', in MPEPIL (online edn), MN 1. The process of separation of colonies or other non-self-governing territories from the metropolitan states is not considered as a series of secessions under international law, since at the time of decolonization these entities were no longer regarded to be integral parts of the metropolitan states, see ibid., MN 26–7.

[16] Crawford, *The Creation of States in International Law* (2006) (n. 14), 158, 393. On Bangladesh's secession from Pakistan see Subrata Roy Chowdhury, *The Genesis of Bangladesh: A Study in International Legal Norms and Permissive Conscience* (New York, NY: Asia Publishing House, 1972). Successful separations outside the colonial context after the Second World War *in agreement* with the parent state include Senegal (1960), Singapore (1965), and South Sudan (2011).

separation.[17] The international community's division on the question whether Kosovo's secession from Serbia was legal in terms of international law became instantly apparent following Kosovo's declaration of independence on 17 February 2008. In the UN Security Council's meeting the next day, Vitaly Churkin, Russia's permanent representative to the United Nations, stated that Kosovo's declaration of independence constitutes 'a blatant breach of the norms and principles of international law—above all the Charter of the United Nations—which undermines the foundations of the system of international relations'.[18] The US delegate, on the other hand, maintained that considering the ultimate failure of all previous attempts to resolve Kosovo's status issue in agreement with Serbia and Russia, Kosovo's declaration of independence was 'a logical, legitimate and legal response to the situation at hand'.[19] Still on the same day, the United States recognized Kosovo as an independent state, referring to the 'unusual combination of factors found in the Kosovo situation—including the context of Yugoslavia's breakup, the history of ethnic cleansing and crimes against civilians in Kosovo, and the extended period of UN administration', which 'are not found elsewhere and therefore make Kosovo a special case'.[20] As of February 2021, 98 out of 193 UN member states recognize Kosovo as an independent state,[21] while at the same time, apart from the Russian Federation and Serbia,[22] quite a number of states (Argentina, Brazil, China, Greece,

[17] Kosovo is a landlocked territory in the Balkan peninsula with a predominantly ethnic Albanian population. From 1945 to 1963, it was an autonomous region of Serbia within Yugoslavia. In 1963, it was elevated to the status of an autonomous province within Serbia, and remained as such until 1989, when Serb president Slobodan Milošević rescinded Kosovo's autonomy. Throughout the 1990s, Kosovo Albanians sought either restoration of autonomy or independence. In 1998, the Serb government launched military actions in Kosovo, resulting in widespread atrocities. After negotiations failed to resolve Kosovo's political status, NATO launched a controversial air campaign to force the Serb government to withdraw from Kosovo (for a recent assessment of the NATO military intervention see Daniel Franchini and Antonios Tzanakopoulos, 'The Kosovo Crisis–1999', in Tom Ruys and Olivier Corten (eds), *The Use of Force in International Law: A Case-based Approach* (Oxford: Oxford University Press, 2018), 594–622). On 10 June 1999, the UN Security Council adopted Resolution 1244, authorizing an international civil and military presence in Yugoslavia, establishing the UN Interim Administration Mission in Kosovo, and setting out a general framework for resolving the final political and legal status of Kosovo. In December 2007, after almost nine years of political negotiations over the final status of Kosovo, the mediation process had ended in an impasse. On the events that led to the declaration of independence see e.g. Henry Perritt, *The Road to Independence for Kosovo: A Chronicle of the Ahtisaari Plan* (Cambridge: Cambridge University Press, 2010); on the almost mythical origins of the conflict see Robert Kaplan, *Balkan Ghosts: A Journey Through History* (New York, NY: St. Martin's Press, 1993).

[18] Russian Federation, UN SC 5839th meeting, 18 February 2008, UN Doc. S/PV.5839, 6. See also 'Путин: независимость Косово повлечёт непредсказуемые последствия' [Putin: Kosovo's Independence Will Lead to Unpredictable Consequences], *RIA Novosti*, 22 February 2008.

[19] United States, S/PV.5839 (n. 18), 18.

[20] U.S. Department of State, 'U.S. Recognizes Kosovo as Independent State', 18 February 2008, https://2001-2009.state.gov/ secretary/rm/2008/02/100973.htm.

[21] Numerous international organizations such as the International Monetary Fund, the World Bank, and the International Olympic Committee also include Kosovo in their member lists, see e.g. International Monetary Fund, 'Press Release: Kosovo Becomes the International Monetary Fund's 186th Member', 29 June 2009, Press Release No. 09/240, http://www.imf.org/en/News/Articles/2015/09/14/01/49/pr09240.

[22] In 2013, Kosovo and Serbia signed the Brussels Agreement, thereby agreeing to begin normalize relations. The process had stalled since November 2018 but regained momentum in September 2020, when Serbia and Kosovo agreed to normalize economic relations, see Anne Gearan, 'Serbia and

India, Iran, Spain, South Africa—to name only a few) continue to reject Kosovo's claim for independent statehood.

1.1 The *Kosovo* Case in Front of the International Court of Justice

On 8 October 2008, the UN General Assembly, on the initiative of Serbia, requested the International Court of Justice (ICJ) to render an advisory opinion on the question whether Kosovo's declaration of independence was 'in accordance with international law'.[23] On 22 July 2010, the ICJ held that Kosovo's declaration 'did not violate general international law',[24] arguing:

> Whether, outside the context of non-self-governing territories and peoples subject to alien subjugation, domination and exploitation, the international law of self-determination confers upon part of the population of an existing State a right to separate from that State is . . . a subject on which radically different views were expressed by those taking part in the proceedings and expressing a position on the question. Similar differences existed regarding whether international law provides for a right of 'remedial secession' and, if so, in what circumstances. There was also a sharp difference of views as to whether the circumstances which some participants maintained would give rise to a right of 'remedial secession' were actually present in Kosovo. The Court considers that it is not necessary to resolve these questions in the present case. The General Assembly has requested the Court's opinion only on whether or not the declaration of independence is in accordance with international law. Debates regarding the extent of the right of self-determination and the existence of any right of 'remedial secession', however, concern the right to separate from a state [and] is beyond the scope of the question posed by the General Assembly.[25]

By contrast, a number of states participating in the *Kosovo* case did consider these debates relevant, and the thirty-five written statements submitted to the ICJ during the proceedings offered partly diametrically opposed views on the scope of the right of self-determination and the concept of secession.[26] The Russian Federation

Kosovo Sign Breakthrough Economic Accord that is Short of Normal Relations', *The Washington Post*, 4 September 2020.

[23] GA Res 63/3 (Request for an Advisory Opinion of the International Court of Justice on whether the Unilateral Declaration of Independence of Kosovo is in Accordance with International Law), 8 October 2008, UN Doc. A/RES/63/3.

[24] ICJ, Accordance with International Law of the Unilateral Declaration of Independence in Respect of Kosovo, Advisory Opinion, 22 July 2010, ICJ Reports 2010, 403, para. 56.

[25] Ibid., paras 82–83.

[26] For a detailed assessment of these statements see James Summers, 'Kosovo', in Christian Walter, Antje von Ungern-Sternberg, and Kavus Abushov (eds), *Self-determination and Secession in*

also submitted a written statement, arguing that 'in 1999, just like in 1991, the international community did not proceed on the premise that Kosovo Albanians, or the whole population of Kosovo, were entitled to self-determination'.[27] The statement includes a chapter entitled 'The Declaration of Independence in the Light of General International Law', containing something like a distillation of the debate around the scope of the right of peoples to self-determination and its relevance with regard to secession.[28] It draws on most major international legal instruments regulating the right of peoples to self-determination (i.e. the UN Charter, the 1970 Friendly Relations Declaration,[29] and the 1975 Helsinki Final Act[30]), quotes from the *East Timor* judgment by the ICJ,[31] cites the legal opinion *Reference Re Secession of Québec* by the Canadian Supreme Court,[32] and makes extensive reference to some of the most authoritative works on the right to self-determination and secession in Western international law scholarship.[33]

1.2 Russia's Written Statement to the ICJ on Territorial Integrity and Self-determination

The chapter in Russia's written statement dealing with the international law aspects of Kosovo's declaration of independence starts with a short section on the principle of territorial integrity (paragraphs 76–78). By way of quoting a passage of Marcelo

International Law (Oxford: Oxford University Press, 2014), 235–54, 244–53. More recently, the content and scope of the right to self-determination was again widely discussed by numerous states in the written proceedings of the ICJ's Legal Consequences of the Separation of the Chagos Archipelago case. For the written statements and comments on these statements see https://www.icj-cij.org/en/case/169/written-proceedings.

27 Written Statement by the Russian Federation, Accordance with International Law of the Unilateral Declaration of Independence by the Provisional Institutions of Self-Government of Kosovo (Request for Advisory Opinion), 16 April 2009, para. 97, available for download at: http://www.icj-cij.org/files/case-related/141/15628.pdf.

28 Ibid., paras 74–104.

29 GA Res 26/25 (XXV) (Friendly Relations Declaration), 24 October 1970, UN Doc. A/RES/25/2625.

30 Helsinki Final Act, 1 August 1975, 1975 ILM 1292.

31 ICJ, East Timor (Portugal v Australia), 30 June 1995, ICJ Reports 1995, 90.

32 Supreme Court of Canada, Reference Re Secession of Québec, Dominion Law Reports 161 (1998), 4th Series, 386.

33 Throughout the text, the Russian written statement refers to the following works: Hurst Hannum, *Autonomy, Sovereignty and Self-determination* (Philadelphia, PA: University of Pennsylvania Press, 1990); Christian Tomuschat (ed.), *Modern Law of Self-determination* (Dordrecht: Nijhoff, 1993); Antonio Cassese, *Self-determination of Peoples: A Legal Reappraisal* (Cambridge: Cambridge University Press, 1995); Oscar Schachter, 'Micronationalism and Secession', in Ulrich Beyerlin, Michael Bothe, Rainer Hofmann, and Ernst-Ulrich Petersmann (eds), *Recht zwischen Umbruch und Bewahrung: Völkerrecht, Europarecht, Staatsrecht* (Berlin: Springer, 1995), 179–86; Julie Dahlitz (ed.), *Secession and International Law: Conflict Avoidance—Regional Appraisals* (The Hague: T.M.C. Asser Press, 2003); Marcelo Kohen (ed.), *Secession: International Law Perspectives* (Cambridge: Cambridge University Press, 2006); Crawford, *The Creation of States in International Law* (2006) (n. 14); and James Summers, *Peoples and International Law* (Leiden: Brill Nijhoff, 2007).

Kohen's introductory chapter in *Secession: International Law Perspectives*, territorial integrity is described as 'an unalienable attribute of a State's sovereignty'.[34] The written statement then mentions article 2(4) of the UN Charter and quotes from the 1970 Friendly Relations Declaration, according to which 'any attempt aimed at the partial or total disruption of the national unity and territorial integrity of a State or country ... is incompatible with the purposes and principles of the Charter'.[35] Further reference is made to the 1975 Helsinki Final Act which also recognizes territorial integrity as one of the principles of modern international relations.

A short description of the right of peoples to self-determination follows (paragraphs 79–81). With reference to the ICJ's *East Timor* judgment, self-determination is considered 'one of the essential principles of contemporary law' which 'is now universally recognised as applicable to all peoples'.[36] 'Besides this general idea', Russia's written statement maintains,

> a consensus seems to exist among States and scholars at least on the following points: the right to self-determination is to be exercised through the free choice by the people concerned without outside interference; it may be exercised through the establishment of an independent State, or through achieving a particular status within an existing State; [and] the right includes the possibility to freely determine the economic, social and cultural development of the people.[37]

With regard to the bearer of the right, the 'people', the written statement maintains that outside the colonial context it is 'widely accepted that a population ... of an existing State, taken as a whole' qualifies as a people entitled to the right to self-determination. The question '[w]hether, and under which conditions, an ethnic or other group within an existing State may qualify as a people is subject to extensive debates', the statement concludes rather vaguely.[38]

[34] Written Statement by the Russian Federation (2009) (n. 27), para. 77, citing Marcelo Kohen, 'Introduction', in Kohen, *Secession* (2006) (n. 33), 1–20, 6 ('For States, respect of their territorial integrity is paramount. This is a consequence of the recognition of their equal sovereign character. One of the essential elements of the principle of territorial integrity is to provide a guarantee against any dismemberment of the territory. It is not only the respect of the territorial sovereignty, but its *integrity*.')

[35] Written Statement by the Russian Federation (2009) (n. 27), para. 77.

[36] Ibid., para. 79.

[37] Ibid., para. 80, quoting Stanislav Chernichenko and Vladimir Kotliar, 'Ongoing Global Legal Debate on Self-determination and Secession', in Dahlitz, *Secession and International Law* (2003) (n. 33), 75–88, 77. On this book chapter by two Russian scholars of international law in more detail see Chapter 5 Section 2 below.

[38] Written Statement by the Russian Federation (2009) (n. 27), para. 81. However, during the public hearings, Kirill Gevorgian, the head representative of the Russian delegation, elaborated a bit further on the question in the context of the 'will of the people' mentioned in the Rambouillet Accords, and argued that the words 'do not necessarily refer to the population of Kosovo only and could very

After these broad overviews on territorial integrity and the right of peoples to self-determination in international law, Russia's written statement sets out to balance the two principles with each other (paragraphs 82–88). The starting point for the discussion is the so-called savings clause in the 1970 Friendly Relations Declaration,[39] from which the general conclusion is drawn that 'a State that respects the right of peoples living in its territory, is protected by the principle of territorial integrity from the implementation of the right to self-determination in the form of secession ("external self-determination")'.[40] This assessment is supported by a statement in *Reference Re Secession of Québec* of the Canadian Supreme Court, the written statement maintains, where it is argued that 'the recognized sources of international law establish that the right of self-determination of a people is normally fulfilled through internal self-determination', and that 'there is no necessary incompatibility between the maintenance of the territorial integrity of existing states ... and the right of a "people" to achieve a full measure of self-determination'.[41] Furthermore, the written statement argues, 'external self-determination', understood as 'self-determination in the form of secession', is generally not recognized in international law doctrine, whereas 'internal self-determination', that is the exercise of that right within an existing state, usually prevails.[42]

well encompass the whole population of the country concerned, or else reflect the general notion of "popular will" as a principle of democracy', ICJ, Accordance with International Law of the Unilateral Declaration of Independence in Respect of Kosovo (Request for Advisory Opinion), Oral Statements, 8 December 2009, Verbatim Record 2009/30, para. 16. (The Rambouillet Agreement was a proposed peace agreement between Yugoslavia and a delegation representing the Albanian majority population of Kosovo drafted by NATO. Yugoslavia's refusal to accept it triggered the NATO bombing during the Kosovo War.)

39 Friendly Relations Declaration (1970) (n. 29), para. 7 of the fifth principle: 'Nothing in the foregoing paragraphs shall be construed as authorizing or encouraging any action which would dismember or impair, totally or in part, the territorial integrity or political unity of sovereign and independent States conducting themselves in compliance with the principle of equal rights and self-determination of peoples and thus possessed with a Government representing the whole population.' See also Chapter 1 Section 2 above.

40 Written Statement by the Russian Federation (2009) (n. 27), para. 84.

41 Ibid., para. 95, quoting Supreme Court of Canada, Reference Re Secession of Québec (1998) (n. 32), paras 127, 130.

42 Written Statement by the Russian Federation (2009) (n. 27), paras 84–85, with references to Crawford, *The Creation of States in International Law* (2006) (n. 14), 415 ('outside the colonial context, the principle of self-determination is not recognized as giving rise to unilateral rights of secession by party of independent States'); Rosalyn Higgins, 'Self-determination and Secession', in Dahlitz, *Secession and International Law* (2003) (n. 33), 21–38, 36 ('[T]he concept of secession is irrelevant to the ongoing entitlement of peoples to self-determination in the post colonial era'); Cassese, *Self-determination of Peoples* (1995) (n. 33), 112 ('The principle of territorial integrity of sovereign States was, and still is, considered sacred ... [A]ny licence to secede must be interpreted very strictly'); and Christian Tomuschat, 'Self-determination in a Post-colonial World', in Christian Tomuschat, *Modern Law of Self-determination* (1993) (n. 33), 1–20, 11 ('[I]n no case should existing governmental structures be put in jeopardy lightly').

1.3 Russia's Written Statement to the ICJ on Secession

'What remains to be analyzed', the written statement sets out to conclude, 'is whether there exists a possibility of secession' in the cases mentioned in the savings clause, in other words whether a right of 'remedial' secession exists when the state concerned does not conduct itself 'in compliance with the principle of equal rights and self-determination of peoples' and is thus not 'possessed with a Government representing the whole population':[43]

> In this regard, the Russian Federation is of the view that the primary purpose of the '[savings] clause' is to serve as a guarantee of territorial integrity of States. It is also true that the clause may be construed as authorizing secession under certain conditions. However, those conditions should be limited to truly extreme circumstances, such as an outright armed attack by the parent State, threatening the very existence of the people in question. Otherwise, all efforts should be taken in order to settle the tension between the parent State and the ethnic community concerned within the framework of the existing State.[44]

This view also finds support in international law doctrine, Russia's written statement correctly observes, where the existence of a right of 'remedial' secession is limited to extreme situations in which 'violent acts of discrimination are continuously committed against the people in question and all the possibilities for a resolution of the problem within the existing State have been exhausted', that is as 'a measure of last resort, where the very existence of the people, or its characteristic features, are in danger'.[45] In sum, in Russia's view a right of remedial secession exists in positive international law, albeit only in very rare and extreme circumstances (which, according to Russia, were however not present in Kosovo).[46]

If one situates this position in the wider scholarly discourse of whether the right of peoples to self-determination confers a right of remedial secession, Russia's view as expressed in its written statement to the ICJ appears rather progressive, considering that the traditional view in international law doctrine is that the principle of territorial integrity either restricts secession, or that international law is at least

[43] Written Statement by the Russian Federation (2009) (n. 27), para. 86.
[44] Ibid., para. 88.
[45] Ibid., para. 87, quoting, *inter alia*, Tomuschat, 'Secession and Self-determination', in Kohen, *Secession* (2006) (n. 33), 41; Cassese, *Self-determination of Peoples* (1995) (n. 33), 119; and Schachter, 'Micronationalism and Secession' (1995) (n. 33), 185.
[46] Written Statement by the Russian Federation (2009) (n. 27), paras 98–103; ICJ, Verbatim Record 2009/30 (n. 38), paras 19–22.

neutral on it in situations outside the colonial context and situations involving foreign occupation.[47] Consequently, a number of states in the *Kosovo* proceedings ruled out the possibility of a right of remedial secession,[48] and the ICJ observed that the states that laid out the conditions for such a right in their written statements raised it 'in almost every instance only as a secondary argument', suggesting the states' lack of confidence in this position.[49]

2. *Case Study 3*: Nagorno-Karabakh

Nagorno-Karabakh is a landlocked territory in the South Caucasus within the mountainous range of Karabakh, a geographic region between present-day eastern Armenia and south-western Azerbaijan. Since the last Soviet census of 1989, the ethnic composition of the population residing in Nagorno-Karabakh shifted from 77 per cent Armenian and 22 per cent Azeri to almost exclusively Armenian in 2015.[50] Nagorno-Karabakh's Armenian population is mostly Christian and adheres to the Armenian Apostolic Church.

2.1 Origins of the Conflict Over Nagorno-Karabakh

The origins of the conflict over Nagorno-Karabakh can be traced back to Russia's victory in the last Russo-Persian War (1826–1828), following which the Russian Empire was able to consolidate its control over the Caucasus region. Since the peace treaty that concluded the war not only provided for the cession of the khanates of Erivan and Nakhchivan to Russia but also for the resettlement of Armenians from the Ottoman Empire and Persia into the Caucasus, a large number of Armenians migrated not only into Erivan and Nakhchivan but also into Karabakh, another Turkic khanate which had already fallen under Russian rule in 1805, to the effect that the share of the Armenian population in the region increased to almost

[47] See e.g. Crawford, *The Creation of States in International Law* (2006) (n. 14), 417; Olivier Corten, 'Are There Gaps in the International Law of Secession?', in Kohen, *Secession* (2006) (n. 33), 231–254; Olivier Corten, 'Territorial Integrity Narrowly Interpreted: Reasserting the Classical Inter-State Paradigm of International Law', *Leiden Journal of International Law* 24 (2011), 87–94.

[48] See Summers, 'Kosovo' (2014) (n. 26), 252.

[49] ICJ, Kosovo Advisory Opinion (2010) (n. 24), para. 82.

[50] State Committee of the USSR on Statistics, *Национальный Состав Населения СССР, по данным Всесоюзной Переписи Населения 1989 г.* [The National Composition of the Population of the USSR According to the All-Union Population Census of 1989] (Moscow: Finansȳ i statistika, 1991); Artsakh Republic National Statistical Service, 'Результаты переписи населения НКР 2015 г.' [The Results of the 2015 Population Census of the Republic of NKR], available at: http://stat-nkr.am/ru/-2015/-2015 (Table 5.1).

50 per cent.[51] The Crimean War (1853–1856), the Serbian-Turkish Wars (1876–1878), and the Russo-Turkish War (1877–1878) led to further migration of ethnic Armenians into Karabakh; conversely, thousands of Muslims left the region.[52]

The resettlement of Armenians was part of a wider Russian policy of Christianization in the Caucasus which was accompanied and supported by an extensive redrawing of administrative boundaries. In the case of Karabakh, the khanate was dissolved and absorbed into the Caspian Oblast in 1840, and made part first of the Shemakha Governorate (the later Baku Governorate) in 1846, before it was finally integrated into the Elisabethpol Governorate in 1868.[53]

During the First World War and following the Russian Revolution, control over Karabakh was fiercely disputed between Armenians and Azeris, but also between Ottoman and British forces, and after initial resistance, Karabakh Armenians had to accept their inclusion into Azerbaijan.[54] In August 1919, a provisional agreement with the government in Baku was signed,[55] subject to a final decision at the Paris Peace Conference, which subsequently recognized Azerbaijan's claim to Karabakh.[56] Over the course of 1920, the Red Army invaded and occupied Transcaucasia, capturing Baku in Azerbaijan in April, Shusha in Karabakh in May, and Dilijan in Armenia by the end of November of that year.[57] Dispute over Karabakh between Armenians and Azeris, however, continued but was eventually brought to a halt on 5 July 1921, when the Caucasian Bureau declared Nagorno-Karabakh to remain part of Azerbaijan, based on 'the need for national peace between Muslims and Armenians and [the existing] economic ties between upper and lower Karabakh, [and] its permanent link with Azerbaijan'.[58] On 7 July 1923, the Nagorno-Karabakh Autonomous Oblast (NKAO) was established within the Azerbaijan SSR.[59]

[51] See George Bournoutian, 'The Ethnic Composition and the Socio-Economic Condition of Eastern Armenia in the First Half of the Nineteenth Century', in Ronald Grigor Suny (ed.), *Transcaucasia, Nationalism and Social Change: Essays in the History of Armenia, Azerbaijan, and Georgia* (Ann Arbor, MI: University of Michigan Press, 1996), 69–86, 79.

[52] See Tim Potier, *Conflict in Nagorno-Karabakh, Abkhazia and South Ossetia: A Legal Appraisal* (The Hague: Kluwer Law International, 2001), 2.

[53] Ibid., 9.

[54] For a more detailed historical account of the events see Arsène Saparov, *From Conflict to Autonomy in the Caucasus: The Soviet Union and the Making of Abkhazia, South Ossetia and Nagorno-Karabakh* (Abingdon: Routledge, 2015), 91–113.

[55] An English translation of the agreement is reprinted in Richard G. Hovannisian, *The Republic of Armenia*, vol. 1 (Berkeley, CA: University of California Press, 1971), 186–7.

[56] Potier, *Conflict in Nagorno-Karabakh, Abkhazia and South Ossetia* (2001) (n. 52), 2.

[57] Saparov, *From Conflict to Autonomy in the Caucasus* (2015) (n. 54), 95–99.

[58] Ibid., 100–1, 110–11. Quotation from the English translation in ibid., 111. The Caucasian Bureau was an organization set up by the Bolsheviks in April 1920 to supervise the subordination of the Caucasus to the Russian Communist Party.

[59] Ibid., 117.

2.2 Karabakh Armenian Resistance During the Soviet Era and War of Independence

During the Soviet period, Karabakh Armenians repeatedly demanded integration of Nagorno-Karabakh into the Armenian SSR. Several petitions and letters were sent to Moscow over the decades but it took until the advent of *perestroĭka* for the movement to gain momentum.[60] In August 1987, a petition calling for a referendum on unification with Armenia was signed by more than 75,000 people, and on 20 February 1988, the local Soviet of the NKAO officially resolved to work towards a transfer of the region to the Armenian SSR.[61] On 15 June 1988, the Armenian Supreme Soviet voted to accept the NKAO into Armenia, a decision which was immediately rejected by the Azerbaijan Supreme Soviet, the Supreme Soviet of the Soviet Union, and the Central Committee of the Communist Party of the Soviet Union with reference to article 78 of the Constitution of the Soviet Union, according to which territorial alterations were inadmissible without the mutual agreement of the affected union republics. These protests notwithstanding, the Armenian Supreme Soviet and the National Council of Nagorno-Karabakh jointly declared the unification of the region with the Armenian SSR, and on 2 September 1991, only three days after Azerbaijan declared independence from the Soviet Union, the National Council declared Nagorno-Karabakh independent from Azerbaijan.[62] On 10 December 1991, a reported 99.9 per cent of the electorate confirmed Nagorno-Karabakh's independence in a referendum, with the Azeri population of Nagorno-Karabakh boycotting the vote.[63]

Parallel to and fuelled by these events, conflict broke out among the Armenian and Azeri population in the entire region with expulsions, violent incursions, and killings on both sides.[64] Following a pogrom on Armenians in the town of Sumqayit in Azerbaijan in February 1988, the situation escalated and ultimately led to an armed conflict between paramilitary units and government forces, producing an estimated 350,000 Armenian and up to 800,000 Azeri refugees and internally displaced persons.[65] By mid-1992, all 40,000 Azeris who lived in Nagorno-Karabakh were forced to flee, and by mid-1994, Nagorno-Karabakh forces (strongly supported by Armenia) succeeded in occupying more than 90 per cent of the former NKAO territory plus seven districts of Azerbaijan as a buffer zone.[66] The war finally

[60] Thomas de Waal, *Black Garden: Armenia and Azerbaijan Through Peace and War* (New York, NY: New York University Press, 2nd edn, 2013), 17–18.
[61] Ibid., 11–12.
[62] Potier, *Conflict in Nagorno-Karabakh, Abkhazia and South Ossetia* (2001) (n. 52), 7.
[63] Ibid., 8. On the referendum see also Anne Peters, *Das Gebietsreferendum im Völkerrecht: seine Bedeutung im Licht der Staatenpraxis nach 1989* (Baden-Baden: Nomos, 1995), 194–8.
[64] See HRW, Seven Years of Conflict in Nagorno-Karabakh (New York, NY: Human Rights Watch, 1994).
[65] Ibid., 99.
[66] Andriy Melnyk, 'Nagorny-Karabakh', in MPEPIL (online edn), MN 3.

ended in May 1994 with a ceasefire agreement between Azerbaijan, Armenia, and the Commander of the Army of Nagorno-Karabakh, mediated by the Russian diplomat Vladimir Kazimirov.[67]

Russia's military involvement in the war is disputed among the conflict parties, but it is safe to say that at least from mid-1992, Russia supported the Armenian side with arm supplies worth an estimated US$1 billion.[68] Beyond this material support, Russia's involvement and claimed partisanship for Armenia is difficult to assess. Thomas de Waal writes in *Black Garden: Armenia and Azerbaijan Through Peace and War*, the authoritative work on the Nagorno-Karabakh conflict:

> Early on in the conflict, in the chaos immediately following the end of the Soviet Union, there were dozens, if not hundreds, of 'Russian' freelancers and mercenaries fighting on both sides. Many of these were not actually 'Russian' in the strictest sense. They were former Soviet soldiers—mainly Russians, but also Ukrainians or Belarussians—who, when their units were withdrawn, had stayed behind . . . to earn a living.[69]

2.3 Russia's Mediation Efforts within the Minsk Group and Beyond

Although the 1994 ceasefire provided more than two decades of relative stability, numerous breaches had been reported by both Armenia and Azerbaijan before the conflict over Nagorno-Karabakh broke out again in September 2020.[70] Russia has been involved in the conflict as a mediator within the framework of the Conference (since 1995: Organization) on Security and Co-operation in Europe (CSCE/OSCE), but also on a trilateral basis with Armenia and Azerbaijan, since the early days of the war.

In 1992, the CSCE set up the so-called Minsk Group to encourage a peaceful, negotiated resolution to the conflict. Since then, Russia, together with France and the United States, has co-chaired various international mediation efforts that have gradually consolidated into a negotiation process. At the Lisbon OSCE summit

[67] Reprinted in V.N. Kazimirov, *Мир Карабаху* [Peace of Karabakh] (Moscow: Mezhdunarodnye otnosheniya, 2009), 396–8. An English translation of the ceasefire agreement is available at: http://nkr.am/en/ceasefire-agreement/147.

[68] The extent of this support became public only in 1997, when the Russian general Lev Rokhlin reported to the Russian State Duma that weaponry worth an estimated US$1 billion was sold to Armenia during the war, of which some had arrived in Armenia as early as summer 1992. See Lev Rokhlin, 'Спецоперация или коммерческая афера?' [A Special Operation or a Commercial Deal?], *Nezavisimoe voennoe obozrenie* (1997), no. 13.

[69] De Waal, *Black Garden* (2013) (n. 60), 213.

[70] For the most detailed report on the 2020 hostilities available at the time of writing see Amnesty International, In the Line of Fire: Civilian Casualties from Unlawful Strikes in the Armenian-Azerbaijani Conflict over Nagorno-Karabakh (London: Amnesty International, 2021). On the so-called Four-Day War of April 2016, the deadliest ceasefire violation prior to the renewed escalation in 2020 see ICG, Europe Report No. 239, Nagorno-Karabakh: New Opening, or More Peril?, 4 July 2016.

in 1996, three principles were worked out that shall guide the process: (1) the territorial integrity of Armenia and Azerbaijan; (2) the legal status of Nagorno-Karabakh 'defined in an agreement based on self-determination which confers on Nagorno-Karabakh the highest degree of self-rule within Azerbaijan'; and (3) the guaranteed security for Nagorno-Karabakh and its whole population.[71] Founded on these principles, a compromise based on the Helsinki Final Act principles of non-use of force, territorial integrity, and the equal rights and self-determination of peoples was worked out at the 2007 OSCE Ministerial Council in Madrid. These so-called Madrid Recommendations call for the return of the occupied territories surrounding Nagorno-Karabakh to Azerbaijan control; an interim status for Nagorno-Karabakh providing guarantees for security and self-governance; a specific arrangement for a corridor linking Armenia and Nagorno-Karabakh; future determination of the final legal status of Nagorno-Karabakh through a legally binding expression of will by referendum; the right of all internally displaced persons and refugees to return to their former places of residence; and internal security guarantees that would include the stationing of peacekeeping forces.[72] In 2009, at the 35th G8 summit, the Minsk Group co-chairs affirmed their 'commitment to support the leaders of Armenia and Azerbaijan', and urged them to 'resolve the few differences remaining between them and finalize their agreement'.[73] Further meetings in Muskoka (2010), Deauville (2011), and Los Cabos (2012) resulted in similar statements, however with no substantial progress on the status question of Nagorno-Karabakh being achieved.[74]

Beyond these efforts within the Minsk Group, Russia has been involved as a mediator on a trilateral basis with the conflict parties. For example, at Meiendorf Castle near Moscow in 2008, the presidents of Armenia and Azerbaijan agreed to reach a 'political settlement ... on the basis of the principles and norms of international law and the decisions and documents' adopted within the Minsk Group framework.[75] Further presidential meetings were held in Kazan in 2011, and again in Sochi in 2012. Most recently, Russia was ultimately able to broker a new ceasefire agreement between Armenia and Azerbaijan following the renewed escalation of

[71] Statement of the OSCE Chairman-in-Office, Annex 1 to Lisbon Document 1996, 3 December 1996, OSCE DOC.S/1/96, 15.

[72] See Statement by the OSCE Minsk Group Co-Chair Countries, L'Aquila, Italy, 10 July 2009, https://www.osce.org/mg/51152.

[73] Ibid.

[74] See Joint Statement on the Nagorno Karabakh Conflict by Dmitry Medvedev, President of the Russian Federation, Barack Obama, President of the United States of America, and Nicolas Sarkozy, President of the French Republic, Muskoka, Canada, 26 June 2010, https://www.osce.org/mg/69515; Joint Statement on the Nagorno-Karabakh Conflict by Dmitry Medvedev, President of the Russian Federation, Barack Obama, President of the United States of America, and Nicolas Sarkozy, President of the French Republic, Deauville, France, 26 May 2011, https://www.osce.org/mg/78195; Joint Statement by the Presidents of the United States, the Russian Federation and France on Nagorno-Karabakh, Los Cabos, Mexico, 19 June 2012, https://www.osce.org/mg/91393).

[75] Joint Declaration of the Republic of Armenia, the Republic of Azerbaijan, and the Russian Federation, Meiendorf Castle, Moscow Province, 2 November 2008, Annex to the letter dated 10 November 2008 from the Permanent Representative of the Russian Federation to the United Nations addressed to the President of the Security Council, UN Doc. 2/2008/702.

the conflict in September 2020, with the agreement providing for the return of the seven districts surrounding the former NKAO territory to Azerbaijani control and the stationing of a Russian peacekeeeping force, tasked to protect the Lachin corridor linking Armenia and Nagorno-Karabakh.[76]

2.4 International Status of the 'Republic of Artsakh'

Since the end of the war in 1994, the self-proclaimed 'Nagorno-Karabakh Republic', renamed the 'Republic of Artsakh' in 2017,[77] is *de facto* independent from Azerbaijan. Artsakh has a president, a parliament, a government, a ministry of foreign affairs, and, since December 2006, also a constitution, approved by referendum by 98.6 per cent of the electorate, on an 87.2 per cent turnout.[78] The preamble states:

> We, the people of Artsakh: Filled with the spirit of freedom; realizing the dream of our ancestors and the natural right of people to lead a free and secure life in the Homeland and to create; Showing a firm will to develop and defend the Republic of Nagorno-Karabakh formed on September 2, 1991 on the basis of the right of self-determination and proclaimed independent by a referendum conducted on December 10, 1991; ... Reviving the historic traditions of statehood in Artsakh; Aspiring to establish good-neighborly relations with all peoples, first of all with our neighbors, on the basis of equality, mutual respect and peaceful co-existence; Staying faithful to the just world order in conformity with the universal values of international law; Recognizing our own responsibility for the fate of our historic homeland before present and future generations; Exercising our sovereign right, For us, for generations to come and for those that will wish to live in Artsakh ...[79]

Article 1 of the constitution describes Artsakh as 'a sovereign, democratic state', based on social justice and the rule of law.[80] References to Nagorno-Karabakh's

[76] Statement by President of the Republic of Azerbaijan, Prime Minister of the Republic of Armenia and President of the Russian Federation, 10 November 2020, http://en.kremlin.ru/events/president/news/64384. For the latest developments since the end of hostilities see ICG, 'The Nagorno-Karabakh Conflict: A Visual Explainer', https://www.crisisgroup.org/content/nagorno-karabakh-conflict-visual-explainer.

[77] Following a 2017 referendum, the republic's official name was changed from the 'Republic of Nagorno-Karabakh' to the 'Republic of Artsakh', implying a claim to areas controlled beyond the former Nagorno-Karabakh Autonomous Oblast, see 'Azerbaijan's Breakaway Nagorno-Karabakh Holds "Illegal" Referendum', *Radio Free Europe/Radio Liberty*, 21 February 2017.

[78] See 'Karabakh Approves Pro-Independence Constitution', *Radio Free Europe/Radio Liberty*, 11 December 2006.

[79] Constitution of the Republic of Nagorno-Karabakh, 10 December 2006. Quotation from the English translation reprinted in Philip Raworth (ed.), *Constitutions of Dependencies and Territories*, vol. 8, Supp 2013-4 (Dobbs Ferry, NY: Oceana Publications), 7–45.

[80] Ibid., 8.

relationship with Armenia (or Azerbaijan) are missing, although cultural ties to Armenia become evident from setting Armenian as the official language and the Armenian Apostolic Church as the national church, 'with a unique spiritual mission in the life of the people of Artsakh, their national cultural development and the nurturing of their national identity'.[81]

Artsakh's formal attributes and claims of statehood notwithstanding, it is doubtful whether the republic qualifies as a state under international law since it probably lacks an effective government which is commonly regarded one of the basic requirements to qualify as a state in international law.[82] Several aspects indicate that the Republic of Artsakh is military, financially, and politically dependent on Armenia to a degree that has been described as 'de facto annexation' by the Council of Europe.[83] Artsakh's military consists of troops from both Armenia and Nagorno-Karabakh, with Armenian nationals reportedly making up half of the defence and occupying force.[84] At a financial level, the Republic of Artsakh introduced the dram, the Armenian currency, and it is estimated that Armenian 'inter-state' loans cover more than half of Artsakh's annual budget.[85] The political intertwining of the Armenian and the Nagorno- Karabakh political systems is reflected in the person of Robert Kocharyan, who not only served as Nagorno-Karabakh's first president from 1994 to 1997 but also as the second president of Armenia from 1998 to 2008.[86]

International and intergovernmental organizations such as the United Nations, the OSCE, the Council of Europe,[87] or the European Union,[88] all uphold the view that Nagorno-Karabakh continues to be an integral part of Azerbaijan, a position which is also widely shared in international law scholarship.[89] In 1993,

[81] Ibid., 10.

[82] Cf. Montevideo Convention on the Rights and Duties of States, 26 December 1933, 165 LNTS 19, art. 1.

[83] PACE Res 1416 (2005), The Conflict over the Nagorno-Karabakh Region Dealt with by the OSCE Minsk Conference, 25 January 2005, IV, para. 2. See also Melnyk, 'Nagorny-Karabakh' (n. 66), MN 10 ('should rather be characterized as "puppet-State" or even a de facto Armenian province').

[84] ICG, Europe Report No. 166, Nagorno-Karabakh: Viewing the Conflict from the Ground, 15 September 2005.

[85] Ibid., 12.

[86] In 2018, Kocharyan was arrested after being charged over the deadly dispersion of opposition protesters following the 2008 presidential elections. He was freed on bail from pre-trial detention in May 2019. On the charges and Russia's reaction towards it see 'Russia "Concerned" About Armenian Arrest of Former Pro-Moscow Leaders', *Radio Free Europe/Radio Liberty*, 1 August 2018.

[87] See PACE Res 1416 (2005) (n. 83). See also PACE Res 2085 (2016), Inhabitants of Frontier Regions of Azerbaijan are Deliberately Deprived of Water, 26 January 2016, paras 4 and 7.1.

[88] See e.g. 'Statement by High Representative Catherine Ashton on Nagorno-Karabakh', 21 May 2010, EU Doc. A 84/10, http://www.consilium.europa.eu//uedocs/cms_data/docs/pressdata/EN/foraff/114603.pdf.

[89] See Melnyk, 'Nagorny-Karabakh' (n. 66), MN 1; Heiko Krüger, *The Nagorno-Karabakh Conflict: A Legal Analysis* (Berlin: Springer, 2010), 92; and Heiko Krüger, 'Nagorno-Karabakh', in Walter, von Ungern-Sternberg, and Abushov, *Self-determination and Secession in International Law* (2014) (n. 26), 214–32, 230. *Contra* Otto Luchterhandt, 'Das Recht Berg-Karabaghs auf staatliche Unabhängigkeit aus völkerrechtlicher Sicht', *Archiv des Völkerrechts* 31 (1993), 30–81, 79–80 (arguing for a 'remedial' right of secession for Nagorno-Karabakh from Azerbaijan). For the views on Nagorno-Karabakh in Russian international law scholarship see Chapter 5 Section 2 below.

the UN Security Council passed four resolutions, reaffirming Azerbaijan's territorial integrity and condemning the occupation of the territory of Azerbaijan by Armenian forces, and demanding their complete, immediate, and unconditional withdrawal.[90] (However, none of these decisions was implemented. Since all four resolutions were passed under Chapter VI of the UN Charter, they are not legally binding.)[91] In 2008, the UN General Assembly furthermore adopted resolution 62/243, affirming 'continued respect and support for the sovereignty and territorial integrity of the Republic of Azerbaijan within its internationally recognized borders'.[92]

As a permanent member of the UN Security Council, Russia supported all four Security Council resolutions mentioned above, and as of February 2021, Russia has not—like any other UN member state, including Armenia—recognized the Republic of Artsakh as an independent state. Consequently, Russia has also no diplomatic relations with the breakaway republic, although the Republic of Artsakh runs a 'permanent representation' in Moscow.[93] It should however be noted that Russia (together with the two other co-chairs of the OSCE Minsk Group, France and the United States) voted against General Assembly resolution 62/243, calling it 'selectively propagating' the territorial integrity of Azerbaijan 'to the exclusion' of the other guiding principles of the Minsk mediation process, that is the territorial integrity also of Armenia, the refraining from the threat or use of force, and the equal rights and self-determination of peoples.[94]

3. *Case Study 4*: Transnistria

Transnistria is a narrow valley stretching along the east bank of the Dniester river, bordering Ukraine to the east and the historical region of Bessarabia, forming most part of modern Moldova, to the west. According to a 2015 census, the ethnic composition of Transnistria is an almost even mix of 33.8 per cent Russians, 33.2 per cent Moldovans, and 26.7 per cent Ukrainians.[95] Ninety-one per cent of the

[90] SC Res 822, 30 April 1993, UN Doc. S/RES/822; SC Res 853, 29 July 1993, UN Doc. S/RES/853; SC Res 874, 14 October 1993, UN Doc. S/RES/874; SC Res 884, 12 November 1993, UN Doc. S/RES/884.

[91] See Sir Michael Wood, 'United Nations, Security Council', MPEPIL (online edn), MN 22.

[92] GA Res 62/243 (The Situation in the Occupied Territories of Azerbaijan), 14 March 2008, UN Doc. A/RES62/243, para. 1.

[93] According to the Artsakh Ministry of Foreign Affairs' website, Artsakh runs 'permanent representations' also in Armenia, Australia, France, Germany, and the United States, see http://www.nkr.am/en/karabakh-permanent-representations.

[94] See GA Press Release, 14 March 2008, UN Doc. GA/10693. The resolution was adopted by a recorded vote of 39 in favour to 7 against, with 100 abstentions. Apart from Armenia and the three co-chairs of the Minsk Group, Angola, India, and Vanuatu were the only states voting against the draft resolution.

[95] Transnistrian State Statistics Service, *Статистический ежегодник 2017* [Statistical Yearbook 2017] (Tiraspol: Transnistrian State Statistics Service, 2017), 19, 28 .

Transnistrian population adheres to Eastern Orthodox Christianity, and Russian is used as an inter-ethnic language.[96]

3.1 Origins of the Conflict Over Transnistria

Unlike the conflict over Nagorno-Karabakh, the Transnistrian conflict originates less in ancient hatreds between different ethnic groups than in a long history of separate political and cultural affiliations on both sides of the Dniester river. In the Middle Ages, the region east of the Dniester river was not part of traditional Romanian settlement, but belonged to the Kyivan Rus' and to the Kingdom of Galicia-Volhynia. Under Ottoman rule since the fourteenth century, Transnistria was ceded to the Russian Empire in 1792. The region west of the Dniester river, on the other hand, formed the Principality of Moldavia and was a vassal state of the Ottoman Empire from the sixteenth century until 1812, when the Russian Empire gained control over it, naming it Bessarabia. However, following the defeat in the Crimean War (1853–1856), Russia was forced to cede Bessarabia, which was included in the Kingdom of Romania, created in 1859. Less than twenty years later, Bessarabia changed hands again, with the Treaty of Berlin providing for the return of Bessarabia to Russia, in exchange for Dobruja to Romania. Now named the Bessarabia Governorate, it became an administrative region of the Russian Empire separate from Transnistria, which belonged to the Podolia and Kherson Governorates.[97]

Following the Russian Revolution and the ensuing Russian Civil War (1917–1922), the two regions east and west of the Dniester river were again separated. In January 1918, Romania occupied Bessarabia, and on 9 April 1918, the National Council of Bessarabia proclaimed the Union of Bessarabia with the Kingdom of Romania. Transnistria, on the other hand, was Sovietized and set up as the Moldavian Autonomous Oblast within the Ukrainian SSR, elevated to the status of an Autonomous Soviet Socialist Republic (ASSR) on 8 October 1924.[98]

3.2 Transnistrian Resistance During the Soviet Era and War of Independence

During the Second World War, the two regions on both sides of the Dniester river were merged once again. Based on a secret additional protocol to the Molotov–Ribbentrop

[96] See Minority Rights Group International, 'World Directory of Minority and Indigenous Peoples – Transnistria (Unrecognised State)', 2007, http://www.refworld.org/docid/4954ce57c.html.
[97] Charles King, *The Moldovans: Romania, Russia, and the Politics of Culture* (Stanford, CA: Hoover Institution Press, 2000), 179–80.
[98] Ibid., 35, 54.

Pact of 1939, the Soviet Union annexed Bessarabia in 1940 and merged it together with Transnistria to the Moldavian SSR, thereby making it the fifteenth union republic within the Soviet Union.[99] According to Charles King's *The Moldovans*, the authoritative account on the history of the Transnistrian conflict, Transnistria played a 'disproportionate important role' in the Moldavian SSR although it accounted for only 12 per cent of the union republic's territory.[100] With its high concentration of military personnel and its heavy industry, this privileged position within the Moldavian SSR continued throughout the Soviet period, and by the late 1980s, the citizens of Bessarabia and Transnistria 'were living in increasingly distinct worlds'.[101]

Conflict over Transnistria finally broke out in 1989, when local ethnic Russians and Ukrainians began to organize an independence movement against increasing fears of Moldovan nationalist policies.[102] On 28 January 1990, a referendum on Transnistrian autonomy was conducted in which a reported 96 per cent favoured a self-governing status for Transnistria within the Moldavian SSR, and, if necessary, the creation of an independent state.[103] On 2 September 1990, shortly after the Moldavian SSR's declaration of sovereignty on 23 June 1990, Transnistrian separatists announced the creation of the 'Pridnestrovian Moldavian Republic' (PMR), and began taking over police stations and government institutions in Transnistria. On 25 August 1991, the Supreme Soviet of the PMR declared independence from Moldova, and on 1 December 1991, presidential elections were held, making ethnic Russian Igor Smirnov the first president of the self-proclaimed republic.[104]

In November 1991, the Transnistria War broke out between pro-Transnistrian and pro-Moldovan forces; combat lasted throughout the spring and early summer of 1992. By May 1992, the Soviet 14th Army, which had been stationed in the Transnistrian city of Tiraspol since the 1980s, became involved, and on the night of 20 June 1992, openly intervened in the conflict on the side of PMR forces in the battle over the city of Bender.[105] Skirmishes continued until early July 1992, but the Moldovan defeat in Bender marked the climax of the Transnistria War. On 21 July 1992, a ceasefire agreement was signed by the presidents of Moldova and Russia.[106]

[99] Treaty of Non-Aggression between Germany and the Union of Soviet Socialist Republics, 23 August 1939, English translation reprinted in J.A.S. Grenville (ed.), *The Major International Treaties 1914–1945: A History and Guide with Texts* (London: Methuen, 1987), 195–6, Secret Additional Protocol, art. 3.

[100] King, *The Moldovans* (2000) (n. 97), 182–3.

[101] Ibid., 183–4.

[102] Ibid., 186–9.

[103] Ibid., 189.

[104] Ibid., 189–91.

[105] King explains Russia's motivation behind this support the following way: 'So long as the Transnistrians were in the winning position, the Russians were content to let things go on as before. The escalation of the conflict, however, not only threatened Russian security interests in the region, but also posed a threat to the position of the Transnistrians, whom the Russian press and Duma had long portrayed as an embattled Russian minority fighting against chauvinistic Moldovan nationalism', ibid., 195.

[106] Соглашение о принципах мирного урегулирования вооружённого конфликта в приднестровском регионе республики молдова [Agreement on Principles of a Peace Settlement of the

It provided for the cessation of hostilities, the creation of a security zone along the Dniester river, and the deployment of the Joint Control Commission, a trilateral peacekeeping force with a joint military command structure of Moldovan, Transnistrian, and Russian forces.

3.3 Russia's Independent Mediation Efforts: The Primakov and Kozak Memoranda

Negotiations for a political settlement between Moldova and Transnistria have been ongoing since late 1992. After bilateral negotiations over the status of the breakaway republic failed in 1993, Russian president Boris Yeltsin initiated the restarting of negotiations.[107] In April 1994, the leaders of Moldova and Transnistria agreed to continue negotiations on Transnistria's future status, based on proposals the CSCE had outlined in an earlier report.[108]

According to this CSCE Report No. 13, granting a special status to Transnistria 'differing from the constitutional condition of other parts of Moldova' was key to the restoration of Moldova's territorial integrity. Consequently, separation of Transnistria from Moldova as a possible outcome of the negotiations was generally dismissed. However, the report proposed that Transnistria would be guaranteed the right of 'external self-determination' in case Moldova chose 'to give up statehood in order to merge with another country', that is Romania.[109] In January 1996, Moldova, Russia, and Ukraine (which had become the third official mediator and eventual 'guarantor' of a settlement in 1995, besides Russia and the—now renamed—OSCE) signed another joint declaration, recognizing the sovereignty and territorial integrity of Moldova.[110] Since then, the negotiations on the status of Transnistria have come close to a solution twice, both times on the initiative and under the leadership of Russia.

The first such proposal was the Memorandum on the Basis for Normalisation of Relations between the Republic of Moldova and Transnistria, signed on 8 May 1997

Armed Conflict in the Transnistrian Region of the Republic of Moldova], 21 June 1992, available for download at: http://www.operationspaix.net/data/document/1651~v~accord_de_cessez_le_feu_entre_la_transnistrie_et_la_moldavie_du_21_juillet_1992_-_document_en_russe_anglais_roumain.pdf.

[107] Marius Vahl and Michael Emerson, 'Moldova and the Transnistrian Conflict', in Bruno Coppieters, Michael Emerson, Michel Huysseune, Tamara Kovziridze, Gergana Noutcheva, Nathalie Tocci, and Marius Vahl, *Europeanization and Conflict Resolution: Case Studies from the European Periphery* (Gent: Academia Press, 2004), 149–90, 164.

[108] Ibid.; CSCE Mission to Moldova, Report No. 13, 13 November 1993, available at: https://www.osce.org/moldova/42307. The CSCE had been concerned with the conflict since the establishment of its mission to Moldova in February 1993.

[109] See ibid., 1, 5.

[110] Vahl and Emerson, 'Moldova and the Transnistrian Conflict' (2004) (n. 107), 164.

in Moscow by Moldovan president Petru Lucinschi and Transnistrian president Igor Smirnov after negotiations based on the CSCE report had stalled.[111] Largely negotiated under the auspices of Russian foreign minister Yevgeny Primakov, the document is commonly referred to as the Primakov Memorandum. According to its paragraph 2, '[t]he Parties shall continue the establishment between them of state-legal relations'; paragraph 3 provides for Transnistria's eligibility to participate in the conduct of Moldova's foreign policy on questions concerning its own interests and the right 'to unilaterally establish and maintain international contacts in the economic, scientific-technical and cultural spheres' as well as in other fields, to be determined by mutual agreement; and according to paragraph 11 of the Primakov Memorandum, '[t]he Parties shall build their relations in the framework of a common state within the borders of the [Moldavian] SSR as of January of the year 1990'.[112] The document was heavily criticized both in Moldova and Transnistria, and there was wide disagreement on what had actually been agreed in Moscow.[113] Disagreement over the meaning of a 'common state' continued over the next years, and when Primakov, now in his capacity as head of the new Russian State Commission on the Settlement of the Transnistrian Conflict, presented yet another draft of the memorandum in August 2000, it received no support either in Moldova or Transnistria.[114]

After negotiations based on the Primakov Memorandum had failed, no substantial progress regarding the status of Transnistria could be achieved in the following years.[115] Only in 2003, when new Moldovan president Vladimir Voronin asked

[111] Меморандум об основах нормализации отношений между Республикой Молдова и Приднестровьем [Memorandum on the Principles of Normalisation of Relations between the Republic of Moldova and Transnistria] (Primakov Memorandum), 8 May 1997, http://mfa-pmr.org/ru/JLK. On the Primakov Memorandum see also Vahl and Emerson, 'Moldova and the Transnistrian Conflict' (2004) (n. 107), 165–6; Bill Bowring, 'Transnistria', in Walter, von Ungern-Sternberg, and Abushov, *Self-determination and Secession in International Law* (2014) (n. 26), 157–74, 163–4.

[112] Primakov Memorandum (1997) (n. 111). Quotation from the English translation available at: https://www.osce.org/moldova/ 42309.

[113] Marius Vahl and Michael Emerson summarize the diverging interpretations at the time as follows: 'On the Moldovan side, the signing of the [Primakov] Memorandum was interpreted as providing Transnistrian acceptance of the territorial integrity of Moldova and thus reunification, while on the left bank it was seen as Moldova's implicit recognition of the Transnistrian republic, which had no intention of becoming an integral part of the Republic of Moldova', Vahl and Emerson, 'Moldova and the Transnistrian Conflict' (2004) (n. 107), 165–6. See also William H. Hill, *Russia, the Near Abroad, and the West: Lessons from the Moldova-Transdniestria Conflict* (Washington, D.C.: Woodrow Wilson Center Press, 2012), 85.

[114] See ICG, Europe Report No. 147, Moldova: No Quick Fix, 12 August 2003, 8.

[115] One notable attempt to solve the conflict in this time period was the Draft Agreement between the Republic of Moldova and Transnistria, proposed at a meeting in Kyiv on 1–3 July 2002 by the OSCE, Russia, and Ukraine. It foresaw the adoption of a new constitution by which Moldova would have been transformed from a unitary into a federal state, with Bessarabia, Transnistria, and possibly also Gagauzia as constituent republics. The decisive question however, whether the federation would consist of two, three, or even more constituent republics, was left open as well as the question whether it would be designed symmetric or asymmetric. An unofficial English translation of the Kyiv document is reprinted in Bruno Coppieters and Michael Emerson, 'Conflict Resolution for Moldova and Transdniestria Through Federalisation?', *CEPS Policy Brief*, no. 25 (August 2002), 10–22. On the details of the Kyiv document see ibid, 2–9; Vladimir Socor, 'Federalization Experiment in Moldova', *Russia*

Russian president Vladimir Putin for assistance in the drafting of a new Moldovan constitution, the process gained new momentum. Dmitry Kozak, at the time deputy head of the Russian presidential administration,[116] was sent to Chişinău, the Moldovan capital, to facilitate negotiations between Moldova and Transnistria, and in November 2003, Russia—much to the surprise of the other two official mediators OSCE and Ukraine, which had been excluded in the entire drafting process[117]—tabled the Memorandum on the Basic Principles of the State Structure of a United State in Moldova (the so-called Kozak Memorandum), in which a federal state structure for Moldova was proposed, with guaranteeing Transnistria a substantial degree of autonomy.[118]

The Kozak Memorandum designed Transnistria as a subject of a federal Moldovan state with its own legislative, executive, and judicial agencies of state power, its own constitution and legislation, property, independent budget and taxation system, and state symbols and other attributes of its state status (paragraph 3.8). It envisaged that the constitutional and legal status as well as the borders of Transnistria cannot be changed without its consent (paragraph 3.10); membership in regional and international organizations for Transnistria would have been allowed as long as 'international legal subjectivity is not a mandatory requirement' and subjects of the planned federation could have maintained international relations, conclude international treaties within the competencies of the subjects, and set up missions 'that do not have the status of diplomatic missions or consulates in other states' (paragraph 3.15). Moreover, the Kozak Memorandum would have provided Transnistria a right to secede from Moldova 'in the event of a decision about the Federation's annexation to another state being taken and (or) on the grounds of the Federation's complete forfeiture of its sovereignty' (paragraph 3.16). In this case (i.e. in the event of Moldova's integration into Romania), the secession would necessarily need to be based on a 'decisions taken in a nationwide referendum of the subject of the federation by a majority of votes of the constituents

and Eurasia Review 1 (2002), no. 4; Vahl and Emerson, 'Moldova and the Transnistrian Conflict' (2004) (n. 107), 169–70; Otto Luchterhandt, 'Transnistrien vor und nach dem Regimewechsel in Kiew und Russlands Krim-Annexion', *Osteuropa-Recht* 62 (2016), 4–29, 19–20.

[116] Kozak served as Russia's deputy prime minister from 2008–2020. Following Russia's annexation of Crimea in 2014, Kozak was appointed to oversee the strengthening of the peninsula's social, political, and economic ties to Russia, see Oleg Sukhov, 'From Olympics to Crimea: Putin Loyalist Kozak Entrusted with Kremlin Mega-Projects', *The Moscow Times*, 28 March 2014.

[117] See the autobiographic account by OSCE Head of Mission Hill, *Russia, the Near Abroad, and the West* (2012) (n. 113), 138–48.

[118] Меморандум об основных принципах государственного устройства объединённого государства [Memorandum on the Basic Principles of the State Structure of a United State in Moldova] (Kozak Memorandum), 17 November 2003, http://regnum.ru/news/458547.html. An English translation of the Kozak Memorandum is reprinted in Hill, *Russia, the Near Abroad, and the West* (2012) (n. 113), 207–220 (Appendix C). See Vahl and Emerson, 'Moldova and the Transnistrian Conflict' (2004) (n. 107), 170–4; Bowring, 'Transnistria' (2014) (n. 111), 163–4; and Luchterhandt, 'Transnistrien vor und nach dem Regimewechsel in Kiew und Russlands Krim-Annexion' (2016) (n. 115), 20–1.

registered on the territory of the subject of the Federation' (paragraph 3.17). The Kozak Memorandum's critical paragraph that ultimately led to its failure concerned possible guarantees for a future settlement: in particular, paragraph 18 of the Kozak Memorandum provided for a security guarantee in the form of a bilateral treaty between Moldova and Russia on the deployment of a Russian peacekeeping force with up to 2,000 troops during a transitional period until 2020. (According to paragraph 19 of the Kozak Memorandum, the European Union, the OSCE, and Ukraine could have joined as co-guarantors, but only with the consent of Moldova and Russia.)

The signing of the Kozak Memorandum had been scheduled for 25 November 2003 in the presence of Russian president Vladimir Putin. However, after diplomatic intervention on the part of the European Union, the Council of Europe, and the OSCE,[119] instead of signing the document, Moldovan president Voronin issued a statement, calling the Kozak Memorandum 'of such strategic importance that it cannot be adopted against the resistance of one or another side', and described the signing 'premature' before the text was not coordinated with the OSCE and other European organizations.[120] When Putin, reportedly already on his way to Moldova, learnt of Voronin's statement he was so offended that the negotiating process subsequently gradually fell apart.[121]

Between 2005 and 2016, negotiation efforts on the status of Transnistria had been effectively suspended, and focused instead on 'confidence-building measures' in a new '5+2' format (with the United States and the European Union as additional observers), in the hope of gradually moving closer to a situation that would allow the resumption of status negotiations.[122] At the beginning of 2017, the definition of a special status for Transnistria within Moldova was restarted within agreements to develop and implement practical outputs to advance the settlement process. To

[119] Voronin reportedly received phone calls by the High Representative of the European Union Javier Solana and the Secretary General of the Council of Europe Walter Schwimmer, warning him of the implications if signing the Kozak Memorandum, see Hill, *Russia, the Near Abroad, and the West* (2012) (n. 113), 152. According to Hill (at the time the head of the OSCE Mission to Moldova), the provisions regarding the security guarantees were included last minute and without prior consultation with the OSCE. Therefore, the OSCE issued a statement, expressing 'serious reservations' with regard to 'some provisions' in the Kozak Memorandum, see ibid., 147–8.

[120] Statement by President Vladimir Voronin on the Memorandum on Basic Principles of State Structure of the Republic of Moldova, 25 November 2003. Quotation from the English translation in Hill, *Russia, the Near Abroad, and the West* (2012) (n. 113), 153

[121] See ibid., 153–5. A last, but ultimately unsuccessful attempt was made under the Bulgarian OSCE chairmanship with the 'Proposals and Recommendations of the Mediators from the OSCE, the Russian Federation, and Ukraine with Regard to the Transdniestrian Settlement', 13 February 2004, CIO.GAL/11/04, https://www.osce.org/moldova/23585.

[122] See Claus Neukirch, 'From Confidence Building to Conflict Settlement in Moldova?', in Institute for Peace Research and Security Policy at the University of Hamburg (ed.), *OSCE Yearbook 2011: Yearbook on the Organization for Security and Co-operation in Europe (OSCE)* (Baden-Baden: Nomos, 2012), 137–50.

this aim, a 'package of eight' priorities was identified, with agreements reached on six of them in November 2017 and April 2018.[123]

Russia's involvement in the 5+2 format has so far remained sporadic, with the notable exception of the co-called Meseberg Memorandum, signed in June 2010 by German chancellor Angela Merkel and Russian president Dmitry Medvedev, in which the parties agreed 'to cooperate in particular towards a resolution of the Transnistria conflict with a view to achieve tangible progress within the established 5+2 format ... This cooperation could include a joint EU–Russia engagement, which would guarantee smooth transition of the present situation to a final stage.'[124]

3.4 International Status of the 'Pridnestrovian Moldavian Republic'

Like in the case of Nagorno-Karabakh, the self-proclaimed 'Pridnestrovian Moldavian Republic' (PMR) has its own president, government, parliament, and military and police forces. PMR authorities have adopted a national anthem, a flag, a coat of arms,[125] and since 1996, Transnistria has also a constitution. According to the preamble, 'the multinational people' of Transnistria established a 'state of law, which would ensure the rule of law as an expression of the will of the people'.[126] The Transnistrian Constitution proclaims 'a sovereign, independent, democratic and constitutional state', with Russian, Ukrainian, and Moldovan as the three official languages of the PMR.[127] Notwithstanding these claims and formal attributes of statehood, it appears however doubtful whether the PMR qualifies as a state under international law, since it lacks an effective government similar to the 'Republic of

[123] See Protocol of the Official Meeting of the Permanent Conference for Political Questions in the Framework of the Negotiating Process on the Transdniestrian Settlement, Berlin, 2–3 June 2016, https://www.osce.org/moldova/244656; Protocol of the Official Meeting of the Permanent Conference for Political Questions in the Framework of the Negotiating Process on the Transdniestrian Settlement; Vienna, 27–28 November 2017, https://www.osce.org/chairmanship/359196; Protocol of the Official Meeting of the Permanent Conference for Political Questions in the Framework of the Negotiating Process on the Transdniestrian Settlement, Rome, 29–30 May 2018, https://www.osce.org/chairmanship/382885.

[124] Memorandum (Meeting of Chancellor Angela Merkel and President Dmitri Medvedev on 4–5 June 2010 in Meseberg), available at: www.russianmission.eu/sites/default/files/user/files/2010-06-05-meseberg-memorandum.pdf. See Vladimir Socor, 'Meseberg Process: Germany Testing EU-Russia Security Cooperation Potential', *Eurasia Daily Monitor* 7 (2010), no. 191.

[125] Although Transnistria is not a socialist republic, the PMR's coat of arms depicts the hammer and sickle, making Transnistria the only republic in the world currently using the symbol.

[126] Конституция Приднестровской Молдавской Республики [Constitution of the Pridnestrovian Moldavian Republic], 17 January 1996. Quotation from the English translation reprinted in Philip Raworth (ed.), *Constitutions of Dependencies and Territories*, vol. 11, Supp 2013-5 (Dobbs Ferry, NY: Oceana Publications), 9–46, 9.

[127] Ibid., art. 1 and 12. Since 1996, the PMR Constitution has been revised several times, most notably in 2000 and 2011, see Luchterhandt, 'Transnistrien vor und nach dem Regimewechsel in Kiew' (2016) (n. 115), 9–13.

Artsakh' in Nagorno-Karabakh.[128] In particular, the European Court of Human Rights (ECtHR) has found Russia to exercise effective control over Transnistria in various instances—an assessment Russia has denied and criticized as 'politicized'.[129] In *Ilaşcu and Others v Moldova and Russia*, the ECtHR held that the PMR 'remains under the effective authority, or at the very least under the decisive influence' of Russia, and in any event survives only 'by virtue of the military, economic, financial, and political support given to it by the Russian Federation'.[130] The assessment was affirmed in *Catan and Others v Moldova and Russia*, in which the ECtHR attested Russia 'continued military, economic and political support' for the authorities of the PMR,[131] and again in two subsequent ECtHR judgments, most recently in *Sandu and Others v Russia and Moldova.*[132]

With regard to Russia's assumed military support it is important to know that Russia's military presence in Transnistria was unusually high at the end of the Soviet period because one of the largest ammunition depots of the Soviet Union was located in Cobasna in Transnistria, not far from the border to Ukraine.[133] The military base was guarded by the 14th Soviet Army, being committed to strict neutrality according to the 1992 ceasefire agreement.[134] In April 1995, the 14th Soviet Army was transferred to the Operational Group of Russian Forces in Moldova, and in 1999, at the OSCE Istanbul Summit, Russia committed itself to the complete withdrawal of Russian forces from Moldovan territory by the end of 2002.[135] Since 2007, Russia insists that it has fulfilled those obligations, stating that remaining

[128] See also Christopher J. Borgen, 'Thawing a Frozen Conflict: Legal Aspects of the Separatist Crisis in Moldova. A Report from the Association of the Bar of the City of New York', *St. John's University School of Law Legal Studies Research Paper #06-0045* (2006), stating at 53 that the PMR 'is an entity that is able to survive only because of certain carefully regulated conditions—in this case the ample economic and security support of the Russian Federation—that would be unable to survive under normal circumstances'.

[129] See Statement by the Russian Ministry of Foreign Affairs Concerning the Ruling of the European Court of Human Rights in Strasbourg on the 'Case of Ilascu', 8 July 2004, http://www.mid.ru/en/foreign_policy/news/-/asset_publisher/cKNonkJE02Bw/content/id/465018. See also Dissenting Opinion of Judge Kovler, in ECtHR, Ilaşcu and Others v Moldova and Russia, judgment, 8 July 2004, application no. 48787/99, 142. (Anatoly Kovler was the judge of the ECtHR in respect of Russia from 1999 until 2012.)

[130] Ibid., para. 392.

[131] ECtHR, Catan and Others v Moldova and Russia, judgment, 18 October 2012, application nos 43370/04; 8252/05; 18454/06, para. 150.

[132] ECtHR, Mozer v the Republic of Moldova and Russia, judgment, 23 February 2016, application no. 11138/10, paras 110–111; ECtHR, Sandu and Others v Russia and Moldova, judgment, 17 July 2018, application nos 21034/05; 41569/04; 41573/04; 41574/04; 7105/06; 9713/06; 18327/06 and 38649/06, paras 36–37. See Konstantsin Dzehtsiarou, 'Sandu and Others v Russia and Moldova: The High Costs of Occupation', Verfassungsblog, 23 July 2018. See also ECtHR, Ivanţoc and Others v Moldova and Russia, judgment, 15 November 2011, application no. 23687/05, paras 116–120.

[133] See Pavel Felgenhauer, 'Гарнизон Приднестровья на подножном корму' [The Transnistrian Garrison Out at Feed], *Novaya gazeta*, 15 June 2015.

[134] Agreement on Principles of a Peace Settlement of the Armed Conflict in the Transnistrian Region of the Republic of Moldova (1992) (n. 106), art. 4.

[135] Istanbul Summit Declaration, 19 November 1999, para. 19, restated in the OSCE Istanbul Document 1999, 46, available at: https://www.osce.org/mc/39569.

troops are serving as peacekeeping forces under the 1992 ceasefire agreement, and are therefore not in violation of the Istanbul commitments. Moldova, on the other hand, regards the continuous stationing of Russian troops in Transnistria as a 'foreign military occupation illegally deployed on the territory of the state'.[136] (In 2017, the Moldovan Constitutional Court declared the continuous presence of Russian military forces in Transnistria unconstitutional.)[137]

In November 2008, NATO reproached Russia for not fulfilling its duties, and urged 'the government and the parliament of Russia . . . to withdraw its illegal military presence from the Transdnestrian region of Moldova in the nearest future'.[138] Russian troops continued to be stationed in Transnistria, and in June 2018, the UN General Assembly urged 'the Russian Federation to complete, unconditionally and without further delay, the orderly withdrawal of the Operational Group of Russian Forces and its armaments from the territory of the Republic of Moldova'.[139] The resolution was adopted by a vote of sixty-four in favour to fifteen against, with eighty-three abstentions. Russia voted against, regretting the outcome of the vote and the 'politicisation' of the problem.[140]

Economically, Transnistria could not sustain without Russia which provides budget support ranging from US$160 to US$200 million per year. Financial support includes humanitarian aid via the Gorchakov Fund or the non-profit organization Eurasian Integration,[141] additional funding of pensions and salaries of state officials,[142] financing of social and cultural institutions, and energy subsidies. (For example, Transnistria is paying almost nothing for gas, resulting in a debt of US$5.8 billion to Gazprom as of 1 January 2017.)[143]

At a political level, Russian influence on the PMR is much more difficult to assess. The limited control over Transnistrian politics became particularly evident in the 2011 presidential elections, when Igor Smirnov, the president of the breakaway republic since its declared independence in 1990, was surprisingly not replaced by Anatoliy Kaminski, the Kremlin-backed candidate, but by Yevgeny Shevchuk, who

[136] Statement by Minister of Foreign Affairs of Moldova Andrei Stratan at the Twelfth Meeting of the Ministerial Council, 6 December 2004, MC.DEL/21/04.

[137] Constitutional Court of Moldova, Decision No. 14/2017, *Interpretarea Constituției Republicii Moldova*, 2 May 2017.

[138] NATO Parliamentary Assembly Res 371 (The Future of NATO Russia Relations), 18 November 2008, para. 11. See 'McCain Backs Demand for Russian Troop Withdrawal from Transdniester', *Radio Free Europe/Radio Liberty*, 13 June 2011.

[139] GA Res 72/282 (Complete and Unconditional Withdrawal of Foreign Military Forces from the Territory of the Republic of Moldova), 26 June 2018, UN Doc. A/RES/72/282.

[140] See 'General Assembly Adopts Text Urging Troop Withdraw from Republic of Moldova, Strengthening Cooperation in Central Asia', UN Press Release, 22 June 2018, UN Doc. GA/12030.

[141] See https://gorchakovfund.ru/en; http://eurasian.su/partner/ano-evraziyskaya-integraciya.

[142] See 'Приднестровье: Российские пенсии для граждан РФ вместо «российских надбавок» для всех?' [Transnistria: Russian Pensions for Citizens of the Russian Federation Instead of 'Russian Allowances' for All?], *Regnum News Agency*, 17 October 2014.

[143] '"Газпром" оставил долг за Молдавией" ['Gazprom' Left a Debt for Moldova], *Kommersant*, 13 February 2017.

was portrayed in Russian media as a protégé of the West.[144] On 11 December 2016, Kaminski was replaced by Vadim Krasnoselsky; Russia reportedly did not favour one of the candidates or interfere in the campaign.[145]

Another indicator to measure Russia's influence on Transnistria is the share of Russian passport holders living in the PMR. According to Dmitry Rogozin, who was appointed the Russian Special Presidential Representative for Transnistria in 2012, 200,000 Transnistrians currently also hold Russian citizenship.[146] If one takes the official numbers of the 2015 census, that number equals over 40 per cent of the entire Transnistrian population. The high numbers are the result of a wider Russian policy of 'passportization' aiming at the conferral of nationality on the citizens of other states in the post-Soviet space without sufficient factual links.[147]

Notwithstanding this fundamental support for and interference in the functioning of the PMR, Russia does not go as far (at least as of February 2021) as to recognize the breakaway republic as an independent state. (To date, no UN member state has recognized Transnistria's independence, and some scholars even argue for a duty of non-recognition due to Russia's involvement in the conflict.)[148] Russia has no embassy in Transnistria, although it opened a consular office in the region's capital, Tiraspol, officially functioning as a remote office of its embassy to Moldova in Chişinău.[149] However, in response to the Transnistrian referendum of 17 September 2006, in which a reported 97 per cent of the electorate voted in favour of independence and 'free association with Russia',[150] the Russian State Duma has expressed its believe that 'the results of the referendum ... should be fully taken

[144] See Andrey Devyatkov, 'Russian Policy Toward Transnistria: Between Multilateralism and Marginalization', *Problems of Post-Communism* 59 (2012), 53–62, 59.

[145] Kamil Całus, 'Transnistrian "House of Cards"', *New Eastern Europe*, 7 June 2016.

[146] 'Рогозин выступил за предоставление гражданства РФ молодёжи Приднестровья' [Rogozin Spoke in Favour of Granting Russian Citizenship to the Youth of Transnistria], *Interfax*, 1 July 2015. The independent *Novaya gazeta* reported much higher numbers, see Elena Racheva, 'Мы готовы быть вашим форпостом' [We Are Ready to be Your Outpost], *Novaya gazeta*, 29 June 2015. On Rogozin, Deputy Prime Minister of Russia for Defence and Space Industry until 18 May 2018, and notoriously known for his ultra-nationalist views see Vladimir Socor, 'Dmitry Rogozin Appointed Special Presidential Representative for Transnistria', *Eurasia Daily Monitor* 9 (2012), no. 59.

[147] The policy is widely considered illegal under international law, see e.g. Anne Peters, 'Extraterritorial Naturalization: Between the Human Right to Nationality, State Sovereignty and Fair Principles of Jurisdiction', *German Yearbook of International Law* 53 (2010), 623–725, 634–45.

[148] See e.g. Borgen, 'Thawing a Frozen Conflict' (2006) (n. 128), 52–61, comparing the situation to Cyprus. See also Chrostopher J. Borgen, 'Imagining Sovereignty, Managing Secession: The Legal Geography of Eurasia's "Frozen Conflicts"', *Oregon Review of International Law* 9 (2007), 477–534, 507–13.

[149] See https://moldova.mid.ru/punkt-vyezdnogo-konsul-skogo-obsluzivania-v-tiraspole. On 23 January 2019, Transnistria opened an 'Official Representation' in Moscow, see http://mfa-pmr.org/en/hyq.

[150] See the official results announced by the Central Election Commission of the PMR, available at: https://www.cikpmr.com/index.php/o-vyborakh-i-referendumakh/informatsiya-o-referendumakh/item/211-rezultaty-referenduma-17-sentyabrya-2006-goda.

into account by the international community', and that 'the Russian Federation must built its policy in the light of free expression of the will by the Pridnestrovie's people'.[151] On the other hand, the Russian parliament's lower house abstained from calling also for Transnistria's independence in a later resolution in support of South Ossetian and Abkhaz independence shortly before the Russo-Georgian War broke out.[152] Asked whether Russia might recognize the independence of Transnistria, Russian Deputy Minister of Foreign Affairs Grigory Karasin reportedly said in 2012: 'We see the future of Transnistria in a special region with special internationally recognised guarantees as part of a neutral Moldovan state.'[153] It was the first time that a high-ranking Russian official outrightly excluded a possible recognition as an independent state or even unification with Russia in the presence of the Transnistrian leadership.

4. *Case Study* 5: South Ossetia

Ossetia is a historic region located on both sides of the Greater Caucasus mountains. While the northern part, the Republic of North Ossetia–Alania, is a federal subject of Russia, sovereignty over the southern part is disputed between Georgia and the self-proclaimed Republic of South Ossetia–the State of Alania.[154] According to a 2016 census, 89.9 per cent of South Ossetia's population are Ossetian and 7.4 per cent Georgian,[155] while at the end of the Soviet period, almost a third were ethnic Georgian and roughly two-thirds Ossetian.[156]

[151] Resolution of the State Duma of Russia No. 3560-4 GD, Об итогах Референдума в Приднестровье [On the Results of the Referendum in Transnistria], 6 October 2006. Quotation from the English translation reprinted in V.V. Ignatiev (ed.), *Pridnestrovie: The Legal Foundation of Independence* (Tiraspol: Ministry of Foreign Affairs of the Pridnestrovian Moldavian Republic, 2017), 17–20, 19–20.

[152] Resolution of the State Duma of Russia No. 245-5 GD, О политике Российской Федерации в отношения Абхазии, Южной Осетии И Приднестровья [On the Policy of the Russian Federation in Relation to Abkhazia, South Ossetia and Transnistria], 21 March 2008. English translation of the resolution reprinted in Ignatiev, *Pridnestrovie* (2017) (n. 151), 21–25.

[153] Vladimir Solovyov, 'Приднестровью отказали в независимости: Россия будет решать приднестровский конфликт через федерализацию Молдавии' [Transnistria Denied Independence: Russia Will Solve the Transnistrian Conflict Through the Federalisation of Moldova], *Kommersant*, 30 July 2012.

[154] On 9 April 2017, a local referendum approved a name change of South Ossetia by 79.5 per cent of the electorate, on a 79.8 per cent turnout. Since then, a reference to Alania has been added to the republic's name after the medieval kingdom of an Iranian nomadic pastoral people, and in analogy to the name of the Russian federal subject to the North, see Liz Fuller, 'South Ossetia Referendum on Name Change Steers Clear of Thornier Unification Issue', *Radio Free Europe/Radio Liberty*, 8 February 2017.

[155] See Tamar Svanidze, 'South Ossetian Authorities Release Results of 1st Census in 26 Years', *Georgia Today*, 12 August 2016.

[156] State Committee of the USSR on Statistics, *The National Composition of the Population of the USSR* (1991) (n. 50).

4.1 Origins of the Conflict Over South Ossetia

The origins of the conflict over South Ossetia date back to 1801, when the Russian Empire annexed the Georgian kingdom of Kartli-Kakheti.[157] In 1824, following various rebellions of Ossetian peasants against their Georgian lords, Russia created the Ossetian Military District, originally encompassing the entire Ossetian populated territory on both sides of the Caucasus mountains.[158] In 1859 however, the military district was dissolved, with the northern part integrated in the Vladikavkaz Military District, whereas the southern part was integrated into the Tiflis Governorate.[159] After the Russian Revolution the separation continued, and South Ossetia became part of the newly independent Democratic Republic of Georgia.

By 1920, an Ossetian political movement had emerged and ultimately led to a rebellion against Georgian rule. After initial success, the resistance was repelled by the Georgian government, leaving up to 20,000 people dead, and some 35,000 Ossetians seeking refuge in the northern part of Ossetia.[160] There, a district committee of the Communist Party was set up by South Ossetian Bolsheviks which, on 25 February 1921, adopted the Resolution on the Self-determination of South Ossetia, thereby declaring the creation of South Ossetia as an autonomous region, after 'the persistent, nearly three-year long struggle of the South Ossetian people against Georgian national-chauvinists for their liberation'.[161] A few days later, Ossetian units moved from the North into South Ossetia and established control over the self-proclaimed autonomous region. By December 1921, the Caucasian Bureau had approved South Ossetia's autonomy and its boundaries, and on 22 April 1922, the South Ossetian Autonomous Oblast was formally established within the Georgian SSR.[162]

4.2 South Ossetian Resistance During the Soviet Era and War of Independence

Unlike North Ossetia, which was accorded the status of an autonomous region within the Russian SFSR in 1924 and upgraded to an autonomous republic in 1936, the status of South Ossetia as an autonomous region within the Georgian SSR was not altered during the entire Soviet period. (An attempt to unite North and South

[157] On the history of Georgia more generally see Ronald Grigor Suny, *The Making of the Georgian Nation* (Stanford, CA: Hoover Institution Press, 1988).

[158] Saparov, *From Conflict to Autonomy in the Caucasus* (2015) (n. 54), 29–30.

[159] Ibid., 30.

[160] Ibid., 66–70, 74.

[161] Quotation from the English translation in ibid., 75.

[162] Ibid., 76, 81. On the Caucasian Bureau see n. 58 above.

Ossetia in 1925 was abandoned after Stalin suggested that a united Ossetia could join the Georgian SSR rather than the Russian SFSR.)[163]

Until the 1980s, South Ossetians and Georgians had lived largely in peaceful coexistence. But when the local South Ossetian Soviet unilaterally proclaimed the region's elevation to an autonomous republic and declared itself 'sovereign' in September 1990,[164] the Georgian parliament abolished South Ossetia's autonomy, and in January 1991, Georgian police forces entered Tskhinvali, the South Ossetian capital, to disarm Ossetian armed groups. The situation escalated and led to a violent armed conflict between Georgian government forces and ethnic Georgian militia on one side, and forces of South Ossetia and ethnic Ossetian militia on the other side, resulting in the expulsion of 23,000 Georgians living in South Ossetia and nearly 100,000 Ossetians from other parts of Georgia.[165] On 18 January 1992, a referendum on South Ossetian independence and 'reunification' with North Ossetia was held, with more than 90 per cent of the electorate voting for secession from Georgia and integration into Russia, on a 98 per cent turnout.[166] On 29 May 1992, based on the results of the referendum, the local South Ossetian Soviet declared 'the independence of South Ossetia and [the] establishment of the independent State of South Ossetia'.[167] On 24 June 1992, Russia was able to broker a ceasefire between the belligerents (the so-called Sochi Agreement).[168]

Apart from establishing a ceasefire between the Georgian and South Ossetian forces, the Sochi Agreement defines a zone of conflict around Tskhinvali and establishes a security corridor along the (unrecognized) border between Georgia and South Ossetia. The agreement furthermore created the Joint Control Commission for Georgian-Ossetian Conflict Resolution, a peacekeeping organization operating in South Ossetia and consisting of Georgian, North Ossetian, Russian, and South Ossetian forces.[169] In addition, the agreement established the Joint Peacekeeping Force, with equal contingents of Russian, Georgian, and South Ossetian military. On 16 May 1996, representatives of Georgia, Russia, South Ossetia, North Ossetia, and the OSCE signed the Memorandum on Measures to Provide Security and Strengthen Mutual Trust between the Parties to the Georgian-Ossetian Conflict in Moscow, thereby leaving the South Ossetian authorities with *de facto* control over

[163] See Saparov, *From Conflict to Autonomy in the Caucasus* (2015) (n. 54), 87, 89 (fn. 31).

[164] See Christopher Waters, 'South Ossetia', in Walter, von Ungern-Sternberg, and Abushov, *Self-determination and Secession in International Law* (2014) (n. 26), 175–90, 176.

[165] HRW, Bloodshed in the Caucasus: Violations of Humanitarian Law and Human Rights in the Georgia-South Ossetia Conflict (Helsinki: Human Rights Watch, 1992), 3.

[166] See Peters, *Das Gebietsreferendum im Völkerrecht* (1995) (n. 63), 209–10.

[167] Angelika Nußberger, 'South Ossetia', in MPEPIL (online edn), MN 21.

[168] Соглашение о принципах мирного урегулирования грузино-осетинского конфликта [Agreement on Principles of a Peace Settlement of the Georgian-Ossetian Conflict] (Sochi Agreement), 24 June 1992, BMD 1993, no. 8, 25. English translation available at: https://peacemaker.un.org/georgia-sochi-agreement92.

[169] Ibid., art. 3.

roughly the territory that formerly constituted the South Ossetian Autonomous Oblast.[170]

4.3 The Russo-Georgian War 2008 and the EU International Fact-Finding Mission

Until the turn of the twenty-first century, Georgia's relations with South Ossetia and Russia were relatively peaceful and stable.[171] Russo-Georgian relations abruptly deteriorated during Vladimir Putin's first term as Russian president starting in 2000. For example, in a letter to the UN Security Council issued on the first anniversary of the 9/11 attacks, Putin accused Georgia of helping Chechen separatists, and threatened to use force on Georgian territory based on article 51 of the UN Charter.[172] (In response, Georgian president Eduard Shevardnadze declared Georgia's intention to join NATO.)[173] Escalation of tensions continued over the following years, and on 8 August 2008, Russia ultimately launched a military operation on Georgian territory.[174] In the following 7 days, about 300 persons were killed on the South Ossetian and Russian sides, as were about 360 persons on the Georgian side.[175] Moreover, some 192,000 persons were displaced, of which 25,000 from South Ossetia and 6,000 from Abkhazia are considered to be permanently unable to return to their original places of residence.[176]

[170] Меморандум о мерах по обеспечению безопасности и укреплению взаимного доверия между сторонами в грузино-осетинском конфликте [Memorandum on Measures to Provide Security and Strengthen Mutual Trust between the Parties to the Georgian-Ossetian Conflict], 16 May 1996, *Diplomaticheskiĭ vestnik* 1996, 6. The OSCE Mission to Georgia was set-up in 1992 and ended in 2008, with no substantial achievements on record, see Silvia Stöber, 'The Failure of the OSCE Mission to Georgia – What Remains?', in Institute for Peace Research and Security Policy at the University of Hamburg (ed.), *OSCE Yearbook 2010: Yearbook on the Organization for Security and Co-operation in Europe* (Baden-Baden: Nomos, 2011), 203–20.

[171] See Andrei Illarionov, 'The Russian Leadership's Preparation for War, 1999–2008', in Svante E. Cornell and S. Frederick Starr (eds), *The Guns of August 2008: Russia's War in Georgia* (Armonk, NY: M.E. Sharpe, 2009), 49–84, 51.

[172] See Letter dated 11 September 2002 from the Permanent Representative of the Russian Federation to the United Nations Addressed to the Secretary-General (Annex), 11 September 2002, UN Doc. S/2002/1012. On the implications of this claim see Roy Allison, *Russia, the West, and Military Intervention* (Oxford: Oxford University Press, 2013), 102–19.

[173] See Jean-Christophe Peuch, 'Georgia: Shevardnadze Officially Requests Invitation to Join NATO', *Radio Free Europe/Radio Liberty*, 22 November 2002.

[174] Between Georgia and Russia, it is debated who started the conflict, both blame each other for breaching the ceasefire. For a timeline of actions see Illarionov, 'The Russian Leadership's Preparation for War, 1999–2008' (2009) (n. 171), 77–80.

[175] PACE Res 1633 (2008), The Consequences of the War between Georgia and Russia, 2 October 2008, para. 16.

[176] Ibid., para. 15. In January 2016, the Prosecutor of the International Criminal Court (ICC) was authorized to open investigation on alleged crimes against humanity and war crimes committed in the context of the Russo-Georgian War in and around South Ossetia, see ICC, Situation in Georgia, Decision on the Prosecutor's Request for Authorization of an Investigation, 27 January 2016, ICC-01/15-12.

On 16 August 2008, a six-point ceasefire agreement between Russia and Georgia was brokered by the European Union. The agreement stipulated a lasting cessation of hostilities, and provided for the withdrawal of Georgian and Russian military forces to their lines prior to the outbreak of the conflict. Pending an international mechanism, Russian peacekeeping forces were allowed to take additional security measures for a six-month time period.[177] In addition to the ceasefire agreement, an EU monitoring group was put in place.[178] It was the first time that the European Union had decided to intervene actively in a serious armed conflict, and also the first time to set up a fact-finding mission as a political and diplomatic follow-up to a conflict. Although labelled a fact-finding mission that was 'strictly limited to establishing facts', the Independent International Fact-Finding Mission on the Conflict in Georgia (IIFFMCG) was additionally charged to assess the facts 'with regard to international law ... humanitarian law and human rights law, and the accusations made in that context'.[179]

In the second part of its three-volume report,[180] the IIFFMCG assessed the legality of the use of force of all parties involved in the conflict. With regard to the military clashes between Georgian troops and South Ossetian militias, it found that on-the-spot reactions by Georgian troops were necessary and appropriate to counter the attacks of the Ossetian militias before 7 August 2008, whereas the large-scale offensive from 7 until 12 August 2008 was not justified as self-defence.[181] Conversely, South Ossetia was found to have violated the prohibition of the use of force before 7 August 2008, whereas its military actions were justified as self-defence as long as the Georgian attack was ongoing.[182] Although the IIFFMCG report refrained from attributing South Ossetian acts to Russia, it considered Russia's own direct involvement in the war contrary to the prohibition of the use of force, which was not justified as self-defence or any other existing or purported exception to this core principle of international law.[183]

[177] Six-point Ceasefire Agreeement, 12 August 2008, restated in Identical Letters Dated 10 June 2009 from the Permanent Representative of Georgia to the United Nations Addressed to the Secretary-General and the President of the Security Council (Annex), 3 June 2009, UN Doc. S/2009/305, 3.

[178] EU Council Decision 2008/901/CESP, 2 December 2008, 2008 OJ 323/66.

[179] Ibid., art. 1(2).

[180] Independent International Fact-Finding Mission on the Conflict in Georgia, Report (IIFFMCG Report), September 2009, 3 vols, available for download at: http://www.mpil.de/en/pub/publications/archive/independent_international_fact.cfm.

[181] Ibid., vol. 2, 229–51.

[182] Ibid., vol. 2, 261–2.

[183] Ibid., vol. 2, 262 et seq. According to the IIFFMCG, Russia had, in principle, a right to self-defence, since it considered Georgia's moving towards Russia's peacekeeping forces stationed in South Ossetia as aggression in the sense of art. 3(d) of the 1970 Definition of Aggression, and, *a fortiori*, an armed attack against Russia in the sense of art. 51 of the UN Charter. But since the IIFFMCG considered Russia's actions to go beyond the repulsion of the Georgian armed attack on the Russian bases in South Ossetia and since it held that the means to achieve this objective were not in a reasonable relationship to use force against Georgia, Russia's actions were found to be neither necessary nor proportionate. Furthermore, the report considered (and ultimately denied) other possible justifications, in particular the use of force as humanitarian intervention (at 283–4) and Russia's claim to have used force as action to rescue and protect nationals abroad (at 285–9). For detailed legal assessments of Russia's actions in

4.4 Russia's Intervention in Georgia as Assistance in an Ossetian War of Liberation?

Of the various justifications for Russia's use of force refuted by the EU fact-finding mission, one argument raised by Russia is particularly interesting for the purposes of this study if viewed against its historical origins: in its Responses to Questions on Military Aspects Posited by the IIFFMCG on the Events That Took Place in the Caucasus in August 2008, Russia argued *inter alia* that it had intervened in the conflict 'following a request from the government of South Ossetia'.[184] At first glance, the argument seems surprising, since only governments of states are commonly regarded capable of inviting foreign troops in an internal armed conflict,[185] and Russia had not (yet) recognized South Ossetia as an independent state at the time of the Russo-Georgian War. However, from the Ossetian point of view, the conflict with Georgia is a 'national-liberation struggle of the people of South Ossetia',[186] and seen this way, the former Soviet doctrine on wars of national liberation instantly comes to mind.[187] Assessing the validity of this claim, the IIFFMCG report states:

> Military force is never admissible as a means to carry out a claim to self-determination, including internal self-determination. There is no support in state practice for the right to use force to attain self-determination outside the context of decolonization or illegal occupation. Still less is there support by states for the right of ethnic groups to use force to secede from existing states. This means that the use of force by secessionist groups is in any case illegal under international law, even assuming that a right to secede exists. The general rule is that South

Georgia see Angelika Nußberger, 'Völkerrecht im Kaukasus—Postsowjetische Konflikte in Russland und in Georgien', *Europäische Grundrechte-Zeitschrift* 35 (2008), 457–66; Angelika Nußberger, 'The War between Russia and Georgia—Consequences and Unresolved Questions', *Göttingen Journal of International Law* 1 (2009), 341–64; Nicolai Petro, 'The Legal Case for Russian Intervention in Georgia', *Fordham International Law Journal* 32 (2009), 1524–49; Gregory Hafkin, 'The Russo-Georgian War of 2008: Developing the Law of Unauthorized Humanitarian Intervention after Kosovo', *Boston University International Law Journal* 28 (2010), 219–39; Hannes Hofmeister, 'Don't Mess with Moscow—Legal Aspects of the 2008 Caucasus Conflict', *San Diego International Law Journal* 12 (2010/2011), 147–73; Robert Chatham, 'Defense of Nationals Abroad: The Legitimacy of Russia's Invasion of Georgia', *Florida Journal of International Law* 23 (2011), 75–102; and Christine Gray, 'The Conflict in Georgia—2008', in Ruys and Corten, *The Use of Force in International Law* (2018) (n. 17), 712–28.

[184] Ответы на вопросы по военным аспектам миссии Европейского союза по расследованию фактов, связанных с событиями на Кавказе в августе 2008 г. [Responses to Questions on Military Aspects Posited by the EU Fact-Finding Mission on the Events in the Caucasus in August 2008], reprinted in IIFFMCG Report (2009) (n. 180), vol. 3, 356–68. Quotation from the English translation in ibid. 369–79, 371.

[185] On the concept of 'intervention by invitation' in international law generally see e.g. Georg Nolte, 'Intervention by Invitation', in MPEPIL (online edn), MN 1.

[186] See e.g. point 1 of the Declaration of the Genocide of 1920 in South Ossetia, issued by the South Ossetian parliament on 19 May 2007, available at: http://www.mfa-rso.su/en/node/362.

[187] See Chapter 1 Sections 2 and 4.

> Ossetian authorities and armed forces were not themselves entitled to use force in order to attain self-determination. This also means that a secessionist party cannot validly invite a foreign state to use force against the army of the metropolitan state.[188]

Similarly, the International Court of Justice found in the *Nicaragua* case that 'no such general right of intervention, in support of an opposition within another State, exists in contemporary international law', adding that 'it is difficult to see what would remain of the principle of non-intervention in international law, if intervention, which is already permissible at the request of a government of a State, were also to be allowed at the request of the opposition'.[189] International law scholarship in the West is also very sceptical about such a right of intervention on the side of a separatist entity, above all because the legal regime of article 2(4) UN Charter is commonly considered to bind only states, and therefore to be inapplicable to struggles deriving from a people's right to self-determination.[190]

4.5 Russia's Recognition of South Ossetia and the Claim of 'Genocide'

On 26 August 2008, Russia recognized South Ossetia as an independent state.[191] (As of February 2021, five other UN member states have so far followed: Nauru, Nicaragua, Syria, Vanuatu, and Venezuela.)[192] The decision was immediately condemned by many states and international organizations. For example, the Parliamentary Assembly of the Council of Europe (PACE) considered Russia's recognition 'a violation of international law and of the Council of Europe's statutory principles', and reiterated 'its call on Russia to withdraw its recognition of the independence of South Ossetia ... and to fully respect the sovereignty and territorial

[188] IIFFMCG Report (2009) (n. 180), vol. 2, 279 (footnote omitted).

[189] ICJ, Military and Paramilitary Activities in and Against Nicaragua (Nicaragua v USA), 27 June 1986, ICJ Reports 1986, 14, paras 209 and 246.

[190] See e.g. Yoram Dinstein, *War, Aggression and Self-Defence* (Cambridge: Cambridge University Press, 2012), para. 249; Albrecht Randelzhofer and Oliver Dörr, 'Art. 2(4)', in Bruno Simma, Daniel-Erasmus Khan, Georg Nolte, and Andreas Paulus (eds), *The Charter of the United Nations: A Commentary*, vol. 1 (Oxford: Oxford University Press, 3rd edn, 2012), MN 62. For a detailed discussion of the inapplicability of the prohibition of the use of force to national liberation struggles see Olivier Corten, *The Law against War: The Prohibition on the Use of Force in Contemporary International Law* (Oxford: Hart Publishing, 2010), 135–49. For views on this doctrine in post-Soviet Russian scholarship see Chapter 5 Section 2 below.

[191] Decree of the President of Russia No. 1261, О признании Республики Южная Осетия [On the Recognition of the Republic of South Ossetia], 26 August 2008, SZRF 2008, no. 35, item 4012.

[192] Tuvalu had recognized South Ossetia as an independent state in 2011, but subsequently withdrew recognition in 2014. With regard to Syria's recognition see 'Georgia Severs Relations With Syria For Recognizing Abkhazia, South Ossetia', *Radio Free Europe/Radio Liberty*, 29 May 2018.

integrity of Georgia, as well as the inviolability of its borders'.[193] The Georgian parliament declared South Ossetia an 'occupied territory', and passed the Law on Occupied Territories of Georgia.[194]

It appears that the central argument of Russia's decision to recognize South Ossetia's independence was essentially that of a 'remedial' right of secession for the Ossetian population. In a statement issued on the day of Russia's recognition, meantime Russian president Dmitry Medvedev argued that it 'represents the only possibility to save human lives', because Georgia had 'opted for genocide to accomplish his political objectives', which 'dashed all the hopes for the peaceful coexistence of Ossetians, Abkhazians and Georgians in a single state'.[195] Already during the war, the Russian government had voiced similar allegations of 'genocide' committed by Georgian forces. On 10 August 2008 for instance, Medvedev reportedly stated that 'the actions of the Georgian side cannot be called anything other than genocide'.[196] Initially, Russian authorities claimed that up to 2,000 ethnic Ossetian civilians were killed by Georgian forces during the war.[197] By December 2008, the numbers were however revised down to a total of 162 South Ossetian casualties.[198] Nevertheless, in its responses to the IIFFMCG, Russia insisted that:

> [r]eferences made by the Russian side to acts of genocide perpetrated against the Ossetian people by the Georgian side in August 2008 should be viewed in the context of the preliminary information that was received during the first hours of the conflict and prior to it. As far as we can judge, there were indeed reasons to believe that the actions undertaken by the Georgians were aimed at exterminating fully or partially the Ossetian ethnic group as such.[199]

[193] PACE Res 1647 (2009), Implementation of Resolution 1633 (2008) on the Consequences of the War between Georgia and Russia, 28 January 2009. Other international organizations and states issued similar statements, see 'Reaction to Russia's Recognition of Rebels', *BBC News*, 26 August 2008. For individual statements see e.g. 'US Condemns Russia over Georgia', *BBC News*, 4 September 2008; 'OSCE Chairman Condemns Russia's Recognition of South Ossetia, Abkhazia Independence', *OSCE Press Release*, 26 August 2008, https://www.osce.org/cio/50011.

[194] On this law see Venice Commission, *Opinion on the Law on Occupied Territories of Georgia Adopted by the Venice Commission at its 78th Plenary Session*, 13–14 March 2009, Doc. CDL-AD(2009)015-e.

[195] 'Statement by President of Russia Dmitry Medvedev', 26 August 2008, http://en.kremlin.ru/events/president/transcripts/1222. Medvedev served as the third president of the Russian Federation from 2008 until 2012, preceded and succeeded by Vladimir Putin, who served as prime minister during Medvedev's presidency.

[196] See 'СКП РФ возбудил уголовное дело по убийствам россиян в Южной Осетии' [SKP RF Opened a Criminal Investigation into the Killings of Russian Citizens in South Ossetia], *Kommersant*, 14 August 2008.

[197] HRW, Up in Flames—Humanitarian Law Violations and Civilian Victims in the Conflict Over South Ossetia, 23 January 2009, 74, available for download at: https://www.hrw.org/sites/default/files/reports/georgia0109web.pdf.

[198] Ibid., 75.

[199] Ответы на вопросы миссии Европейского союза по расследованию фактов, связанных с событиями на Кавказе в августе 2008 г. (гуманитарные аспекты) [Responses to Questions Posited by the EU Fact-Finding Mission on the Events that Took Place in the Caucasus in August 2008 (Humanitarian Aspects)], reprinted in IIFFMCG Report (2009) (n. 180), vol. 3, 458–74. Quotation from the English translation in ibid., 475–90, 475.

According to the 1948 Genocide Convention, acts such as killings or the causing of serious bodily or mental harm have to be 'committed with intent to destroy, in whole or in part, a national, ethnical, racial or religious group' in order to qualify as genocide.[200] Therefore, the acts must be carried out with intent to destroy the group as such, in whole or in part. In its report, the IIFFMCG found that this specific intent required for acts to be qualified as genocide was not present in the Russo-Georgian War,[201] and the PACE Rapporteur of the Committee on Legal Affairs and Human Rights had already noted earlier that 'the facts do not seem to support the genocide allegations against Georgia', and that 'the number of Ossetian (civilian) victims of the Georgian assault . . . seem to be much exaggerated'.[202]

Since claims of Ossetian 'genocide' committed by Georgian forces therefore soon proved to be untenable, Russia tuned down its argument in later statements. Referring to paragraph 5 of the fifth principle of the Friendly Relations Declaration,[203] Russian foreign minister Sergey Lavrov stated for example in an article for the *Diplomatic Yearbook* of the Russian MFA that '[t]he possession of sovereignty presupposes the duty of a state to refrain from any forcible action which deprives people living on its territory of their right to self-determination, freedom and independence'. 'By giving an order to bomb Tskhinvali and planning to use force against Abkhazia', Lavrov maintained, Georgia 'trampled underfoot this norm of international law, enshrined in the 1970 UN Declaration' and 'undermined the territorial integrity of its state in the immediate neighbourhood of Russia',[204] thereby openly disputing Georgia's territorial integrity and sovereignty.

4.6 International Status of the 'Republic of South Ossetia'

Like Nagorno-Karabakh and Transnistria, the 'Republic of South Ossetia' developed all formal aspects of statehood during the 1990s.[205] State practice in the negotiation process over the conflict furthermore shows that South Ossetia was at least treated as a partial subject of international law: South Ossetia was accepted as one

[200] Convention on the Prevention and Punishment of the Crime of Genocide, 9 December 1948, art. 2(a), 1951 UNTS 278.

[201] IIFFMCG Report (2009) (n. 180), vol. 2, 427.

[202] PACE Res 1633 (2008) (n. 175), para. 14.

[203] Cf. Friendly Relations Declaration (1970) (n. 29), para. 5 of the fifth principle: 'Every State has the duty to refrain from any forcible action which deprives peoples referred to in the elaboration of the principle of equal rights and self-determination of their right to self-determination and freedom and independence . . . .'

[204] Sergey Lavrov, 'Внешняя политика России и новое качество геополитической ситуации' [Russian Foreign Policy and New Quality of the Geopolitical Situation], *Diplomaticheskiĭ vestnik* 4 (2008), 7–14, quotation from the English translation in 'Russian Foreign Minister Assesses New Geopolitical Situation, *BBC Monitoring Former Soviet Union*, 30 December 2008, available at: http://r2plive.org/russian-foreign-minister-assesses-new-geopolitical-situation.

[205] See Christopher Waters, 'Rule of Law in the Secessionist States' in Christopher Waters (ed.), *The State of Law in the South Caucasus* (London: Palgrave Macmillan, 2005), 59–80.

of the parties of the Joint Peacekeeping Force and also as one of the parties in the 1996 Memorandum on Measures to Provide Security and Strengthen Mutual Trust between the Parties to the Georgian-Ossetian Conflict.[206] However, despite partial recognition in the negotiation process and formal attributes of statehood, the Republic of South Ossetia cannot be qualified as a state in terms of international law for the same reason that has foreclosed statehood already in the earlier two case studies on Nagorno-Karabakh and Transnistria, that is the lack of an effective government.[207]

The IIFFMCG report found that Russia had *de facto* control over South Ossetia's institutions already before the outbreak of the war in 2008,[208] and since then Russia has even further increased its military, political, and economic influence. An estimated 5,000 Russian military troops are based in South Ossetia, and 900 Russian FSB border guards are stationed along the boundary with Georgia.[209] South Ossetia is financially dependent on Russia. It is South Ossetia's virtually only trading partner, and there is no indication that there are any other investors in South Ossetia but Russia.[210] Moreover, Russia provides financial aid amounting to 99 per cent of South Ossetia's annual budget.[211] In addition, Russians hold key posts in the administration of South Ossetia. For example, at the eve of the Russo-Georgian War the South Ossetian prime minister, the minister of the interior, and the head of the secret service were all ethnic Russians,[212] and according to a 2010 report published by the International Crisis Group, Russia controls South Ossetia's decision making in key spheres such as border, public order, and external relations, with more than half of the government staff originating from Russia.[213]

Since the Russo-Georgian War, Russia formalized this influence by the signing of various 'treaties' and agreements with the government of the breakaway republic: on 15 August 2008, that is already *prior* to Russia's recognition of South Ossetia as an independent state, the Treaty on Military Cooperation between the

[206] Memorandum on Measures to Provide Security and Strengthen Mutual Trust between the Parties to the Georgian-Ossetian Conflict (1996) (n. 170). This aspect should however not be overestimated, since North Ossetia (an integral part of the Russian Federation) was granted the same status, and the Sochi Agreement was concluded only between Russia and Georgia, Nußberger, 'South Ossetia' (n. 167), MN 23.

[207] This point is typically ignored in Russian scholarship, making divergent assessments possible. See e.g. V.D. Dzidzoev, 'Национальный суверенитет и право нации на самоопределение (на примере Абхазии и Южной Осетии)' [National Sovereignty and the Right of Nations to Self-determination (e.g. of Abkhazia and South Ossetia], *Severo-Kavkazskiĭ yuridicheskiĭ vestnik* (2016), no. 4, 18–30.

[208] IIFFMCG Report (2009) (n. 180), vol. 2, 131–3.

[209] ICG, 'South Ossetia: Rise of a New Politics and Foreign Policy', 17 February 2012, https://www.crisisgroup.org/europe-central-asia/caucasus/georgia/south-ossetia-rise-new-politics-and-foreign-policy. The Federal Security Service of the Russian Federation (FSB) is the principal security agency of Russia.

[210] Andre W.M. Gerrits and Max Bader, 'Russian Patronage over Abkhazia and South Ossetia: Implications for Conflict Resolution, *East European Politics* 32 (2016), 297–313, 300–1.

[211] Ibid., 302.

[212] See Illarionov, 'The Russian Leaderships Preparation for War' (2009) (n. 171), 81–2 (Box 4.1).

[213] ICG, Europe Report No. 205, South Ossetia: The Burden of Recognition, 7 June 2010.

Russian Federation and South Ossetia was signed and subsequently published in the official Bulletin of International Treaties of Russia.[214] In September 2008, the Treaty on Friendship, Cooperation and Mutual Assistance followed,[215] and in April 2010, an Agreement on the Creation of a Joint Military Base on the Territory of the Republic of South Ossetia was concluded.[216]

In early 2015, the Russo-South Ossetian Border Treaty and the Treaty on Alliance and Strategic Partnership followed.[217] According to article 1 of the latter agreement, Russia and South Ossetia pursue an 'agreed foreign policy that involves the mutual consideration of the interests of the Contracting Parties in various areas of cooperation, inform each other about the actions taken in this regard, and closely cooperate in strengthening peace, enhancing stability and security in the Caucasus region'. The agreement includes provisions incorporating the South Ossetian military into Russia's armed forces, integrating the customs service of South Ossetia into that of the Russian Federation, and commit Russia to paying officials salaries in South Ossetia at rates equal to those in the North Caucasian Federal District.[218]

The Georgian Ministry of Foreign Affairs condemned the signing of the Treaty on Alliance and Strategic Partnership as 'factual annexation' of South Ossetia by Russia.[219] The European Union and the United States also criticized the signing of the agreement, stating that they 'do not recognise the legitimacy of any so-called "treaty" on alliance and integration'.[220] Russia, on the other hand, plainly denies control over South Ossetia. Most prominently, it submitted to the International Court of Justice in *Georgia v Russian Federation* that it 'does not at present, nor will

[214] Соглашение между Российской Федерацией и Республикой Южная Осетия о сотрудничестве в военной области [Agreement between the Russian Federation and the Republic of South Ossetia on Military Cooperation], 15 August 2009, BMD 2013, no. 3, 57.

[215] Договор о дружбе, сотрудничестве и взаимной помощи между Российской Федерацией и Республикой Южная Осетия [Treaty on Friendship, Cooperation and Mutual Assistance between the Russian Federation and the Republic of South Ossetia], 17 September 2008, BMD 2009, no. 5, 68. See 'Statements following Signing of the Treaties on Friendship, Cooperation and Mutual Assistance with the Republics of Abkhazia and South Ossetia', http://en.kremlin.ru/events/president/transcripts/1136.

[216] Соглашение между Российской Федерацией и Республикой Южная Осетия об объединённой российской военной базе на территории Республики Южная Осетия [Agreement between the Russian Federation and the Republic of South Ossetia on the Creation of a Joint Military Base on the Territory of the Republic of South Ossetia], 7 April 2010, BMD 2010, no. 10, 34.

[217] Договор между Российской Федерацией и Республикой Южная Осетия о государственной границе [Treaty on the State Border between the Russian Federation and the Republic of South Ossetia], 18 February 2015, BMD 2017, no. 1, 74; Договор между Российской Федерацией и Республикой Южная Осетия о союзничестве и интеграции [Treaty between the Russian Federation and the Republic of South Ossetia on Alliance and Strategic Partnership], 18 March 2015, BMD 2015, no. 12, 77.

[218] The North Caucasian Federal District is one of the eight federal districts of the Russian Federation. It borders South Ossetia to the North and includes Chechnya, Dagestan, Ingushetia, Kabardino-Balkaria, Karachay-Cherkessia, North Ossetia-Alania, and the Stavropol Krai.

[219] Statement of the Ministry of Foreign Affairs Regarding the Signature of the So Called 'Treaty on Alliance and Integration' between Moscow and the Russian Occupation Regime of Tskhinvali, 18 March 2015, available at: http://www.poland.mfa.gov.ge/default.aspx?sec_id=440&lang=12&NewsID=104877.

[220] See 'U. S. does not Recognize Moscow-Tskhinvali Treaty, Concerned over Timing of its Signing', *Civil Georgia*, 18 March 2015, https://old.civil.ge/eng/article.php?id=28140.

it in the future, exercise effective control over South Ossetia'.[221] (In 2011, the ICJ dismissed the case, in which Georgia accused Russia of ethnic cleansing during the Russo-Georgian War, on the grounds of jurisdiction.)[222]

5. *Case Study* 6: Abkhazia

Abkhazia lies on the eastern coast of the Black Sea, south of the Greater Caucasus mountains and the Russian Federation. Since the last Soviet census of 1989, the composition of the two largest ethnic groups residing in Abkhazia almost reversed from 45.7 per cent Georgian and 17.8 per cent Abkhaz to 50.8 per cent Abkhaz and 18.0 per cent Georgian in 2011.[223]

5.1 Origins of the Conflict Over Abkhazia

The origins of the conflict over Abkhazia can be traced back to 1810, when Abkhazia became a Russian dependency following the Russo-Turkish War (1806–1812). In the following decades, the Russian Empire retained control over Abkhazia but ended its autonomous status and transformed it into the Sukhumi Military District in 1883. Thereafter, repressive measures against the Abkhaz population led to mass emigration into the Ottoman Empire. In turn, ethnic Russian, Armenian, Greek, and Georgian settlers arrived in Abkhazia to colonize free land.[224]

During the Russian Revolution, the Abkhaz People's Council was founded 'to protect the national and cultural-economic interests and political rights of the Abkhaz people', and 'to prepare the ground for self-determination of the Abkhaz people'.[225] On 31 March 1921, the Abkhaz SSR was created, distinct from and recognized by the Georgian SSR. In December 1921, the two Soviet republics however concluded the so-called Union Treaty, thereby establishing a military, political, and financial-economic cooperation with joint commissariats, but placing the foreign

[221] Submission of the Russian Federation, quoted in ICJ, Case Concerning Application of the International Convention on the Elimination of All Forms of Racial Discrimination (Georgia v Russian Federation), Request for the Indication of Provisional Measures, Order, 15 October 2008, ICJ Reports 2008, 353, para. 74.

[222] ICJ, Georgia v Russian Federation, Preliminary Objections, judgment, 1 April 2011, ICJ Reports 2011, 70. See Phoebe Okawa, 'The International Court of Justice and the Georgia/Russia Dispute', *Human Rights Law Review* 11 (2011), 739–757.

[223] State Committee of the USSR on Statistics, *The National Composition of the Population of the USSR* (1991) (n. 50); Abkhazian State Statistics Office, *Абхазия в цифрах за 2011 год* [Abkhazia in Numbers 2011] (Sukhumi: Abkhazian State Statistics Office, 2011), 23 (Table 1.9).

[224] Saparov, *From Conflict to Autonomy in the Caucasus* (2015) (n. 54), 24–27.

[225] Конституция Абхазского Народного Совета Принятая на Съезде Абхазского Народа [Constitution of the Abkhaz People's Council Adopted by the Abkhaz People's Congress], 8 November 1917, article 4. Quotation from the English translation available at: http://rrc.ge/law/abkonst_1917_11_08_e.htm?lawid=8&lng_3=en.

policy of the union fully within the competence of the Georgian SSR.[226] The resulting complicated relationship between the two republics was reflected in the 1925 Abkhaz Constitution, according to which the Abkhaz SSR was 'united on the basis of the Union Treaty with the Georgian SSR', and entered the Transcaucasian SFSR 'through the Georgian SSR and as a member of [the] latter, the USSR'.[227] According to article 5 of the Abkhaz Constitution, the Abkhaz SSR was, however, a sovereign state, 'which exercises state authority on its territory independently from any other powers'. Conversely, the 1927 Georgian Constitution stated that Abkhazia was an integral part of Georgia 'on the basis' of the Union Treaty, conferred with the special status of a 'contractual' (*dogovornaya*) autonomous republic.[228]

5.2 Abkhaz Resistance During the Soviet Era and War of Independence

Abkhazia's unique status in the Soviet Union lasted until 1931, when it was downgraded to an autonomous republic (ASSR) within the Georgian SSR, on the order of Stalin.[229] In the following two decades, ethnic Abkhaz were the subject of mass repression and discrimination. For example, the Abkhaz alphabet was changed from the earlier used Latin script to the Georgian script, all Abkhaz schools were closed and replaced by Georgian ones, and the Abkhaz language was banned from administration and publication. In 1953, after the death of Stalin, the Abkhaz were 'rehabilitated'; a new Abkhaz script based on Cyrillic was introduced, and Abkhaz schools were reopened.[230]

In 1978, Abkhaz intellectuals sent a letter to Moscow, asking for separation from the Georgian SSR, and in 1989, 30,000 people signed a similar petition, demanding the restoration of Abkhazia's status as a union republic of the Soviet Union. When Georgian authorities attempted to open a local branch of Tbilisi State University in Abkhazia later that year, open conflict between Georgians and Abkhaz broke

226 Союзный Договор Социалистической Советской Республики Грузии и Социалистической Советской Республики Абхазии [Union Treaty between the Soviet Socialist Republic of Georgia and the Soviet Socialist Republic of Abkhazia] (Union Treaty), 16 December 1921. English translation available at: https://www.rrc.ge/law/union_1921_12_16_e.htm?lawid=123&lng_3=en.

227 Конституция Социалистической Советской Республики Абхазии [Constitution of the Soviet Socialist Republic of Abkhazia], 1 April 1925, Quotation from the English translation available at http://rrc.ge/law/konst_1992_01_04_e.htm?lawid=139 8&lng_3=en. The Transcaucasian SFSR was a constituent republic of the Soviet Union that existed from 1922 to 1936. It consisted of Armenia, Azerbaijan, and Georgia.

228 Основной Закон (Конституция) Социалистической Советской Республики Грузии [Basic Law (Constitution] of the Soviet Socialist Republic of Georgia], 3 April 1927, art. 9 and 83–91. Quotation from the English translation available at http://rrc.ge/law/Gkon_1926_07_05_e.htm?lawid=1109&lng_3=en.

229 Angelika Nußberger, 'Abkhazia', in MPEPIL (online edn), MN 8.

230 Saparov, *From Conflict to Autonomy in the Caucasus* (2015) (n. 54), 151–2.

out. Although the violence soon subsided, the situation was quickly aggravated again by the adoption of a Georgian election law preventing regional political parties from participation.[231] On 23 July 1992, the situation finally escalated when the Abkhaz Supreme Soviet reinstated the 1925 Abkhaz Constitution, and declared the restoration of the Abkhaz SSR. (Earlier, Georgia had declared that the 1922 Treaty on the Establishment of the Soviet Union was invalid for Georgia and had restored its pre-Bolshevik constitution of 1921.)[232] On 14 August 1992, Georgian troops entered into Abkhazia, quickly culminating into a full-scale military conflict between Abkhaz and Georgian forces. The war lasted until May 1994 and resulted in the eviction of the Georgian population from Abkhazia, with gross human rights violations committed on both sides.[233]

As in the other secessionist conflicts that broke out when the Soviet Union collapsed, Russia's role in the Georgian-Abkhaz conflict was ambivalent. Officially, Russia maintained neutrality throughout the war, and imposed even sanctions on both Georgia and Abkhazia in response to their misconduct. Nevertheless, according to a 1995 Human Rights Watch report, 'Russian arms found their way into Abkhaz hands, Russian planes bombed civilian targets in Georgian-controlled territory, Russian military vessels, manned by supporters of the Abkhaz side, were made available to shell Georgian-held Sukhumi, and at least a handful of Russian-trained and Russian-paid fighters defended Abkhaz territory in Tkvarcheli.'[234]

5.3 Russia's Mediation Efforts within the Group of Friends and Beyond

Unlike in the Georgian-Ossetian conflict, the international community was actively involved in the attempts to solve the Georgian-Abkhaz conflict, and Russia played an important and in many respects crucial role in these efforts.[235] After the signing of the Agreement on a Ceasefire in Abkhazia and Arrangements to Monitor its Observance on 27 July 1993,[236] Russia was able to broker a final ceasefire agreement in which Georgia and Abkhazia agreed to the deployment of a—mainly Russian—CIS peacekeeping force and about 120 military observers of

[231] Ibid., 156.
[232] Nußberger, 'Abkhazia' (n. 229), MN 11.
[233] See Report of the Secretary-General's Fact-finding Mission to Investigate Human Rights Violations in Abkhazia, Republic of Georgia, 17 November 1993, UN Doc. S/26795 (Annex).
[234] HRW, Georgia/Abkhazia: Violations of the Law of War and Russia's Role in the Conflict, March 1995, 7.
[235] See IIFFMCG Report (2009) (n. 180), vol. 2, 76 et seq.
[236] Соглашение о прекращении огня в Абхазии и механизме контроля за его соблюдением [Agreement on a Ceasefire in Abkhazia and Arrangements to Monitor its Observance], 27 July 1993, English translation reprinted in Report of the Secretary-General in Pursuance of Security Council Resolution 849 (1993) (Annex I), 6 August 1993, UN Doc. S/26250, 6–8.

the United Nations Observer Mission in Georgia (UNOMIG).[237] The Abkhaz-Georgian ceasefire agreement was recognized by UN Security Council Resolution 934, and UNOMIG's mandate was established by UN Security Council Resolution 858, based on the expectation 'to reach a comprehensive political settlement of the conflict, including on the political status of Abkhazia, respecting fully the sovereignty and territorial integrity of the Republic of Georgia'.[238]

A first framework document on the question of Abkhazia's future legal status was the Declaration on Measures for a Political Settlement of the Georgian-Abkhaz Conflict, adopted on 4 April 1994 in Moscow.[239] In 1995 and again in 1997, Russia proposed draft protocols for possible legal relations between Abkhazia and Georgia which were reportedly accepted by the parties already on a working level, but in both instances consent was subsequently withdrawn by one or the other side.[240] With regard to these attempts, the IIFFMCG report notes:

> One of the most difficult issues for the parties proved to be not only the very concept of a future arrangement (federation or confederation) or its denomination, but also or mainly the right to secession. The Abkhaz insisted on such a right, arguing that it would constitute the most viable guarantee that their rights and positions within the agreed state arrangement would not be disregarded in the future. The Georgians, on the contrary, seemed to see serious potential risks to themselves deriving from their acceptance of the right to secession.[241]

In 1999, it was decided to address the status issue also in the framework of the UN-sponsored peace process, which had until then focused on practical issues.[242] In 2001, the Group of Friends of the UN Secretary-General on Georgia (comprising France, Germany, Russia, the United Kingdom, and the United States) adopted a document entitled 'Basic Principles for the Distribution of Competences between Tbilisi and Sukhumi', commonly known as the Boden Paper, named after Dieter Boden, the Special Representative of the Secretary-General at the time. The Boden Paper considered Abkhazia to be a sovereign entity within the Georgian state. A right of secession for Abkhazia was not included, and unilateral changes to a

[237] Соглашение о прекращении огня и разъединении сил [Agreement on a Ceasefire and Separation of Forces] (Abkhaz-Georgian Ceasefire Agreement), 17 May 1994, UN Doc. S/1994/583, 2–4 (Annex I).

[238] SC Res 858, 24 August 1993, UN Doc. S/RES/858; SC Res 934, 30 June 1994, UN Doc. S/RES/934.

[239] Заявление о мерах по политическому урегулированию грузино-абхазского конфликта [Declaration on Measures for a Political Settlement of the Georgian-Abkhaz Conflict], 4 April 1994, UN Doc. S/1994/397, 2–3 (Annex 1).

[240] See Potier, *Conflict in Nagorno-Karabakh, Abkhazia and South Ossetia* (2001) (n. 52), 118–19. The 1995 Protocol on Georgian-Abkhaz Conflict Settlement is reprinted in Tamaz Diasamidze, *Regional Conflicts in Georgia (The Autonomous Oblast of South Ossetia; The Autonomous SSR of Abkhazia 1989–2011). Collection of Political-Legal Acts* (Tbilisi: Regionalism Research Centre, 2008).

[241] IIFFMCG Report (2009) (n. 180), vol. 2, 83–4.

[242] SC Res 1255, 30 July 1999, UN Doc. S/RES/1255.

future federal agreement were also not allowed.[243] Consequently, Abkhazia repeatedly refused to receive the Boden Paper for consideration, and in October 1999 formally declared its independence from Georgia.[244] From 2001, Abkhazia virtually suspended its participation in the UN-sponsored peace negotiations. Russia, who had initially supported the Boden Paper as part of the Group of Friends, also started questioning its usefulness from January 2006 onwards.[245]

In 2008, as a consequence of the Russo-Georgian War, Georgia declared the 1994 ceasefire agreement null and void.[246] Moreover, Georgia terminated its membership to the Commonwealth of Independent States, which in turn declared the withdrawal of its peacekeeping force in Abkhazia.[247] In June 2009, UNOMIG's mandate expired due to a Russian veto in the UN Security Council.[248] 'There is no point in extending it since it is built on old realities', Vitaly Churkin, Russia's permanent representative to the UN, said about the mission's mandate before the voting on the draft resolution that would have extended it, later adding that it 'would have established a new security regime with politically incorrect provisions and old, contradictory terms' which 'was aimed at affirming the territorial integrity of Georgia and at denying the existence of Abkhazia as a State. Obviously', Churkin stated, 'the Russian side could not agree to that.'[249] On 31 October 2009, UNOMIG personnel left Abkhazia.

5.4 International Status of the 'Republic of Abkhazia'

Like in the case of South Ossetia, no UN member state had recognized the 'Republic of Abkhazia' as an independent state prior to the 2008 Russo-Georgian War. To the contrary, a substantial number of UN Security Council resolutions that were passed in the context of the Georgia-Abkhaz conflict explicitly recognized and reaffirmed Georgia's territorial integrity. For instance, UN Security Council Resolution 896 of 31 January 1994 prescribed that the status of Abkhazia was to be defined by respecting 'the sovereignty and the territorial integrity of the Republic

243 On the Boden Paper in more detail see Bruno Coppieters, 'The Georgian-Abkhaz Conflict', in Coppieters, Emerson, Huysseune, Kovziridze, Noutcheva, Tocci, and Vahl, *Europeanization and Conflict Resolution* (2004) (n. 107), 191–232, 203–9.

244 Акт о Государственной Независимости Республики Абхазия [Act on the National Independence of the Republic of Abkhazia], 12 October 1999, English translation reprinted in Diasamidze, *Regional Conflicts in Georgia* (2008) (n. 240).

245 See Vladimir Socor, 'Moscow Kills Boden Paper, Threatens to Terminate UNOMIG in Georgia', *Eurasia Daily Monitor* 3 (2006), no. 26.

246 Nußberger, 'Abkhazia' (n. 229), MN 21. However, UN Security Council Resolution 1866 still refers to it and calls for it to be respected, SC Res 1866, 13 February 2009, UN Doc. S/RES/1866.

247 Nußberger, 'Abkhazia' (n. 229), MN 22.

248 See Nikola Krastev, 'Georgia Slams Russia For Shutting Down UN Mission', *Radio Free Europe/Radio Liberty*, 16 June 2009.

249 Russian Federation, SC 6143rd meeting, 15 June 2009, UN Doc. S/PV.6143, 2–3.

of Georgia',[250] and Security Council Resolution 1808 of 15 April 2008 continued to reaffirm the commitment of all UN member states to 'the sovereignty, independence and territorial integrity of Georgia within its internationally recognized borders'.[251]

Russia supported all these resolutions in the Security Council,[252] but changed its approach in the aftermath of the Russo-Georgian War, arguing that Georgia had 'ended' its territorial integrity by attacking the Ossetian town of Tskhinvali, resulting in the emergence of two new states, South Ossetia and Abkhazia.[253] Consequently, on the same day that Russia recognized South Ossetia as an independent state, Russian president Medvedev signed also a separate decree recognizing Abkhazia's independence.[254] Similar to the situation in South Ossetia, as of February 2021, four UN member states other than Russia have recognized the Republic of Abkhazia as an independent state: Nauru, Nicaragua, Syria, and Venezuela.[255]

As in the earlier case studies on Nagorno-Karabakh, Transnistria, and South Ossetia, Abkhazia has all formal attributes of statehood, including a constitution. Adopted on 26 November 1994 and confirmed by referendum on 3 October 1999, the Abkhaz Constitution refers to the right of peoples to self-determination in the preamble and article 1 proclaims 'a sovereign, democratic state, established historically pursuant to the right of a people to free self-determination and functioning

[250] SC Res 896, 31 January 1994, UN Doc. S/RES/896.

[251] SC Res 1808, 15 April 2008, UN Doc. S/RES/1808, para. 1.

[252] In total, the Security Council passed thirty-nine resolutions between 1993 and 2008 on the situation in Abkhazia: SC Res 849, 9 July 1993, UN Doc. S/RES/849; SC Res 854, 6 August 1993, UN Doc. S/RES/854; SC Res 858, 24 August 1993, UN Doc. S/RES/858; SC Res 876, 19 October 1993, UN Doc. S/RES/876; SC Res 881, 4 November 1993, UN Doc. S/RES/881; SC Res 892, 22 December 1993, UN Doc. S/RES/892; SC Res 896 (n. 250); SC Res 901, 4 March 1994, UN Doc. S/RES/901; SC Res 906, 25 March 1994, UN Doc. S/RES/906; SC Res 934, 30 June 1994, UN Doc. S/RES/934; SC Res 937, 21 July 1994, UN Doc. S/RES/937; SC Res 971, 12 January 1995, UN Doc. S/RES/971; SC Res 993, 12 May 1995, UN Doc. S/RES/993; SC Res 1036, 12 January 1996, UN Doc. S/RES/1036; SC Res 1065, 12 July 1996, UN Doc. S/RES/1065; SC Res 1077, 22 October 1996, UN Doc. S/RES/1077; SC Res 1096, 30 January 1997, UN Doc. S/RES/1096; SC Res 1124, 31 July 1997, UN Doc. S/RES/1124; SC Res 1150, 30 January 1998, UN Doc. S/RES/1150; SC Res 1187, 30 July 1998, UN Doc. S/RES/1187; SC Res 1225, 29 January 1999, UN Doc. S/RES/1225; SC Res 1255 (n. 242); SC Res 1287, 31 January 2000, UN Doc. S/RES/1287; SC Res 1311, 28 July 2000, UN Doc. S/RES/1311; SC Res 1339, 31 January 2001, UN Doc. S/RES/1339; SC Res 1364, 30 March 2001, UN Doc. S/RES/1364; SC Res 1393, 31 January 2002, UN Doc. S/RES/1393; SC Res 1427, 29 July 2002, UN Doc. S/RES/1427; SC Res 1462, 30 January 2003, UN Doc. S/RES/1462; SC Res 1494, 30 July 2003, UN Doc. S/RES/1494; SC Res 1524, 30 January 2004, UN Doc. S/RES/1524; SC Res 1554, 29 July 2004, UN Doc. S/RES/1554; SC Res 1582, 28 January 2005, UN Doc. S/RES/1582; SC Res 1615, 29 July 2005, UN Doc. S/RES/1615; SC Res 1656, 31 March 2006, UN Doc. S/RES/1656; SC Res 1716, 13 October 2006, UN Doc. S/RES/1716; SC Res 1752, 13 April 2007, UN Doc. S/RES/1752; SC Res 1781, 15 October 2007, UN Doc. S/RES/1781; SC Res 1808 (n. 251).

[253] See e.g. Russian Federation, SC 6143rd meeting, 15 June 2009, UN Doc. S/PV.6143, 2–3.

[254] Decree of the President of Russia No. 1260, О признании Республики Абхазия [On the Recognition of the Republic of Abkhazia], 26 August 2008, SZRF 2008, no. 35, item 4011.

[255] As in the case of South Ossetia, Tuvalu had recognized Abkhazia as an independent state in 2011, but subsequently withdrew recognition in 2014.

in accordance with law'.[256] Article 3 refers to the Republic of Abkhazia as a subject of international law. According to article 6 of the Abkhaz Constitution, the official language is Abkhazian, although Russian is also recognized as 'the language of the government and public and other institutions'. (The Georgian language is not explicitly mentioned, but 'the state shall guarantee all ethnic groups living in Abkhazia the right to use freely their own language'.)

Formal attributes of statehood and recognition by five UN member states therefore raise the question whether the Republic of Abkhazia qualifies as a state under international law. As in the previous case studies on Transnistria and South Ossetia, several aspects indicate that the Republic of Abkhazia is military, financially, and politically dependent on Russia, although probably to a lesser degree than the other two republics. According to a 2013 report by the International Crisis Group, there are around 2,500 Russian military and 1,500 FSB border guards stationed in Abkhazia.[257] Furthermore, although Russia is not Abkhazia's only trading partner, it is by far its biggest: more than 70 per cent of Abkhazia's exports go to Russia, and up to 80 per cent of what is consumed in Abkhazia originates from there. In addition, a reported 99 per cent of foreign direct investments in Abkhazia come from Russia, and Russian financial aid amounts to 60 per cent of the Abkhaz budget. Moreover, nearly the entire Abkhaz population reportedly holds Russian citizenship, and ethnic Russians hold key posts in government.[258]

The IIFMCG has noted in its report that 'Abkhazia is more advanced than South Ossetia in the process of state-building and might be seen to have reached the threshold of effectiveness. It may therefore be qualified as a state-like entity'.[259] 'Weighing the factors differently', Angelika Nußberger considered in 2013 in her entry on Abkhazia for the *Max Planck Encyclopedia of Public International Law*, it could also be argued 'that the criteria of statehood were already satisfied before the outbreak of the 2008 war and Abkhazia could be qualified as a "stabilized de facto regime", which was denied recognition and membership in international organizations for political reasons only'.[260] However, at least for the period after the Russo-Georgian War, both assessments are arguably outdated due to the subsequent conclusion of several agreements that make Abkhazia similarly dependent on Russia like South Ossetia.

[256] Конституция Республики Абхазия [Constitution of the Republic of Abkhazia], 26 November 1994. English translation reprinted in Philip Raworth (ed.), *Constitutions of Dependencies and Territories*, vol. 1, Supp 13-4 (Dobbs Ferry, NY: Oceana Publications, 2013), 7–23.

[257] ICG, Europe Report No. 224, Abkhazia: The Long Road to Reconciliation, 10 April 2013.

[258] ICG, Europe Report No. 202, Abkhazia: Deepening Dependence, 26 February 2010.

[259] IIFFMCG Report (2009) (n. 180), vol. 2, 134. Earlier in the report, the term is defined as 'fulfilling the relevant criteria [for statehood], but which are not, or not universally, recognised', ibid., 128.

[260] Nußberger, 'Abkhazia' (n. 229), MN 27. On the concept of *de facto* regimes in international law generally see Jochen Abr. Frowein, *Das de facto-Regime im Völkerrecht. Eine Untersuchung zur Rechtsstellung "nichtanerkannter Staaten und ähnlicher Gebilde* (Cologne: Carl Heymanns, 1968).

On 17 September 2008, the Treaty on Friendship, Cooperation and Mutual Assistance was concluded in Moscow.[261] In 2009–2010, further agreements on joint efforts in the field of protection of the border of Abkhazia, on cooperation in the military field, and on a Russian basis on the territory of Abkhazia followed. Abkhaz-Russian relations were further intensified in response to the signing of an association agreement between the European Union and Georgia in June 2014, with Russia and Abkhazia agreeing on a Treaty on Alliance and Strategic Partnership in November the same year.[262] (The agreement was signed on 18 March 2015, the day of the first anniversary of Russia's annexation of Crimea.) In its article 3, the agreement sets forth six goals for the development of a strategic partnership between Abkhazia and the Russian Federation: (1) a 'coordinated' foreign policy; (2) the creation of a 'common space for defence and security'; (3) the formation of a 'common social and economic space'; (4) Russian assistance to the socio-economic development of Abkhazia; (5) the 'creation of conditions of Abkhazia for full participation in the integration process in the post-Soviet space, implemented on the initiative of and (or) with the assistance of the Russian Federation'; and (6) the preservation of a 'common cultural, spiritual, and humanitarian space'.

Article 4 of the Treaty on Alliance and Strategic Partnership sets out the establishment of a 'coordinated' Abkhaz-Russian foreign policy in more detail. It involves 'mutual consideration of the interests of the Contracting Parties in various areas of cooperation' and 'informing each other about the actions taken in this regard' as well as 'close cooperation in strengthening peace, increasing stability and security in the Caucasus region'. Moreover, the commitment to a 'coordinated' foreign policy entails that

> [t]he Russian Federation will contribute in every possibly way to strengthening the international relations of the Republic of Abkhazia, including expanding the circle of officially recognised states, and creating conditions for the accession of the Republic of Abkhazia to international organisations and associations, including those created on the initiative and/or with the assistance of the Russian Federation.

[261] Договор о дружбе, сотрудничестве и взаимной помощи между Российской Федерацией и Республикой Абхазия [Treaty on Friendship, Cooperation and Mutual Assistance between the Russian Federation and the Republic of Abkhazia], 17 September 2008, BMD 2009, no. 5, 59. See also 'Statements following Signing of the Treaties on Friendship, Cooperation and Mutual Assistance with the Republics of Abkhazia and South Ossetia' (2008) (n. 215).

[262] Договор между Российской Федерацией и Республикой Абхазия о союзничестве и стратегическом партнёрстве [Treaty between the Russian Federation and the Republic of Abkhazia on Alliance and Strategic Partnership], 24 November 2014, BMD 2015, no. 7, 23. On the agreement see also 'Moscow, Sokhumi Endorse Final Text of New Treaty', *Civil Georgia*, 22 November 2014, https://old.civil.ge/eng/article.php?id=27841.

The creation of a 'common space for defence and security' is lined out in the next section of the agreement. Articles 5 and 7(1) foresee the creation of a joint force of Russian and Abkhazian troops within one year from the date of entry into force of the agreement to 'repel aggression (armed attack) in accordance with article 51 of the UN Charter' and 'to protect the state border of the Republic of Abkhazia with Georgia' as well as the maritime borders under the jurisdiction of the Republic of Abkhazia. In the event of an 'immediate threat of aggression', the joint force will be put into operation, with a commander appointed by the Russian Federation, and a deputy appointed by the Republic of Abkhazia, article 7(2). The decision on the joint use of force on Abkhaz territory shall be coordinated with the Abkhaz president, article 7(3). Furthermore, article 6 provides for a collective defence clause, according to which 'aggression (armed attack) by a state or group of states' against one contracting party 'will be considered aggression (armed attack)' also against the other contracting party of the agreement, which then shall provide 'necessary assistance, including military', as well as 'support with the means at its disposal in the exercise of the right of collective self-defence in accordance with article 51 of the UN Charter'.

Against the background of these agreements concluded since the Russo-Georgian War, in particular the Treaty on Alliance and Strategic Partnership of 2014, arguing for the effectiveness of the Abkhaz government appears almost impossible.[263]

6. Conclusions

This chapter has shown that prior to Russia's annexation of Crimea in 2014, Russia's state practice in the post-Soviet space with regard to the right of peoples to self-determination and secession appeared relatively consistent, notwithstanding valid critique of hypocrisy. Until Kosovo's declaration of independence, Russia did not recognize any of the secessionist republics in the post-Soviet space as independent states but affirmed the inviolability of borders and the territorial integrity of their parent states in various UN resolutions and international agreements. At the same time, Russia shaped the negotiation processes of all four conflicts as a mediator andsecured the agreement by the conflict parties to deploy (or remain in the format of) Russian peacekeeping forces.[264] Russia thereby maintained the

[263] Some Russian scholars seem to suggest the exact opposite: 'Today, the state and legal system of the Republic of Abkhazia exists as a transitional type system, being in the process of its synchronisation with the state legal system of the Russian Federation in accordance with the aim of building a sovereign state', P.I. Kvacheva and S.V. Petrova, 'Политико-правовой статус непризнанного государства в современном мире: историко-правовой аспект (на примере Республики Абхазия) [Political and Legal Status of an Unrecognized State in the Modern World: Historical and Legal Aspect (on the Example of the Republic of Abkhazia], *Vestnik Permskogo universiteta. Yuridicheskie nauki* 35 (2017), 56–65.

[264] On the underlying policy of these deployments see Allison, *Russia, the West, and Military Intervention* (2013) (n. 172), 126–30.

status quo it helped to create in the first place, since Russian support on the side of the secessionist parties when the Soviet Union collapsed was critical for the successful separation of the breakaway republics from their parent states in the early 1990s. In the following years, strong influencing on a military, political, and financial level led the ECtHR and the IIFFMCG to conclude that Russia had effective control over the authorities in Transnistria, South Ossetia, and, with some reservations, also Abkhazia—an assessment which Russia plainly denies and repudiates as 'politicized'.

With the recognition of Abkhazia and South Ossetia in 2008 shortly after Kosovo's declaration of independence, Russia's approach towards the secessionist conflicts in the post-Soviet space shifted fundamentally. According to the official Russian reasoning, Georgia had lost its sovereignty over the two breakaway republics following the attack on the Ossetian town of Tskhinvali on 8 August 2008. As has been noted, the claim of a right of secession of the population of South Ossetia was however based on highly exaggerated numbers and must therefore appear hypocritical.

The underlying legal view, on the other hand, that a right to 'remedial' secession exists in modern international law *de lege lata*, was consistent with Russia's views voiced in the *Kosovo* case in front of the ICJ with regard to the right of peoples to self-determination and secession. Section 1 clearly showed that Russia approves of the concept of remedial secession (even if the expression 'remedial' is rarely used), and denies Kosovo recognition not because of a different view on self-determination and secession but because it refuses to accept the logic of some states to view Kosovo as a 'special' or 'unique' case that cannot be compared with other secessionist conflicts. In fact, Russia had warned the international community in the emergency session of the UN Security Council on the day after Kosovo's declaration of independence that recognition of Kosovo might set a dangerous precedent, whereas many states in the same session stressed that Kosovo should not be construed as such.[265] It is therefore important to note what Russian foreign minister Sergey Lavrov stated with regard to the possible impact of Russia's recognition of South Ossetia and Abkhazia for the other two secessionist conflicts in the post-Soviet space, Nagorno-Karabakh and Transnistria. In September 2008, Lavrov stated in the Federation Council, the upper house of the Russian parliament:

> We intend to continue actively facilitating the peaceful resolution of the conflicts in the CIS space on the basis of international law, respect for all the principles of the UN Charter and all the previously reached agreements and of a search for consensus between the parties in conflict. We are going to responsibly carry out our mediation mission in the negotiation process and peacemaking. This fully

[265] See the various statements summarized in 'Security Council Meets in Emergency Session Following Kosovo's Declaration of Independence, with Members Sharply Divided on Issue', *UN Press Release*, 18 February 2008, UN Doc. SC/9252.

> applies to Transnistria and Nagorno-Karabakh—each place has its specific features, its formats and mechanisms of mediation. But the South Ossetian crisis creates no precedent for them. None of those concerned with Nagorno-Karabakh and Transnistrian settlement plan to violate international law, tear up existing accords, destroy the agreed settlement formats and bomb civilian residents and peacekeepers. There is no one there who would like to ensure territorial integrity by mass killing of people whom you consider your citizens, residents of your own country.[266]

Why Abkhazia too should have a right to secede, even if the allegation of 'genocide' or 'mass killing' of the Ossetian population were true, remained largely unclear. Generally, the issue of recognition of the two republics was treated as if it concerned a single question, and the arguments raised in favour of South Ossetia's independence were often extended also to Abkhazia without further distinction or explanation. One notable exception in this regard is a remark by Vladimir Putin (at the time Russian prime minister), in which he openly challenged the legitimacy of the application of the *uti possidetis* principle for the dissolution process of the Soviet Union. Referring to the downgrading of the Abkhaz SSR on the order of Stalin from a union republic to an autonomous republic within the Georgian SSR in 1931, Putin stated in a televized interview with CNN that 'those who insist that those territories must continue to belong to Georgia are Stalinists—they stick to Josef Vissarionovich Stalin's decision'.[267] On first sight, Putin seems to have a point here, since it calls into question the legitimacy of the application of the *uti possidetis* principle in cases where administrative borders of a given state are the result of historical injustices and oppression. However, the *uti possidetis* principle was developed and applied in the process of decolonization precisely with the aim of guaranteeing the immutability of arbitrarily established borders by colonial powers, fixed for the sake of stability.[268] Or, in the words of Anne Peters: 'It is exactly the function of *uti possidetis* to terminate arguments about prior territorial

[266] 'Transcript of Remarks by Sergey Lavrov, Minister of Foreign Affairs of the Russian Federation, at an Enlarged Meeting of the Federation Council International Affairs Committee, Moscow, September 18, 2008', http://www.mid.ru/en/press_service/minister_speeches/-/asset_publisher/7OvQR5KJWVmR/content/id/324594.

[267] See 'Transcript: CNN Interview with Vladimir Putin', *CNN*, 29 August 2008, http://edition.cnn.com/2008/world/europe/ 08/29/putin.transcript.

[268] See ICJ, Burkina Faso v Republic of Mali (1986) (n. 6), para. 25: 'However, it may be wondered how the time-hallowed principle has been able to withstand the new approaches to international law as expressed in Africa, where the successive attainment of independence and the emergence of new States have been accompanied by a certain questioning of traditional international law. At first sight this principle conflicts outright with another one, the right of peoples to self-determination. In fact, however, the maintenance of the territorial status quo in Africa is often seen as the wisest course, to preserve what has been achieved by peoples who have struggles for their independence, and to avoid a disruption which would deprive the continent of the gains achieved by much sacrifice. The essential requirement of stability in order to survive, to develop and gradually to consolidate their independence in all fields, has induced African States judiciously to consent to the respecting of colonial frontiers, and to take account of it in the interpretation of the principle of self-determination of peoples.'

illegality.'[269] Similar considerations must therefore also prevail in the context of the dissolution process of the Soviet Union.[270]

Nevertheless, apart from occasional references to historical arguments, the case studies on Abkhazia and South Ossetia proved that rather than withdrawing from legal rhetoric, Russia started to construct its own legal framework.[271] This approach could be observed in the Russo-Georgian War 2008 with regard to the sudden appreciation of formerly refuted doctrines as justifications for Russia's use of force like 'humanitarian intervention',[272] but also with regard to claims of self-determination and secession. In this context, Russia's response to the IIFFMCG that it had intervened 'following a request from the government of South Ossetia' is particularly interesting since it can be interpreted as a revitalization of the former Soviet doctrine of the right to use force to assist wars of national liberation.

[269] Anne Peters, 'The Principle of *Uti Possidetis Juris*: How Relevant is it for Issues of Secession?', in Walter, von Ungern-Sternberg, and Abushov, *Self-determination and Secession in International Law* (2014) (n. 26), 95–137, 123.

[270] Nußberger, 'Völkerrecht im Kaukasus' (2008) (n. 183), 458; Nußberger, 'The War between Russia and Georgia' (2009) (n. 183), 361.

[271] See also Christopher J. Borgen, 'Law, Rhetoric, Strategy: Russia and Self-determination Before and After Crimea', *International Law Studies* 91 (2015), 216–80, 235–6.

[272] See n. 183 above and Nußberger, 'Völkerrecht im Kaukasus' (2008) (n. 183), 464.

4

Russia, the Right to Self-Determination and Annexation

On 15 April 1994, the members of the Commonwealth of Independent States (CIS) adopted the Declaration on the Respect for Sovereignty, Territorial Integrity, and Inviolability of Borders, thereby confirming their commitment to recognize and respect the inviolability of each other's existing borders already stipulated in the founding documents of the CIS.[1] This affirmation notwithstanding, a number of territorial disputes arose among some of the former Soviet republics, in particular between Russia and Ukraine, but also between Russia and the three Baltic states Estonia, Latvia, and Lithuania.

The border dispute between Russia and Lithuania was settled with the Lithuanian-Russian Border Treaty, signed in Moscow on 24 October 1997.[2] Negotiations with Estonia and Latvia were more complicated, since both states initially relied on their respective peace treaties with the Soviet Union, signed in 1920, whereas Russia proceeded from the border limitations of the Estonian and Latvian Soviet republics at the time of the dissolution of the Soviet Union. The dispute between Russia and Latvia could be settled on 27 March 1997 with the signing of the Latvian-Russian Border Treaty.[3] As of September 2020, Russia's border dispute with Estonia remains however unresolved. In 2005, a first border treaty was signed, but Russia subsequently declared that it did not see itself bound by it after the Estonian parliament had added a preamble before ratifying it, declaring that the peace treaty of 1920 remained valid.[4] In 2012, negotiations resumed, and in 2014 the Estonian-Russian Border Treaty was signed, but as of February 2021, the treaty has not been ratified.[5]

[1] Декларация о соблюдении суверенитета, территориальной целостности и неприкосновенности границ государств [Declaration on the Respect for Sovereignty, Territorial Integrity, and Inviolability of Borders of Member States], 15 April 1994, BMD 1994, no. 7, 9.

[2] Treaty between the Republic of Lithuania and the Russian Federation concerning the State Border between Lithuania and Russia, 24 October 1997, *Valstybes žinios* 1997, no. 100-2891.

[3] Treaty between the Republic of Latvia and the Russian Federation on the Latvian and Russian State Border, 27 March 2007, *Latvijas Vēstnesis* 2007, no. 85.

[4] See 'Россия отозвала подписи под договорами о границе с Эстонией' [Russia Withdrew Signatures on Border Treaties with Estonia], *Rossiĭskaya gazeta*, 1 September 2005.

[5] Договор между Эстонской Республикой и Российской Федерацией о государственной границе [Treaty between the Republic of Estonia and the Russian Federation on State Border]. English translation available at: http://vm.ee/sites/default/files/content-editors/web-static/394/Est-Rus_border_treaty.pdf.

Russia and the Right to Self-Determination in the Post-Soviet Space. Johannes Socher, Oxford University Press.
 DOI: 10.1093/oso/9780192897176.003.0005

The most complex territorial dispute following the dissolution of the Soviet Union arose between Russia and Ukraine concerning the status of Crimea and the city of Sevastopol, notwithstanding affirmations of the respect for each other's borders in numerous bilateral and multilateral agreements: already prior to the break up of the Soviet Union, a first agreement was signed in November 1990 between the Russian Soviet Federative Socialist Republic (SFSR) and the Ukrainian Soviet Socialist Republic (SSR) in which the territorial integrity within the existing border framework of the Soviet Union was recognized.[6] On 23 June 1992, a second treaty was concluded between the Russian Federation and independent Ukraine in Sochi, confirming these commitments.[7] In 1994, the so-called Budapest Memorandum was signed between Russia, Ukraine, the United Kingdom, and the United States, in return for Ukraine joining the Treaty on the Non-Proliferation of Nuclear Weapons,[8] declaring that the signatories 'reaffirm their commitment to Ukraine, in accordance with the principles of the Helsinki Final Act, to respect the Independence and Sovereignty and the existing borders of Ukraine'.[9] The commitment to respect each other's territorial integrity and inviolability of existing borders was reaffirmed between Russia and Ukraine in the 1997 Treaty on Friendship, Cooperation, and Partnership,[10] and again in an additional treaty on the Russian-Ukrainian border concluded on 28 January 2003.[11] On 24 December 2003, the Treaty between the Russian Federation and Ukraine on Cooperation on the Use of the Sea of Azov and the Kerch Strait was concluded.[12]

These agreements and commitments notwithstanding, the status of Crimea and the city of Sevastopol were a continuous issue in Russo-Ukrainian relations. In 1993 for example, the Supreme Soviet of the Russian Federation tried to declare Sevastopol a Russian city, an attempt immediately denounced by the president of the UN Security Council.[13] Another concern after the dissolution of the

[6] Treaty between the Russian Soviet Federative Socialist Republic and the Ukrainian Soviet Socialist Republic, 19 November 1990, 1641 UNTS 228, art. 6.

[7] See Serge Schmemann, 'Main Russia–Ukraine Disputes Settled', *The New York Times*, 24 June 1992.

[8] Treaty on the Non-Proliferation of Nuclear Weapons, 1 July 1968, 729 UNTS 161.

[9] Memorandum on Security Assurances in Connection with Ukraine's Accession to the Treaty on the Non-Proliferation of Nuclear Weapons (Budapest Memorandum), 5 December 1994, UN Doc. A/49/765. It is debated whether the memorandum constitutes legal obligations or merely expresses political commitments.

[10] Договор о дружбе, сотрудничестве и партнёрстве между Российской Федерацией и Украиной [Treaty on Friendship, Cooperation and Partnership between Ukraine and the Russian Federation], 31 May 1997, BMD 1999, no. 7, 50, art. 2. English translation: *Harvard Ukrainian Studies* 20 (1996), 319–29. The treaty expired on 1 April 2019.

[11] Договор между Российской Федерацией и Украиной о российско-украинской государственной границе [Treaty between the Russian Federation and Ukraine on the Russian-Ukrainian State Border], 28 January 2003, BMD 2004, no. 7, 47.

[12] Договор между Российской Федерацией и Украиной о сотрудничестве в использовании Азовского моря и Керченского пролива [Treaty between the Russian Federation and Ukraine on Cooperation on the Use of the Sea of Azov and the Kerch Strait], 24 December 2003, BMD 2004, no. 7, 46.

[13] 'Note by the President of the Security Council', 20 July 1993, UN Doc. S/26118.

Soviet Union was the partition and the continuous stationing of the Black Sea Fleet in Crimea, which was solved only in 1997 with the signing of three agreements allowing for Russian military presence on the peninsula under limited conditions.[14]

This chapter discusses Russia's state practice with regard to these territorial disputes in the context of the right of peoples to self-determination and annexation. After briefly outlining the general commitment of the international community to outlaw annexation, a short Section 1 situates Russia's retrospect reading of the Soviet Union's incorporation of the Baltic states in 1940 in the wider spectrum of international state practice following the dissolution of the Soviet Union. Section 2 then sets out to depict the conflict over Crimea in more detail, and analyses Russia's attempts to use the right of peoples to self-determination as a pretext to justify its annexation of Crimea in 2014.

1. Russia's Retrospective View on the Baltic States' Annexation in 1940

Under modern international law, the forcible acquisition of territory by one state at the expense of another state is illegal since it violates the prohibition of the threat or use of force enshrined in article 2(4) of the UN Charter.[15] Various resolutions by the UN Security Council and General Assembly confirm this position,[16] and

[14] Соглашения между Российской Федерацией и Украиной о параметрах раздела Черноморского флота [Agreement between the Russian Federation and Ukraine on the Parameters of the Division of the Black Sea Fleet], 28 May 1997, BMD 1999, no. 10, 34; Соглашение между Российской Федерацией и Украиной о статусе и условиях пребывания Черноморского флота Российской Федерации на территории Украины [Agreement between the Russian Federation and Ukraine on the Status and Conditions of the Stay of the Black Sea Fleet of the Russian Federation on the Territory of Ukraine], 28 May 1997, BMD 1999, no. 10, 74; Соглашение между Правительством Российской Федерации и Правительством Украины о взаиморасчетах, связанных с разделом Черноморского флота и пребыванием Черноморского флота Российской Федерации на территории Украины [Agreement between the Government of the Russian Federation and the Government of Ukraine on Mutual Settlements Related to the Division of the Black Sea Fleet and the Stay of the Black Sea Fleet of the Russian Federation on the Territory of Ukraine], 28 May 1997, BMD 1999, no. 10, 80. English translations: Centre for Research on Canadian-Russian Relations (ed.), *Russia & Eurasia Documents Annual* (1997), no. 1, 129. On the details of the agreements see Veronika Bílková, 'The Use of Force by the Russian Federation in Crimea', *Zeitschrift für ausländisches öffentliches Recht und Völkerrecht* 75 (2015), 27–50, 31–4 and Thomas D. Grant, 'Annexation of Crimea', *American Journal of International Law* 109 (2015), 68–95, 78–80. Russia unilaterally declared the agreements terminated on 2 April 2014, see Federal Law of Russia No. 38-FZ, О прекращении действия соглашений, касающихся пребывания Черноморского флота Российской Федерации на территории Украины [On the Termination of Agreements Concerning the Stay of the Black Sea Fleet of the Russian Federation on the Territory of Ukraine], 2 April 2014, SZRF 2014, no. 14, item 1530.

[15] See e.g. Rainer Hofmann, 'Annexation', in MPEPIL (online edn), MN 1 et seq. The reference work on the topic is still Robert Yewdall Jennings, *The Acquisition of Territory in International Law* (Manchester: Manchester University Press, 1963).

[16] See SC Res 242, 22 November 1967, UN Doc. A/RES/242 ('Emphasizing the inadmissibility of the acquisition of territory by war ...'); GA Res 26/25 (XXV) (Friendly Relations Declaration), 24 October 1970, UN Doc. A/RES/25/2625 ('The territory of a State shall not be the object of acquisition by another State resulting from the threat or use of force ...'); GA Res 3314 (XXIX) (Definition of Aggression), 13 December 1974, UN Doc. A/RES/29/3314 ('No territorial or special advantage resulting from

the Vienna Convention on the Law of Treaties (VCLT) rejects the validity of even a treaty-based annexation by stating that such an agreement is void 'if its conclusion has been procured by the threat or use of force in violation of the principles of international law embodied in the Charter of the United Nations'.[17] The Russian Federation is party to the VCLT and also backed Security Council Resolutions 1244 and 1472, the two most recent resolutions reflecting the international community's commitment to outlaw annexations.[18]

1.1 The International Community's Reaction on the Baltic States' Independence in 1991

Following the dissolution of the Soviet Union, the international community had to deal with the question of annexation when Estonia, Latvia, and Lithuania did not declare themselves independent from the Soviet Union (like all other union republics except Russia), but proclaimed instead the 'restoration' or the 'renewal' of the pre-Soviet republics' independence that had existed prior to their incorporation by the Soviet Union in 1940. According to the Baltic states' view, the republics of Estonia, Latvia, and Lithuania continued to exist throughout the Soviet period. The Soviet Union committed acts of aggression in June 1940, they argued, and their subsequent annexation by the Soviet Union in August 1940 must therefore be qualified as illegal acts. As a result, the Baltic states claimed, their existence was terminated only *de facto*, but continued to exist *de jure*. Accordingly, the Soviet Union never acquired sovereign title over the Baltic states, and thus remained solely the occupying power until the independence of the *de jure* existing Baltic states was finally restored also *de facto* in 1991, the Baltic states argued.[19]

While practice as related to the membership in international organizations was somewhat inconsistent with regard to that question, most Western states followed the Baltic states' claim of state identity and gave their support to this so-called continuity thesis when they restored their diplomatic relationships in 1991 (or established them anew, if they had accorded *de jure* recognition to the incorporation by the Soviet Union earlier).[20] The European Community, for instance, welcomed 'the

aggression is or shall be recognized as lawful ...'); SC Res 662, 9 August 1990, UN Doc. A/RES/662 ('... decides that annexation of Kuwait by Iraq under any form and whatever pretext has no legal validity, and is considered null and void').

[17] Vienna Convention on the Law of Treaties, 23 May 1969, 1155 UNTS 331, art. 52.

[18] SC Res 1244, 10 June 1999, UN Doc. S/RES/1244 ('Reaffirming the commitment of all Member States to the sovereignty and territorial integrity of the Federal Republic of Yugoslavia and the other States of the region'); SC Res 1472, 28 March 2003, UN Doc. S/RES/1472 ('Reaffirming the commitment of all member states to the sovereignty and territorial integrity of Iraq').

[19] See Lauri Mälksoo, *Illegal Annexation and State Continuity: The Case of the Incorporation of the Baltic States by the USSR: A Study of the Tension Between Normativity and Power in International Law* (Leiden: Martinus Nijhoff, 2003), 46–7.

[20] See ibid., 62 et seq.

restoration of the sovereignty and independence of the Baltic States which they lost in 1940',[21] and the United States announced the immediate establishment of diplomatic relations which would mark 'the culmination of the Unites States' 52 year refusal to accept the forcible incorporation of the independent Baltic States' by the Soviet Union.[22] Interestingly, Czechoslovakia, Poland, Romania, and Hungary—all states formerly part of the Eastern Bloc—also recognized the independence of the Baltic states based on the principle of state continuity.[23]

1.2 Russia's Position on the Baltic States' Annexation by the Soviet Union in 1940

The only state that openly rejected the thesis that the Baltic states are identical with the three republics prior to their incorporation by the Soviet Union in 1940 was the Russian Federation.[24] At times, not only the state continuity of the Baltic states but also the illegality of their annexation was debated. In May 1992, for example, Russian foreign minister Andrey Kozyrev stated in front of the Council of Europe that '[t]he events of 1940, and the situation, which developed in the succeeding decades in Latvia, Lithuania, and Estonia cannot be interpreted unequivocally. As is known, various political assessments exist in this respect'.[25] Other senior Russian officials made similar statements, at times denying outright the Soviet occupation of the Baltic states or even upholding the Soviet reading of the events that the Baltic parliaments had 'requested' to join the Soviet Union.[26] On 9 July 2000, for example, the illegality of the annexation was explicitly denied in a statement of the Russian Ministry of Foreign Affairs (MFA), in reaction to Lithuanian reparation claims towards Russia:

> The introduction of the forces of the USSR in 1940 was carried out with the agreement of the supreme leadership of this country, an agreement which was

[21] Declaration of European Community Foreign Ministers on the Baltic States, 27 August 1991, *British Yearbook of International Law* 62 (1991), 558.

[22] State Department Press Statement, 2 September 1991, quoted in Thomas D. Grant, 'United States Practice Relating to the Baltic States, 1940–2000', *Baltic Yearbook of International Law* 1 (2001), 23–110, 93.

[23] See Ineta Ziemele, 'The Role of State Continuity and Human Rights in Matters of Nationality of the Baltic States', in Tālavs Jundzis (ed.), *The Baltic States at Historical Crossroads: Political, Economic, and Legal Problems and Opportunities in the Context of International Cooperation at the Beginning of the 21st Century* (Riga: Latvian Academy of Sciences, 2001), 248–71.

[24] See e.g. Declaration of the Russian Ministry of Foreign Affairs, 4 July 1994, *Diplomaticheskiĭ vestnik* (1994), no. 13–14, 52–3.

[25] Speech by A.V. Kozyrev at the Committee of Ministers of the Council of Europe, 7 May 1992, *Diplomaticheskiĭ vestnik* (1992), no. 9–10, 19–22, 21. Quotation from the English translation in Boris Meissner, 'The Occupation of the Baltic States from a Present-Day Perspective', in Jundzis, *The Baltic States at Historical Crossroads* (2001) (n. 23), 437–51, 437.

[26] See the statements restated in ibid., 437–8.

> received/obtained (*polucheno*) within the framework of international law as practised at the time. The authoritative/competent functions in the Soviet period here were carried out by the national organs of authority. The decision of the USSR Supreme Soviet of August 3, 1940 concerning the acceptance of Lithuania into the framework of the Soviet Union was preceded by corresponding requests of the highest representative organs of the Baltic states. In this way, it is unjust/illegal (*nepravomerno*) to qualify the entrance of Lithuania into the make-up of the USSR as the result of unilateral actions by the latter.[27]

Since then, this line of argument has been reaffirmed on various occasions.[28] Most recently, Russian president Vladimir Putin maintained in an article entitled 'The Real Lessons of the 75th Anniversary of World II' that the Baltic states' 'accession to the USSR was implemented on a contractual basis, with the consent of the elected authorities' which 'was in line with international and state law of that time'.[29] At this point, one can therefore note a remarkable continuity in the Soviet and post-Soviet assessments of the incorporation of the Baltic states into the Soviet Union: the continuous insistence that Estonia, Latvia, and Lithuania had not been illegally annexed, but had rather voluntarily 'requested' to become part of the Soviet Union. As has been shown earlier,[30] it is precisely this reading of the events that had made it possible for the Soviet Union to portray the annexation of the Baltic states as an exercise of the right to self-determination of the peoples of Estonia, Latvia, and Lithuania.

2. *Case Study 7*: Crimea

Crimea is a peninsula on the northern coast of the Black Sea. According to a 2014 Russian census, 65.3 per cent of the Crimean population belong to the Russian ethnic group, 15.1 per cent are ethnic Ukrainian, and 10.8 per cent Crimean Tatar, a Turkic ethnic group with predominantly Sunni Islam religion.[31] Compared to the last Soviet census of 1989, the share of the Russian population remained relatively stable (67.0 per cent), while the percentage of ethnic Ukrainians living in Crimea

[27] Statement by the Russian Ministry of Foreign Affairs, 9 July 2000. Quotation from the English translation in Alfred Senn, 'What Happened in Lithuania in 1940?', *Lithuanian Foreign Policy Review* 6 (2000), 179–95, 179–80 (line breaks omitted).

[28] See e.g. 'Russia Denies Baltic "Occupation"', *BBC News*, 5 May 2005.

[29] Vladimir Putin, 'The Real Lessons of the 75th Anniversary of World War II', *The National Interest*, 18 June 2020, https://nationalinterest.org/feature/vladimir-putin-real-lessons-75th-anniversary-world-war-ii-162982.

[30] See Chapter 1 Section 3.

[31] Russian Federal State Statistics Service, *Итоги переписи населения в Крымском федеральном округе* [Results of the Census in the Crimean Federal District] (Moscow: Statistika Rossii, 2015).

was much higher (25.8 per cent), and the Crimean Tatar ethnic group significantly lower (1.6 per cent).[32]

2.1 Origins of the Conflict Over Crimea

The origins of the conflict over Crimea date back to 1783, when the Russian Empire under Catherine the Great annexed the Crimean Khanate, the longest-lived Turkic khanate originally created as a result of the dismemberment of the Golden Horde and from 1475 onwards a protectorate of the Ottoman Empire.[33] In 1802, the Crimean khanate was dissolved and integrated into the newly established Taurida Governorate of the Russian Empire.[34] Subsequently, the city of Sevastopol was expanded to become the largest naval port on the Black Sea, and it became one of the most important places of military power in the Russian Empire.[35] Around the same time, politically and religiously motivated emigration of Crimean Tatars into the Ottoman Empire coincided with migration to the peninsula from the Russian Empire.[36]

Following the Russian Revolution and during the ensuing Russian Civil War (1917–1922), Crimea changed hands numerous times. In April 1919, Soviet troops reoccupied Crimea, and, by October 1920, ultimately gained control over the territory.[37] Following the recommendations of the Tatar Bolshevik Mirsaid Sultan-Galiev, Crimea received the status of administrative autonomy, and on 18 October 1921, the Crimean Autonomous Soviet Socialist Republic (ASSR) of the Russian SFSR was established.[38]

2.2 The Dispute Over Crimea during the Soviet Era

The subsequent Sovietization of Crimea led to the removal of all Crimean Tatars in administration deemed untrustworthy from their posts and the forced collectivization and attempted destruction of Tatar agricultural life, and by 1933

[32] State Committee of the USSR on Statistics, *Национальный Состав Населения СССР, по данным Всесоюзной Переписи Населения 1989 г.* [The National Composition of the Population of the USSR According to the All-Union Population Census of 1989] (Moscow: Finansy̆ i statistika, 1991).

[33] See Alan Fisher, *The Crimean Tatars* (Stanford, CA: Hoover Institution Press, 1987), 1–47.

[34] See ibid., 82–3.

[35] On the importance of Sevastopol during the Crimean War (1853–1856) between the Russian Empire and the Ottoman Empire, France, Britain, and Sardinia see Orlando Figes, *Crimea: The Last Crusade* (London: Allan Lane, 2010), 230 et seq.

[36] See Chantal Lemercier-Quelquejay, 'The Tatars of the Crimea: A Retrospective Summary', *Central Asian Review* 16 (1968), 15–25, 15–19.

[37] Richard Pipes, *The Formation of the Soviet Union* (Cambridge, MA: Harvard University Press, 6th edn, 1997), 185–9.

[38] Ibid., 190.

approximately 50 per cent of the Tatar population had either been killed or forced to leave Crimea.[39] On a cultural level, Sovietization effectively meant Russification, and in 1938, the Latin alphabet was replaced with Cyrillic script.[40] During the Second World War, from September 1942 to October 1943, Crimea was under *de facto* control of Nazi Germany as part of the Reichskommissariat Ukraine,[41] but by May 1944, Soviet troops had regained control, resulting in the deportation of around 200,000 Crimean Tatars to Central Asia under the pretext of alleged collaboration with the Nazi occupation regime, on the order of Stalin.[42]

The deportation led to a dramatic change in the ethnic composition of Crimea, with Crimean Tatars being allowed to return to the peninsula only in the late 1980s.[43] In June 1945, the Crimean ASSR was downgraded to the Crimean Oblast within the Russian SFSR, but on 25 January 1954, the Bureau of the Central Committee of the Communist Party of the Soviet Union decided under the chairmanship of Nikita Khrushchev to cede Crimea to the Ukrainian SSR.[44] The Presidium of the Supreme Soviet of the Soviet Union ordered a respective decree, confirmed by a law on the amendment of the 1936 Soviet Constitution.[45] Although this sequence of events was in reverse order to the procedure set out in the Soviet Constitution, it was arguably regarded as irrelevant at the time.[46] (In 1992, the Russian State Duma nevertheless resolved that the cession was illegal.)[47] Thereafter, the status of Crimea was codified in article 77 of the Constitution of the Ukrainian SSR, listing the Crimean Oblast among the various regions of the Ukrainian union republic.[48]

[39] See Fisher, *The Crimean Tatars* (1987) (n. 33), 140–7.
[40] Ibid., 147.
[41] See ibid., 155–7.
[42] Ibid., 165–7. For a detailed account on the deportation of the Crimean Tatars see e.g. Brian Glyn Williams, 'Hidden Ethnocide in the Soviet Muslim Borderlands: The Ethnic Cleansing of the Crimean Tatars', *Journal of Genocide Research* 4 (2002), 357–73.
[43] See Edward Allworth (ed.), *The Tatars of Crimea: Return to the Homeland* (Durham, NC: Duke University Press, 2nd edn, 1998).
[44] This 'gift' by Khrushchev marked the 300th anniversary of the Pereyaslav Council of 1654, by which the Cossacks had sworn an oath of allegiance to the Tsar of Muscovy in exchange for military support in their battle with Poland. On the details of the transferral see Roman Solchanyk, *Ukraine and Russia: The Post-Soviet Transition* (Lanham, MD: Rowman & Littlefield, 2000), 162 et seq, and Gwendolyn Sasse, *The Crimea Question: Identity, Transition, and Conflict* (Cambridge, MA: Harvard University Press, 2007), 107–26. The underlying rationale of the decision is debated, and a full protocol of the session is missing. For a shortened documentation of the transferral see 'Как это делалось' [How it Was Done], *Rossiĭskaya gazeta*, 19 February 2004.
[45] Decree of the Presidium of the Supreme Soviet of the Soviet Union, О передаче Крымской области из состава РСФСР в состав УССР [On the Transfer of the Crimean Oblast from the Russian SFSR to the Ukrainian SSR], 19 February 1954, VVS SSSR 1954, no. 4, item 64; Law on the Amendment of the Constitution of the Soviet Union, 26 April 1954, VVS SSSR 1954, no. 10, item 211.
[46] Otto Luchterhandt, 'Der Anschluss der Krim aus völkerrechtlicher Sicht', *Archiv des Völkerrechts* 52 (2014), 137–74, 145–6. On the procedure set out in article 146 of the 1936 Soviet Constitution see Reinhard Maurach, *Handbuch der Sowjetverfassung* (Munich: Isar Verlag, 1955), 173–4, 422.
[47] See Serge Schmemann, 'Russia Votes to Void Cession of Crimea to Ukraine', *The New York Times*, 22 May 1992.
[48] Конституція (Основний Закон) Української Радянської Соціалістичної Республіки [Constitution (Basic Law) of the Ukrainian Soviet Socialist Republic], 20 April 1978.

The issue of Crimean autonomy became politically salient again during the time of *perestroĭka*, when a Russian national movement was formed and started to advocate a 'Crimea first' policy.[49] After the Ukrainian SSR had declared itself sovereign on 22 July 1990, the political elite of Crimea responded by declaring the restoration of the Crimean ASSR, a decision approved by a Crimea-wide referendum on 20 January 1991 by 93 per cent of the electorate, on an 81 per cent turnout, with the Crimean Tatars boycotting the vote.[50] In an attempt to contain the situation, the Supreme Soviet of the Ukrainian SSR reacted with a law affirming Crimea's autonomous status within the Ukrainian SSR, and amended the Ukrainian Constitution accordingly.[51]

2.3 Crimean Autonomy in Independent Ukraine

With Ukraine gaining independence in December 1991, Crimea's new autonomy status had to be adjusted to post-Soviet realities. In April 1992, the Verkhovna Rada (parliament) of Ukraine proposed a draft Law on the Delimitation of Powers between Ukraine and the Republic of Crimea, conferring on Crimea a symbolic status with vaguely defined competences. Unsatisfied with the proposal, the Verkhovna Rada of Crimea adopted the Act on State Independence of the Republic of Crimea on 5 May 1992, thereby declaring Crimea's independence/autonomy,[52] conditional upon approval by another Crimean-wide referendum scheduled for the beginning of August 1992. In the name of 'the multinational people of Crimea', a constitution was passed, defining the Republic of Crimea as a state with sovereign powers over its territory and free disposition over international relations in accordance with international law (article 1), while at the same time affirming that it was part of Ukraine, on the basis of future bilateral agreements (article 9).[53] Under the pressure of the Ukrainian central government, the scheduled referendum was however suspended,[54] but on 27 March 1994, the day of the first elections to the Verkhovna Rada of Ukraine since independence, the Crimean authorities decided to conduct simultaneously a consultative opinion poll in which the population of Crimea was asked whether the suspended regulation in article 9 of the

[49] Sasse, *The Crimea Question* (2007) (n. 44), 133.

[50] Ibid., 133–8. On the referendum see also Anne Peters, *Das Gebietsreferendum im Völkerrecht: seine Bedeutung im Licht der Staatenpraxis nach 1989* (Baden-Baden: Nomos, 1995), 190–1.

[51] Sasse, *The Crimea Question* (2007) (n. 44), 138–9.

[52] The text speaks of *samostoyatel'nost'*, thereby arguably denoting an undefined degree of autonomy rather than the more common *nezavisimost'* in the sense of full legal and political independence, see ibid., 145.

[53] Конституция Республики Крым [Constitution of the Republic of Crimea], 6 May 1992. On the ambiguity of the 1992 Crimean Constitution see Sasse, *The Crimea Question* (2007) (n. 44), 146.

[54] See Doris Wydra, 'The Crimean Conundrum: The Tug of War Between Russia and Ukraine on the Questions of Autonomy and Self-determination', *International Journal on Minority and Group Rights* 10 (2003), 111–30, 116 et seq.

1992 Crimean Constitution should be re-established. Reportedly, 90 per cent of the electorate agreed, and on 20 May 1994, the 1992 Constitution was reinstated—a step the Verkhovna Rada of Ukraine declared null and void almost a year later.[55]

Tensions between the Ukrainian central government and the local authorities in Crimea eased with the adoption of the Constitution of Ukraine on 28 June 1996, thereby finally providing for a constitutional framework for Crimea's status in independent Ukraine. According to article 136 of the Ukrainian Constitution, the Autonomous Republic of Crimea (ARC) forms 'an inseparable constituent part of Ukraine and decides on the issues ascribed to its competence within the limits of authority' determined by the Ukrainian Constitution.[56] Article 135 guarantees the ARC the right to have its own constitution, and pursuant to article 137 the ARC 'exercises normative regulation' in a number of policy areas. In cases of nonconformity of normative legal acts of the ARC with those of Ukraine, the latter prevail.

With the adoption of the Constitution of the Autonomous Republic of Crimea, set up by the Verkhovna Rada of the ARC on 21 October 1998, and approved by the Verkhovna Rada of Ukraine on 23 December of the same year, Crimea's status within the Ukrainian legal system was finally settled.[57] According to article 1 of the 1998 Crimean Constitution, the ARC is an 'integral part of Ukraine and it shall solve, within the powers conferred upon it by the Constitution of Ukraine, any and all matters coming within the scope of its powers'. At the same time, '[t]he legal foundation of the status and powers of the Autonomous Republic of Crimea ... shall be the Constitution of Ukraine, Ukrainian laws and the Constitution of the Autonomous Republic of Crimea' (article 2). Finally, article 3 of the 1998 Crimean Constitution establishs the 'concord of the interests of the Autonomous Republic of Crimea and the national interests of Ukraine' as one of the fundamental principles of the ARC.

[55] Ibid., 119. On the opinion poll see also Peters, *Das Gebietsreferendum im Völkerrecht* (1995) (n. 50), 213.

[56] Конституція України [Constitution of Ukraine], 28 June 1996, Vidomosti Verkhovnoï Radi Ukraïni 1996, no. 30, 141. This and all following quotations from the Ukrainian Constitution in the English translation in Rüdiger Wolfrum, Rainer Grote, and Charles M. Fombad (eds), *Constitutions of the Countries of the World*, vol. 15, Supp 2015-4 (Oxford: Oxford University Press). On the drafting history and the subsequent amendments since its denouncement see Rainer Grote, 'The Ukraine: Introductory Note', in ibid., 3–11. See also Wydra, 'The Crimean Conundrum' (2003) (n. 54), 124–6; Bill Bowring, 'The Crimean Autonomy: Innovation or Anomaly?', in Marc Weller and Stefan Wolff (eds), *Autonomy, Self-governance and Conflict Resolution: Innovative Approaches to Institutional Design in Divided Societies* (London: Routledge, 2005), 75–97, 84–9; and Sasse, *The Crimea Question* (2007) (n. 44), 202–3.

[57] Конституция Автономной Республики Крым [Constitution of the Autonomous Republic of Crimea], 21 October 1998; Law of Ukraine on Approval of the Constitution of the Autonomous Republic of Crimea, 23 December 1998, Vidomosti Verkhovnoï Radi Ukraïni 1999, no. 5–6, 43. All quotations from the English translation in Philip Raworth (ed.), *Constitutions of Dependencies and Territories*, vol. 11, Supp 2014-3 (Oxford: Oxford University Press). On the 1998 Crimean Constitution see also Wydra, 'The Crimean Conundrum' (2003) (n. 54), 126–7; Bowring, 'The Crimean Autonomy' (2005) (n. 56), 89–92; and Sasse, *The Crimea Question* (2007) (n. 44), 138–9.

A comparison of the 1998 Crimean Constitution with the Ukrainian Constitution offers some important ambiguities and contradictions. This regards a broad range of issues such as the competence to organize elections or the status of the Verkhovna Rada of Crimea, and is particularly sensitive with regard to the status conferred on the Russian language.[58] According to the Ukrainian Constitution, 'the free development, use and protection of Russian, and other languages of national minorities of Ukraine' is guaranteed next to Ukrainian as the state language of Ukraine.[59] The 1998 Crimean Constitution, on the other hand, states that 'Russian, being the language spoken by the majority of the population and the language acceptable for purposes of interethnic communication, shall be used in all spheres of public life' of the ARC.[60] Therefore, the Russian language is arguably 'privileged in the Crimean Constitution in a way which is in doubtful accord' with the Ukrainian Constitution, as Bill Bowring notes in his study *The Crimean Autonomy: Innovation or Anomaly?*.[61]

2.4 The 2014 Ukrainian Revolution and Russia's Intervention in Crimea

From the mid-2000s onwards, Crimea was again under pressure from the central government in Kyiv, with a vigorous policy of Ukrainization leading to growing reservations of the non-Ukrainian population.[62] In 2009 for example, the OSCE High Commissioner on National Minorities noted concerns about a reported 'tendency towards increasing radicalisation and xenophobia on the peninsula'.[63] Ukraine's relations with Russia, on the other hand, eased substantially with the election of Viktor Yanukovych as new Ukrainian president in 2010.[64] This was also reflected in the extension of the agreements regulating the stationing of the Russian Black Sea Fleet in Crimea, in exchange for substantive economic assistance until 2042, with an additional five-year renewal option.[65] In late 2013, Yanukovych decided

[58] See ibid., 204–6 for further examples.

[59] Constitution of Ukraine (n. 56), art. 10. On the controversy over this article in the Ukrainian Constitution see Andrew Wilson, *The Ukrainians: Unexpected Nation* (New Haven, CT: Yale University Press, 4th edn, 2015), 208–9.

[60] Constitution of the Autonomous Republic of Crimea (n. 57), art. 10(2).

[61] Bowring, 'The Crimean Autonomy' (2005) (n. 56), 90.

[62] See Frank Evers, 'Damaged Prospects/Damaged Dialogue in Ukraine and Crimea: The Current Situation in Ukraine and Future Co-operation with the OSCE', in Institute for Peace Research and Security Policy at the University of Hamburg (ed.), *OSCE Yearbook 2010: Yearbook on the Organization for Security and Cooperation in Europe (OSCE)* (Baden-Baden: Nomos, 2012), 221–43, 222–4.

[63] OSCE High Commissioner on National Minorities to the Permanent Council, Report, 18 June 2009, 4, http:/www.osce.org/hcnm/37812.

[64] See Evers, 'Damaged Prospects/Damaged Dialogue in Ukraine and Crimea' (2012) (n. 62), 227–8.

[65] Соглашение между Российской Федерацией и Украиной по вопросам пребывания Черноморского флота Российской Федерации на территории Украины [Agreement between the Russian Federation and Ukraine on the Stay of the Black Sea Fleet of the Russian Federation on the Territory of Ukraine], 21 April 2010, BMD 2010, no. 10, 74.

to suspend preparations for signing an association agreement with the European Union, and agreed instead with Russian president Vladimir Putin on a Ukrainian-Russian Action Plan, whereby Russia would buy Ukrainian Eurobonds worth US$15 billion, and the cost of Russian natural gas supplied to Ukraine would be cut by a third.[66] The decision led to massive protests in Kyiv for closer ties between Ukraine and the European Union, and ultimately culminated in the Ukrainian Revolution and the ousting of Yanukovych as president on 22 February 2014.[67]

Asked about the situation in Ukraine, Putin stated during an interview on 4 March 2014: 'If this is a revolution, what does this mean? In such a case it is hard not to agree with some of our experts who say that a new state is now emerging on this territory', Putin maintained, adding, '[t]his is just like what happened when the Russian Empire collapsed after the 1917 revolution and a new state emerged.'[68] Considering that changes of government, coups d'état, and similar revolutionary situations are commonly regarded as irrelevant for questions of state continuity,[69] the assessment becomes comprehensible only against its historical background: after the Russian Revolution, the Soviet Union had claimed discontinuity with the Russian Empire, an assessment contrary to the view of the majority of states at the time which assumed state continuity between the Russian Empire and the Russian SFSR.[70]

Right after Yanukovych's ousting, Putin reportedly convened an all-night meeting with security services chiefs in which he remarked at the end that 'we must start working on returning Crimea to Russia'.[71] 'Little green men', Russian special forces operating in uniforms of the local pro-Russian militias or in green uniforms similar to those worn by Russian soldiers, started to appear on the peninsula, setting up blockades and occupying government buildings.[72] On 27 February 2014, masked gunmen seized the parliament building of the Verkhovna Rada of the

[66] See 'Russia Offers Ukraine Major Economic Assistance', *BBC News*, 17 December 2013.

[67] See 'Ukraine Crisis: Timeline', *BBC News*, 13 November 2014.

[68] 'Vladimir Putin answered Journalists' Questions on the Situation in Ukraine', 4 March 2014, http://en.kremlin.ru/events/president/news/20366.

[69] See Andreas Zimmermann, 'Continuity of States', in MPEPIL (online edn), MN 9. For earlier and more detailed pronunciations of this well-established rule of customary international law see Krystyna Marek, *Identity and Continuity of States in Public International Law* (Geneva: Droz, 1954), 24–73; Wilfried Fiedler, *Das Kontinuitätsproblem im Völkerrecht: zum funktionalen Zusammenhang zwischen Völkerrecht, Staatsrecht und Politik* (Freiburg: Alber, 1978), 46–51.

[70] See Marek, *Identity and Continuity of States in Public International Law* (1954) (n. 69), 34–38; Rein Müllerson, 'The Continuity and Succession of States, by Reference to the Former USSR and Yugoslavia', *International and Comparative Law Quarterly* 42 (1993), 473–93, 476.

[71] See the Russian documentary 'Crimea: Path to the Homeland' which was aired on 15 March 2015 on the state-owned news channel Russia-24, available at: https://www.youtube.com/watch?v=3Mw4Y9jRwCQ (in Russian, with English subtitles).

[72] See Vitaly Shevchenko, '"Little Green Men" or "Russian Invaders"?', *BBC News*, 11 March 2014; Pavel Felgenhauer, 'Операция «Русский Крым»' [Operation 'Russian Crimea'], *Novaya gazeta*, 1 March 2014. The involvement of Russian special forces was initially denied, but later openly admitted by the Russian president, see 'Direct Line with Vladimir Putin', 17 April 2014, http://en.kremlin.ru/events/president/news/20796.

ARC in Simferopol, Crimea's capital, barricading themselves inside and raising the Russian flag, whilst Sergey Aksyonov was elected new prime minister of the ARC in an emergency session.[73]

On 1 March 2014, the representative of Ukraine to the UN reported in the Security Council that 'Russian troops had illegally entered the territory of Ukraine in the Crimean peninsula', amounting to 'an act of aggression against the State of Ukraine'.[74] The assessment was widely shared within the international community. The Council of the European Union for instance condemned 'the clear violation of Ukrainian sovereignty and territorial integrity by acts of aggression by the Russian Federation'.[75] Similar views were expressed by Australia, the United Kingdom, and the United States in the meeting of the UN Security Council on 3 March 2014,[76] after the Russian representative to the UN had reported that Vladimir Putin had requested the Russian Federation Council, the Russian parliament's upper house, for authorization to deploy Russian armed forces in the territory of Ukraine following a request by Yanukovych and Aksyonov 'to help restore calm in Crimea'.[77] (The permission was never officially used in practice and was later revoked, at the request of Putin.)[78]

2.5 Crimea's Declaration of Independence against the Backdrop of the *Kosovo* Advisory Opinion

Less than two weeks later, on 11 March 2014, the Verkhovna Rada of the ARC and the Sevastopol City Council jointly declared 'an independent and sovereign state', in the case that a future referendum 'shows as a direct expression of the peoples of Crimea' that the ARC should join the Russian Federation.[79] The declaration refers to the right of peoples to self-determination, and explicitly draws on the

[73] 'How the Separatists Delivered Crimea to Moscow', *Reuters*, 13 March 2014, https://in.reuters.com/article/ukraine-crisis-russia-aksyonov-idINL6N0M93AH20140313.

[74] Ukraine, UN SC 7124th meeting, 1 March 2014, UN Doc. S/PV.7124, 3.

[75] Council of the European Union, Council Conclusions on Ukraine, 3 March 2014, para. 1, https://www.consilium.euro pa.eu/media/28853/141291.pdf.

[76] UN SC 7125th meeting, 3 March 2014, UN Doc. S/PV.7125, at 10, 6, 5, respectively.

[77] Russia, UN SC 7125th meeting, 3 March 2014, UN Doc. S/PV.7125, 3, referring to Decree of the Council of Federation of the Federal Assembly of Russia No. 48-SF, Об использовании Вооружённых Сил Российской Федерации на территории Украины [On the Use of the Armed Forces of the Russian Federation on the Territory of Ukraine], 1 March 2014, http://council.gov.ru/activity/documents/39979. For an assessment of this purported justification for the use of force following an 'invitation to intervention' see Grant, 'Annexation of Crimea' (2015) (n. 14), 81–3.

[78] Decree of the Council of Federation of the Federal Assembly of Russia No. 296-SF, Об отмене постановления Совета Федерации Федерального Собрания Российской Федерации от 1 марта 2014 года № 48-СФ «Об использовании Вооружённых Сил Российской Федерации на территории Украины» [On the Repeal of the Resolution of the Council of Federation of the Federal Assembly of Russia dated March 1, 2014 No. 48-SF 'On the Use of the Armed Forces of the Russian Federation on the Territory of Ukraine'], 25 June 2014, http://council.gov.ru/activity/documents/44424.

[79] Декларация о независимости Автономной Республики Крым и г. Севастополя [Declaration of Independence of the Autonomous Republic of Crimea and the City of Sevastopol], 11 March 2014, https://www.rada.crimea.ua/news/11_03_ 2014_1.

International Court of Justice's (apparent) finding in the *Kosovo* case that unilateral declarations of independence do 'not violate international law'.[80] A statement issued on the same day by the Russian MFA embraced the joint declaration, stating that Russia 'believes that the decision of the Crimean Parliament is absolutely within its rights'.[81] This view was upheld in numerous subsequent statements, most prominently in the Russian president's address to State Duma deputies and Federation Council members, held on 18 March 2014 in Moscow (the so-called Crimea Speech):

> [T]he Crimean authorities referred to the well-known Kosovo precedent – a precedent our western colleagues created with their own hands in a very similar situation, when they agreed that the unilateral separation of Kosovo from Serbia, exactly what Crimea is doing now, was legitimate and did not require any permission from the country's central authorities. Pursuant to Article 2, Chapter 1 of the United Nations Charter, the UN International Court agreed with this approach and made the following comment in its ruling of July 22, 2010, and I quote: 'No general prohibition may be inferred from the practice of the Security Council with regard to declarations of independence', and 'General international law contains no prohibition on declarations of independence'.[82]

This line of argument is questionable for a number of reasons. First of all, the *Kosovo* advisory opinion is not a 'ruling' and has, as the term already implies, no binding force.[83] Second, Putin's reference to the International Court of Justice's (ICJ) finding in the *Kosovo* advisory opinion is in sharp contrast to Russia's own views expressed after Kosovo's unilateral declaration of independence in 2008, and appears therefore inconsistent.[84] Third, to conclude from this statement that *all* unilateral declarations of independence don't violate international law would

[80] See ICJ, Accordance with International Law of the Unilateral Declaration of Independence in Respect of Kosovo, Advisory Opinion (Kosovo Advisory Opinion), 22 July 2010, ICJ Reports 2010, 403, para. 56.

[81] Statement by the Russian Ministry of Foreign Affairs Regarding the Adoption of the Declaration of Independence of the Autonomous Republic of Crimea and Sevastopol, 11 March 2014, http://www.mid.ru/ru/press_service/spokesman/official_statement/-/asset_publisher/t2GCdmD8RNIr/content/id/71274.

[82] Address by President of the Russian Federation, 18 March 2014, http://en.kremlin.ru/events/president/news/20603.

[83] See ICJ, Difference Relating to Immunity from Legal Process of a Special Rapporteur of the Commission on Human Rights, Advisory Opinion, 29 April 1999, ICJ Reports 1999, 62, para. 25 ('A distinction should . . . be drawn between the advisory nature of the Court's task and the particular effects that parties to an existing dispute between the advisory nature of the Court's task and the particular effects that parties to an existing dispute may wish to attribute, in their mutual relations, to an advisory opinion of the Court, which, "as such, . . . has no binding force"'). On the nature and importance of advisory opinions see e.g. Hugh Thirlway, 'Advisory Opinion', in MPEPIL (online edn).

[84] See Chapter 3 Section 1above. Ukraine even argued that Russia has lost its right to refer to the ICJ's conclusion as a result of the principle of estoppel, see Position of Ukraine on the Russian Federation MFA's Statement of 11 March on the Declaration of Independence of the Autonomous Republic of

mean to ignore another passage in the *Kosovo* advisory opinion in which the court explicitly affirmed the illegality of other unilateral declarations of independence in the past whose illegality 'stemmed not from the unilateral character of these declarations as such but from the fact that they were, or would have been, connected with the unlawful use of force or other egregious violations of norms of general international law, in particular those of a peremptory character (*jus cogens*)'.[85] Arguably, Crimea's declaration of independence must therefore be considered illegal for the same reasons.[86] Russia's admitted deployment and use of special forces and regular military troops in Crimea amount to a *prima facie* violation of the use of force in the sense of article 2(4) of the UN Charter, and constitutes an act of aggression under the 1974 Definition of Aggression.[87] Moreover, the mere authorization by the Russian Federation Council to deploy Russian armed forces in the territory of Ukraine can possibly be qualified as an act of unlawful threat of force against Ukraine, equally prohibited under article 2(4) of the UN Charter.[88]

2.6 The Crimean Vote as an Abuse of the Institution of Referendum

The planned 'referendum' initially should have taken place on 25 May 2014, but was rescheduled first for 30 March 2014, and then again for 16 March 2014.[89] In the vote, the population of Crimea was asked to choose between the following alternatives: '1) Do you support the reunification of Crimea with Russia as a subject of the Russian Federation?', and '2) Do you support the restoration of the

Crimea and Sevastopil, 2, http://www.europarl.europa.eu/meetdocs/2009_2014/documents/d-ua/dv/dua_2014_0319_14_/dua_2014_0319_14_en.pdf.

[85] ICJ, Kosovo Advisory Opinion (2010) (n. 80), para. 81.

[86] See also Jure Vidmar, 'The Annexation of Crimea and the Boundaries of the Will of the People', *German Law Journal* 3 (2015), 365–83, 374–6.

[87] Bilková, 'The Use of Force by the Russian Federation in Crimea' (2015) (n. 14), 30–3. See also Antonello Tancredi, 'The Russian Annexation of the Crimea: Questions Relating to the Use of Force', *Questions of International Law* 1 (2014), 16–23; Mary Ellen O'Connell, 'The Crisis in Ukraine–2014', in Tom Ruys and Olivier Corten (eds), *The Use of Force in International Law: A Case-based Approach* (Oxford: Oxford University Press, 2018), 855–72.

[88] Bilková, 'The Use of Force by the Russian Federation in Crimea' (2015) (n. 14), 30–1. For Russia's purported justifications with regard to the use of force see Grant, 'Annexation of Crimea' (2015) (n. 14), 80–3. See also Hans-Joachim Heintze, 'Völkerrecht und Sezession—Ist die Annexion der Krim eine zulässige Wiedergutmachung sowjetischen Unrechts?', *Journal of International Law of Peace and Armed Conflict* 27 (2014), 129–38, 133–4, and Peter Hilpold, 'Ukraine, Crimea and New International Law: Balancing International Law with Arguments Drawn from History', *Chinese Journal of International Law* 14 (2015), 237–70, 247–56.

[89] Resolution of the Verkhovna Rada of the Autonomous Republic of Crimea No. 1702-6/14, Про проведення загальнокримського референдуму [On Holding an All-Crimean Referendum], 6 March 2014. The Ukrainian president suspended the decree one day later, see 'Letter Dated 15 March 2014 from the Permanent Representative of Ukraine to the United Nations Addressed to the President of the Security Council', 17 March 2014, UN Doc. S/2014/193.

Constitution of the Republic of Crimea of 1992 and the status of Crimea as part of Ukraine?'[90] Only one day later, Russian news agencies reported that 96.77 per cent of the electorate had opted for Crimea's 'reunification' with Russia, on an 83.1 per cent turnout.[91] The OSCE had refused to observe the vote because 'basic criteria for a decision in a constitutional framework' had not been met,[92] and large parts of the international community rejected the vote as irrelevant or illegal. For example, the Parliamentary Assembly of the Council of Europe issued a statement declaring the result of the vote to have 'no legal effect',[93] and the presidents of the European Council and the European Commission jointly declared that the European Union 'does neither recognise the illegal and illegitimate referendum in Crimea nor its outcome'.[94] On 27 March 2017, UN General Assembly Resolution 68/262 was adopted, by a vote of 100 in favour and 11 against, with 58 abstentions, stressing that 'the referendum held in the Autonomous Republic of Crimea and the city of Sevastopol on 16 March 2014, having no validity, cannot form the basis for any alteration of the status of the Autonomous Republic of Crimea or the city of Sevastopol'.[95]

When assessing the legality of the Crimean vote under international law, it is first of all important to note that constitutional aspects are irrelevant in this regard.[96] Moreover, plebiscites or referendums are traditionally not regarded as

[90] See Constitutional Court of Ukraine, *У справі за конституційними поданнями виконуючого обов'язки Президента України, Голови Верховної Ради України та Уповноваженого Верховної Ради України з прав людини щодо відповідності Конституції України (конституційності) Постанови Верховної Ради Автономної Республіки Крим «Про проведення загальнокримського референдуму»* [In the Case on the Constitutional Petition of the Acting President of Ukraine, the Chairman of the Verkhovna Rada of Ukraine, the Ukrainian Parliament Commissioner for Human Rights Concerning the Compliance with the Constitution of Ukraine (Constitutionality) of the Resolution of the Verkhovna Rada of the Autonomous Republic of Crimea 'On Holding of the All-Crimean Referendum'], 14 March 2014, Decision No. 2-rp/2014, para. 1.

[91] See e.g. 'Crimea Declares Independence, seeks UN Recognition', *Russia Today*, 17 March 2014, http://on.rt.com/prw9tz. The numbers are debated; for example, a report by the Presidential Council for Civil Society and Human Rights initially reported significantly lower numbers. Following corresponding media reports, one of the authors of the report indicated its 'unofficial' nature, see Evgeny Bobrov, 'Проблемы жителей Крыма' [Problems of the Inhabitants of Crimea], 22 April 2014, http://president-sovet.ru/members/blogs/bobrov_e_a/problemy-zhiteley-kryma- (the original report of 21 April 2014 has been deleted from the council's website).

[92] OSCE, 'OSCE Chair says Crimean Referendum in its Current Form is Illegal and Calls for Alternative Ways to Address the Crimean Issue', *OSCE Press Release*, 11 March 2014, https://www.osce.org/cio/116313.

[93] PACE Res 1988 (2014), Recent Developments in Ukraine: Threats to the Functioning of Democratic Institutions, 9 April 2014, para. 16.

[94] Joint Statement on Crimea by President of the European Council Herman Van Rompuy and President of the European Commission José Manuel Barroso, 18 March 2014, EUCO 63/14.

[95] GA Res 68/262 (Territorial Integrity of Ukraine), 27 March 2014, UN Doc. A/RES/68/262. See Sergey Sayapin, 'The United Nations General Assembly Resolution 68/262 in the Context of General International Law', *European Politics and Law Discourse* 2 (2015), 19–30.

[96] The Ukrainian Constitutional Court as well as the Venice Commission determined that the referendum was unconstitutional under Ukrainian law, see Constitutional Court of Ukraine, Decision No. 2-rp/2014 (n. 90); Venice Commission, *Whether the Decision Taken by the Supreme Council of the Autonomous Republic of Crimea in Ukraine to Organize a Referendum on Becoming a Constituent*

necessary requirements for territorial alignments.[97] However, an important strand in international law scholarship argues in favour of a democratic legitimization of all territorial alignments, preferably through a direct democratic decision, that is by territorial referendum.[98] Notably, this view was also taken by the Badinter Commission in the dissolution process of Yugoslavia, holding in its Opinion No. 4 that the independence of Bosnia and Herzegovina should not be recognized since it—unlike the other republics seeking independence—had not yet held a referendum on independence.[99]

Arguably, these rules are transferable to the situation in Crimea,[100] but in any case, Anne Peters' reasoning is persuasive that '*[i]f* a state decides to hold a referendum, *then* it must satisfy international standards. And when these standards are not respected, a territorial referendum cannot serve as a legal basis for a territorial change.'[101] Therefore, since a vote did take place in Crimea, the question arises whether it satisfied international standards.

According to Peters, at least four procedural standards for referendums can be identified:[102] peacefulness; universal, equal, free, and secret suffrage;[103] framework conditions of freedom of media and neutrality of the authorities;[104] and

Territory of the Russian Federation or Restoring Crimea's 1992 Constitution is Compatible with Constituional Principles, 21 March 2014, Opinion No. 762/2014, CDL-AD(2014)002.

[97] See e.g. Alfred Verdross and Bruno Simma, *Universelles Völkerrecht: Theorie und Praxis* (Berlin: Duncker & Humblot, 3rd edn, 1984), MN 1159; Robert Jennings and Arthur Watts (eds), *Oppenheim's International Law* (Harlow: Longman, 9th edn, 1993), vol. 1, part 2, MN 248; James Crawford, *Brownlie's Principles of Public International Law* (Oxford: Oxford University Press, 8th edn, 2012), 243.

[98] See e.g. Peters, *Das Gebietsreferendum im Völkerrecht* (1995) (n. 50), 470; Steven R. Ratner, 'Drawing a Better Line: *Uti Possidetis* and the Borders of New States', *American Journal of International Law* 90 (1996), 590–624, 622–3; Antonello Tancredi, 'A Normative "Due Process" in the Creation of States Through Secession', in Marcello Kohen (ed.), *Secession: International Law Perspectives* (Cambridge: Cambridge University Press, 2006), 171–207, 190–1.

[99] Conference on Yugoslavia Arbitration Commission, *On International Recognition of the Socialist Republic of Bosnia-Hercegovina by the European Community and its Member States*, Opinion No. 4, 14 January 1992, 1992 ILM 1501.

[100] Anne Peters, 'The Crimean Vote of March 2014 as an Abuse of the Institution of the Territorial Referendum', in Christian Calliess (ed.), *Staat und Mensch im Kontext des Völker- und Europarechts: Liber Amicorum für Torsten Stein* (Baden-Baden: Nomos Verlag, 2015), 255–80, 268. Concurring Luchterhandt, 'Der Anschluss der Krim aus völkerrechtlicher Sicht' (2014) (n. 46), 156.

[101] Peters, 'The Crimean Vote of March 2014 as an Abuse of the Institution of the Territorial Referendum' (2015) (n. 100), 272.

[102] Ibid., 280. On the procedural requirements of referendums under international customary law in more detail see Sarah Wambaugh, *Plebiscites Since the World War* (Washington, D.C.: Washington Carnegie Endowment of Peace, 1933), 506–507; Harold S. Johnson, *Self-determination within the Community of Nations* (Leiden: Sijthoff, 1967), 135–58; Peters, *Das Gebietsreferendum im Völkerrecht* (1995) (n. 50), 499–501.

[103] Cf. International Covenant on Civil and Political Rights, 1967 ILM 368, art. 25: 'Every citizen shall have the right and the opportunity ...: (b) To vote and to be elected at genuine periodic elections which shall be universal and equal suffrage and shall be held by secret ballot, guaranteeing the free expression of the will of the electors ...'.

[104] Cf. Venice Commission, *On the Compatibility of the Existing Legislation in Montenegro Concerning the Organization of Referendums with Applicable International Standards*, 19 December 2005, Doc. CDL-AD(2005)041, para. 12: 'the authorities must provide objective information; the public media

international referendum observation.[105] Arguably, none of these international legal standards were respected in the Crimean vote of 16 March 2014, Russia's claim in the Security Council notwithstanding that 'a free referendum' was held, in 'strict compliance with international law and democratic procedure, [and] without outside interference'.[106]

The universal, equal, free, and secret suffrage as well as the framework conditions of freedom of media and neutrality of the authorities were questionable, and international monitoring of the Crimean referendum did not take place.[107] But most importantly, the vote was not held under peaceful conditions, *the* classic requirement for unimpeded voting on territorial issues.[108] (Although initially denied, Russian president Putin had later admitted the military presence of Russian forces in Crimea, arguing that 'Russia created conditions—with the help of special armed groups and the Armed Forces, I will say it straight—but only for the free expression of the will of the people living in Crimea and Sevastopol'.)[109] One can therefore only agree once more with Anne Peters, who arrives at the following conclusion in her legal analysis on the Crimean vote:

> The basic rule of pacification and neutralisation is of paramount importance for the assessment of the 2014 referendum in Crimea. It was held in front of the guns and tanks of the Russian army and unidentified troops. For this reason alone, the referendum cannot deploy a legal value under international law. It cannot be said that, against the background of the history of Crimea, even in the absence of Russian and unknown troops, a majority of the voters would in any case have voted in favour of joining Russia, even if the exact rate of approval might have been lower. Such an argument is unacceptable, because the prohibition of conducting a referendum in a non-pacified territory, under threat of force, is exactly

have to be neutral, in particular in news coverage; the authorities must not influence the outcome of the vote by excessive, one sided campaigning; the use of public funds by the authorities for campaigning; the use of public funds by the authorities for campaigning purposes must be restricted'.

[105] Cf. Venice Commission, *Guidelines on the Holding of Referendums*, 20 January 2009, Doc. CDL-AD(2007)008rev, point 3.2: 'b. Observation must not be confined to election day itself, but must include the referendum campaign and, where appropriate, the voter registration period and the signature collection period. It must make it possible to determine whether irregularities occurred before, during or after the vote. It must always be possible during vote counting. c. Observers should be able to go everywhere where operations connected with the referendum are taking place (for example, vote counting and verification). The places where observers are not entitled to be present should be clearly specified by law, with the reasons for their being banned.'

[106] Russia, UN SC 7144th meeting, 19 March 2014, UN Doc. S/PV.7144, 8.

[107] Peters, 'The Crimean Vote of March 2014 as an Abuse of the Institution of the Territorial Referendum' (2015) (n. 100), 274–8. See also Luchterhandt, 'Der Anschluss der Krim aus völkerrechtlicher Sicht' (2014) (n. 46), 157–9.

[108] See already Wambaugh, *Plebiscites Since the World War* (1933) (n. 102), 507: 'A plebiscite not effectively neutralized is a crime against the inhabitants of the area as well as against political science itself.'

[109] 'Direct Line with Vladimir Putin' (2014) (n. 72).

a procedural and formal device to forestall speculations about an ostensible real will of the concerned population.[110]

2.7 The 'Legal Arguments for Russia's Position on Crimea and Ukraine'

On 17 March 2014, the day after the vote and the day of the announcement of its result, the Republic of Crimea was proclaimed as an independent state, immediately recognized as such by the Russian Federation.[111] Following the 'coup' in Kyiv, Russia argued, Crimea had a right to secede. The argument was first raised by the Russian foreign minister,[112] and has consistently been affirmed since. On the occasion of the 'three-year anniversary of Crimea's unification with Russia', for example, the spokesperson of the Russian MFA claimed that Crimea's independence was a 'legitimate exercise of the right of the people of Crimea to self-determination following an armed coup in Ukraine and the mayhem wreaked by radical national forces that did not hesitate to use terror and intimidation on both political opponents and the population of entire regions of that country', and concluded that '[t]he legality and validity of this exercise of the right to self-determination are on graphic display today, in light of the disgraceful bloody campaign waged by the Kiev regime against its own people'.[113]

The most detailed legal argument in this vein was provided in a document disseminated by the Russian MFA via various Russian embassies' websites. According to this paper, dated 27 October 2014 and entitled 'Legal Arguments for Russia's Position on Crimea and Ukraine', Crimea's secession is 'a legitimate form of the implementation of the right to self-determination by the people of Crimea in the situation when a coup accompanied by the use of force was carried out in Ukraine with an external support'.[114] Grasping this finding in terms of international law is difficult for a number of reasons:

[110] Peters, 'The Crimean Vote of March 2014 as an Abuse of the Institution of the Territorial Referendum' (2015) (n. 100), 274.

[111] Decree of the President of Russia No. 63, О признании Республики Крым [On the Recognition of the Republic of Crimea], 17 March 2014, SZRF 2014, no. 12, item 1259.

[112] See Speech by the Russian Foreign Minister, Sergey Lavrov, and his Answers to Questions from Deputies during the Plenary Session of the State Duma of the Russian Federation, 20 March 2014, http://www.mid.ru/en/web/guest/foreign_policy/news/-/asset_publisher/cKNonkJE02Bw/content/id/69626.

[113] Briefing by Foreign Ministry Spokesperson Maria Zakharova, 16 March 2017, http://www.mid.ru/en/web/guest/foreign_policy/news/-/asset_publisher/cKNonkJE02Bw/content/id/2687802.

[114] Правовые обоснования позиции России по Крыму и Украине [Legal Arguments for Russia's Position on Crimea and Ukraine], 27 October 2014, available at: http://russische-botschaft.ru/wp-content/uploads/2014/10/Krym-pravovye-osnovy.doc. An English translation of the document was published on the website of the Permanent Delegation of the Russian Federation to UNESCO, see http://russianunesco.ru/eng/article/1637. See Oleksandr Zadorozhnii, 'To Justify against all Odds: The Annexation of Crimea in 2014 and the Russian Legal Scholarship', *Polish Yearbook of International Law*

A first hurdle is the terminology used in the document. Standard notions of international law like 'secession', 'use of force', or 'territorial integrity' are used throughout the text in a very flexible or even distorted manner. For instance, the separation of South Sudan from Sudan in 2011 is cited as an example of successful secession, notwithstanding that the former withdrew *with the consent* from the latter.[115] Later in the document, Ukraine's territorial integrity is claimed to be 'destroyed' as a result of the policies pursued by the Ukrainian interim government, and the stated 'use of force' mentioned in the overall finding turns out to be the ousting of Yanukovych 'by force' later in the text—and not the use of force by one state against another state enshrined in article 2(4) of the UN Charter and prohibited under international law.[116]

A second aspect concerns the depth of the discussion on the right of peoples to self-determination provided at the beginning of the document. Although far less detailed than the considerations in Russia's written statement to the ICJ in the *Kosovo* case, the 'Legal Arguments for Russia's Position on Crimea and Ukraine' at least refer to the main international instruments dealing with the right to self-determination, i.e. article 1(2) of the UN Charter, common article 1 of the Human Rights Covenants as well as the most relevant resolutions by the UN General Assembly and judgments and advisory opinions by the ICJ.[117] However, in a way similar to the Russian Constitutional Court's findings in the *Tatarstan* and *Chechnya* decisions,[118] there is no differentiation between the different sources of the international documents the text refers to nor does it discuss their binding nature or general relevance. As such, the crucial question whether the right of peoples to self-determination may also confer a right of secession under international law is reduced to the savings clause of the Friendly Relations Declaration, resulting to the straightforward statement that the '[i]mplementation of the right to secession may occur in three cases: in a colonial context, in situations of foreign occupation

35 (2015), 139–70, 157–60; Maria Issaeva, 'Quarter of a Century on From the Soviet Era: Reflections on Russian Doctrinal Responses to the Annexation of Crimea', *Russian Law Journal* 5 (2017), no. 3, 87–112, 99–104; Bill Bowring, 'Who Are the "Crimea People" or "People of Crimea"? The Fate of the Crimean Tatars, Russia's Legal Justification for Annexation, and Pandora's Box', in Sergey Sayapin and Evhen Tsybulenko (eds), *The Use of Force against Ukraine and International Law* (The Hague: T.M.C. Asser Press, 2018), 21–40, 24–5.

115 Legal Arguments for Russia's Position on Crimea and Ukraine (2014) (n. 114), para. 1.
116 Ibid., para. 5.
117 See ibid., fnn. 1–2, referring to the Friendly Relations Declaration (n. 16); the Colonial Independence Declaration, GA Res 1514(XV), 14 December 1960, UN Doc. A/4684, 66–7; ICJ, Legal Consequences for States of the Continued Presence of South Africa in Namibia (South West Africa) notwithstanding Security Council Resolution 276 (1970), Advisory Opinion, 21 June 1971, ICJ Reports 1971, 16, paras 52–53; ICJ, East Timor (Portugal v Australia), Judgment, 30 June 1995, ICJ Reports 1995, 90, para. 29; ICJ, Legal Consequences of the Construction of a Wall in the Occupied Palestinian Territory, Advisory Opinion (Israeli Wall Advisory Opinion), 9 July 2004, ICJ Reports 2004, 136, para. 88; and ICJ, Kosovo Advisory Opinion (2010) (n. 80), para. 72.
118 See Chapter 2 Sections 2 and 3.

and in "the most extreme situations"'.[119] The claim is substantiated with a loose reference to *Reference Re Secession of Québec* of the Canadian Supreme Court, which however *at no point* in its legal opinion maintains the existence of a right to secede in 'the most extreme situations' (as the court is quoted in the document), but only ponders on the question if, 'as a last resort', such a right exits 'when a people is blocked from the meaningful exercise of its right to self-determination internally'—*without* ultimately answering it.[120]

A third and arguably the most problematic aspect regards the fundamentally different reading of the situation on the ground in Crimea following the Ukrainian Revolution, purportedly giving rise to a right to secede in the case at hand. In the 'Legal Arguments for Russia's Position on Crimea and Ukraine', Russia maintains that 'it is a fact that Crimea's secession from Ukraine and its accession to Russia took place in extreme conditions of impossibility to implement the right to self-determination within the framework of Ukraine'.[121] The assessment enabling this reading of events was established in the White Book on Violations of Human Rights and the Rule of Law in Ukraine, published by the Russian MFA in April 2014:

> [U]nder the influence of extremists from ultranationalistic and neo-Nazi forces, with the active multidimensional support of the USA and the European Union and its members, the protests in Ukraine which bore an initially peaceful character rapidly escalated into a coercive rebellion and, in the end, the forceful seizure of power and unconstitutional coup d'etat. These dramatic events were accompanied by widespread and gross violations of human rights and freedoms on the part of the self-proclaimed government and its supporters. As a result, manifestations of extremist, ultranationalist, and neo-Nazistic sentiments, religious intolerance, xenophobia, blatant blackmail, threats, pressure placed by the Maidan leaders on their opponents, 'purges' and arrest among them, repression, physical violence, and sometimes plain criminal lawlessness have become commonplace in Ukraine.[122]

A few days earlier and in sharp contrast to this assessment, the Office of the UN High Commissioner for Human Rights had published its Report on the Human Rights Situation in Ukraine, observing succinctly that 'it is widely assessed that

[119] Legal Arguments for Russia's Position on Crimea and Ukraine (2014) (n. 114), para. 1.

[120] See Supreme Court of Canada, *Reference Re Secession of Québec*, DLR 1998, 4th Series, 386, paras 134–138.

[121] Legal Arguments for Russia's Position on Crimea and Ukraine (2014) (n. 114), para. 1.

[122] 'White Book on Violations of Human Rights and the Rule of Law in Ukraine (November 2013–March 2014)', April 2014, 63, available at: http://www.mid.ru/documents/10180/698385/White+Book.pdf/d806eb55-5a78-459b-950c-2072ebbcf7fe. Similar assessments of the situation in Ukraine were made on numerous occasions, see e.g. Russia, UN SC 7125th meeting, 3 March 2014, 3, UN Doc. S/PV.7125, and Russia, UN SC 7138th meeting, 14 March 2014, 2, UN Doc. S/PV.7138.

Russian-speakers have not been subject to threats in Crimea'.[123] Since a report of an international organization is *prima facie* more reliable than a report issued by a regional power involved in a conflict, the argument of a right to secede, even if in theory accepted, must therefore be rejected.[124]

2.8 Annexation and Incorporation of Crimea into the Russian Federation

On 18 March 2014, the Treaty on the Accession of the Republic of Crimea to the Russian Federation was signed between Russia and the Republic of Crimea.[125] On the same day, Russian president Vladimir Putin submitted a request to the Russian Constitutional Court to verify its compliance with the Russian Constitution.[126] In its *Crimea* decision of 19 March 2014, the court limited itself to conclude that the accession agreement 'cannot be regarded as breaking the Constitution of the Russian Federation as to the procedure of signing, conclusion and entry into force', arguing that it is not the court's duty to 'assess the political expediency associated with the execution of an international treaty'.[127]

[123] Office of the United Nations High Commissioner for Human Rights, Report on the Human Rights Situation in Ukraine, 15 April 2014, para. 89, https://www.ohchr.org/Documents/Countries/UA/Ukraine_Report_15April2014.doc.

[124] Anne Peters, 'Das Völkerrecht der Gebietsreferenden. Das Beispiel der Ukraine 1991–2014', *Osteuropa* 64 (2014), no. 5–6, 101–33, 120–4. On Russia's claim of Crimea having a right to secede see also Heintze, 'Völkerrecht und Sezession' (2014) (n. 88), 135–6; Luchterhandt, 'Der Anschluss der Krim aus völkerrechtlicher Sicht' (2014) (n. 46), 153; Theodore Christakis, 'Self-determination, Territorial Integrity and *Fait Accompli* in the Case of Crimea', *Zeitschrift für ausländisches öffentliches Recht und Völkerrecht* 75 (2015), 75–100, 88–9; Grant, 'Annexation of Crimea' (2015) (n. 14), 71; Hilpold, 'Ukraine, Crimea and New International Law' (2015) (n. 88), 265; Vidmar, 'The Annexation of Crimea and the Boundaries of the Will of the People' (2015) (n. 86), 371–2.

[125] Договор между Российской Федерацией и Республикой Крым о принятии в Российскую Федерацию Республики Крым и образовании в составе Российской Федерации новых субъектов [Treaty between the Russian Federation and the Republic of Crimea on the Accession of the Republic of Crimea into the Russian Federation and on Creation of New Federative Entities within the Russian Federation], 18 March 2014, BMD 2014, no. 6, 88. English translation: Anatoly Pronin, 'Republic of Crimea: A Two-Day State', *Russian Law Journal* 3 (2015), no. 1, 133–42, 137–41 (Annex).

[126] Запрос о проверке соответствия Конституции Договора о принятии Республики Крым в Российскую Федерацию [Request to Verify the Compliance of the Treaty on Accession of the Republic of Crimea to the Russian Federation with the Constitution], 18 March 2014. English translation: http://en.kremlin.ru/acts/news/20614.

[127] Constitutional Court of Russia, *По делу о проверке конституционности не вступившего в силу международного договора между Российской Федерацией и Республикой Крым о принятии в Российскую Федерацию Республики Крым и образовании в составе Российской Федерации новых субъектов* [In the Case on the Verification of the Constitutionality of an International Treaty that has not Entered into Force between the Russian Federation and the Republic of Crimea on the Admission to the Russian Federation of the Republic of Crimea and the Formation of New Subjects within the Russian Federation] (Crimea Decision), Decision No. 6-P, 19 March 2014, SZRF 2014, no. 13, item 1527. English summary available at: http://ksrf.ru/en/decision/judgments/documents/resume19032014.pdf.

Leaving constitutional aspects and procedural deficiencies of the decision aside,[128] the Russian Constitutional Court's *Crimea* decision is remarkable also with regard to international law aspects for at least two reasons. First, by calling the accession agreement an 'international treaty' and by furthermore assuming the eligibility of its provisional application with reference to article 25 of the Vienna Convention on the Law of Treaties,[129] the Russian Constitutional Court apparently considers the self-proclaimed Republic of Crimea to qualify as a state, since only states can conclude treaties under the Vienna Convention.[130] Second, it may be recalled from Chapter 2 that article 15(4) of the Russian Constitution prescribes '[u]universally recognized principles and norms of international law as well as international agreements of the Russian Federation' to be an 'integral part of its legal system'.[131] It seems therefore highly doubtful whether the Russian Constitutional Court could ignore international obligations of Russia towards Ukraine enshrined in the 1997 Treaty on Friendship and other bilateral and multilateral agreements of Russia when assessing the constitutionality of the accession agreement under the Russian Constitution.

On 21 March 2014, the accession agreement was ratified and formalized in two federal constitutional laws, thereby making Sevastopol and the Republic of Crimea the eighty-fourth and eighty-fifth federal subject of the Russian Federation, respectively.[132] In response, international organizations such as the European Union

[128] For assessments of the Crimea decision under Russian constitutional law see Carmen Schmidt, 'Das russische Verfassungsgericht zum Beitritt der Krim und Sewastopol—das Urteil vom 19. März 2014', *Osteuropa-Recht* 60 (2014), 254–5; Elena Lukyanova, 'On the Rule of Law in the Context of Russian Foreign Policy', *Russian Law Journal* 3 (2015), no. 2, 10–36.

[129] Constitutional Court of Russia, Crimea Decision (2014) (n. 127), para. 3.

[130] Cf. Vienna Convention on the Law of Treaties (VCLT), 23 May 1969, 1155 UNTS 331, art. 2(1)(a): 'For the purposes of the present Convention ... "treaty" means an international agreement concluded between States in written form and governed by international law ...'. Misleading therefore Grant, *Annexation of Crimea* (2015) (n. 14), 71, who, apparently unaware of the court's explicit reference to article 25 VCLT, discusses the possibility of the court qualifying Crimea not as a state, but merely as one of 'other subjects of international law' in the sense of article 3(c) VCLT.

[131] Конституция Российской Федерации [Constitution of the Russian Federation], 12 December 1993, *Rossiĭskaya gazeta*, 25 December 1995. Quotation from the English translation available on the Russian Constitutional Court's website: http://www.ksrf.ru/en/info/legalbases/constitutionrf/documents/constitution-eng.pdf.

[132] Federal Constitutional Law of Russia No. 6-FKZ, О принятии в Российскую Федерацию Республики Крым и образовании в составе Российской Федерации новых субъектов—Республики Крым и города федерального значения Севастополя [On the Admission to the Russian Federation of the Republic of Crimea and the Formation within the Russian Federation of New Subjects—the Republic of Crimea and the City of Federal Importance Sevastopol], 21 March 2014, SZRF 2014, no. 12, item 1201; Federal Constitutional Law of Russia No. 36-FKZ, О ратификации Договора между Российской Федерацией и Республикой Крым о принятии в Российскую Федерацию Республики Крым и образовании в составе Российской Федерации новых субъектов [On Ratification of the Treaty between the Russian Federation and the Republic of Crimea on the Admission to the Russian Federation of the Republic of Crimea and the Formation of New Entities Within the Russian Federation], 21 March 2014, SZRF 2014, no. 12, item 1202. On the incorporation process in more detail see Sebastian Pritzkow, 'Dokumentation zur Integration der Krim in die Russische Föderation', *Osteuropa-Recht* 60 (2014), 426–36, and Otto Luchterhandt, 'Die Krim-Krise von 2014. Staats- und völkerrechtliche Aspekte', *Osteuropa* 64 (2014), no. 5–6, 61–86, 84 et seq.

and numerous states explicitly condemned the process as annexation,[133] and there is broad consensus in Western international law scholarship that the incorporation of Crimea and Sevastopol into Russia qualifies as the forceful acquisition of territory by one state at the expense of another state, that is annexation illegal under international law.[134]

Russia, by contrast, follows a different line of argument. The following excerpt from the Russian president's Crimea Speech illustrates the official rationale of the incorporation of Crimea into the Russian Federation:

> In people's hearts and minds, Crimea has always been an inseparable part of Russia. This firm conviction is based on truth and justice and was passed from generation to generation, over time, under any circumstances, despite all the dramatic changes our country went through during the entire 20th century. After the revolution, the Bolsheviks, for a number of reasons—may God judge them—added large sections of the historical South of Russia to the Republic of Ukraine. This was done with no consideration for the ethnic make-up of the population, and today these areas form the southeast of Ukraine. Then, in 1954, a decision was made to transfer [the] Crimean Region to Ukraine, along with Sevastopol, despite the fact that it was a federal city. This was the personal initiative of the Communist Party head Nikita Khrushchev. . . .
>
> What matters now is that this decision was made in clear violation of the constitutional norms that were in place even then. The decision was made behind the scenes. Naturally, in a totalitarian state nobody bothered to ask the citizens of Crimea and Sevastopol. They were faced with the fact. People, of course, wondered why all of a sudden Crimea became part of Ukraine. But on the whole—and we must state this clearly, we all know it—this decision was treated as a formality of sorts because the territory was transferred within the boundaries of a single state. Back then, it was impossible to imagine that Ukraine and Russia may split up and become two separate states. However, this has happened. Unfortunately, what seemed impossible became a reality. The USSR fell apart. Things developed

[133] See e.g. 'Joint Statement on Crimea by President of the European Council Herman Van Rompuy and President of the European Commission José Manuel Barroso' (2014) (n. 94); 'G-7 Leaders' Statement on Ukraine', 26 April 2014, available for download at: https://www.g7germany.de/Content/DE/_Anlagen/G7_G20/G7-leaders_statement-ukr-2014-04-26-eng___blob=publicationFile&v=6.pdf. For further reactions by other states and international organizations see the overview by Grant, 'Annexation of Crimea' (2015) (n. 14), 87–91.

[134] See e.g. Luchterhandt, 'Der Anschluss der Krim aus völkerrechtlicher Sicht' (2014) (n. 46), 171; Tancredi, 'The Russian Annexation of the Crimea' (2014) (n. 87); Christian Walter, 'Postscript: Self-determination, Secession, and the Crimean Crisis 2014', in Christian Walter, Antje von Ungern-Sternberg, and Kavus Abushov (eds), *Self-determination and Secession in International Law* (Oxford: Oxford University Press, 2014), 293–312, 310; Bilková, 'The Use of Force by the Russian Federation in Crimea' (2015) (n. 14), 35; Christakis, 'Self-determination, Territorial Integrity and Fait Accompli in the Case of Crimea' (2015) (n. 124), 100; Grant, 'Annexation of Crimea' (2015) (n. 14), 68; Hilpold, 'Ukraine, Crimea and New International Law' (2015) (n. 88); Peters, 'The Crimean Vote of March 2014 as an Abuse of the Institution of the Territorial Referendum' (2015) (n. 100), 257.

> so swiftly that few people realised how truly dramatic those events and their consequences would be. Many people both in Russia and in Ukraine, as well as in other republics hoped that the Commonwealth of Independent States that was created at the time would become the new common form of statehood. They were told that there would be a single currency, a single economic space, joint armed forces; however, all this remained empty promises, while the big country was gone. It was only when Crimea ended up as part of a different country that Russia realised that it was not simply robbed, it was plundered.[135]

There is no need here to argue against these claims, since they are above all historical, moral, and political rather than legal. What is important here is that in terms of international law, they mark nothing less than the open renunciation of the view that the dissolution process of the Soviet Union followed the *uti possidetis* principle, notwithstanding earlier proclamations assuming the contrary in the founding documents of the CIS and the 1994 Declaration on Respect of Sovereignty, Territorial Integrity and Inviolability of Boundaries. Furthermore, the claim to right a perceived historical wrong raises the question of how far back in time one should go when assessing territorial claims in light of the right of peoples to self-determination.[136] However, how arbitrary such considerations must appear also in the case of Crimea was stressed by France in the UN Security Council:

> Crimea was Russian from 1783 to 1954. What does that mean? Will we take out our history books to review our borders or challenge or defend them? What date will we go back to? After all, Crimea was Russian for 170 years but a vassal of Turkey for three centuries. We know only too well that anything can be justified by history, particularly the unjustifiable.[137]

2.9 International Status of the 'Republic of Crimea'

Already prior to the completion of Crimea's incorporation into the Russian Federation, a number of states stated in the UN Security Council that they would not recognize Crimea as part of Russia,[138] and General Assembly resolution 68/262

[135] Crimea Speech (2014) (n. 82).

[136] See Christakis, 'Self-determination, Territorial Integrity and Fait Accompli in the Case of Crimea' (2015) (n. 124), 85.

[137] France, UN SC 7138th meeting, 15 March 2014, UN Doc. S/PV.7138, 5.

[138] France, 19 March 2014, UN Doc. S/PV.7144, 7; ('[W]e will never accept the fait accompli that [Russia] has just imposed on the ground'); United States, ibid., 11 ('We must stand together denying recognition and imposing consequences for that illegal act'); Australia, ibid., 13 ('The international community will not recognize Russia's annexation of Crimea'); Luxemburg, ibid., 17 ('The international community does not recognize any measure to integrate the Ukrainian Autonomous Republic of Crimea within the Russian Federation via the referendum').

later explicitly called upon 'all states, international organizations and specialized agencies not to recognize any alteration of the status of the Autonomous Republic of Crimea and the city of Sevastopol on the basis of the ... referendum and to refrain from any action or dealing that might be interpreted as recognizing any such altered status'.[139] As has been mentioned earlier, the vote was however not unanimous, with eleven states voting against the resolution, and as many as fifty-eight states abstaining, which raises the question whether third states are possibly even obliged not to recognize the status of Crimea as an integral part of Russia due to serious breaches of international law.

According to the ICJ's *Israeli Wall* advisory opinion, states are obliged not to recognize illegal situations resulting from breaches of 'important' international norms.[140] Similarly, article 41(2) of the Articles on Responsibility of States for Internationally Wrongful Acts obliges states not to recognize situations created by a 'serious breach' of an obligation 'arising under a peremptory norm of general international law'.[141] Numerous scholars of international law argue in a similar vein.[142] John Dugard, for instance, maintained as early as 1987 that '[a]n act in violation of a norm having the character of jus cogens is illegal and is therefore null and void', singling out the creation of states and the acquisition of territory as examples in which states are under a duty not to recognize such acts.[143] Proceeding from the earlier assessments that Russia's military intervention in Crimea qualifies as an act of aggression and as a violation of the prohibition of the use of force, and that, as a result, Crimea's declaration of independence was illegal under international law as was Russia's subsequent annexation of Crimea, one can only conclude that states have an obligation not to recognize Russia's annexation of Crimea from Ukraine.[144]

[139] GA Res. 68/262 (Territorial Integrity of Ukraine) (2014) (n. 95), para. 6. Non-recognition of Crimea's annexation by Russia was reaffirmed by GA Res 71/205 (Situation of Human Rights in the Autonomous Republic of Crimea and the City of Sevastopol (Ukraine)), 19 December 2016, UN Doc. A/RES/71/205 as well as GA Res 74/17 (Problem of the Militarization of the Autonomous Republic of Crimea and the City of Sevastopol, Ukraine, as well as Parts of the Black Sea and the Sea of Azov), 9 December 2019, UN Doc. A/RES/74/17.

[140] ICJ, Israeli Wall Advisory Opinion (2004) (n. 117), para. 159.

[141] Articles on Responsibility of States for Internationally Wrongful Acts, Annex to GA Res 56/83, 12 December 2001, UN Doc. A/RES/56/83.

[142] See e.g. Stefan Talmon, *Die kollektive Nichtanerkennung illegaler Staaten: Grundlagen und Rechtsfolgen einer internationalen koordinierten Sanktion, dargestellt am Beispiel der Türkischen Republik Nord-Zypern* (Tübingen: Mohr Siebeck, 2006); Stefan Talmon, 'The Duty Not to 'Recognize as Lawful' a Situation Created by the Illegal Use of Force or Other Serious Breaches of a Jus Cogens Obligation: An Obligation without Real Substance?', in Christian Tomuschat and Jean-Marc Thouvenin (eds), *The Fundamental Rules of the International Legal Order: Jus Cogens and Obligations Erga Omnes* (Leiden: Nijhoff, 2006), 99–126.

[143] John Dugard, *Recognition and the United Nations* (Cambridge: Grotius Publications, 1987), 135.

[144] See Enrico Milano, 'The Non-Recognition of Russia's Annexation of Crimea: Three Different Legal Approaches and One Unanswered Question', *Questions of International Law* 1 (2014), 35–55. Concurring Walter, 'Postscript: Self-determination, Secession, and the Crimean Crisis' (2014) (n. 134), 310; Grant, 'Annexation of Crimea' (2015) (n. 14), 91–2; Hilpold, 'Ukraine, Crimea and New International Law' (2015) (n. 88), 268–9; Peters, 'The Crimean Vote of March 2014 as an Abuse of the Institution of the Territorial Referendum' (2015) (n. 100), 280; Vidmar, 'The Annexation of Crimea and the Boundaries of the Will of the People' (2015) (n. 86), 376.

The possibilities of implementing such a collective obligation of non-recognition is of course another matter, and is in any event blocked on the level of the United Nations by the veto power of the Russian Federation in the Security Council.[145]

Since February 2014, the European Union, the United States, and other international organizations and states have imposed sanctions against individuals, businesses, and officials from Russia; as of February 2021, the sanctions by the European Union and the United States continue to be in effect.[146] Furthermore, the Russian delegation to the Parliamentary Assembly of the Council of Europe (PACE) had been stripped of its key rights since April 2014, including the right to vote and to take part in the assembly's governing bodies.[147] In response, Russia decided in 2016 that it would no longer participate in the assembly and would stop paying its annual contribution of €33 million, roughly 7 per cent of the Council of Europe's budget; in 2018, Russian foreign Mminister Sergey Lavrov stated that Russia will quit the Council of Europe 'if its opponents insist on its expulsion' and later justified the announcement as a legitimate method of blackmailing.[148] On 25 June 2019, the Russian delegation's rights were restored after a controversial resolution was adopted that added to PACE's rules of procedure a passage according to which the 'members' rights to vote, to speak and to be represented in the Assembly and its bodies shall not be suspended or withdrawn in the context of a challenge to or reconsideration of credentials'.[149]

Ukraine, on its part, has declared Crimea a temporarily occupied territory, and seeks remedy in a number of international courts and arbitral tribunals for Russia's actions. In September 2016, it filed a claim at the Permanent Court of Arbitration (PCA) under Annex VII of the 1982 United Nations Convention on the Law of the Sea (UNCLOS)[150] concerning the coastal state rights in the Black Sea, Sea of Azov, and Kerch Strait. In its preliminary objections, Russia argued, *inter alia*, that the tribunal does not have jurisdiction to determine Ukraine's claims because the dispute 'relates essentially to the sovereignty over Crimea, but also because Ukraine maintains that Russian sovereignty was acquired through unlawful use of military force'.[151] On 21 February 2020, the PCA issued its award on preliminary objections,

[145] See in particular the draft resolution on Ukraine of 15 March 2014, vetoed by Russia, UN Doc. S/2014/189.

[146] 'White House Extends Russia Sanctions Over Ukraine Situation For One Year', *Radio Free Europe/Radio Liberty*, 26 February 2020; 'EU Extends Sanctions Crimea Sanctions By One More Year', *Radio Free Europe/Radio Liberty*, 18 June 2020.

[147] PACE Res 1990 (2014), Reconsideration on Substantive Grounds of the Previously Ratified Credentials of the Russian Delegation, 10 April 2014.

[148] See 'Russia Will Quit Council of Europe if Opponents Insist on Its Expulsion, Says Lavrov', *TASS*, 16 October 2018; 'Council of Europe Realized Current Status of Russia Unacceptable, Says Lavrov', *TASS*, 17 May 2019.

[149] PACE Res 2287 (2019), Strengthening the Decision-making Process of the Parliamentary Assembly Concerning Credentials and Voting, 25 June 2019, para. 10.

[150] United Nations Convention on the Law of the Sea (UNCLOS), 10 December 1982, 1833 UNTS 3.

[151] PCA, Dispute Concerning Coastal State Rights in the Black Sea, Sea of Azov, and Kerch Strait (Ukraine v Russian Federation), Case No. 2017-06, vol. 1, Preliminary Objections of the Russian Federation, 19 May 2018, para. 148. On the dispute see Dmytro Koval and Valentin J. Schatz, 'Ukraine

finding that it lacks jurisdiction over the dispute 'to the extent that a ruling of the Arbitral Tribunal on the merits of Ukraine's claims necessarily requires it to decide, expressly or implicitly, on the sovereignty of either Party over Crimea'.[152]

In January 2017, Ukraine furthermore filed an application against Russia before the ICJ, claiming violations of the International Convention for the Suppression of the Financing of Terrorism (ICSFT) and the International Convention on the Elimination of All Forms of Racial Discrimination (CERD).[153] Parallel to the case in front of the PCA, Russia argued in its preliminary objections that the ICJ has no jurisdiction since the real issue in dispute between the parties does not concern racial discrimination but the status of Crimea, and Ukraine's invocation of the CERD was therefore 'artificial'.[154] On 8 November 2019, the ICJ found that it has jurisdiction to entertain the claims made by Ukraine and that the application in relation to those claims is admissible.[155]

3. Conclusions

This chapter has shown how Russia (ab)used the right of peoples to self-determination as a pretext to justify territorial acquisitions by the threat and use of force. Although different with regard to its historical, political, and cultural context, the assessments provided by Russia after the dissolution of the Soviet Union

v. Russia: Passage through Kerch Strait and the Sea of Azov', *Völkerrechtsblog*, 10 January 2018; Otto Luchterhandt, 'Gegen das Völkerrecht. Die Eskalation des Konflikts am Asowschen Meer', *Osteuropa* 69 (2019), no. 1–2, 3–21. In April 2019, Ukraine furthermore submitted a request to the International Tribunal for the Law of the Sea (ITLOS), seeking provisional measures under UNCLOS concerning the detention of three Ukrainian naval vessels following the so-called Kerch Strait incident. On 25 May 2019, ITLOS prescribed provisional measures ordering Russia to release the vessels and their servicemen, ITLOS, Case Concerning the Detention of Three Ukrainian Naval Vessels (Ukraine v Russian Federation), Request for the prescription of provisional measures, Order, 25 May 2019. By November 2019, all ships and their servicemen were returned to Ukraine.

152 PCA, Dispute Concerning Coastal State Rights in the Black Sea, Sea of Azov, and Kerch Strait (Ukraine v Russian Federation), Case No. 2017-06, Award Concerning the Preliminary Objections of the Russian Federation, 21 February 2020, para. 197.

153 International Convention for the Suppression of the Financing of Terrorism (ICSFT), 9 December 1999, 2178 UNTS 197; International Convention on the Elimination of All Forms of Racial Discrimination (CERD), 4 January 1969, 660 UNTS 195.

154 ICJ, Application of the International Convention for the Suppression of the Financing of Terrorism and the International Convention on the Elimination of All Forms of Racial Discrimination (Ukraine v Russian Federation), Preliminary Objections Submitted by the Russian Federation, vol. 1, 12 September 2018, paras 295–298.

155 ICJ, Ukraine v Russian Federation (n. 154), Judgment, 8 November 2019, ICJ Reports 2019, 558. See Iryna Marchuk, 'Green Light from the ICJ to Go Ahead with Ukraine's Dispute against the Russian Federation Involving Allegations of Racial Discrimination and Terrorism Financing, *EJIL:Talk!*, 22 November 2019. As of February 2021, Russia had not yet filed its counter-memorial, for which the time limit for filing was extended to July 2021 following requests by Russia based on 'ongoing difficulties and related delays in the preparation of that pleading resulting from restrictions due to the coronavirus pandemic'. For the latest developments see https://www.icj-cij.org/en/case/166.

with regard to the annexation of the Baltic states by the Soviet Union in 1940 on the one hand and the annexation of Crimea by the Russian Federation in 2014 on the other hand offered a clear parallel in the way the incorporations were legally justified: with the argument that the parliaments of the Baltic states back in 1940 and the population of Crimea in 2014 voluntarily asked to join the Soviet Union/the Russian Federation, and the portrayal of these 'requests' as an exercise of the right to self-determination. In the case of Crimea, as in the Baltic states before, facts were denied or even invented in order to arrive at these conclusions, making creative legal assessments possible.

Russia's main legal argument for the legality of Crimea's incorporation into the Russian Federation—the claim that Crimea has a right to secede—was based on the reading of the Ukrainian Revolution having created an 'extreme situation' in which Crimea's right to self-determination could not be exercised any longer in the constitutional framework of Ukraine, whose territorial integrity was purportedly 'destroyed' by the Ukrainian interim government. This reasoning clearly reminded of the argument raised in the Russo-Georgian War 2008, where a similar point was made in the context of the recognition of South Ossetia as an independent state, with Russia arguing that the bombing of Tskhinvali amounted to 'genocide' and Georgia therefore having 'ended' its sovereignty. As in the Russo-Georgian War 2008, the claim of a right to secede had however no sufficient factual basis, and therefore appeared hypocritical. The underlying legal view, on the other hand, that is that the right to self-determination of peoples may confer a right to secede in 'extreme situations', was consistent with earlier state practice, in particular Russia's written statement in the *Kosovo* proceedings before the ICJ and Russia's responses to the EU International Fact-Finding Mission in the Conflict in Georgia. On the other hand, one cannot fail to note that a right to secede was not even considered in solving the single most violent secessionist conflict in the post-Soviet space, Chechnya, and Russia's support for such a right for situations outside the territory of the Russian Federation seems therefore arbitrary and politicized.

Comparing Crimea to the other case studies in Chapters 2 and 3 offers other interesting differences and changes over time. A first observation regards the role of the Russian Constitutional Court. Whereas the court at least dealt with international law aspects of the secessionist conflicts in Tatarstan and Chechnya, balancing the territorial integrity of the Russian Federation with the right of peoples to self-determination, its role in Russia's annexation of Crimea was arguably reduced to a procedural fig leaf serving to justify the 'political expediency' of Russian state action.[156]

[156] See Elena Lukyanova, О праве налево: К вопросу о верховенстве права в контексте российской внешней политики, или Почему, согласно закону Российской Федерации, Крым все-таки не совсем наш [From the Right to the Left: On the Question of the Rule of Law in the Context of Russian Foreign Policy, or Why, According to Russian Law, Crimea is Still not Quite Ours], *Novaya gazeta*, 19

This decreasing importance of international law in the justifications of Russia's state practice could be observed also on a more general level. Although the incorporation of Crimea into the Russian Federation formally followed a legal process and was accompanied by the use of international legal arguments (the right of peoples to self-determination, use of a referendum to determine the 'will of the people' of Crimea, formal signing of an accession agreement with the self-proclaimed Republic of Crimea, etc.), the main resource for legitimacy was no longer law but history. Putin's Crimea Speech starts with the following—almost mythical—statement:

> Everything in Crimea speaks of our shared history and pride. This is the location of ancient Khersones, where Prince Vladimir was baptised. His spiritual feat of adopting Orthodoxy predetermined the overall basis of the culture, civilisation and human values that unite the peoples of Russia, Ukraine and Belarus. The graves of Russian soldiers whose bravery brought Crimea into the Russian empire are also in Crimea. This is also Sevastopol—a legendary city with an outstanding history, a fortress that serves as the birthplace of Russia's Black Sea Fleet.[157]

This and similar statements were voiced on numerous occasions, producing an official Russian narrative of why 'Crimea is Ours',[158] in which legal reasoning is replaced by a rhetoric of historical and nationalist claims. Take, for example, Putin's remarks at a meeting with young academics and history teachers at the Museum of Contemporary History of Russia in Moscow, made on 5 November 2014:

> [F]or ethnic Russians (I mean that particular segment of our multi-ethnic peoples—ethnic, Orthodox Russians), Crimea has a kind of sacred significance. After all, it was in Crimea, in Hersonissos, that Prince Vladimir was baptised, subsequently baptising Rus. The first, initial font of Russia's Baptism is there. And what is Hersonissos? It is Sevastopol. You can see the connection between the spiritual source and state component, meaning the fight for Crimea overall and for Sevastopol, for Hersonissos. In essence, the Russian people have been fighting for many years to gain a firm foothold in its historical font. This is extremely important.[159]

March 2015, and the reply to Lukyanova by the chairman of the Russian Constitutional Court, Valery Zorkin, Право—и только право [Law—and only Law], *Rossiĭskaya gazeta*, 23 March 2015.

[157] Crimea Speech (2014) (n. 82).

[158] On this popular meme in Russian social media see Mikhail D. Suslov, '"Crimea is Ours!" Russian Popular Geopolitics in the New Media Age', *Eurasian Geography and Economics* 55 (2014), 588–609. On the official narrative more broadly Yuri Teper, 'Official Russian Identity Discourse in Light of the Annexation of Crimea: National or Imperial?', *Post-Soviet Affairs* 32 (2016), 378–96.

[159] Meeting with Young Academics and History Teachers. Vladimir Putin met with Young Academics and History Teachers at the Museum of Modern Russian History, 5 November 2014, http://en.kremlin.ru/events/president/news/46951. The core argument here, i.e. that Russia's special relationship with

In sum, 'Crimea' arguably marks a shift away from legal arguments towards eclectic historical claims and restoration of hegemonic power, in which the right of peoples to self-determination continues to function as a central legal argument, but legal reasoning more generally loses its dominant position in the official justification of Russia's state practice in the post-Soviet space.

Crimea goes back to the tenth century (the fact that Vladimir was baptized in Crimea), is disputed. On the accuracy of Putin's statement see e.g. Masha Lipman, 'A Museum Survives in Crimea', *The New Yorker*, 3 August 2015: 'The theory that Grand Prince Vladimir (whose death a thousand years ago was marked by the Kremlin this month) was baptized in Chersonesus is not the only version of this event. Another, equally well-known theory has it that Vladimir was baptized in Kiev, the birthplace of the history of Old Rus', but Kiev, for obvious reasons, has become a politically inconvenient place of origin for Russian Orthodox Christianity. Even if Vladimir had been baptized in Chersonesus, Crimea in the tenth century lay far beyond Rus', in the Byzantine Empire. Finally, in the many centuries since Vladimir's conversion, Chersonesus has never been a special place of worship for Orthodox Christians.'

5
Post-Soviet Russian Scholarship on Self-Determination

With the Soviet Union's collapse, Marxist-Leninist ideology also disappeared from Russian textbooks of international law. Post-Soviet Russian international law scholarship however continues to assume the existence of a national doctrine, distinct from Western literature. In 2013, the Russian Association of International Law even adopted a resolution on a Russian doctrine of international law,[1] and Oleg Khlestov (1923–), professor of international law at the Diplomatic Academy of the Russian MFA, dedicated an article to the topic in the *Eurasian Law Journal*, describing the doctrine's relation to Russian foreign policy as follows:

> International legal doctrine is closely connected with the foreign policy doctrine of the state, its foreign policy, and usually reflects the goals and tasks that the latter pursues in the international arena.... Depending on the character of the foreign policy of the state, the doctrine gives bigger or smaller importance to certain or other norms of international law.... The Russian doctrine of international law is progressive. In many ways, it corresponds to the official positions of our country.[2]

Although such a self-understanding is arguably no longer characteristic for all international lawyers in post-Soviet Russia and is more widespread among the older generation educated in Soviet times,[3] the assumed existence of a distinct Russian doctrine is virtually unquestioned, resulting in a clear division between 'domestic' (*otechestvennyĭ*) and 'foreign' or 'Western' international law scholarship in Russian academic literature similar to the former 'socialist'/'bourgeois' division during the Soviet period.[4] As Lauri Mälksoo has shown in *Russian Approaches to*

[1] See L.V. Korbut, 'Аналитический обзор работы 56-го Ежегодного Собрания Российской Ассоциации международного права 26-28 июня 2013 г.' [Analytical Review of the Work of the 56th Annual Meeting of the Russian Association of International Law 26–28 June 2013], *Rossiĭskiĭ ezhegodnik mezhdunarodnogo prava* (2013), 408–35, 409.

[2] O.N. Khlestov, 'Российская доктрина международного права' [Russian Doctrine of International Law], *Evraziĭskiĭ yuridicheskiĭ zhurnal* 58 (2013), no. 3, 19–22, 19, 22.

[3] See Lauri Mälksoo, *Russian Approaches to International Law* (Oxford: Oxford University Press, 2015), 81–2.

[4] See ibid., 87, with numerous examples cited in fn. 54. On this continuity see also Maria Issaeva, 'Quarter of a Century on from the Soviet Era: Reflections on Russian Doctrinal Responses to the Annexation of Crimea', *Russian Law Journal* 5 (2017), no. 3, 86–112, 109, observing that '[w]hen a new edition of the most authoritative Soviet international law textbook co-authored by Tunkin was published in 1999, most of its chapters repeated the previous 1981 version of the same textbook

Russia and the Right to Self-Determination in the Post-Soviet Space. Johannes Socher, Oxford University Press.
 DOI: 10.1093/oso/9780192897176.003.0006

International Law, this domestic/Western division also has substantial implications, leading to different understandings of human rights law, what domestic affairs of a state include, or who can be subjects of international law.[5]

Against this background of a purported Russian doctrine, close to Russian foreign policy and at times substantially different from Western international law scholarship, this chapter analyses how this self-perception affects the discourse on the right to self-determination in post-Soviet Russian scholarship. (Note in this context that 'Russian international law scholarship' and 'scholarship of international law in Russia' will be used synonymously, denoting all literature published by scholars affiliated with an academic institution seated in the Russian Federation. The exception to this rule is a cameo appearance of Rein Müllerson, for reasons that will become clear when reading Section 3 below.) Section 1 will provide a general overview of international law scholarship in post-Soviet Russia by introducing the main protagonists and leading institutions in the field. Additionally, some core features and continuous peculiarities of Russian international law scholarship will be outlined. Section 2 then analyses at how the right to self-determination is theorized in Russian international law literature. In doing so, the views expressed in that literature will be situated in the wider spectrum of international law scholarship, with a focus on highlighting peculiarities that existed already prior to Russia's annexation of Crimea in 2014. Section 3 finally illustrates the various attempts made in Russian scholarship in accommodating legal assessments of these events with prior positions on state sovereignty, the right to self-determination, secession, and annexation, without contradicting itself or even criticizing the Russian government for its actions.

1. Post-Soviet Scholarship of International Law in Russia: An Overview

At the turn of the twenty-first century, with Boris Yeltsin's resignation as the first president of the Russian Federation and Vladimir Putin's succession as new head of state, the initial post-Soviet enthusiasm of Western doctrines in Russian

word-for-word, with references to "bourgeois" science of international law in the 1981 edition simply replaced by global change to "Western" science of international law in the 1999 edition. The ideological split between the "communist" and the "capitalist" systems invented by the USSR... thus remained untouched in the Russian international law mentality despite Russia's declared transition to democracy and free market in the 1990s.'

[5] See Mälksoo, *Russian Approaches to International Law* (2015) (n. 3), 88–9, 104–10, 122–32. With regard to the latter question see also Lauri Mälksoo, 'International Legal Theory in Russia: A Civilizational Perspective, or Can Individuals be Subjects of International Law?', in Anne Orford and Florian Hoffmann (eds), *The Oxford Handbook of the Theory of International Law* (Oxford: Oxford University Press, 2016), 257–75.

international law scholarship came to an end and arguably marked a turning point in the perception of international law in Russia.[6] In 2003, Tarja Långström observed in *Transformation in Russia and International Law* that compared to the former Soviet doctrine, Russian scholarship of international law is (again) 'closely intertwined with the state' and 'official political thinking' plays a far more dominant role in Russia than for example in the United States, 'where academic lawyers perceive their role more as critics of government than its advocates'.[7] More than a decade later, this finding seems to be still accurate when Lauri Mälksoo argues in *Russian Approaches to International Law* that '[s]ome leading international lawyers of the older generation in Russia see it as their vocation to support the Kremlin with all the weight of the "science" of international law'.[8]

1.1 Protagonists and Main Institutions in the Field of International Law in Russia

The sometimes explicitly assumed close interaction between international law scholarship and foreign policy in Russia is also reflected in a strong personal link between academia and practice. Many senior international law professors hold or held important government positions in addition to their academic posts, often moving on to international courts and tribunals: Vladlen Vereshchetin (1932–), professor of international law at the Institute of State and Law of the Russian Academy of Sciences (IGP RAN), was a member of the International Law Commission from 1992 until 1995 and judge at the ICJ from 1995 until 2006; Bakhtiar Tuzmukhamedov (1955–) was professor of international law at the Diplomatic Academy and advisor to the Russian Constitutional Court until 2009, when he was appointed to serve as judge at the International Criminal Tribunal for Rwanda; and Roman Kolodkin (1960–) held numerous senior positions in the Russian Ministry of Foreign Affairs (MFA) while simultaneously being professor of international law at the Moscow State Institute of International Relations (MGIMO) before becoming judge at the International Tribunal of the Law of the Sea in 2017.

In the 'post-Tunkin' era of the 1990s and early 2000s, Igor Lukashuk (1926–2007) of IGP RAN was considered the unofficial doyen in the field of international law scholarship in Russia.[9] Following Lukashuk's death in 2007, Stanislav

[6] See Rima Tkatova, 'Russian Spirit, Soviet Heritage and Western Temptation: "Un-'Peaceful Coexistence'" in Russia's International Doctrine and Practice', *Baltic Yearbook of International Law* 12 (2012), 1–28, 15–16.

[7] Tarja Långström, *Transformation in Russia and International Law* (Leiden: Martinus Nijhoff Publishers, 2003), 169.

[8] Mälksoo, *Russian Approaches to International Law* (2015) (n. 3), 81.

[9] See, in particular, I.I. Lukashuk, *Нормы международного права в международной нормативной системе* [The Norms of International Law in the International Normative System] (Moscow: SPARK, 1997); I.I. Lukashuk, *Международное право* [International Law] (Moscow: Wolters Kluwer, 3rd edn,

Chernichenko (1935–) of the Diplomatic Academy, arguably succeeded in assuming the title. Chernichenko is the author of two major books on the foundations of international law, *Theory of International Law*, published in 1999, and *Essays on Philosophy and International Law*, published in 2009.[10] Chernichenko is also a former editor of the Diplomatic Academy's own international law textbook,[11] which—together with MGIMO—is considered the most prestigious Russian institution in the field.[12] Like the Diplomatic Academy, MGIMO is run by the Russian MFA.[13] Its international law department was founded in 1948 and sees itself in clear continuity to its Soviet past.[14] In particular Fyodor Kozhevnikov, who led the department for more than twenty years, continues to be regarded as the department's figurehead. Like most leading institutions in the field in Russia, MGIMO publishes its own international law textbook. Since 2010, it appears under the general editorship of Alexander Vylegzhanin, the head of the international law department.[15] MGIMO is also home to the most prestigious international law journal in Russia, the *Moscow Journal of International Law*.[16] Other academic journals with a focus on international law include the *Eurasian Law Journal*,[17] *International Justice*,[18] the *Kazan Journal of International Law*,[19] and the *Russian Law Journal*.[20]

Apart from MGIMO and the Diplomatic Academy, a third important institution is RAMP, the Russian Association of International Law.[21] RAMP is the

2010), 2 vols. Lukashuk was a leading research fellow at IGP RAN and a member of the International Law Commission from 1995 until 2001. For an assessment of Lukashuk's conception of international law see Långström, *Transformation in Russia and International Law* (2003) (n. 7), 138–47.

[10] S.V. Chernichenko, *Теория международного права* [Theory of International Law] (Moscow: NIMP, 1999), 2 vols; S.V. Chernichenko, *Очерки по философии и международному праву* [Essays on Philosophy and International Law] (Moscow: Nauchnaya kniga, 2009).

[11] A.A. Kovalev and S.V. Chernichenko (eds), *Международное право* [International Law] (Moscow: Prospekt, 3rd edn, 2008). Since 2014, the textbook has been edited by Sergei Egorov: S.A. Egorov (ed.), *Международное право* [International Law] (Moscow: Statut, 5th edn, 2014).

[12] Other leading institutions include Kutafin Moscow State Law University, the Higher School of Economics (HSE), the law faculties of Moscow State University and the Peoples' Friendship University of Russia (all in Moscow), as well as the law faculties of Saint Petersburg and Kazan State University, Anthea Roberts, *Is International Law International?* (New York, NY: Oxford University Press, 2017), 42–3. See also Mälksoo, *Russian Approaches to International Law* (2015) (n. 3), 86, with a slightly different list.

[13] On MGIMO as an elite academic institution see Martin Müller, *Making Great Power Identities in Russia: An Ethnographic Discourse Analysis of Education at a Russian Elite University* (Münster: Lit., 2009).

[14] See the self-description on the institute's website, available at: http://english.mgimo.ru/international-law-department.

[15] A.N. Vylegzhanin (ed.), *Международное право* [International Law] (Moscow: Yuraĭt, 2010). A second edition was published in 2014, and a third in 2016: A.N. Vylegzhanin (ed.), *Международное право* [International Law] (Moscow: Yuraĭt, 3rd edn, 2016), 2 vols.

[16] Russian: *Moskovskiĭ zhurnal mezhdunarodnogo prava*, see https://www.mjil.ru.

[17] Russian: *Evraziĭskiĭ yuridicheskiĭ zhurnal*, see http://eurasialaw.ru.

[18] Russian: *Mezhdunarodnoe pravosudie*, see http://ilpp.ru/journal.

[19] Russian: *Kazanskiĭ zhurnal mezhdunarodnogo prava i mezhdunarodnȳkh otnosheniĭ*, see http://www.kjil.ru.

[20] See https://www.russianlawjournal.org.

[21] Russian: *Rossiĭskaya Assotsiatsiya mezhdunarodnogo prava*, see http://www.ilarb.ru.

successor of the Soviet Association of International Law and publishes the *Russian Yearbook of International Law*. In addition, the textbook *International Law—A Russian Introduction* was published in 2009 under its auspices, with Bakhtiar Tuzmukhamedov as general editor.[22] The RAMP textbook has been praised as 'substantially superior to the competition, being better researched and broader in scope' than any other Russian international law textbook.[23] Due to its showcase character with a foreword by the Russian foreign minister and contributions by almost every leading scholar of international law in Russia, the textbook makes an almost canonical impression, and will therefore be used as a starting point for most of the discussions on specific topics analysed below.

1.2 Some Core Features and Continuing Particularities of Russian Scholarship

Generally speaking, Russian scholarship of international law tends to be theoretically and dogmatically oriented rather than focused on practice of states and national or international courts.[24] References to foreign literature are rare, whereas works by Soviet authorities of international law remain respected sources. An extreme example is the 2008 edition of the Diplomatic Academy textbook, in which as few as five non-Russian publications are cited in a total of 800 pages.[25] Other textbooks show a similar isolation from international scholarly debates.[26]

Russian international law textbooks are usually structured like their Soviet antecedents, that is around principles of international law, roughly reflecting the principles enumerated in the Friendly Relations Declaration of 1970.[27] In

[22] V.I. Kuznetsov and B.R. Tuzmukhamedov (eds) (William E. Butler transl.), *International Law—A Russian Introduction* (Utrecht: Eleven International Publishing, 2009), 3. The RAMP textbook is an extended and revised translation of a textbook edited by Valery Kuznetsov (1940–2002), who died long before publication in 2009 but nevertheless appears as one of the two general editors in commemoration to his death. Kuznetsov was professor of international law at the Diplomatic Academy, member of the UN Committee for Economic, Social, and Cultural Rights (1992–2002) and the International Law Commission (2002).

[23] Boris N. Mamlyuk, 'Book Review', *Review of Central and East European Law* 35 (2010), 111–15, 112.

[24] Mälksoo, *Russian Approaches to International Law* (2015) (n. 3), 77–97; Lauri Mälksoo, 'Case Law in Russian Approaches to International Law', in Anthea Roberts, Paul B. Stephan, and Pierre-Hugues Verdier (eds), *Comparative International Law* (New York, NY: Oxford University Press, 2018), 337–52, 338–41.

[25] Kovalev and Chernichenko, *International Law* (2008) (n. 11).

[26] See Roberts, *Is International Law International?* (2017) (n. 12), 346–53 (Table 12).

[27] Cf. GA Res 26/25 (XXV) (Friendly Relations Declaration), 24 October 1970, UN Doc. A/RES/25/2625, enlisting the following seven principles: 'a. The principle that States shall refrain in their international relations from the threat or use of force against the territorial integrity or political independence of any State, or in any other manner inconsistent with the purposes of the United Nations, b. The principle that States shall settle their international disputes by peaceful means in such a manner that international peace and security and justice are not endangered, c. The duty not to intervene in matters within the domestic jurisdiction of any State, in accordance with the Charter, d. The duty of States to co-operate with one another in accordance with the Charter, e. The principle of equal rights and

the RAMP textbook, principles of international law are described as 'having both customary-law and treaty nature' which work like 'a kind of constitutional principles of the world community'. Principles of international law form part of *jus cogens* and

> (1) bring together and juridically consolidate the most general and important rules of inter-state relations formed as a result of lengthy practice; (2) create the normative-legal foundation for the entire system of international law and ensure the normal functioning thereof; (3) facilitate the stabilization of international relations, juridically limiting them within strictly determined normative legal frameworks; [and] (4) promote the further development of international relations, generalizing the normatively consolidating new generally-significant roles of international practice.[28]

According to the author of this passage, Vitaly Ivanenko of Saint Petersburg State University, the emergence and existence of principles of international law is a 'major system-forming factor', with international law having been transformed 'from an aggregate of various norms into a unified, internally consistent and orderly normative system'.[29]

1.3 In Particular: Dominance of Statism

With regard to theory, the core feature of post-Soviet Russian scholarship is the continuing dominance of a 'statist' understanding of international law to a degree Lauri Mälksoo has described as 'nineteenth-century Hegelian' in the sense that Russian scholarship often glorifies the state as such, as 'an embodiment of the Absolute Idea, often detaching the state from its democratic legitimacy'.[30] According to Mälksoo, this dominant statist school of thought is essentially positivist, sceptical towards modern Western influences in international law (in particular human rights), and more likely to be nostalgic towards achievements of the Soviet Union and the Russian Empire compared to the more liberal-leaning minority in post-Soviet Russian scholarship.[31]

self-determination of peoples, f. The principle of sovereign equality of States, g. The principle that States shall fulfil in good faith the obligations assumed by them in accordance with the Charter.' On the origins of the Friendly Relations Declaration as a result of the Soviet endeavours in the codification of the principles of 'peaceful coexistence' see Chapter 1 Section 2.

[28] Kuznetsov and Tuzmukhamedov, *International Law* (2009) (n. 22), 132.
[29] Ibid.
[30] Mälksoo, *Russian Approaches to International Law* (2015) (n. 3), 100.
[31] Ibid., 99–100.

The most important effect of this dominant statist thinking is the conceptualization of state sovereignty in near-absolutist terms.[32] A typical example for this understanding is the monograph *State Sovereignty in International Law* by Aleksei Moiseev, professor of international law at the Diplomatic Academy.[33] Moiseev contends that 'one needs to recognise that sovereignty as a category bears absolute character. State sovereignty does not have limits. It cannot be divided and it symbolizes the united will of the people—it either exists or not.... Contemporary international law is based on the absolute nature of sovereignty.'[34] Similar positions can be found in other works, for example in the *Essays on Philosophy and International Law*, where Chernichenko maintains that sovereignty 'cannot be divided or limited'.[35]

Somewhat paradoxical to this dominant understanding of state sovereignty it is often simultaneously stressed that the sovereign equality of states exists only as a formality. In the *Essays* for example, Chernichenko takes the view that the states of the world are 'de facto unequal', and that the stability in international relations depends on the interaction between powerful nations.[36] In a similar vein, the RAMP textbook maintains that '[t]he juridical equality of States does not mean [that] they are actually equal, which is taken into account in the realities of international relations'.[37] Moreover, it is claimed that the concept of 'great powers' has still some validity,[38] although—'[a]s a general rule'—this would have no legal significance due to the principle of sovereign equality of states.[39]

[32] On the evolution of sovereignty as a concept of international law generally see e.g. Martti Koskenniemi, *From Apology to Utopia: The Structure of International Legal Argument* (Cambridge: Cambridge University Press, 2005), 228–33, 240–5. Cf. with the perspective of a Russian scholar: N.I. Grachev, *Происхождение суверенитета. Верховная власть в мировоззрении и практике государственного строительства традиционного общества* [The Origin of Sovereignty. Supreme Power in the Worldview and Practice of State-building of a Traditional Society] (Moscow: Zertsalo, 2009).

[33] A.A. Moiseev, *Суверенитет государства в международном праве* [State Sovereignty in International Law] (Moscow: Vostok-Zapad, 2009). See also A.A. Moiseev, 'Критика концепции относительного государственного суверенитета' [Criticism of the Concept of Relative State Sovereignty], *Moskovskiĭ zhurnal mezhdunarodnogo prava* 67 (2007), no. 3, 16–32.

[34] Moiseev, *State Sovereignty in International Law* (2009) (n. 33), 59.

[35] Chernichenko, *Essays on Philosophy and International Law* (2009) (n. 10), 755. Other, more pro-individual views exist, embodied for example in the work of Gennady Ignatenko (1927–2012) of Ural State Law Academy (now Ural State Law University) in Yekaterinburg. See Gennady Ignatenko, *Международное право и внутригосударственное право: проблемы сопряженности и взаимодействия* [International Law and Domestic Law: Problems of Interconnection and Interaction] (Moscow: Norma, 2012). On the dominance of the statist over the pro-individual school in Russian scholarship in more detail see Mälksoo, *Russian Approaches to International Law* (2015) (n. 3), 98–110. On post-Soviet Russian positions on sovereignty see also Lauri Mälksoo, 'Contemporary Russian Perspectives on Non-State Actors: Fear of the Loss of State Sovereignty', in Jean d'Aspremont (ed.), *Participants in the International Legal System: Multiple Perspectives on Non-state Actors in International Law* (London: Routledge, 2011), 126–38, 130–6.

[36] Chernichenko, *Essays on Philosophy and International Law* (2009) (n. 10), 676–8, 690.

[37] Kuznetsov and Tuzmukhamedov, *International Law* (2009) (n. 22), 137.

[38] Ibid., 47. On the relevance of the concept of 'great powers' in modern international law see Jörg Kammerhofer, 'Superpowers and Great Powers', in MPEPIL (online edn); Gerry J. Simpson, *Great Powers and Outlaw States: Unequal Sovereigns in the International Legal Order* (Cambridge: Cambridge University Press, 2004).

[39] Kuznetsov and Tuzmukhamedov, *International Law* (2009) (n. 22), 137.

2. Self-Determination in Post-Soviet Russian Scholarship

In Russian textbooks of international law, the legacy of the Russian Revolution is usually portrayed in an ambiguous fashion. In the introductory chapter of the RAMP textbook, for example, Roman Kolodkin maintains that the Russian Revolution 'proved to have a material, but contradictory impact on international relations and international law' which 'not only cardinally changed Russia, but also became an additional stimulus in the struggle for social, economic, and political transformations in other States'.[40] Lenin's promotion of the principle of self-determination is highlighted and the Decree on Peace as well as the Declaration of the Rights of the Peoples of Russia are mentioned as important contributions to the evolution of the concept.[41] Kolodkin then points at the practical significance the principle had played when Estonia, Finland, Latvia, and Lithuania gained independence from the Russian Empire in 1920—although, however, without mentioning the Soviet Union's subsequent annexation of the Baltic states two decades later.[42]

2.1 Post-Soviet Russian Scholarship on Self-Determination

In the first decade following the dissolution of the Soviet Union, the Russian literature on the right of peoples to self-determination was dominated by the work of Yuri Barseghov,[43] who had started to argue for the independence of Nagorno-Karabakh on the basis of self-determination already in the 1980s and continued to do so throughout the following years in his capacity as director of the Armenian Institute of International Law and Political Science in Moscow.[44] On a more abstract level, the general understanding of the concept was however more conservative, with most Russian scholars being careful in limiting the right to self-determination

[40] Kuznetsov and Tuzmukhamedov, *International Law* (2009) (n. 22), 3.

[41] Ibid., 10.

[42] Ibid. See also V.I. Kuznetsov, 'Октябрь и международное право' [October and International Law], *Mezhdunarodnaya zhizn'* (1997), no. 11–12; Vladislav Tolstykh, 'Марксизм, Октябрьская революция и правоведение' [Marxism, October Revolution and Jurisprudence], *Rossiĭskiĭ yuridicheskiĭ zhurnal* 118 (2018), no. 1, 9–20.

[43] On Barseghov's contribution to the Soviet doctrine of international law, see Chapter 1 Section 4 above.

[44] See Yu.G. Barseghov, *Право на самоопределение: основа демократического решения международных проблем; к проблеме Нагорного Карабаха* [The Right to Self-determination: the Basis of a Democratic Solution of International Problems; on the Problem of Nagorno-Karabakh] (Yerevan: Ayastan, 1989); Yu.G. Barseghov, *Обязательная сила права народов на самоопределение и средства его обеспечения* [The Binding Force of the Right to Self-determination and the Means to Ensure it] (Moscow: International Humanitarian Fund of Armenology, 1993); Yu.G. Barseghov (ed.), *Нагорный Карабах в международном праве и мировой политике: документы и комментарии* [Nagorno-Karabakh in International Law and World Politics: Documents and Commentary] (Moscow: KRUG Publishers, 2008).

to autonomy and 'internal' self-determination rather than arguing for a right to independence outside the colonial context.[45] Open disagreement with Russia's state practice was possible, as the conference materials on 'Legal Aspects of the Chechen Crisis', organized in March 1995 by Russian NGO Memorial, show.[46] In his general assessment of the Chechen conflict, Igor Petrukhin (1926–2009) of IGP RAN, for instance, explicitly argued for the population of Chechnya to have a right to self-determination, that this right 'was not systematically respected' in the First Chechen War, and that Russia 'had no right to force Chechnya ... to enter the Russian Federation'.[47] Similarly, Vil Kikot (1924–) of the Moscow State Academy of Law (now Kutafin Moscow State Law University) argued in his presentation that 'the people of Chechnya have the right to secede' on the basis of international law.[48]

Later, such explicit criticism disappeared, and more recent Russian textbooks argue instead that inside the Russian Federation, the issue of self-determination is 'consolidated' in the Russian Constitution.[49] Consequently—and in line with the official discourse of the Russian government[50]—the question, for example, whether the population of Chechnya has a right to self-determination is discussed (if at all) as a matter of terrorism rather than secession. Without explicitly referring to the conflict in Chechnya, the RAMP textbook states, for example:

> One cannot fail to note that in recent years the threat of abusing [the principle of self-determination] has arisen and become a reality. Political, nationalist,

[45] See, in particular, the contributions in A.G. Ossipov (ed.), *Право Народов на Самоопределение: Идеи и Воплощение* [Right of Peoples to Self-determination: Idea and Embodiment] (Moscow: Zven'ya, 1997). See also Yu. A. Reshetov, 'Право на самоопределение и отделение' [The Right to Self-determination and Secession], *Moskovskiĭ zhurnal mezhdunarodnogo prava* (1994), no. 1, 3–20; S.V. Chernichenko, 'Принцип самоопределения (современная интерпретация)' [The Principle of Self-determination (Modern Interpretation)], *Moskovskiĭ zhurnal mezhdunarodnogo prava* (1996), no. 4, 9–21; and A.V. Avdokushkin and V.G. Mayurov, 'Право наций на самоопределение следует конкретизировать' [The Right of Nations to Self-determination Should be Concretised], *Moskovskiĭ zhurnal mezhdunarodnogo prava* 35 (1999), no. 3, 20–2. For a complete bibliography of the Russian literature on the right to self-determination published between 1991 and 2005 see the works listed under the headings 'Нормы и принципы международного права' [Norms and Principles of International Law] and 'Субъекты международного права' [Subjects of International Law] in L.N. Galenskaya, G.I. Kurdyukov, and S.V. Bakhin (eds), *Международное право. Библиография, 1991-2005* [International Law. Bibliography 1991–2005] (Saint Petersburg: Rossiya-Neva, 2010), 46–65.

[46] N.A. Kravchenko (ed.), *Правовые аспекты чеченского кризиса: Материалы семинара* [Legal Aspects of the Chechen Crisis: Workshop Materials] (Moscow: Memorial, 1995). See also Andrei Illarionov and Boris Lvin, 'Should Russia Recognize Chechnya's Independence?', *The Moscow News*, 24 February–2 March 1995, reprinted in Tony Wood, *Chechnya: The Case for Independence* (London: Verso, 2007), 183–90.

[47] I.L. Petrukhin, 'Правовая оценка военного конфликта в Чечне' [Legal Assessment of the Military Conflict in Chechnya], in Kravchenko, *Legal Aspects of the Chechen Crisis* (1995) (n. 46), 8–18, 11.

[48] V.A. Kikot, 'Проблемы самоопределения. Право и приказ' [Problems of Self-determination. Right and Order], in Kravchenko, *Legal Aspects of the Chechen Crisis* (1995) (n. 46), 40–7, 44.

[49] See e.g. Kuznetsov and Tuzmukhamedov, *International Law* (2009) (n. 22), 151.

[50] See Roy Allison, *Russia, the West, and Military Intervention* (Oxford: Oxford University Press, 2013), 91–4.

> separatist, criminal, and other factors often are becoming the driving force for using the principle for mercenary purposes. For many States a real threat to territorial integrity has been created. Therefore, the realization of this principle should not lead to the destruction of existing States.[51]

At the same time, the same textbook observes a lacking consistency in state practice, 'recognizing the lawfulness of the struggle of some peoples (for example, Kosovo) and considering others to be unlawful (for example, Abkhazia or Dniestr Region)'.[52]

On a more abstract level, the right to self-determination is usually discussed in the system of principles of international law, that is by stressing that the right is a basic principle that needs to be balanced with other such principles, in particular state sovereignty and the territorial integrity of states.[53] Taking again the RAMP textbook as a representative example, self-determination is defined as 'the right of a people or any ethnic group to decide autonomously the question of the forms of its socio-political life', and as the 'right of peoples to choose that path of development which to the greatest degree corresponds to their historical, geographical, cultural, and other traditions and concepts'.[54] All major international legal instruments in which the right to self-determination is laid down are mentioned and restated,

[51] Kuznetsov and Tuzmukhamedov, *International Law* (2009) (n. 22), 150–1.

[52] Ibid., 151. There seems to be consensus among Russian scholars of international law that Kosovo's declaration of independence in 2008 and its subsequent recognition as an independent state by large parts of the international community has set a 'precedent' in international law, see e.g. A.A. Moiseev, 'Косовский прецедент и система международного права' [The Kosovo Precedent and the System of International Law], *Mezhdunarodnaya zhizn'* (2008), no. 5, 79–89; I.S. Marusin, 'О соотношении принципа нерушимости границ и права народов на самоопределение' [On the Relationship between the Principle of Inviolability of Borders and the Right of Peoples to Self-determination], *Pravovedenie* (2014), no. 1, 109–19. For an extensive argument in favour of Abkhaz independence see the monograph by the Abkhaz-Russian scholar Taras Shamba (jointly written with Alexander Neproshin), *Абхазия. Правовые основы государственности и суверенитета* [Abkhazia. Legal Basis for Statehood and Sovereignty] (Moscow: Izd-vo RGTEU, 2004). For a collection of arguments in favour of recognizing Transnistria's independence see V.V. Ignatiev (ed.), *Политико-правовые основы международного признания независимости Приднестровской Молдавской Республики* [Political and Legal Framework for International Recognition of Independence of the Pridnestrovian Moldavian Republic] (Tiraspol: Ministry of Foreign Affairs of the Pridnestrovian Moldavian Republic, 2018), available for download (in Russian and English) at: http://mfa-pmr.org/en/publish.

[53] Kovalev and Chernichenko, *International Law* (2008) (n. 11), 72–73; Kuznetsov and Tuzmukhamedov, *International Law* (2009) (n. 22), 146–51; Vylegzhanin, *International Law* (2014) (n. 15), 69–70, 104–5. See also R.P. Zokhrabyan, 'Принцип равноправия и самоопределения народов: эволюция содержания в системе принципов международного права' [The Principle of Equality and Self-determination of Peoples: Evolution of the Content in the System of Principles of International Law], *Vestnik Moskovskogo universiteta. Pravo.* (2009), no. 2, 61–73; G.M. Velyaminov, 'Соотношение принципов самоопределения народов и территориальной целостности, а также проблемы признания' [The Ratio of the Principles of Self-determination of Peoples and Territorial Integrity, as Well as the Problems of Recognition], *Gosudarstvo i pravo* (2010), no. 10, 101–4; R.P. Zokhrabyan, 'Формы реализации права народов на самоопределение в международном праве и доктрине' [Forms of Realisation of the Right to Self-determination in International Law and Doctrine], *Vestnik Moskovskogo universiteta. Pravo.* (2010), no. 2, 75–85. On the post-Soviet Russian approach to self-determination see also Mälksoo, *Russian Approaches to International Law* (2015) (n. 3), 125–6.

[54] Kuznetsov and Tuzmukhamedov, *International Law* (2009) (n. 22), 147, 150.

although however without assessing the content or discussing the binding character of these instruments. By contrast (and in line with the general view in Russian scholarship),[55] the Helsinki Final Act is explicitly considered legally binding in that context.[56]

Another particularity in post-Soviet Russian scholarship with regard to the theory of self-determination is the definition of 'peoples' in terms of nationality and ethnicity, something which (although not entirely uncommon)[57] tends to be avoided in more recent Western scholarship, sometimes even up to the point that the notion is replaced entirely for 'units to which the principle applies'.[58] The most influential discussion of the concept of 'peoples' in Russian scholarship is probably a passage in Stanislav Chernichenko's *Theory of International Law*.[59] According to Chernichenko, a people is characterized by its residence in a common territory, its economic and social integrity, the presence of certain elements of a common culture, and the subjective awareness of these aspects. Additional factors may be racial or linguistic proximity or a common religion, although a part of a population which has the same 'general national roots' has no right to self-determination, Chernichenko maintains.[60]

2.2 Post-Soviet Russian Scholarship on Secession

In clear continuity with the former Soviet doctrine, there is broad consensus in post-Soviet Russian scholarship that secession is not a separate concept of international law, but the ultimate expression of the right of peoples to self-determination. Taking again the RAMP textbook as a typical example that illustrates that consensus, self-determination is said to include that 'every people in any state has the right autonomously, without any interference or pressure from without, to decide whether to maintain the existing socio-political system and structure within a particular State or to demand the change thereof, to transform their political status within this State, *or to withdraw from it*'.[61]

55 See e.g. Yu. R. Reshetov, 'К вопросу о «Мягком праве»' [On the Question of 'Soft Law'], *Moskovskiĭ zhurnal mezhdunarodnogo prava* 34 (1999), no. 2, 26–31, 26–7. For the possible reasons for this view Conclusions in Chapter 1.

56 Kuznetsov and Tuzmukhamedov, *International Law* (2009) (n. 22), 148. See also ibid., 673–4.

57 See e.g. Juliane Kokott, 'The Development of the Human Rights Situation in Kosovo 1989–1999', in Christian Tomuschat (ed.), *Kosovo and the International Community: A Legal Assessment* (The Hague: Kluwer Law International, 2002), 1–35, 6: 'The definition of a people includes objective elements such as a separate culture, possibly a separate language or ethnic origins different from the majority population in the State.'

58 James Crawford, *The Creation of States in International Law* (Oxford: Oxford University Press, 2nd edn, 2006), 127. For one of the latest attempts to characterize what defines a 'people' in international law see Frédéric Mégret, 'The Right to Self-determination. Earned, Not Inherent', in Fernando R. Téson (ed.), *The Theory of Self-determination* (Cambridge: Cambridge University Press, 2016), 45–69.

59 Chernichenko, *Theory of International Law* (1999) (n. 10), vol. 2, 175–9.

60 Ibid., 177.

61 Kuznetsov and Tuzmukhamedov, *International Law* (2009) (n. 22), 149 (emphasis added).

The legal basis for this claim is usually sought in an *a contrario* argument of the savings clause in the Friendly Relations Declaration.[62] From this clause, the RAMP textbook draws the conclusion that 'the world community does not deny the right to self-determination even leading to a disruption of territorial integrity, but only in those States where the principle of equality and self-determination of peoples is not observed, the entire people are not represented in agencies of power, and individual ethno-territorial parts of the State are subjected to discrimination'.[63] As has been discussed earlier in this book, a right to secede is also widely discussed and has prominent supporters in Western international law scholarship under the concept of 'remedial' secession.[64] In these writings, the savings clause of the Friendly Relations Declaration is also regularly quoted, typically as evidence of *opinio juris* that such a right of secession exists under positive international law. In this context, it is however important to note that the position expressed in the RAMP textbook differs significantly from these writings in so far as the application of a remedial right to secession is commonly restricted to the most extreme cases of oppression, that is only as a last resort when gross violations of human rights occur.[65]

This difference in the understanding commonly found in Russian scholarship vis-à-vis the standard literature on secession in the context of self-determination in Western international law scholarship was also observed in a chapter by Chernichenko and Vladimir Kotliar in a book published in 2003, based on a series of regional conferences on secession in The Hague (Europe), Santa Clara, California (Americas), and Moscow (CIS area).[66] In their contribution, entitled 'Ongoing Global Legal Debates on Self-determination and Secession: Main Trends', Chernichenko and Kotliar find it 'somewhat surprising that... Western lawyers assert that international law remains neutral on the matter of the right to secession'.[67]

[62] Friendly Relations Declaration (1970) (n. 27), para. 7 of the fifth principle: 'Nothing in the foregoing paragraphs shall be construed as authorizing or encouraging any action which would dismember or impair, totally or in part, the territorial integrity or political unity of sovereign and independent States conducting themselves in compliance with the principle of equal rights and self-determination of peoples as described above and thus possessed of a government representing the whole people belonging to the territory without distinction as to race, creed or colour.'

[63] Kuznetsov and Tuzmukhamedov, *International Law* (2009) (n. 22), 149–50.

[64] See Conclusions of Chapter 2, with reference to e.g. Antonio Cassese, *Self-determination of Peoples: A Legal Reappraisal* (Cambridge: Cambridge University Press, 1995), 119–20, and Christian Tomuschat, 'Secession and Self-determination', in Marcello Kohen (ed.), *Secession: International Law Perspectives* (Cambridge: Cambridge University Press, 2006), 1–45, 41.

[65] See e.g. ibid., 35: 'Although for a right to secession to arise, the threshold indicated by [the Friendly Relations Declaration] must certainly be higher; a mere lack of representativeness of a government would not suffice to bring about a right to secession as a form of a right of resistance. The phrase employed rightly conveys the idea that exceptional circumstances are capable of sustaining a claim for secession – circumstances which may roughly be summarized as a grave and massive violation of the human rights of a specific group in a discriminatory fashion.'

[66] Julie Dahlitz (ed.), *Secession and International Law: Conflict Avoidance—Regional Appraisals* (The Hague: T.M.C. Asser Press, 2003). The conclusions and recommendations from the regional conferences are reprinted at the end of the book, see ibid., 259–3 (CIS); 263–8 (Americas); 269–74 (Europe).

[67] Stanislav Chernichenko and Vladimir Kotliar, 'Ongoing Global Legal Debate on Self-determination and Secession', in Julie Dahlitz (ed.), *Secession and International Law: Conflict Avoidance—Regional Appraisals* (The Hague: T.M.C. Asser Press, 2003), 75–88, 83.

While Western scholars usually regard self-determination and secession as two distinct concepts, Chernichenko and Kotliar observe, Russian scholars of international law tend to understand secession as an expression of self-determination.[68] In line with this general observation, Chernichenko and Kotliar argue that 'self-determination (including secession)' entails the possibility of a given people to choose freely between 'internal self-determination, i.e. to obtain the status of a subject of a federation, autonomy or other form self-determination' within an existing state, and external self-determination in the form of secession, resulting either in the creation of a new state or in the accession to an existing state.[69]

2.3 Continuance of the Soviet Doctrine on Wars of National Liberation in Russian Scholarship?

In line with its near-absolutist conception of sovereignty, post-Soviet Russian scholarship was initially very conservative towards possible exceptions to the prohibition of the threat or use of force enshrined in article 2(4) of the UN Charter. As such, Russian scholarship used to argue fiercely against the legality of 'so-called humanitarian intervention' or pre-emptive use of force, and permitted self-defence only if carried out against an armed attack or when authorized by the UN Security Council.[70] It is therefore interesting to note that one exception to the prohibition of the use of force maintained by the former Soviet doctrine, wars of national liberation, may still occasionally be found in contemporary Russian scholarship, although no uniform position seems to have been formed.[71] At one point in the RAMP textbook for instance, it is argued that

[68] Ibid., 82–3. Although the authors don't refer to any specific work or authority, the following statement by Rosalyn Higgins in the same book may suffice to provide a representative example for this widespread view among Western scholars: '[T]he concept of secession is irrelevant to the ongoing entitlement of peoples to self-determination in the post colonial era', and 'disintegration (and by implication secession too) [are] matters of fact, not law'. In a final comment on Kosovo, the possibility of a remedial right to secession in extreme cases of abuse is raised, but ultimately left unanswered. Rosalyn Higgins, 'Secession and International Law', in Dahlitz, *Secession and International Law* (2003) (n. 66), 21–38, 36–7.

[69] Chernichenko and Kotliar, 'Ongoing Global Legal Debate on Self-determination and Secession' (2003) (n. 67), 77.

[70] In line with Russian government policy documents, this strict approach underwent a considerable readjustment in recent years. On the different debates see B.R. Tuzmukhamedov, 'Упреждающее применение силы: возможные критерии допустимости' [Pre-emptive Use of Force: Possible Criteria for Admissibility], *Rossiĭskiĭ ezhegodnik mezhdunarodnogo prava* (2005), 36–55; Sergei Marochkin, 'Contemporary Approaches of the Russian Doctrine in International Law' *Baltic Yearbook of International Law* 12 (2012), 29–56, 38–9 (discussing the changing attitude towards humanitarian intervention); and Bakhtiar Tuzmukhamedov, 'Legislative Regulation of Trans-boundary Use of Armed Force: Russian Case Study', *Baltic Yearbook of International Law* 12 (2012), 57–74, 68–9 (with regard to a possible right to save co-nationals abroad).

[71] As outlined in Johannes Socher, 'Lenin, (Just) Wars of National Liberation, and the Soviet Doctrine on the Use of Force', *Journal of the History of International Law* 19 (2017), 219–45, 231, this position always faced strong opposition in Western academia for a number of reasons, above all because the legal regime of article 2(4) of the UN Charter is commonly thought to bind only states and therefore to be

> [a]ll States are obliged to refrain from any coercive actions depriving peoples of their right to self-determination. If any State by force obstructs a struggling people from realizing their right to self-determination, this people has the right to resist and has the right to seek support and receive if from other States and international organizations in accordance with the principles and norms of international law.[72]

Later in the same textbook, however, it is maintained that in separatist conflicts 'participation on the side of the rebels is regarded as illegal interference in the internal affairs of the respective State and consequently, as a violation of fundamental norms of international law'.[73] Although it would therefore seem unfair to conclude that the Soviet doctrine on wars of national liberation continues to be unanimously approved in post-Soviet Russian scholarship, it should nevertheless be noted that the doctrine was raised in the past in an attempt to help justify Russia's state practice by one of the most eminent Russian scholars of international law: shortly after the Russo-Georgian War in 2008, Bakhtiar Tuzmukhamedov wrote in a newspaper article that 'it would not hurt to recall ... the right of peoples striving for national liberation and their own statehood' in line with the 'traditional canons of the domestic doctrine of international law' which 'one does not always find in the newest textbooks on international law'.[74]

2.4 Self-Determination and Acquisition of Territory in Post-Soviet Russian Scholarship

Arguably the most astonishing continuity between the Soviet and post-Soviet Russian scholarship on self-determination can be observed with regard to the claimed relevance of the right in determining the legality of territorial acquisitions.[75] As will be recalled from Chapter 1 of this book, the former Soviet doctrine regarded not the agreement of the affected state, but the will of the population residing in the disputed territory as decisive for determining the legality of territorial acquisitions.[76] A look into the RAMP textbook suggests that this understanding

inapplicable to struggles deriving from a people's right to self-determination. For a detailed discussion of the problem see Olivier Corten, *The Law against War: The Prohibition on the Use of Force in Contemporary International Law* (Oxford: Hart Publishing, 2010), 135–49. See also Chapter 1 Sections 2 and 4, and Chapter 3 Section 4 above.

[72] Kuznetsov and Tuzmukhamedov, *International Law* (2009) (n. 22), 148.

[73] Ibid., 638.

[74] B.R. Tuzmukhamedov, 'От политических деклараций – к правовым доводам' [From Political Declarations to Legal Arguments], *Nezavisimaya gazeta*, 2 September 2008.

[75] On the different 'modes' of acquisition generally see James Crawford, *Brownlie's Principles of Public International Law* (Oxford: Oxford University Press, 8th edn, 2012), 220–44.

[76] See Chapter 1 Section 4 above.

continues to be the dominant view in post-Soviet Russian scholarship. Although it is acknowledged that if use of force is applied, territorial acquisitions are unlawful,[77] the view expressed in the textbook is consistent with the former Soviet doctrine in so far as it continues to maintain that

> [i]t is virtually unanimously recognized in Russian doctrinal writings that the legal grounds for the affiliation of a territory to a specific State is the freely expressed wish of the population of this territory. In accordance with the right to self-determination, *a people may decide the question of forming an autonomous State or being part of another State.*[78]

Clearly, such an understanding is at odds with the consensus view in Western international law scholarship, which commonly highlights that international practice does not regard the will of the *population* but the agreement of the affected *state* as decisive for the legality of cessions or other territorial changes.[79]

3. Positions on 'Crimea' in Russian Scholarship

Already prior to Russia's annexation of Crimea in 2014, some Russian scholars treated the peninsula's status as sort of a 'special case' that was open for discussion.[80] The majority view in Russian international law scholarship before 2014 was clearly that Crimea was an integral part of Ukraine. In *The Dissolution of the USSR: International Legal Problems* for instance, Petr Kremnev (1954–) of Moscow State University leaves no doubt about Crimea being part of Ukraine. Referring to the reaffirmation of each other's territorial integrity and inviolability of borders in the 1997 Treaty on Friendship, Cooperation and Partnership between the Russian Federation and Ukraine,[81] Kremnev explicitly states that Ukraine thereby 'for the first time receives the treaty norm on the right to Crimea (including Sevastopol),

[77] Kuznetsov and Tuzmukhamedov, *International Law* (2009) (n. 22), 405.
[78] Ibid., 405–6 (emphasis added).
[79] See e.g. Oliver Dörr, 'Cession', in MPEPIL (online edn), MN 17. This question should not be confused with the seemingly similar, but actually very different question whether plebiscites or referendums are regarded necessary *additional* requirements for territorial alignments. On this question see Chapter 4 Section 2 above.
[80] See e.g. V.V. Pokhlebkin, 'К вопросу о геополитическом и международно-правовом положении Крыма' [On the Question of the Geopolitical and International Legal Position of Crimea], *Moskovskiĭ zhurnal mezhdunarodnogo prava* (1996), no. 2, 165–81.
[81] Договор о дружбе, сотрудничестве и партнёрстве между Российской Федерацией и Украиной [Treaty on Friendship, Cooperation and Partnership between the Russian Federation and Ukraine], 31 May 1997, BMD 1999, no. 7, 50, art. 2. English translation: *Harvard Ukrainian Studies* 20 (1996), 319–29.

and Russia at the same time loses the possibility to present any legally grounded claims to territory'.[82]

3.1 Representing the Official View at International Conferences: Anatoly Kapustin

A first defence of Russia's actions in Crimea came from Anatoly Kapustin (1954–), president of RAMP and first deputy director of the Institute of Legislation and Comparative Law under the Government of the Russian Federation, who issued a circular letter to the members of the International Law Association.[83] Kapustin appeared earlier as a leading authority representing and promoting a distinct Russian perspective on international law abroad, for example with a lecture in the 'national perspectives' series of the UN Audiovisual Library of International Law.[84] In the circular letter, Kapustin describes the events in Ukraine in February 2014 along the lines of the Russian government's official interpretation, that is that the Ukrainian Revolution was an 'anticonstitutional coup d'etat'; that the Crimean vote was an exercise of the 'right of the Crimean nation to self-determination'; that the secession of Kosovo from Serbia set a 'precedent' in international law; and that denying Crimea the right to join the Russian Federation 'is apprehended as quasi-legal hypocrisy and application of double standards'.[85] Moreover, and similarly in line with the Russian president's arguments laid out in his Crimea Speech,[86] the bulk of Kapustin's letter is not a legal assessment of the events but appears rather like a call for international recognition of Russian historical-irredentist claims. Kapustin states:

> Many people in Ukraine speak Russian as a first language and consider Russia a closely related country rather than a foreign one.... This is the land of their parents and ancestors. Ukraine is their Slavic motherland.... [A]nti-Russian rhetoric and

[82] P.P. Kremnev, *Распад СССР: международно-правовые проблемы* [The Dissolution of the USSR: International Legal Problems] (Moscow: Zertsalo, 2005), 77. With regard to the status of Sevastopol see also E.S. Krichikova, '«Круглый стол» в МГИМО-У по Севастополю' [Round Table at MGIMO on Sevastopol], *Moskovskiĭ zhurnal mezhdunarodnogo prava* 27 (1997), no. 3, 136–41.

[83] Anatoly Kapustin, 'Открытое письмо: В Исполнительный совет Ассоциации международного права' [Circular Letter: To the Executive Council of the International Law Association], 6 June 2014, Russian original and English translation available at: http://www.ilarb.ru/html/news/2014/5062014.pdf. See also Caroline von Gall, 'Ist die Krim wirklich russisch? Russische Juristen diskutieren über die Rechtmäßigkeit der Aufnahme der Krim', *Russland-Analysen* 295 (2015), 2–7, 2.

[84] Anatoly Kapustin, 'В поисках системного понимания международного права: взгляд из России' [A Systemic Understanding of International Law: The Russian Perspective], UN Office of Legal Affairs, Audiovisual Library of International Law, 2017, http://legal.un.org/avl/ls/Kapustin_IL_video_1.html.

[85] Kapustin, 'Circular Letter' (2014) (n. 83), 7–9.

[86] See Chapter 4 Section 2.

> actions of Kiev authorities couldn't be ignored by Crimea people of the Crimea. In such conditions holding the Crimean referendum, will expression in form of return of Crimea people to the historical homeland—Russia—became the restoration of historical justice, realization of historically developed legal grounds.[87]

Kapustin's circular letter was only the first in a series of interventions in the international academic debate on Crimea, giving Kapustin the appearance of Russia's quasi-official advocate in the case. In this capacity, Kapustin participated in all three major international conferences in which 'Crimea' was discussed in the light of international law: in a session at the annual meeting of the American Society of International Law in Washington, D.C., on 9 April 2014; in a symposium organized by the Max Planck Institute for Comparative Public Law and International Law in Heidelberg, on 2–3 September 2014; and in a seminar organized by the Center for Polish-Russian Dialogue and Understanding in Warsaw, on 19–20 March 2015. Unfortunately, Kapustin's contributions during these events were not subsequently published,[88] with the notable exception of an article in a 'special issue' on Crimea in the *Heidelberg Journal of International Law*, based on his presentation at the Heidelberg symposium.

In the article, entitled 'Crimea's Self-determination in the Light of Contemporary International Law', Kapustin outlines the right of peoples to self-determination in line with the general Russian understanding of self-determination as a basic principle of international law, guaranteeing all peoples the right to determine freely and without external influence their own destiny, *including the right to secession.*[89] From the savings clause of the Friendly Relations Declaration,[90] Kapustin concludes that a right of secession exists however only in 'exceptional circumstances'.[91] Furthermore, Kapustin regards the secessions of Kosovo from Serbia, South Ossetia, and Abkhazia from Georgia, and Crimea from Ukraine as evidence of emerging state practice confirming the existence of such a right.[92]

With regard to Crimea, Kapustin maintains that its population 'developed a political-ethnic community' that qualifies as a people under international law,[93] a

[87] Kapustin, 'Circular Letter' (2014) (n. 83), 9.

[88] The contributions in Washington and Warsaw were, however, recorded, see American Society of International Law, '2014 Annual Meeting Videos: Is International Law Effective? The Case of Russia and Ukraine', Washington, D.C., 9 April 2014, https://www.asil.org/resources/2014-annual-meeting-videos; Center for Polish-Russian Dialogue and Understanding, 'Conferences and Seminars: The Case of Crimea in the Light of International Law: Its Nature and Implications', Warsaw, 19–20 March 2015, http://cprdip.pl/en,events,conferences_and_seminars,61,the_case_of_crimea_in_the_light_of_international_law_its_nature_and_implications.html.

[89] Anatoly Kapustin, 'Crimea's Self-determination in the Light of Contemporary International Law', *Zeitschrift für ausländisches öffentliches Recht und Völkerrecht* 75 (2015), 101–18, 104.

[90] See n. 62 above.

[91] Kapustin, 'Crimea's Self-determination in the Light of Contemporary International Law' (2015) (n. 89), 106–8.

[92] Ibid., 107. The precedential value of the Kosovo case is however qualified in a footnote (fn. 23).

[93] Ibid., 115.

concept he defines (with reference to Chernichenko) as 'close to the concept of the "nation" '.[94] Moreover, Kapustin claims that 'the physical existence of the people [of Crimea] was at stake and therefore secession from Ukraine was justified', and 'only an appeal to neighbouring states, in this case Russia, for assistance in ensuring the basic right to life and the right to freedom of expression, promised to secure the right to self-determination of the Crimean people'.[95] As such, Kapustin thereby not only follows the alternative interpretation of the events along the lines of the White Book on Violations of Human Rights and the Rule of Law in Ukraine published by the Russian MFA,[96] but arguably also hints at the occasional revitalization of the former Soviet doctrine of wars of national liberation that could be observed in the RAMP textbook and elsewhere.

Although Kapustin's contribution to the *Heidelberg Journal of International Law* draws on legal rhetoric in an attempt to justify Russia's actions in Ukraine, it simultaneously introduces historical-irredentist claims into the debate similar to the circular letter sent to the International Law Association. At one point in the article for instance, Kapustin claims that in 'deciding on their reunification', Russia and the self-proclaimed Republic of Crimea 'recalled the historic community of their people and took into account the existing connections between them'. Acknowledging that '[g]enerally, a reference to the historical basis is extremely rare in international law', Kapustin nevertheless maintains:

> It also cannot be ignored when it comes to reuniting historically united nations. The division of Russia and Crimea was largely artificial and in the process of the disintegration of the USSR a satisfactory legal statement of territorial issues was, for historical reasons, not implemented. Subsequently the conclusion of bilateral agreements between the Russian Federation and Ukraine, as well as documents of the Commonwealth of Independent States ... stated only the *status quo* and did not address the question of the legal status of some of the disputed territories, which means that there are still some unresolved territorial disputes and conflicts on the territory of CIS member states.[97]

As has been noted earlier, such considerations to right perceived historical wrongs are irrelevant for matters of international law.

[94] Ibid., 105, referring to Chernichenko, *Theory of International Law* (1999) (n. 10), vol. 2, 177.

[95] Kapustin, 'Crimea's Self-determination in the Light of Contemporary International Law' (2015) (n. 89), 117.

[96] Ministry of Foreign Affairs of Russia, White Book on Violations of Human Rights and the Rule of Law in Ukraine (November 2013–March 2014), April 2014, available at: http://www.mid.ru/documents/10180/698385/White+Book.pdf/d806eb55-5a78-459b-950c-2072ebbcf7fe. On the reliability of that report see Chapter 4 Section 2 above.

[97] Kapustin, 'Crimea's Self-determination in the Light of Contemporary International Law' (2015) (n. 89), 117.

3.2 Vladislav Tolstykh's 'Letter to the Editors' in the Chinese Journal of International Law

Apart from the above mentioned international conferences, Russia's annexation of Crimea was also the subject of various 'special issues' or series of articles in international law journals. Contributions by Russian international law scholars in periodicals published in English language were however rare. One of the very few exceptions apart from Kapustin's article in the Heidelberg journal was a series of contributions by Vladislav Tolstykh, professor of international law at Novosibirsk State University, of which the first was published as a 'Letter to the Editors' in the *Chinese Journal of International Law*. Interestingly, Tolstykh's letter is a response to an article in the same journal by Rein Müllerson, the co-author of the two seminal articles published at the time of *perestroĭka* which proclaimed the 'new thinking' in international law, discussed in Chapter 1.[98] Following the dissolution of the Soviet Union, Müllerson continued his career abroad and became professor of international law first in London and then in Tallinn. During that time, Müllerson published widely on various topics of international law,[99] including a book chapter and an article on self-determination and secession.[100]

In the article 'Ukraine: Victim of Geopolitics' for the *Chinese Journal of International Law*, Müllerson argues that the recognition of Kosovo as an independent state by large parts of the international community has set a 'negative precedent' which, in turn, has made it easier for Russia to recognize Abkhazia and South Ossetia as independent states.[101] Although Müllerson considers Russia's actions in Crimea to qualify as an act of aggression and as a violation of the prohibition of the use of force, and concludes that the Crimean vote was therefore illegal, he nevertheless maintains that Russia's annexation of Crimea may be seen as legitimate in a similar way NATO's intervention in Kosovo in 1999 has been described as 'illegal but legitimate'.[102] Above all, Müllerson maintains, Russia's actions have to be understood as reactions to a geopolitical threat posed by NATO and the United States:

> Ukraine under President Yushchenko, like Georgia under Saakashvili, was about to sign with NATO a Membership Action Plan (MAP) that would have led to full

[98] See Chapter 1 Section 4 above.

[99] See e.g. Rein Müllerson, *Constitutional Reform and International Law in Central and Eastern Europe* (The Hague: Kluwer Law International, 1998); Rein Müllerson, *Ordering Anarchy: International Law in International Society* (The Hague: Nijhoff, 2000); Rein Müllerson, *Regime Change: From Democratic Peace Theories to Forcible Regime Change* (Leiden: Nijhoff, 2013).

[100] Rein Müllerson, 'Then and Now, Here and There', in Dalitz, *Secession and International Law* (2003) (n. 66), 125–65; Rein Müllerson, 'Precedents in the Mountains: On the Parallels and Uniqueness of the Cases of Kosovo, South Ossetia and Abkhazia', *Chinese Journal of International Law* 8 (2009), 2–15.

[101] Rein Müllerson, 'Ukraine: Victim of Geopolitics', *Chinese Journal of International Law* 13 (2014), 133–45, 139.

[102] Ibid., 140–1.

> membership. NATO, in contradistinction to the EU, is a geopolitical and military alliance and its movement closer to Russian borders serves geopolitical aims.... And Moscow is responding. In 2008 it did that in Georgia and now in Ukraine. This is *in concrecto*. But in *grosso modo* Russia is responding to the encroachment of the United States and its NATO allies closer and closer to the Russian borders.... And Russia, in responding to Washington, is also breaching various norms of international law, as we have shown above. In that respect, i.e. bending and breaching international law, Russia has had good teachers.[103]

In response to Müllerson's article (and without actually engaging with his positions), Tolstykh explicitly aims to provide a 'Russian perspective' on Crimea.[104] Like Kapustin, Tolstykh argues that the population of Crimea exercised its right to self-determination following the ousting of Viktor Yanukovych as Ukrainian president by way of secession from Ukraine and reunification with Russia. However, Tolstykh's reasoning differs from that of Kapustin in the way he arrives at that conclusion. Drawing extensively from Hobbes, Locke, and Rousseau, Tolstykh argues that the right to self-determination can be understood as an expression of the general will. As such, self-determination has to be viewed against the theoretical background of the concept of the social contract: when a government of a given state ceases to obey the laws, Tolstykh maintains, the state undergoes 'contraction' which, in the case of Ukraine following the 'coup' (i.e. the ousting of Yanukovych as president of Ukraine), resulted in the creation of a smaller Ukraine, 'consisting of those who supported the coup and excluding those who did not support it'.[105] As has been noted earlier, the assumption that revolutionary changes of government can result in the extinction of states is contrary to the consensus view in international law scholarship, but in line with the former Soviet doctrine.[106]

[103] Ibid., 143. Müllerson later qualified his assessment, now denying that Russia's threat to use force amounted to aggression, but otherwise upholding his view that Russia's actions were essentially a response to attempts of containment by Western powers, see Rein Müllerson, 'One Man's Separatist—Another Man's Independentist: Self-determination Claims from Scotland to Ukraine', in Peter Hilpold (ed.), *Autonomie und Selbstbestimmung in Europa und im internationalen Vergleich* (Zurich: Nomos, 2016), 68–83; Peter Hilpold, *Dawn of a New Order: Geopolitics and the Clash of Ideologies* (London: Tauris, 2017), 95–122. For a review of the latter work see Lauri Mälksoo, 'The Annexation of Crimea and Balance of Power in International Law', *European Journal of International Law* 30 (2019), 303–19, 311–19.

[104] Vladislav Tolstykh, 'Reunification of Crimea with Russia: A Russian Perspective', *Chinese Journal of International Law* 13 (2014), 879–86. The article is a slightly revised version of Vladislav Tolstykh, 'Воссоединение Крыма с Россией: правовые квалификации' [The Reunification of Crimea with Russia: Legal Qualifications], *Evraziĭskiĭ yuridicheskiĭ zhurnal* 72 (2014), 40–6. Tolstykh's ideas were further developed in Vladislav Tolstykh, 'Three Ideas of Self-determination in International Law and the Reunification of Crimea with Russia', *Zeitschrift für ausländisches öffentliches Recht und Völkerrecht* 75 (2015), 119–39, 123–8, a slightly revised version of 'Три идеи самоопределения в международном праве' [Three Ideas of Self-determination in International Law], *Evraziĭskiĭ yuridicheskiĭ zhurnal* 76 (2014), 65–72.

[105] Tolstykh, 'Reunification of Crimea with Russia' (2014) (n. 104), 881.

[106] See Chapter 4 Section 2 above. For a representative example of this view in Soviet scholarship see G.I. Tunkin (William E. Butler transl.), *Theory of International Law* (London: Wildy, Simmonds and Hill Publishing, 2nd edn, 2003), 3.

Proceeding from this questionable (to say the least) theoretical conceptualization of the right to self-determination, Tolstykh argues that in international law the idea of 'contraction' of the state is reflected in the savings clause of the Friendly Relations Declaration. Proceeding form that view, Tolstykh maintains that 'the right to secession arises when a nation is excluded from the internal political dialogue, when its will is not taken into account when making policy decisions'.[107] According to Tolstykh, such a situation existed in Ukraine in February 2014, when 'some events' (he lists 'an attempt to cancel the law on regional languages, numerous cases of demolition of monuments to Lenin, anti-Russian proclamations and speeches') led to the exclusion of the population of Crimea from the political process in Ukraine, 'carried out through the establishment of cultural qualification' which, in Tolstykh's assessment, amounted to 'genocide'—albeit 'not in the narrow sense in which the term is defined by the Convention of 1948, but in the broad sense in which it is determined by R[aphael] Lemkin'.[108]

The determination of the general will of the people in the phase of contraction of a state may be achieved by way of referendum, Tolstykh continues.[109] However, referendums are only an accurate expression of the general will if 'the choice of the nation was made with full knowledge of all relevant circumstances and in the absence of fraud or coercion by a third party'.[110] According to Tolstykh, Russia's military presence in Crimea during the referendum was no coercion in that sense since it 'was not designed to intervene in the process of formation of the will of [the] Crimean population', and therefore 'cannot be considered as violence'.[111] Moreover, in Tolstykh's view, 'failure to observe the freedoms of expression and assembly, even if true, can hardly be regarded as fraud', and international standards for holding referendums 'have value only if they ensure the coincidence of solutions expressed in the referendum with the actual will of the people' which, in the case of the Crimean referendum, is beyond doubt: 'it is natural to assume that, considering themselves as part of the Russian world, the residents of Crimea were initially predisposed in favor of political union with Russia'.[112] Lastly, in Tolstykh's view, Crimea's choice is not only a political but also a civilizational decision, because the 'liberal systems of the West' dominate other peoples and are a 'tool of colonialism of the XX–XXI centuries'.[113] He concludes:

[107] Tolstykh, 'Reunification of Crimea with Russia' (2014) (n. 104), 879.

[108] Ibid., 884, On Raphael Lemkin's notion of genocide see William A. Schabas, *Genocide in International Law: The Crime of Crimes* (Cambridge: Cambridge University Press, 2000), 26–30.

[109] Tolstykh, 'Reunification of Crimea with Russia' (2014) (n. 104), 881.

[110] Ibid. Cf. these requirements with the international standards outlined in Chapter 4 Section 2 above.

[111] Ibid., 882.

[112] Ibid.

[113] Ibid., 885.

> The Ukrainian crisis has not only political and legal, but also ideological, cultural, historical and civilizational dimensions. The result of the coup was not only the separation of Crimea from Ukraine, but also the separation of Ukraine from the Russian world. However, in contrast to Crimea becoming part of Russia, Ukraine did not and will not become a part of Europe or the Western world; for this it would have to completely give up its language, history and genetic memory.[114]

3.3 The Debate on Crimea in the Domestic Academic Discourse in Russia

Inside Russia, a first occasion in which 'Crimea' was discussed in terms of international law was a round table event in April 2014, jointly organized by the Diplomatic Academy of the Russian MFA and the Russian Association of International Law, and attended by some of the most eminent Russian academics in the field (Stanislav Chernichenko, Anatoly Kapustin, Oleg Khlestov, and others).[115] Chernichenko's statements during the conference are particularly interesting, since they appear to be a condensed reaffirmation of the official Russian position as expressed by Kapustin in the circular letter and at international conferences, blended with Tolstykh's theory (and Putin's remark)[116] reminiscent of the former Soviet doctrine that the Ukrainian state (at least partly) ceased to exist following the Ukrainian Revolution. At one point during the discussion, Chernichenko states:

> Who did we have to enter an agreement regarding the transfer of Crimea to Russia with? [There was] no one.... Yes, Ukraine is a subject of international law, yes, we indeed had an agreement with Ukraine concerning the territorial integrity of Ukraine.... In the situation that we faced, in a legal sense, there was no public authority in Ukraine, it did not exist. This is our position. Who could we negotiate with? Hence, in this situation we could only be guided by the expression of will of the Crimean population. Only after [Crimea's declaration of

[114] Ibid., 886. Tolstykh later qualified some of his assessments, but upheld most of his core theses, see Vladislav Tolstykh, 'Book Review Notes: Difficult Search for Truth', *Russian Law Journal* 6 (2018), no. 4, 154–65. See also Vladislav Tolstykh, 'Revisiting the Principle of Self-determination' in Władysław Czapliński, Sławomir Dębski, Rafał Tarnogórski, and Karolina Wierczyńska (eds), *The Case of Crimea's Annexation under International Law* (Warsaw: Scholar Publishing House, 2017), 99–108.

[115] Diplomatic Academy of the Russian Ministry of Foreign Affairs, 'Круглый стол на тему: «Международно-правовые аспекты присоединения Крыма к России»' [Round Table: International Legal Aspects of Integration of Crimea into Russia], 10 April 2014, https://www.youtube.com/watch?v=4k620BZKyto. The discussions are summarized in Anton Moiseienko, 'Guest Post: What do Russian Lawyers Say about Crimea?', *Opinio Juris*, 24 September 2014.

[116] See Chapter 4 Section 2 above.

independence and the referendum] we could speak of restoration of our historical rights to Crimea.[117]

Apart from the roundtable event, the Russian academic discourse on Crimea occurred primarily in Russian law journals. Georgiy Velyaminov (1925–) for instance, professor of international law at IGP RAN, published an article on 'The Reunification of Crimea with Russia' in the prestigious Russian public law journal *State and Law*.[118] In the article, Velyaminov argues for the legitimacy of the Crimean referendum, and refutes any claims according to which the vote took place 'at gunpoint of Russian soldiers' as lacking any evidence.[119] Furthermore, in Velyaminov's view, a referendum on state independence held in part of a territory of a state is an exercise of the right to self-determination, to the necessary effect of a 'change of the territorial integrity' of the affected state.[120] Lastly, Velyaminov argues that the envisaged guarantees and the agreed state borders of Ukraine in the Budapest Memorandum of 1994 are subject to the general legal principle of *rebus sic stantibus*, the legal doctrine allowing for international agreements to become inapplicable because of a fundamental change of circumstances: 'The general political situation in Ukraine, both internally and externally, but also in terms of ensuring public security and the rule of law, has changed as a result of the coup in February 2014.'[121] Such an assessment is astonishing since Velyaminov thereby ignores not only Russia's further commitments to respect Ukraine's borders in the agreements and treaties of 1990, 1992, 1997, and 2003,[122] but also the second paragraph of article 62 of the Vienna Convention of the Law of Treaties, which explicitly states that a fundamental change of circumstances may not be invoked as a ground for terminating or withdrawing from a treaty if the treaty establishes a boundary or if the fundamental change is the result of a breach by the party invoking it either of an obligation under the treaty or of any other international obligation owed to any other party to the treaty.[123]

[117] Stanislav Chernichenko, in 'Round Table' (2014) (n. 115). Quotation from the English transcription in Issaeva, 'Quarter of a Century on from the Soviet Era' (2017) (n. 4), 95. On Chernichenko's views on Russia's actions in Crimea see also the recorded lecture published by the Diplomatic Academy: Stanislav Chernichenko, 'Лекция Черниченко: Нерешенные проблемы международного права' [Chernichenko Lecture: Unresolved Problems of International Law], 14 November 2014, https://www.youtube.com/ watch?v=T7ohudXoXU8.

[118] G.M. Velyaminov, 'Воссоединение Крыма с Россией: правовой ракурс' [The Reunification of Crimea with Russia: Legal Perspective], *Gosudarstvo i pravo* (2014), no. 9, 12–18. German translation: G.M. Velyaminov, (Alexander Trunk transl.), 'Wiedervereinigung der Krim mit Russland—eine Skizze aus russischer Sicht', *Kieler Ostrechts-Notizen* 18/19 (2014/2015), no. 1/2, 10–14.

[119] Ibid., 11–12.

[120] Ibid., 12.

[121] Ibid., 13. On the 'déjà vu element' of this claim see Lauri Mälksoo, 'Crimea and (the Lack of) Continuity in Russian Approaches to International Law', *EJIL: Talk!*, 28 March 2014.

[122] See Chapter 4 Section 2 above.

[123] Vienna Convention on the Law of Treaties, 23 May 1969, 1155 UNTS 331, art. 62(2). On the interpretation of article 62 VCLT see Malcolm N. Shaw and Caroline Fournet, 'Article 62', in Olivier Corten and Pierre Klein (eds), *The Vienna Conventions on the Law of Treaties*, vol. 2 (Oxford: Oxford University Press, 2011), 1411–36.

Further assessments on Crimea appeared in particular in the *Eurasian Law Journal*, all unanimously justifying Russia's actions in Ukraine and arguing for the legality of Crimea's 'reunification' with Russia one way or another.[124] Arguably the most interesting contribution did however not deal with 'Crimea' directly, but was a possibly farsighted article essentially comprising an argument for the revitalization of the concept of historical consolidation of title by Alexander Vylegzhanin (jointly published with Ekaterina Sokolova), the head of the international law department of MGIMO, in the April/June 2014 issue of the *Moscow Journal of International Law*.[125] With this article, published right at a time when the incorporation of Crimea into the Russian Federation was barely completed, Vylegzhanin and Sokolova seem to cautiously argue in favour of the consideration of historical rights within the framework of the concept of prescription in international law, based on the right of peoples to self-determination.

The basic question behind prescription is to what extent can a lapse of time 'cure' an initially illegal act, in particular: create title to territory acquired by the use of force?[126] Following a historical overview of the concept, Vylegzhanin and Sokolova proceed from a statement in the 2004 edition of the textbook of Kutafin Moscow State Law University, according to which 'it has been proposed to consider a permissible way of changing state territory the "returning of a territory as a result of the restoration of historical rights to previously illegally detached parts of a territory" '.[127] Although Vylegzhanin and Sokolova concede that 'this doctrinal position does not find confirmation in the decisions of international courts and

[124] See in particular the contributions by Vladislav Tolstykh discussed above (n. 104) as well as K.B. Tolkachev, '«Крымский вопрос» и современное право: к дискуссии о легитимности референдума' ['The Crimean Question' and Contemporary Law: On the Discussion on the Legitimacy of the Referendum], *Evraziĭskiĭ yuridicheskiĭ zhurnal* 72 (2014), 90–2, and I.Z. Farhutdinov, 'Евразийская интеграция и испытание украинской государственности в системе международного права' [Eurasian Integration and Test of Ukrainian Statehood in International Law], *Evraziĭskiĭ yuridicheskiĭ zhurnal* 79 (2014), 15–20. Articles published in other Russian law journals includeA.A. Moiseev, 'О некоторых международно-правовых позициях по крымскому вопросу' [On Some International Law Positions on the Crimean Issue], *Mezhdunarodnaya zhizn'* (2014), no. 5, 53–65; Vladimir Tomsinov, 'Международное право с точки зрения воссоединения Крыма с Россией' [International Law from the Point of View of the Reunification of Crimea with Russia], *Zakonodatel'stvo* (2014), no. 7, 11–26; Evgeny R. Voronin, Vyacheslav N. Kulebyakin, and Alexy V. Nikolaev, 'Государственный переворот в Киеве в феврале 2014 г.: международно-правовые оценки и последствия' [The Coup d'État in Kyiv in February 2014: International Law Context and Consequences], *Moskovskiĭ zhurnal mezhdunarodnogo prava* 97 (2015), no. 1, 11–28.

[125] Alexander Vylegzhanin and Ekaterina Sokolova, 'Приобретательская давность в международном праве' [Prescription in International Law], *Moskovskiĭ zhurnal mezhdunarodnogo prava* 94 (2014), no. 2, 37–58.

[126] For a general discussion of the relevance of a fait accompli in international law see Carl Bilfinger, 'Vollendete Tatsache und Völkerrecht—eine Studie', *Zeitschrift für ausländisches öffentliches Recht und Völkerrecht* 15 (1953/1954), 453–81. For the beginnings of this doctrine surrounding 'the normative force of the factual' (*die normative Kraft des Faktischen*) see Georg Jellinek, *Allgemeine Staatslehre* (Berlin: Häring, 3rd edn, 1914), 340 et seq.

[127] Vylegzhanin and Sokolova, 'Prescription in International Law' (2014) (n. 125), 38, quoting R.A. Kalamkaryan and Yu.I. Migachev (eds), *Международное право: Учебник* [International Law: Textbook] (Moscow: Eksmo, 2004), 468.

tribunals on territorial disputes', they also stress that 'there is no doubt that historical rights ... and not only the exercise of state authority are often referred to by states to substantiate their rights to a specific territory'.[128]

Vylegzhanin and Sokolova continue with a review of different doctrinal positions on prescription in international law scholarship, in particular the Soviet works of Yuri Barseghov and Boris Klimenko on territorial acquisition discussed in Chapter 1 of this book.[129] (Barseghov's referred work is actually limited to the problem of acquisition of titles to historic waters, an important limitation the authors do not mention and thereby tacitly extend to general considerations.)[130] They write:

> Barseghov notes that 'historical legal grounds, considered by themselves as a law-forming factor, are very close, if not identical, with the institution of acquisitive prescription in terms of content, assessment criteria and formation conditions', but still these are two different concepts.... In contrast to the opinion of Yu. G. Barseghov, B. M. Klimenko writes that 'acquisitive prescription has been subjected to thorough criticism on the grounds that it justifies the unlawful seizure of territory and thus contradicts the principle of self-determination and the prohibition of the use of force'. But still, if the use of acquisitive prescription is possible without the forcible seizure of foreign territories and without violating the principle of self-determination, then 'acquisitive prescription may cause a different attitude'.[131]

The article goes on (with further reference to Klimenko) to restate the conditions necessary to make acquisitive prescription effective, in particular under which circumstances the conduct of the affected state having lost part of its territory might be interpreted as a manifestation of tacit agreement with the 'events' which had led to that loss.[132] In a next section, the concept of historical consolidation of title is discussed, in which Vylegzhanin and Sokolova seem to agree with Klimenko that this concept is so similar to that of prescription that the two are essentially identical.[133]

[128] Vylegzhanin and Sokolova, 'Prescription in International Law' (2014) (n. 125), 39.

[129] See Chapter 1 Section 4 above.

[130] Vylegzhanin's field of expertise is the law on the Antarctic. See e.g. A.N. Vylegzhanin and V.K. Zilanov (eds), (William E. Butler transl.), *Spitsbergen: Legal Regime of Adjacent Marine Areas* (Utrecht: Eleven International Publishing, 2007). On Vylegzhanin's positions on the Antarctic see Mälksoo, *Russian Approaches to International Law* (2015) (n. 3), 139–40.

[131] Vylegzhanin and Sokolova, 'Prescription in International Law' (2014) (n. 125), 46, referring to Yu.G. Barseghov, 'Вопрос о правовом статусе и правовых основаниях приобретения титулов на исторические воды в современном международном морском праве' [The Issue of the Legal Status and Legal Foundations for Acquisition of Titles to Historic Waters in Modern Law of the Sea', *Sovetskiĭ ezhegodnik mezhdunarodnogo prava* (1987), 201–22, 209–10, and B.M. Klimenko, *Государственная территория* [State Territory] (Moscow: Mezhdunarodnye otnosheniya, 1974), 110, respectively.

[132] Vylegzhanin and Sokolova, 'Prescription in International Law' (2014) (n. 125), 47.

[133] Ibid., 48–50, referring to Klimenko, *State Territory* (1974) (n. 131), 111–12.

A review of the relevant case law in which historical considerations were discussed in the past by international courts and tribunals conclude the article.[134]

At first sight, Vylegzhanin's and Sokolova's article appears as a descriptive restatement of different, but generally affirmative positions on prescription and historical consolidation of title—of which especially the latter is otherwise a *very* contested concept in international law doctrine (James Crawford, for example, discusses the concept in *Brownlie's Principles of Public International Law* under the heading 'An Epitaph').[135] It is the timing and the prominent placing of the article that is astonishing: right at the time of Russia's annexation of Crimea, one of the leading international law scholars in Russia sets out to revitalize a doctrine formerly embraced in Soviet scholarship in the leading Russian international law journal, supposedly with the aim of offering an additional argument Russia could raise for claiming title to Crimea at some point in the future.

4. Conclusions

This chapter has shown that post-Soviet Russian scholarship on self-determination forms a separate epistemic community, with peculiar features and doctrinal positions having existed already prior to Russia's annexation of Crimea in 2014, and the willingness to adjust these positions to official assessments of the Russian government, if necessary. Before Russia's annexation of Crimea, the discourse on self-determination in Russian scholarship of international law showed some distinctive features, of which most could be explained by a lasting legacy of the former Soviet doctrine, but in sum stayed more or less inside the canon of the 'invisible college of international lawyers', in Oscar Schachter's famous terminology.[136] With 'Crimea', the company arguably parted again, and once Russia's actions made it impossible for Russian scholarship to stay within the consensus view without criticizing the Russian government, former consensus was partly replaced by historical-irredentist claims, creative re-readings of self-determination in light of the social contract theory of early modern political philosophy, and attempts in revitalizing the concept of consolidation of historical titles.

Moreover, the assessment of 'Crimea' in Russian scholarship clearly showed that the views expressed in the academic debate—at home and abroad—by and large

[134] Ibid., 50–5, with reference to PCA, Island of Palmas Case (Unites States v Netherlands), 4 April 1928, RIAA 1949, vol. 2, 829; PCA, Clipperton Island Arbitration (France v Mexico), 28 January 1931, RIAA 1949, vol. 2, 1105; PCIJ, Legal Status of Eastern Greenland (Denmark v Norway), 5 April 1933, Publications of the Permanent Court of International Justice Series A/B, 53; ICJ, Minquiers and Ecrehos (France v United Kingdom), 17 November 1953, ICJ Reports 1953, 47; ICJ, Kasikili/Sedudu Island (Botswana v Namibia), 13 December 1999, ICJ Reports 1999, 1045.

[135] Crawford, *Brownlie's Principles of Public International Law* (2012) (n. 75), 235–6.

[136] Oscar Schachter, 'The Invisible College of International Lawyers', *Northwestern University Law Review* 72 (1977–1978), 217–26.

correlated with the official positions purported by the Russian government. An interesting exception of this correlation in positions between academia and practice was the contribution by the head of MGIMO's international law department in the most prestigious Russian international law journal, published shortly after Russia's annexation of Crimea. By revitalizing the concept of consolidation of historical titles in the framework of acquisitive prescription, Alexander Vylegzhanin seemingly attempted to set the legal ground for what one day, based on the demands of effectiveness in international law, might turn out as the ultimate challenge for Ukraine's territorial title to Crimea.[137]

The widespread readiness to justify Russia's annexation of Crimea in Russian scholarship raises the question of academic freedom in Russia.[138] In the leading institutions in the field of international law criticism seemed almost impossible. In March 2014, for example, Andrey Zubov, professor of history at MGIMO, was fired after having published an article in the Russian newspaper *Vedomosti* in which he criticized Russia's policy towards Ukraine and compared the incorporation of Crimea into the Russian Federation to Hitler's *Anschluss* of Austria into Nazi Germany.[139] (Although MGIMO was later forced to reinstate Zubov on a technicality, the institution's administration insisted that this did not in any way change the fact that Zubov had 'violated the main principles of professional conduct'.)[140] This is noteworthy as such, but appears even more worrying against the background of the 1995 workshop on Chechnya organized by Russian NGO Memorial—a similar academic event on Crimea in Putin's Russia, with scholars from some of the leading Russian academic institutions participating and openly criticizing the Russian government, was simply beyond imagination.

Nevertheless, criticism was not completely absent, and in particular scholars from the younger generation in Russia were not ready to accept the official interpretation of the events. Probably the most prominent intervention was a newspaper article in the Russian newspaper *Novaya gazeta* by Elena Lukyanova, in which the prominent professor of constitutional law, then still at the Higher School of Economics, criticized Crimea's incorporation into the Russian Federation as illegal

[137] With regard to the parallel question for the Baltic states between 1940 and 1991 see Lauri Mälksoo, *Illegal Annexation and State Continuity: The Case of the Incorporation of the Baltic States by the USSR: A Study of the Tension Between Normativity and Power in International Law* (Leiden: Martinus Nijhoff, 2003), 108–65.

[138] For a discussion of totalitarian traits in contemporary Russia more generally see Masha Gessen, *The Future is History: How Totalitarianism Reclaimed Russia* (New York, NY: Riverhead Books, 2017), 289 et seq.

[139] A.B. Zubov, 'Это уже было. Мы на пороге полного разрушение системы международных договоров, экономического хаоса и политической диктатуры' [It Happened Before. We are on the Verge of a Complete Destruction of the System of International Treaties, Economic Chaos and Political Dictatorship], *Vedomosti*, 1 March 2014.

[140] See Matthew Bodner, 'Professor Says Sacked Over Opinion Article Against Possible Ukraine Invasion', *The Moscow Times*, 5 March 2014.

under Russian constitutional law.[141] Critical contributions dealing with international law aspects appeared in particular in the *Russian Law Journal*. Although Russia's actions in Ukraine were also defended and justified in that journal,[142] it was virtually the only academic forum in Russia where there was also room for criticism. Anatoly Pronin of Voronezh State University suggested for instance that those scholars who argue that 'Crimea is Ours' must have 'either forgotten their knowledge in the sphere of law or used it in accordance with the proverb "Little thieves are hanged but great ones escape"'.[143] Unfortunately however, Pronin doesn't engage with any of the positions raised in that discourse of 'Crimea is Ours' substantially, and one is therefore left with an angry polemic rather than a legal assessment.

Another critical contribution appeared in the same journal in 2017 by Maria Issaeva, a practising lawyer from Moscow who has made quite a name for herself internationally for criticizing the Russian academic international law elite following Russia's annexation of Crimea.[144] After having reviewed the various doctrinal responses by Chernichenko, Kapustin, Tolstykh, and others, Issaeva arrives at the following conclusion:

> Building upon a legacy of strong Soviet rhetoric, guardians of the closed system of 'Russian international law' continue, domestically, to view and present it as the leading 'science' of international law in the world—a world that unfairly fails to likewise accord it such status. A fair question can be (and indeed has been) asked as to whether international scholars adhering to 'Western' paradigms may indeed be more biased in favouring of blaming Russia for violations committed by a 'Western' state. Indeed, there does appear to be a certain distrust of the Russian positions voiced.... [I]s such distrust coming from 'the West' and is due to Russia's position as a country on the world stage—as some post-Soviet scholars are trying to claim,—or does it come from a professional legal community and is due to logical, communicational and even linguistic fallacies in the rhetoric of Russian international legal doctrine (and of the Russian government)? In other words, can we assess if the Russian doctrinal scholars play the instrument of international

[141] Elena Lukyanova, 'О праве налево. К вопросу о верховенстве права в контексте российской внешней политики, или Почему, согласно закону Российской Федерации, Крым все-таки не совсем наш' [About the Right to the Left: On the Question of the Rule of Law in the Context of Russian Foreign Policy, or Why, According to the Law of the Russian Federation, Crimea is Not Quite Ours], *Novaya gazeta*, 19 March 2015.

[142] See John J.A. Burke and Svetlana Panina-Burke, 'Eastern and Southern Ukraine's Right to Secede and Join the Russian Federation', *Russian Law Journal* 3 (2015), no. 1, 33–57.

[143] Anatoly Pronin, 'Republic of Crimea: A Two-Day State', *Russian Law Journal* 3 (2015), no. 1, 133–42, 133–4.

[144] See e.g. Maria Issaeva, 'Does "Russian International Law" Have an International Academic Future?', *EJIL Talk!*, 21 September 2015; Maria Issaeva, 'A Nationalized Approach to International Law: The Case of Russia', *Völkerrechtsblog*, 5 January 2018.

> law, or if they simply smash on its keys pretending that this is some form of avant-garde music?[145]

And Gleb Bogush of the Higher School of Economics, wrote in a review of Mälksoo's *Russian Approaches to International Law*:

> Taking into account the low popularity of Russian international law among Russian law students in the past two decades, ... and with imitation as one of the main features of Russian social and political life in the 2000s, one may wonder if it is fair to treat the 'official' Russian doctrine as the 'Russian school of international law'. It is suggested that the representatives of Russian international law can be more properly identified as a group of diligent servants and power players, and the excess of the authoritarian power-politics should be identified and treated as such.[146]

Indeed, this could be a valid critique, since one of the inherent dangers in attempting to ascertain national approaches to international law is obviously the exclusion of sub-national, sub-regional, or separatist voices: it validates one particular view as dominant to the exclusion of others.[147] But then, on the other hand, one wonders: if academic freedom was really not the issue (as these younger scholars unanimously claimed),[148] why were legal judgments of Russia's state actions and/or critical substantial engagements with the positions promoted by this 'group of diligent servants and power players' virtually non-existent in the Russian international law discourse on Crimea?

[145] Issaeva, 'Quarter of a Century on from the Soviet Era' (2017) (n. 4), 111–12.

[146] Gleb Bogush, 'Book Review Notes: The Illusive Nature of "Russian International Law"', *Russian Law Journal* 3 (2015), no. 4, 165–9, 169.

[147] See Boris M. Mamlyuk and Ugo Mattei, 'Comparative International Law', *Brookings Journal of International Law* 36 (2011), 385–452, 431.

[148] Asked by the author during a conference on 9–10 November 2018 in Cologne on 'Law and Revolution: Disruption and Continuity of Legal Development in Central and Eastern Europe' organized by the German Association for East European Studies, both Issaeva and Bogush maintained that academic freedom in Russia was not an issue.

Final Conclusions

According to the Foreign Policy Concept of the Russian Federation of 30 November 2016, Russia 'consistently advocates strengthening the legal foundations of international relations and complies with its international legal obligations in good faith. Maintaining and strengthening international rule of law is among its priorities in the international arena.' To achieve this goal, Russia intends to 'counter attempts to revise' and to 'arbitrarily interpret' fundamental principles of international law such as 'non-use of force or threat of force, peaceful settlement of international disputes, respect for sovereignty and territorial integrity of States, [and the] right of peoples to self-determination'.[1]

After having analysed Russia's post-Soviet approach to the right of peoples to self-determination, one could of course be inclined to call this self-portrayal of Russia as a guardian of international law blunt hypocrisy. But there is also another, arguably more insightful way of interpreting this statement, namely to acknowledge that when Vladimir Putin, Sergey Lavrov, Anatoly Kapustin, or Vladislav Tolstykh speak of international law, they actually mean different things than their Western colleagues, and what one can observe is not (only) Russian power politics disguised as legal rhetoric but traits of a regional (re-)fragmentation of international law.

This book provided more than one example that there is reason to believe that even basic agreement on what self-determination as a concept of international law means and what role related concepts such as territorial integrity, secession, referendum, or the prohibition of the use of force do or should play in that context seems almost unattainable, to the effect that international law as a single epistemological frame is arguably in a similar danger as in Soviet times. An increasing difficulty to establish a common understanding of historical facts on which legal assessments can be based exacerbates this danger, with diverging assessments of historical events fitting into a broader trend in Russia where alternative official narratives and historiographies are being established.[2]

[1] The Foreign Policy Concept of the Russian Federation, 30 November 2016, para. 26, available at the website of the Embassy of the Russian Federation to the United Kingdom at: https://www.rusemb.org.uk/rp_insight.

[2] To doubt these official Russian interpretations is not only disfavoured, but increasingly criminalized. Most notoriously, an amendment to the Russian Criminal Code from 2014 prohibits the public 'dissemination of knowingly false information about the activities of the USSR during World War II'. Moreover, since 2020, article 67[1](3) of the Russian Constitution ensures the 'protection of historical truth' and prohibits the '[d]iminution of the heroic deed of the people defending the Fatherland', see

Russia and the Right to Self-Determination in the Post-Soviet Space. Johannes Socher, Oxford University Press.
 DOI: 10.1093/oso/9780192897176.003.0007

At the outset of this book, it has been stated that one interesting continuity in the reading of Soviet and post-Soviet Russian approaches to international law is the suggested usefulness of understanding these approaches in terms of assumed spheres of influences or even regional normative orders in the sense of Carl Schmitt's theory of *Großraum*. And indeed, through this logic, it is possible to make sense of some of the inconsistencies that could be observed in Russia's arguments on the right to self-determination since the dissolution of the Soviet Union: going back to Martti Koskenniemi's basic differentiation of two opposing conceptions of self-determination, one could say that for situations *inside* the Russian Federation, self-determination is understood in its classic conception, with the 'multinational people of the Russian Federation' as the only bearer of that right. For situations *outside* the Russian Federation, on the other hand, self-determination is conceptualized in its romantic or nationalist variant, arguably in order to support the idea of a greater Russian *Reich* or *derzhava*. This nationalist approach to self-determination in the post-Soviet space is supported by a policy of 'passportization' illegal under international law,[3] aiming at the conferral of nationality on the citizens of other states without sufficient factual links in Abkhazia, Crimea, South Ossetia, Transnistria, and, since 2019, also in the Donetsk and Lugansk regions of Eastern Ukraine,[4] thereby trying to extend Russia's sphere of influence by a kind of 'creeping' annexation.

But even the logic of *Großraum* has its obvious flaws: Russia recognized Abkhazia and South Ossetia as independent states but so far did not recognize Transnistria's and Nagorno-Karabakh's independence from Moldova and

Johannes Socher, 'Farewell to the European Constitutional Tradition: The 2020 Russian Constitutional Amendments', *Zeitschrift für ausländisches öffentliches Recht und Völkerrecht* 80 (2020), 615–48, 631–3.

[3] See e.g. Anne Peters, 'Extraterritorial Naturalization: Between the Human Right to Nationality, State Sovereignty and Fair Principles of Jurisdiction', *German Yearbook of International Law* 53 (2010), 623–725; Enrico Milano, 'The Conferral of Citizenship en masse by Kin-States: Creeping Annexation or Responsibility to Protect?', in Francesco Palermo and Natalie Sabanadze (eds), *National Minorities in Inter Sate Relations* (Leiden: Martinus Nijhoff, 2011), 145–66. On the rationale of this policy see Scott Littlefield, 'Citizenship, Identity and Foreign Policy: The Contradictions and Consequences of Russia's Passport Distribution in the Separatist Regions of Georgia', *Europe-Asia Studies* 61 (2009), 1461–82, 1476 et seq.

[4] On 24 and 29 April 2019, Vladimir Putin issued two presidential decrees identifying groups entitled to a 'fast-track procedure' when applying for Russian citizenship otherwise regulated by the Russian Law of Citizenship (Federal Law of Russia No. 62-FZ, О гражданстве Российской Федерации [On Citizenship of the Russian Federation], 31 May 2002, SZRF 2002, no. 22, 2031). The two decrees facilitate the acquisition of Russian nationality by residents from various districts of Ukraine's Donetsk and Lugansk regions without taking residency in Russia: Decree of the President of Russia No. 183, Об определении в гуманитарных целях категорий лиц, имеющих право обратиться с заявлениями о приёме в гражданство России в упрощённом порядке [On the Definition for Humanitarian Purposes of Categories of Persons Entitled to Apply for Admission to Russian Citizenship in a Simplified Manner], 24 April 2019, SZRF 2019, no. 17, item 2071; Decree of the President of Russia No. 187, Об отдельных категориях иностранных граждан и лиц без гражданства, имеющих право обратиться с заявлениями о приёме в гражданство Российской Федерации [On Certain Categories of Foreign Citizens and Stateless Persons Entitled to a Fast-Track Procedure when Applying for Russian Citizenship], 29 April 2019, SZRF 2019, no. 18, item 2226.

Azerbaijan, respectively. In addition, the rationales underlying these decisions appear inconsistent, because if, for example, Russia's main reason for recognizing Abkhazia was really to right a perceived historical wrong during Stalin's reign (the downgrading from a union republic of the Soviet Union to an autonomous republic within the Georgian Soviet Socialist Republic (SSR) in 1931), why has Russia then not also recognized Transnistria's independence, which became part of the newly created Moldavian SSR due to an arguably similarly arbitrary decision (its merger with Bessarabia in 1939)?

Another way of trying to make sense of Russia's approach to the right to self-determination in the post-Soviet space could be to understand it in terms of an assumed exceptionalism, based on balance-of-power considerations.[5] After Russia ultimately had to accept that it could not prevent Kosovo's secession from Serbia and its recognition as an independent state by large parts of the international community, it started to use Kosovo as a kind of tit-for-tat argument, first in Abkhazia and South Ossetia, and then also in Crimea, along the lines of if the Western powers can call Kosovo a 'special case', then Russia can call Crimea a 'special case', too.[6] In order to assess the normative value of this assumed regional hegemony, one needs to look at its 'legitimacy', internationally but also regionally. While internationally, Russia's justifications were (at least in the short run) largely unsuccessful, one probably has to acknowledge a limited degree of acceptance in the post-Soviet space by those over whom Russia's power is exercised.

First of all, one cannot fail to note that the acceptance of Russia's support for the secessionist republics' claims for self-determination among the governments and populations of these breakaway republics themselves is very high, in some cases even up to the point of requests for admission into the Russian Federation. For example, according to a 2010 study, support for reunification with Georgia among the ethnic Abkhaz population was as low as 1 per cent, and even among the ethnic Georgian population living in Abkhazia almost 50 per cent preferred the republic to remain independent.[7] South Ossetia's parliament even adopted a

[5] See Lauri Mälksoo's review essay of Rein Müllerson, *Dawn of a New World Order: Geopolitics and the Clash of Ideologies* (London: I.B. Tauris, 2017). In Mälksoo's view, 'Müllerson's project in this book seems to be that of normatively supporting great powers outside the West, especially Russia' by arguing 'that international law also needs the revival of balance-of-power thinking', Lauri Mälksoo, 'The Annexation of Crimea and Balance of Power in International Law', *European Journal of International Law* 30 (2019), 303–19, 313–14. According to Mälksoo, Müllerson's monograph can be seen as a reflection of a renaissance of balance of power, 'a historical meta-principle related to international law [which] is a dangerous idea and should be rejected lest the international community risk losing the constraining effects of Article 2, paragraph 4 of the UN Charter', ibid., 319. On Müllerson's views on Crimea see also Chapter 5 Section 3 above.

[6] Cf. only the statement by Sergey Lavrov, the Russian foreign minister, in an interview in September 2014, that he believes that 'Crimea was a very special case, a unique case from all points of view. Historically, geopolitically, and patriotically, if you wish', ('Sergey Lavrov: Throwing Russia off Balance is Ultimate Aim', *ITAR-TASS*, 11 September 2014) with the statement by the US Department of State of 18 February 2008 when recognizing Kosovo as an independent state (see Chapter 3 Section 1 above).

[7] Gerald Toal and John O'Loughlin, 'How People in South Ossetia, Abkhazia and Transnistria Feel About Annexation by Russia', *The Washington Post*, 20 March 2014.

resolution to admit South Ossetia into the Russian Federation, and the government of Transnistria made a similar request following Russia's annexation of Crimea in 2014.[8]

On the other hand, Russia's claimed regional hegemony among the states directly affected by these secessionist conflicts is fiercely disputed: in 2001, Georgia, Ukraine, Azerbaijan, and Moldova formed the Organization for Democracy and Economic Development—GUAM, which has since repeatedly pushed to discuss the conflicts of Abkhazia, Nagorno-Karabakh, South Ossetia, and Transnistria in the CIS Foreign Ministers Council and the UN General Assembly, against the declared will of Russia.[9] In 2007, GUAM member states agreed to form a 500-personnel joint peacekeeping force to battle separatism; Russia observed the project with suspicion.[10] In turn, lacking support for granting Russia a special role as a guarantor of peace and security in the post-Soviet space became evident when CIS mandated peacekeeping missions were envisaged: only five other CIS member states other than Russia signed the 1996 Regulations on Collective Peacekeeping Forces in the Commonwealth of Independent States,[11] and subsequently formed national CIS peacekeeping units could only be deployed under a UN mandate.[12]

Furthermore, not a single state from the post-Soviet space so far followed the Russian Federation in recognizing Abkhazia or South Ossetia as independent states. Russia notably also failed to obtain endorsement of its actions in Georgia at the summit of the Shanghai Cooperation Organisation (SCO) held in Dushanbe in August 2008, only two weeks after the war had ended.[13] To the contrary: the summit's final declaration, signed by China, Russia, and the four other post-Soviet states Kazakhstan, Kyrgyzstan, Tajikistan, and Uzbekistan, took a neutral stance on the war, and even reaffirmed the SCO member states' commitment to 'efforts aimed to preserve in accordance to international law unity and territorial integrity of states'.[14]

[8] See generally John O'Loughlin, Gerald Toal, and Vladimir Kolosov, 'Who Identifies with the "Russian World"? Geopolitical Attitudes in Southeastern Ukraine, Crimea, Abkhazia, South Ossetia, and Transnistria', *Eurasian Geography and Economics* 57 (2016), 745–78.

[9] Nikola Krastev, 'UN: GUAM Brings Frozen Conflicts to World Stage', *Radio Free Europe/Radio Liberty*, 27 September 2006.

[10] See 'GUAM Peacekeeping', *Russian Peacekeepers*, 19 June 2007, http://www.peacekeeper.ru/en/?module=news&action= view&id=4105.

[11] Положение о Коллективных силах по поддержанию мира в Содружестве Независимых Государств [Regulations on Collective Peacekeeping Forces in the Commonwealth of Independent States], 19 January 1996, *Diplomaticheskiĭ vestnik* (1996), no. 2, 47. The Regulations were signed by Armenia, Georgia, Kyrgyzstan, Russia, Uzbekistan, and Tajikistan.

[12] See Roy Allison, *Russia, the West, and Military Intervention* (Oxford: Oxford University Press, 2013), 133.

[13] The Shanghai Cooperation Organisation was created in 2001 and is a Eurasian political, economic, and security alliance spearheaded by Russia and China, with the four Central Asian states Kazakhstan, Kyrgyzstan, Tajikistan, and Uzbekistan as additional members. In 2017, India and Pakistan also joined, making it the largest regional organization in the world in terms of both geographical coverage and population.

[14] Dushanbe Declaration of Heads of SCO Member States, 27 August 2008, http://en.kremlin.ru/supplement/287.

In the case of Russia's annexation of Crimea, the reactions in the region were however more ambivalent: UN General Assembly Resolution 68/262 of 27 March 2014 was approved by only seven states from the post-Soviet space and Armenia and Belarus were even among the eleven states that voted against it, thereby not subscribing to the resolution's call 'to refrain from any action or dealing that might be interpreted as recognizing' any alteration of the status of Crimea.[15] Later, the government of Kyrgyzstan also said that it recognizes Crimea's decision to join the Russian Federation as 'legitimate'.[16] Moreover, General Assembly Resolution 71/205 of 19 December 2016 was approved by only six states from the post-Soviet space, whereas this time even four states (Belarus, Armenia, Kazakhstan, and Uzbekistan) followed Russia and voted against it, thereby refraining from condemning the 'temporary occupation' of Crimea by Russia.[17]

In Russian international law scholarship, Russia's assumed regional hegemony is supported by the proclamation of a national ('domestic') doctrine in line with Russian foreign policy but distinct and detached from other academic discourses abroad. Commenting on this phenomenon, the organizers of the Heidelberg symposium on Crimea discussed in Chapter 5 observed that the arguments of the participating Russian scholars 'relied above all on domestic law, on historical considerations, on political arguments, or on readings of international legal norms which—in our view—depart from prior scholarly consensus, not only among western scholars but shared around the globe', adding that the 'crisis is matched by the absence of a serious legal dialogue among international legal scholars of both camps'.[18] And even where dialogue took place, one could get the impression that the participants were talking about increasingly different things: while Western scholars framed the discussion mainly as questions of annexation and Russian use of force, scholars from Russia focused on the right to self-determination.[19]

[15] GA Res. 68/262 (Territorial Integrity of Ukraine), 27 March 2014, UN Doc. A/RES/68/262. Azerbaijan, Estonia, Georgia, Latvia, Lithuania, Moldova, and Ukraine voted in favour of the resolution, the remaining five states from the post-Soviet space either abstained (Kazakhstan, Uzbekistan) or were absent (Kyrgyzstan, Tajikistan, Turkmenistan), see Voting Record on Draft Resolution A/68/L.39, 27 March 2014, https://papersmart.unmeetings.org/en/ga/68th-session/plenary-meetings/documents/voting-record/resolution-68262.

[16] See 'Kyrgyzstan Says Crimea Referendum "Legitimate"', *Radio Free Europe/Radio Liberty*, 20 March 2014.

[17] UN GA Res 71/205 (Situation of Human Rights in the Autonomous Republic of Crimea and the City of Sevastopol (Ukraine)), 19 December 2016, UN Doc. A/RES/71/205. Estonia, Georgia, Kyrgyzstan, Latvia, Lithuania, and Ukraine voted in favour of the resolution. Tajikistan abstained, and Azerbaijan and Turkmenistan were absent, see Voting Record on Draft Resolution A/C.3/71/L.26, 'Situation of Human Rights in the Autonomous Republic of Crimea and the City of Sevastopol (Ukraine)', 15 November 2016, https://www.un.org/en/ga/third/71/docs/voting_sheets/L.26.pdf.

[18] Christian Marxsen, Anne Peters, and Matthias Hartwig, 'Symposium: "The Incorporation of Crimea by the Russian Federation in the Light of International Law"', *Zeitschrift für ausländisches öffentliches Recht und Völkerrecht* 75 (2015), 1–5, 4.

[19] See American Society of International Law, '2014 Annual Meeting Videos: Is International Law Effective? The Case of Russia and Ukraine', Washington, D.C., 9 April 2014, recording available at: https://www.asil.org/ resources/2014-annual-meeting-videos, and Center for Polish-Russian Dialogue and Understanding, 'Conferences and Seminars: The Case of Crimea in the Light of International Law: Its Nature and Implications', Warsaw, 19–20 March 2015, recording available

The apparent inability to understand each other is exacerbated by a translation problem in a more literal sense: unlike in many other countries, the Russian academic discourse of international law occurs almost exclusively in Russian language. As a consequence, debates in Russian scholarship usually happen in a self-referential, autarchic forum, with no connections to or exchange with the outside, English-speaking 'invisible college of international lawyers'. One possible explanation for this detachment is of course the existing language barrier which can serve as a convenient excuse to escape global academic competition of ideas and arguments. Another possibility to explain Russia's isolated academic discourse is to understand it as a reflection of a more general determination to emphasize the country's mental and geopolitical independence from the West. And at least with regard to the scholarly debates on Crimea, a third reason that obstructed more academic dialogue could have been the peer-review system of most international law journals, which either did not include views expressed by Russian scholars at all or, if they chose to do so, only with sort of a disclaimer.[20]

However, the translation problem between the Russian and western international law discourses can also be viewed from yet another perspective: today, most Western scholars are more or less ignorant about what Russian scholars of international law think and write. Again, the language barrier might be one explanatory factor, but Russian scholarship of international law written or translated in English exists,[21] and modern information technology makes understanding foreign literature possible.[22] Arguably, therefore, this point deserves some more critical self-reflection. During the Cold War period, one of the reasons why Western scholars were interested in the Soviet doctrine of international law was of course that the Soviet Union was one of two superpowers, and the necessity to make an effort in understanding Soviet thinking

at: http://cprdip.pl/en,events,conferences_and_seminars,61,the_case_of_crimea_in_the_light_of_international_law_its_nature_and_implications.html. See also Anthea Roberts, 'Crimea and the South China Sea: Connections and Disconnects among Chinese, Russian, and Western International Lawyers', in Anthea Roberts, Paul B. Stephan, and Pierre-Hugues Verdier (eds), *Comparative International Law* (New York, NY: Oxford University Press, 2018), 111–39, 116–21.

20 See Marxsen, Peters, and Hartwig, 'Symposium' 2015 (n. 18), 5: 'The papers did not undergo a peer review in a strict sense. They thus reflect the authentic positions of the authors, independently from what the symposium editors would have preferred as a legal approach.... The fact of publication does not imply any substantive approval by the editors of the symposium and of the Heidelberg Journal of International Law', Vladislav Tolstykh, 'Reunification of Crimea with Russia: A Russian Perspective', *Chinese Journal of International Law* 13 (2014), 879–86, 879 (*): 'Note by the Editors: Letters to the Editors are not reviewed on the same criteria as the other materials and are intended to provoke debate.'

21 See e.g. the many translations listed in William E. Butler, *International and Comparative Law: A Personal Bibliography* (London: Wildy, Simmonds & Hill, 2015), 47–66.

22 On this point see also Sergei Yu. Marochkin, 'Contemporary Approaches of the Russian Doctrine in International Law: Identical to Western Ones?', *Baltic Yearbook of International Law* 12 (2012), 29–56, 55, noting that 'one would not like to think that there is some snobbery of Western colleagues concerning reading and knowing the Russian doctrine'.

was therefore perceived as almost existential in character.[23] Consequently, one of the side effects of the Soviet Union's demise was a decreasing interest in the West in possibly prevailing peculiarities in the post-Soviet Russian approach to international law, and with the assumed 'end of history',[24] many were confident that they could now also stop thinking about a distinct Russian understanding of the field. Today, apart from Lauri Mälksoo's work and occasional contributions by a handful of other scholars in the West, analyses of Russia's post-Soviet state practice and doctrine usually confine themselves to assess the legality of Russia's actions in terms of positive international law. However, while judging Russia's actions is certainly a highly important exercise—and large parts of this book were also concerned with this task—such a limited approach fails to attempt to understand diverging views on international law, something which was perceived as self-evident during the Cold War period.

Already more than a decade ago, Anne Peters, one of the organizers of the Heidelberg symposium on Crimea, warned of a re-emerging 'epistemic nationalism' in international law doctrine, and argued instead for the necessity and feasibility of making arguments about international law that can be understood and replicated by individuals independent from their national background.[25] Arguably, the way towards such a utopian 'epistemic universalism' can only lead via conscious efforts in bridging existing translation problems between different national approaches to international law. Generally, but maybe especially with regard to the Russian approach, one should however also be careful not to over-interpret national-specific peculiarities. Because in the end, the difficulty with understanding the post-Soviet Russian approach to international law might not only lie in a prevailing reluctance to acknowledge that the Russian government and her advocates actually 'believe' in their arguments. It could also lie in the complicated and long history in the West of seeing Russia as an exotic Other, not only but also with regard to international law.[26]

[23] William E. Butler for example explained the past efforts to make sense of the Soviet doctrine the following way: 'In this era, Soviet legal studies to an appreciable degree were a part of the "know thyne enemy" syndrome: to comprehend how he lives, to facilitate means of understanding and communication so as to avoid miscalculations, to identify and clarify opposed positions and values', William E. Butler, 'International Law and the Comparative Method', in William E. Butler (ed.), *International Law in Comparative Perspective* (Alphen aan den Rijn: Sijthoff & Noordhoff, 1980), 25–40, 31.

[24] Francis Fukuyama, *The End of History and the Last Man* (New York, NY: Free Press, 1992).

[25] Anne Peters, 'Die Zukunft der Völkerrechtswissenschaft: Wider den epistemischen Nationalismus', *Zeitschrift für ausländisches öffentliches Recht und Völkerrecht* 67 (2007), 721–76, 765 et seq.

[26] On this history with regard to the question of Russia being a truly European and 'civilized' nation in international relations see Martin Malia, *Russia under Western Eyes: From the Bronze Horseman to the Lenin Mausoleum* (Cambridge, MA: Harvard University Press, 1999), 27 et seq. On this history more generally see Iver B. Neumann, *Uses of the Other: 'The East' in European Identity Formation* (Minneapolis, MN: University of Minnesota Press, 1999), 65–112.

Acknowledgements

This book is an updated version of my doctoral thesis, submitted to the German University of Administrative Sciences in June 2019. Although mainly written in Berlin, it is also the product of regular exchanges with my supervisor in Speyer, Karl-Peter Sommermann, whom I wish to thank for his unconditional support in this project.

Participation in the workshop 'A Century after the Russian Revolution: Its Legacy in International Law' at the Max Planck Institute for Comparative Public Law and International Law in Heidelberg in 2016 turned out to be crucial for the evolution of this study: Anne Peters, who co-organized the event, showed interest in my work, eventually became the thesis' second examiner, and later encouraged me to propose the manuscript for publication with Oxford University Press. It was also in Heidelberg where I met Bill Bowring and Lauri Mälksoo for the first time in person after having read almost everything they had published up to that point on Russian approaches to international law. Inspiring exchanges on the topic developed from that meeting, and I am grateful that I have had two such experts reading and commenting on my own contribution to the field. Discussions with the organizers and panellists of two subsequent events on the legal legacy of the Russian Revolution in Saint Petersburg in 2017 and in Cologne in 2018 further shaped my views on the subject. At the latter conference, I also first met Caroline von Gall, whom I wish to thank not only for reading and discussing with me the constitutional law parts of this study but also for supporting its proposal for the Klaus Mehnert Prize 2021 awarded by the German Association for East European Studies.

I would furthermore like to acknowledge the financial support I received from the German Academic Exchange Service DAAD in the form of two travel grants that helped financing my participations in the 5th Martens Summer School on International Law in Pärnu, Estonia, and in an intensive Russian language course at Kazan Federal University, in the summer of 2016.

Lastly, this book could not have been written or would, in any case, look different without the support of fellow doctoral students, friends, and family. But above all, I am indebted to my partner Marija—thank you for accompanying me throughout this long and sometimes arduous journey.

Bibliography

Newspaper articles (online and print), news agency reports, and other news-related online resources as well as online encyclopaedia and blog entries are not listed individually. When not stated in the respective footnotes, references to these resources can be retrieved via the following websites and their archives:

BBC News: https://bbc.co.uk/news.
The Economist: https://www.economist.com.
EJIL: Talk!: https://www.ejiltalk.org.
Eurasia Daily Monitor: https://jamestown.org/programs/edm.
Interfax: https://www.interfax.ru.
Izvestiya: https://iz.ru.
Kommersant: https://www.kommersant.ru.
Max Planck Encyclopedia of Comparative Constitutional Law: http://www.mpeccol.com.
Max Planck Encyclopedia of Public International Law: http://www.mpepil.com.
The Moscow Times: https://www.themoscowtimes.com.
New Eastern Europe: http://neweasterneurope.eu.
Nezavisimaya gazeta: http://www.ng.ru.
The New Yorker: https://www.newyorker.com.
The New York Times: https://www.nytimes.com.
Novaya gazeta: https://www.novayagazeta.ru.
Opinio Juris: http://opiniojuris.org.
Pravda: https://www.pravda.ru.
Radio Free Europe/Radio Liberty: https://www.rferl.org.
Regnum News Agency: https://regnum.ru.
RIA Novosti: https://ria.ru.
Rossiĭskaya gazeta: https://rg.ru.
TASS: http://tass.ru.
Vedomosti: https://www.vedomosti.ru.
Verfassungsblog: https://verfassungsblog.de.
Völkerrechtsblog: https://voelkerrechtsblog.org.
The Washington Post: https://www.washingtonpost.com.

Reports by International and Non-governmental Organizations

Amnesty International, In the Line of Fire: Civilian Casualties from Unlawful Strikes in the Armenian-Azerbaijani Conflict over Nagorno-Karabakh (London: Amnesty International, 2021).

Commission on Security and Cooperation in Europe. Presidential Elections and Independence Referendums in the Baltic States, the Soviet Union and Successor States: A Compendium of Results 1991–1992 (Washington, D.C.: Commission on Security and Cooperation in Europe, 1992).

Cristescu, Aureliu. The Right to Self-determination: Historical and Current Development on the Basis of United Nations Instruments, United Nations, 1981, UN Doc. E/CN.4/Sub.2/404/Rev.1.

CSCE Mission to Moldova. Report No. 13, 13 November 1993.

Gros Espiell, Héctor. The Right to Self-determination: Implementation of United Nations Resolutions, United Nations, 1980, UN Doc. E/CN.4/Sub.2/405/Rev.1.

Human Rights Watch. Bloodshed in the Caucasus: Violations of Humanitarian Law and Human Rights in the Georgia-South Ossetia Conflict (Helsinki: Human Rights Watch, 1992).

Human Rights Watch. Seven Years of Conflict in Nagorno-Karabakh (New York, NY: Human Rights Watch, 1994).

Human Rights Watch. Georgia/Abkhazia: Violations of the Law of War and Russia's Role in the Conflict, March 1995.

Human Rights Watch. Up in Flames—Humanitarian Law Violations and Civilian Victims in the Conflict Over South Ossetia, 23 January 2009.

International Crisis Group. Europe Report No. 147, Moldova: No Quick Fix, 12 August 2003.

International Crisis Group. Europe Report No. 166, Nagorno-Karabakh: Viewing the Conflict from the Ground, 15 September 2005.

International Crisis Group. Europe Report No. 202, Abkhazia: Deepening Dependence, 26 February 2010.

International Crisis Group. Europe Report No. 205, South Ossetia: The Burden of Recognition, 7 June 2010.

International Crisis Group. Europe Report No. 224, Abkhazia: The Long Road to Reconciliation, 10 April 2013.

International Crisis Group. Europe Report No. 236, Chechnya: The Inner Abroad, 30 June 2015.

International Crisis Group. Europe Report No. 239, Nagorno-Karabakh: New Opening, or More Peril?, 4 July 2016.

International Law Commission. Fragmentation of International Law: Difficulties Arising from the Diversification and Expansion of International Law, 13 April 2006, UN Doc. A/CN.4/L-682.

Office of the UN High Commissioner for Human Rights. Report on the Human Rights Situation in Ukraine, 15 April 2014.

OSCE High Commissioner on National Minorities to the Permanent Council. Report, 18 June 2009.

Report of the Secretary-General in Pursuance of Security Council Resolution 849 (1993), 6 August 1993, UN Doc. S/26250, 6–8 (Annex I).

Report of the Secretary-General's Fact-finding Mission to Investigate Human Rights Violations in Abkhazia, Republic of Georgia, 17 November 1993, UN Doc. S/26795 (Annex).

UNESCO. International Meeting of Experts on Further Study of the Concept of the Rights of Peoples, 27–30.November 1989, Final Report and Recommendations, SHS-89/CONF.602/7.

Monographs and Edited Books

Abkhazian State Statistics Office. *Абхазия в цифрах за 2011 год* [Abkhazia in Numbers 2011] (Sukhumi: Abkhazian State Statistics Office, 2011).

Allison, Roy. *Russia, the West, and Military Intervention* (Oxford: Oxford University Press, 2013).

Allworth, Edward (ed.). *The Tatars of Crimea: Return to the Homeland* (Durham, NC: Duke University Press, 2nd edn, 1998).

Anderson, Benedict. *Imagined Communities: Reflections on the Origin and Spread of Nationalism* (London: Verso, 2nd edn, 1991).

Anghie, Antony. *Imperialism, Sovereignty and the Making of International Law* (Cambridge: Cambridge University Press, 2005).

Anzilotti, Dionisio [Д. Анцилотти] (A.L. Saketti and É.M. Fabrikova transl.). *Курс международного права* [Course of International Law], vol. 1 (Moscow: Izdatel'stvo inostrannoĭ literaturȳ, 1961).

Avakyan, S.A. *Конституционное право России* [Constitutional Law of Russia], 2 vols (Moscow: Norma, 5th edn, 2014).

Baddeley, John Frederick. *The Russian Conquest of the Caucasus* (London: Longmans, Green & Co., 1908).

Bakhin, S.V. (ed.). *Российская ассоциация международного права 1957–2007* [Russian Association of International Law 1957–2007. Biographical Directory] (Saint Petersburg: Izdatel'skiĭ Tsentr Akademiya, 2007).

Barseghov, Yu.G. *Территория в международном праве* [Territory in International Law] (Moscow: Gos. Izd. yurid. lit., 1958).

Barseghov, Yu.G. *Право на самоопределение: основа демократического решения международных проблем; к проблеме Нагорного Карабаха* [The Right to Self-determination: the Basis of a Democratic Solution of International Problems; on the Problem of Nagorno-Karabakh] (Yerevan: Ayastan, 1989).

Barseghov, Yu.G. *Обязательная сила права народов на самоопределение и средства его обеспечения* [The Binding Force of the Right to Self-determination and the Means to Ensure it] (Moscow: International Humanitarian Fund of Armenology, 1993).

Barseghov, Yu.G. *Нагорный Карабах в международном праве и мировой политике: документы и комментарии* [Nagorno-Karabakh in International Law and World Politics: Documents and Commentary] (Moscow: KRUG Publishers, 2008).

Batsell, Walter Russell. *Soviet Rule in Russia* (New York, NY: The Macmillan Company, 1929).

Bauer, Otto. *Die Nationalitätenfrage und die Sozialdemokratie* (Vienna: Brand, 1907).

Bayefsky, Anne. *Self-determination in International Law, Quebec and Lessons Learned* (The Hague: Kluwer Law International, 2000).

Beirne, Piers and Sharlet, Robert (eds). *Pashukanis: Selected Writings on Marxism and Law* (London: Academic Press, 1980).

Blum, Mark E., (ed.). *Austro-Marxism: The Ideology of Unity*, 2 vols (Leiden: Brill, 2016).

Bluntschli, Johann Caspar. *Allgemeine Staatslehre* (Stuttgart: Cotta, 5th edn, 1875).

Bourdieu, Pierre. *Outline of a Theory of Practice* (Cambridge: Cambridge University Press, 1977).

Bourdieu, Pierre and Wacquant, Loïc J.D. *An Invitation to Reflexive Sociology* (Chicago, IL: University of Chicago Press, 1992).

Bowring, Bill. *Law, Rights and Ideology in Russia: Landmarks in the Destiny of a Great Power* (Abingdon: Routledge, 2013).

Brezhnev, L.I. *Speech by L.I. Brezhnev at the 5th Congress of the Polish United Workers' Party on 12 November 1968* (Moscow: Novosti Press Agency Publishing House, 1968).

Buchanan, Allen. *The Morality of Political Divorce from Fort Sumter to Lithuania and Quebec* (Boulder, CO: Westview, 1991).

Buchheit, Lee C. *Secession: The Legitimacy of Self-determination* (New Haven, CT: Yale University Press, 1978).

Buharin, N. and Preobrazhensky, E. (Eden and Cedar Paul transl.). *The ABC of Communism: A Popular Explanation of the Program of the Communist Party of Russia* (Ann Arbor, MI: University of Michigan Press, 1966).

Butler, William E. (ed.). *Collected Legislation of the Union of Soviet Socialist Republics and the Constituent Union Republics*, 7 vols (Dobbs Ferry, NY: Oceana Publications, 1979–1988).

Butler, William E. *Collected Legislation of Russia* (Dobbs Ferry, NY: Oceana Publications, 1992–).

Butler, William E. *Russian Law* (Oxford: Oxford University Press, 3rd edn, 2009).

Butler, William E. *International and Comparative Law: A Personal Bibliography* (London: Wildy, Simmonds & Hill, 2015).

Butler, William E. and Henderson, Jane (eds). *Russian Legal Texts: The Foundations of a Rule-of-Law State and a Market Economy* (London: Simmonds & Hill, 1998).

Cassese, Antonio. *Self-determination of Peoples: A Legal Reappraisal* (Cambridge: Cambridge University Press, 1995).

Chernichenko, S.V. *Теория международного права* [Theory of International Law], 2 vols (Moscow: NIMP, 1999).

Chernichenko, S.V. *Очерки по философии и международному праву* [Essays on Philosophy and International Law] (Moscow: Nauchnaya kniga, 2009).

Chowdhury, Subrata Roy. *The Genesis of Bangladesh: A Study in International Legal Norms and Permissive Conscience* (New York, NY: Asia Publishing House, 1972).

Corten, Olivier. *The Law against War: The Prohibition on the Use of Force in Contemporary International Law* (Oxford: Hart Publishing, 2010).

Crawford, James. *The Creation of States in International Law* (Oxford: Oxford University Press, 2nd edn, 2006).

Crawford, James. *Brownlie's Principles of Public International Law* (Oxford: Oxford University Press, 8th edn, 2012).

Dahlitz, Julie (ed.). *Secession and International Law: Conflict Avoidance—Regional Appraisals* (The Hague: T.M.C. Asser Press, 2003).

Degras, Jane (ed.). *Soviet Documents on Foreign Policy*, 3 vols (London: Oxford University Press, 1951–1953).

Diasamidze, Tamaz. *Regional Conflicts in Georgia (The Autonomous Oblast of South Ossetia; The Autonomous SSR of Abkhazia 1989–2011). Collection of Political-Legal Acts* (Tbilisi: Regionalism Research Centre, 2008).

Dinstein, Yoram. *War, Aggression and Self-Defence* (Cambridge: Cambridge University Press, 2012).

Dohna, Bernt Graf zu. *Die Grundprinzipien des Völkerrechts über die freundschaftlichen Beziehungen und die Zusammenarbeit zwischen den Staaten* (Berlin: Duncker & Humblot, 1973).

Dugard, John. *Recognition and the United Nations* (Cambridge: Grotius Publications, 1987).

Dugin, Alexander. *Геополитика постмодерна* [Postmodern Geopolitics] (Saint Petersburg: Amfora, 2007).

Dunlop, John. *Russia Confronts Chechnya: Roots of a Separatist Conflict* (Cambridge: Cambridge University Press, 1998).

Ebzeev, B.S., Krasnoburytsev, S.L., and Levakin, I.V. *Государственное единство и целостность Российской федерации, Конституционно-правовые проблемы* [State Unity and Integrity of the Russian Federation, Constitutional Problems] (Moscow: Ekonomika, 2005).

Egorov, S.A. (ed.), *Международное право* [International Law] (Moscow: Statut, 5th edn, 2014).

Fiedler, Wilfried. *Das Kontinuitätsproblem im Völkerrecht: zum funktionalen Zusammenhang zwischen Völkerrecht, Staatsrecht und Politik* (Freiburg: Alber, 1978).
Figes, Orlando. *Crimea: The Last Crusade* (London: Allan Lane, 2010).
Fisch, Jörg. *Das Selbstbestimmungsrecht der Völker: Die Domestizierung einer Illusion* (Munich: C.H. Beck, 2010).
Fisch, Jörg, (Anita Mage transl.). *A History of the Self-determination of Peoples: The Domestication of an Illusion* (Cambridge: Cambridge University Press, 2015).
Fisher, Alan. *The Crimean Tatars* (Stanford, CA: Hoover Institution Press, 1987).
Flanz, Gisbert, Grote, Rainer, and Wolfrum, Rüdiger (eds). *Constitutions of the Countries of the World* (New York: Oceana Publications, 1971–).
Fligstein, Neil and McAdam, Doug. *A Theory of Fields* (Oxford: Oxford University Press, 2012).
Frowein, Jochen Abr. *Das de facto-Regime im Völkerrecht. Eine Untersuchung zur Rechtsstellung "nichtanerkannter Staaten und ähnlicher Gebilde* (Cologne: Carl Heymanns 1968).
Fukuyama, Francis. *The End of History and the Last Man* (New York, NY: Free Press 1992).
Galenskaya, L.N., Kurdyukov, G.I., and Bakhin, S.V. (eds). *Международное право. Библиография, 1991–2005* [International Law. Bibliography 1991–2005] (Saint Petersburg: Rossiya-Neva, 2010).
Gall, Caroline von. *Die Konzepte 'staatliche Einheit' und 'einheitliche Macht' in der russischen Theorie von Staat und Recht. Der Einfluss des Gemeinschaftsideals auf die russische Verfassungsentwicklung* (Berlin: Duncker & Humblot, 2010).
Gammer, Moshe. *Muslim Resistance to the Tsar: Shamil and the Conquest of Chechnia and Dagestan* (London: Cass, 1994).
Gati, Charles. *Failed Illusions: Moscow, Washington, Budapest, and the 1956 Hungarian Revolt* (Stanford, CA: Stanford University Press, 2006).
Gellner, Ernest. *Nations and Nationalism* (Ithaca, NY: Cornell University Press, 2nd edn, 2008).
Gessen, Masha. *The Future is History: How Totalitarianism Reclaimed Russia* (New York, NY: Riverhead Books, 2017).
Ginsburgs, George. *From Soviet Russian to Russian International Law: Studies in Continuity and Change* (Leiden: Nijhoff, 1998).
Golan, Galia. *The Soviet Union and National Liberation Movements in the Third World* (Boston, MA: Unwin Hyman, 1988).
Gorbachev, Mikhail. *Перестройка и новое мышление для нашей страны и для всего мира* [Restructuring and New Thinking for Our Country and the Whole World] (Moscow: Politizdat, 1987).
Gorbachev, Mikhail. *Perestroika: New Thinking for Our Country and the World* (New York, NY: Harper & Row Publishers, 1988).
Grabar, V.E. (William E. Butler transl.). *The History of International Law in Russia, 1647–1917: A Bio-Bibliographical Study* (Oxford: Clarendon Press, 1990).
Grachev, N.I. *Происхождение суверенитета. Верховная власть в мировоззрении и практике государственного строительства традиционного общества* [The Origin of Sovereignty. The Supreme Power in the Worldview and Practice of State Building] (Moscow: Zertsalo, 2009).
Granville, Johanna. *The First Domino: International Decision Making During the Hungarian Crisis of 1956* (College Station, TX: A&M University Press, 2004).
Grenville, J.A.S. (ed.). *The Major International Treaties 1914–1945: A History and Guide with Texts* (London: Methuen, 1987).

Grzybowski, Kazimierz. *Soviet Public International Law. Doctrines and Diplomatic Practice* (Leiden: Sythoff, 1970).

Hannum, Hurst. *Autonomy, Sovereignty and Self-determination* (Philadelphia, PA: University of Pennsylvania Press, 1990).

Hannum, Hurst (ed.). *Documents on Autonomy and Minority Rights* (Dordrecht: Nijhoff, 1993).

Henderson, Jane. *The Constitution of the Russian Federation: A Contextual Analysis* (Oxford: Hart Publishing, 2011).

Head, Michael. *Evgeny Pashukanis: A Critical Reappraisal* (Abingdon: Routledge-Cavendish, 2008).

Hill, William H. *Russia, the Near Abroad, and the West: Lessons from the Moldova-Transdniestria Conflict* (Washington, D.C.: Woodrow Wilson Center Press, 2012).

Hobsbawm, Eric J. *Nations and Nationalism since 1780: Programme, Myth, Reality* (Cambridge: Cambridge University Press, 2nd edn, 1992).

Hovannisian, Richard G. *The Republic of Armenia*, 4 vols (Berkeley, CA: University of California Press, 1971–1996).

Ignatenko, G.V. *Международное право и внутригосударственное право: проблемы сопряженности и взаимодействия* [International Law and Domestic Law: Problems of Interconnection and Interaction] (Moscow: Norma, 2012).

Ignatiev, V.V. (ed.). *Pridnestrovie: The Legal Foundation of Independence* (Tiraspol: Ministry of Foreign Affairs of the Pridnestrovian Moldavian Republic, 2017).

Ignatiev, V.V. (ed.). *Политико-правовые основы международного признания независимости Приднестровской Молдавской Республики* [Political and Legal Framework for International Recognition of Independence of the Pridnestrovian Moldavian Republic] (Tiraspol: Ministry of Foreign Affairs of the Pridnestrovian Moldavian Republic, 2018).Jellinek, Georg. *Allgemeine Staatslehre* (Berlin: Häring, 3rd edn, 1914).

Jennings, Robert. *The Acquisition of Territory in International Law* (Manchester: Manchester University Press, 1963).

Jennings, Robert and Watts, Arthur (eds). *Oppenheim's International Law*, 2 vols (Harlow: Longman, 9th edn, 1993).

Johnson, Harold S. *Self-determination within the Community of Nations* (Leiden: Sijthoff, 1967).

Kahn, Jeffrey. *Federalism, Democratization, and the Rule of Law in Russia* (Oxford: Oxford University Press, 2002).

Kalamkaryan, R.A. and Migachev, Yu.I. (eds), *Международное право: Учебник* [International Law: Textbook] (Moscow: Eksmo, 2004).

Kaplan, Robert. *Balkan Ghosts: A Journey Through History* (New York, NY: St. Martin's Press, 1993).

Kaslas, Bronis J. (ed.). *The USSR-German Aggression against Lithuania* (New York, NY: Speller & Sons, 1973).

Kazimirov, V.N. *Мир Карабаху* [Peace of Karabakh] (Moscow: Mezhdunarodnÿe otnosheniya, 2009).

Kembayev, Zhenis. *Legal Aspects of the Regional Integration Processes in the Post-Soviet Area* (Berlin: Springer, 2009).

King, Charles. *The Moldovans: Romania, Russia, and the Politics of Culture* (Stanford, CA: Hoover Institution Press, 2000).

Klimenko, B.M. *Государственная территория* [State Territory] (Moscow: Mezhdunarodnÿe otnosheniya, 1974).

Klimenko, B.M. *Мирное решение территориальных споров* [Peaceful Resolution of Territorial Disputes] (Moscow: Mezhdunarodnȳe otnosheniya, 1982).

Kohen, Marcelo (ed.). *Secession: International Law Perspectives* (Cambridge: Cambridge University Press, 2006).

Korovin, E.A. *Международное право переходного времени* [International Law of the Transitional Period] (Moscow: Gosyurizdat, 1st edn, 1923).

Korovin, E.A. *Современное международное публичное право* [Modern Public International Law] (Moscow: Gosudarstvennoe izdatel'stvo, 1926).

Korovin, E.A. [E.A. Korowin] (J. Robinson-Kaunas transl.). *Das Völkerrecht der Übergangszeit: Grundlagen der völkerrechtlichen Beziehungen der Union der Sowjetrepubliken* (Berlin: Rothschild, 1929).

Koskenniemi, Martti. *The Gentle Civilizer of Nations: The Rise and Fall of International Law 1870–1960* (Cambridge: Cambridge University Press, 2001).

Koskenniemi, Martti. *From Apology to Utopia: The Structure of International Legal Argument* (Cambridge: Cambridge University Press, 2005).

Kovalev, A.A. and Chernichenko, S.V. (eds). *Международное право* [International Law] (Moscow: Prospekt, 3rd edn, 2008).

Kozhevnikov, F.I. *Русское государство и международное право* [The Russian State and International Law] (Moscow: Yurizdat, 1947).

Kozhevnikov, F.I. *Советское государство и международное право. 1917–1947 гг. (Опыт историко-правового исследования)* [The Soviet State and International Law. 1947–1947 (Experience of Historical and Legal Research)] (Moscow: Yuridicheskoe izdatel'stvo, 1948).

Kozhevnikov, F.I. (ed.). *Международное право* [International Law] (Moscow: Gosyurizdat, 1957).

Kozhevnikov, F.I. [F.I. Koschewnikow] (Lothar Schultz transl.). *Völkerrecht* (Hamburg: Hansischer Gildenverlag, 1960).

Kravchenko, N.A. (ed.). *Правовые аспекты чеченского кризиса: Материалы семинара* [Legal Aspects of the Chechen Crisis: Workshop Materials] (Moscow: Memorial, 1995).

Kremnev, P.P. *Распад СССР: международно-правовые проблемы* [The Dissolution of the USSR: International Legal Problems] (Moscow: Zertsalo, 2005).

Krüger, Heiko. *The Nagorno-Karabakh Conflict: A Legal Analysis* (Berlin: Springer, 2010).

Krylov, S.B. *История создания Организации Объединённых Наций: разработка текста устава Организации Объединённых Наций* (1944–1945) [History of the Creation of the United Nations: The Development of the Text of the Charter of the United Nations] (Moscow: IMO, 1960).

Krylov, S.B. and Durdenevsky, V.N. (eds). *Международное право* [International Law] (Moscow: Gosyurizdat, 1947).

Kuznetsov, V.I. and Tuzmukhamedov, B.R. (eds) (William E. Butler transl.). *International Law—A Russian Introduction* (Utrecht: Eleven International Publishing, 2009).

Lalonde, Suzanne. *Determining Boundaries in a Conflicted World: The Role of Uti Possidetis* (Montreal: McGill-Queen's University Press, 2002).

Långström, Tarja. *Transformation in Russia and International Law* (Leiden: Martinus Nijhoff, 2003).

Lapenna, Ivo. *Conceptions soviétiques de droit international public* (Paris: Pedone, 1954).

Lazarev, L.V. (ed.). *Комментарий к Конституция Российской Федерации* [Commentary on the Constitution of the Russian Federation] (Moscow: Prospekt, 3rd edn, 2010).

Lazarev, V.V. (ed.). *Научно-практический комментарий к Конституции Российской Федерации* [Scientific-practical Commentary on the Constitution of the Russian Federation] (Moscow: Yuraĭt, 4rd edn, 2009).

Levin, D.B. and Kalyuzhnaya, G.P. (eds). *Международное право* [International Law] (Moscow: Yurid. literatura, 1960).

Levin, I.D. *Принцип суверенитета в советском и международном праве* [The Principle of Sovereignty in Soviet and International Law] (Moscow: Pravda, 1947).

Levin, I.D. *Суверенитет* [Sovereignty] (Moscow: Yurid. izd-vo, 1948).

Lisovsky, V.I. *Международное право и XV сессия Генеральной Ассамблеи ООН* [International Law and the XVth Session of the General Assembly] (Moscow: Gosyurizdat, 1961).

Lisovsky, V.I. *Международное право* [International Law] (Moscow: Vÿsshaya shkola, 3rd edn, 1970).

Lukashuk, I.I. *Нормы международного права в международной нормативной системе* [The Norms of International Law in the International Normative System] (Moscow: SPARK, 1997).

Lukashuk, I.I. *Международное право* [International Law], 2 vols (Moscow: Wolters Kluwer, 3rd edn, 2010).

Malia, Martin. *Russia under Western Eyes: From the Bronze Horseman to the Lenin Mausoleum* (Cambridge, MA: Harvard University Press, 1999).

Mälksoo, Lauri. *Illegal Annexation and State Continuity: The Case of the Incorporation of the Baltic States by the USSR: A Study of the Tension Between Normativity and Power in International Law* (Leiden: Martinus Nijhoff, 2003).

Mälksoo, Lauri. *Russian Approaches to International Law* (Oxford: Oxford University Press, 2015).

Marek, Krystyna. *Identity and Continuity of States in Public International Law* (Geneva: Droz, 1954).

Martin, Terry. *The Affirmative Action Empire: Nations and Nationalism in the Soviet Union, 1923–1939* (Ithaca, NY: Cornell University Press, 2001).

Mayall, James. *Nationalism and International Society* (Cambridge: Cambridge University Press, 1990).

Maurach, Reinhard. *Handbuch der Sowjetverfassung* (Munich: Isar Verlag, 1955).

McWhinney, Edward. *'Peaceful Coexistence' and Soviet-western International Law* (Leiden: Sythoff, 1964).

Meissner, Boris. *Die Sowjetunion, die baltischen Staaten und das Völkerrecht* (Cologne: Verlag für Politik und Wirtschaft, 1956).

Meissner, Boris. *Sowjetunion und Selbstbestimmungsrecht* (Cologne: Verlag Wissenschaft und Politik, 1962).

Meissner, Boris. *Die 'Breschnew-Doktrin'. Das Prinzip des proletarisch-sozialistischen Internationalismus und die Theorie von den 'verschiedenen Wegen zum Sozialismus'* (Cologne: Verlag Wissenschaft und Politik, 1969).

Meissner, Boris, Frenzke, Dietrich, and Chilecki, Erika (eds). *Sowjetunion und Völkerrecht 1962–1973. Bibliographie und Analyse* (Cologne: Verlag Wissenschaft und Politik, 1977).

Miéville, China. *Between Equal Rights: A Marxist Theory of International Law* (Leiden: Brill, 2005).

Moiseev, A.A. *Суверенитет государства в международном праве* [State Sovereignty in International Law] (Moscow: Vostok-Zapad, 2009).

Morré, Peter. *Die Änderung der staatlichen Gebietshoheit nach sowjetischer Völkerrechtslehre und Völkerrechtspraxis mit besonderer Berücksichtigung des Annexionsverbots* (Münster: PhD thesis, 1967).

Morsink, Johannes. *The Universal Declaration of Human Rights: Origin, Drafting and Intent* (Philadelphia, PA: University of Philadelphia Press, 1999).

Movchan, A.P. *Кодификация и прогрессивное развитие международного права* [Codification and Progressive Development of International Law] (Moscow: Yuridicheskaya literatura, 1972).
Movchan, A.P. [Anatol Petrowitsch Mowtschan] (J. Kirsten and K. Wolf transl.). *Kodifizierung und Weiterentwicklung des Völkerrechts* (Berlin: Staatsverlag der DDR, 1974).
Müller, Martin. *Making Great Power Identities in Russia: An Ethnographic Discourse Analysis of Education at a Russian Elite University* (Münster: Lit., 2009).
Müllerson, Rein. *Constitutional Reform and International Law in Central and Eastern Europe* (The Hague: Kluwer Law International, 1998).
Müllerson, Rein. *Ordering Anarchy: International Law in International Society* (The Hague: Nijhoff, 2000)
Müllerson, Rein. *Regime Change: From Democratic Peace Theories to Forcible Regime Change* (Leiden: Nijhoff, 2013).
Müllerson, Rein. *Dawn of a New Order: Geopolitics and the Clash of Ideologies* (London: Tauris, 2017).
Neumann, Iver B. *Uses of the Other: 'The East' in European Identity Formation* (Minneapolis, MN: University of Minnesota Press, 1999).
Nimni, Ephraim. *Marxism and Nationalism: Theoretical Origins of a Political Crisis* (London: Pluto Press, 1991).
Nimni, Ephraim. *National Cultural Autonomy and its Contemporary Critics* (London: Routledge, 2005).
Ossipov, A.G. (ed.). *Право Народов на Самоопределение: Идеи и Воплощение* [Right of Peoples to Self-determination: Idea and Embodiment] (Moscow: Zven'ya, 1997).
Ouimet, Matthew J. *The Rise and Fall of the Brezhnev Doctrine in Soviet Foreign Policy* (Chapel Hill, NC: The University of North Carolina Press, 2003).
Pashukanis, E.B. *Общая теория права и марксизм* [General Theory of Law and Marxism] (Moscow: Izdatel'stvo Kommunisticheskoĭ Akademii, 1927).
Pashukanis, E.B. *Очерки по международному праву* [Essays on International Law] (Moscow: Gosudarstvennoe izdatel'stvo 'Sovetskoe zakonodatel'stvo', 1935).
Pashukanis, E.B. (Peter B. Maggs transl.). *The General Theory of Law & Marxism* (New Brunswick, NJ: Transaction Publishers, 2002).
Perritt, Henry. *The Road to Independence for Kosovo: A Chronicle of the Ahtisaari Plan* (Cambridge: Cambridge University Press, 2010).
Peters, Anne. *Das Gebietsreferendum im Völkerrecht: seine Bedeutung im Licht der Staatenpraxis nach 1989* (Baden-Baden: Nomos, 1995).
Pipes, Richard. *The Formation of the Soviet Union* (Cambridge, MA: Harvard University Press, 6th edn, 1997).
Pomerance, Michla. *Self-determination in Law and Practice: The New Doctrine of the United Nations* (The Hague: Martinus Nijhoff, 1982).
Potier, Tim. *Conflict in Nagorno-Karabakh, Abkhazia and South Ossetia: A Legal Appraisal* (The Hague: Kluwer Law International, 2001).
Raworth, Philip (ed.). *Constitutions of Dependencies and Territories* (Dobbs Ferry, NY: Oceana Publications, 1998).
Renner, Karl [Synopticus]. *Nation und Staat: Staatsrechtliche Untersuchungen über die möglichen Principien einer Lösung und die juristischen Voraussetzungen eines Nationalitäten-Gesetzes* (Vienna: Dietl, 1899).
Roberts, Anthea. *Is International Law International?* (New York, NY: Oxford University Press, 2017).

Roberts, Anthea, Stephan, Paul B., Verdier, Pierre-Hugues, and Versteeg, Mila (eds). *Comparative International Law* (New York, NY: Oxford University Press, 2018).

Rorlich, Azade-Ayşe. *The Volga Tatars: A Profile in National Resilience* (Stanford, CA: Hoover Institution Press, 1986).

Rückert, Wiebke. *Das Völkerrecht in der Rechtsprechung des russischen Verfassungsgerichts* (Berlin: Berliner Wissenschaftsverlag, 2005).

Russell, Ruth B. and Muther, Jeanette E. *A History of the United Nations Charter, The Role of the United States, 1940–1945* (Washington, D.C.: Brookings Institution, 1958).

Russian Federal State Statistics Service. *Итоги переписи населения в Крымском федеральном округе* [Results of the Census in the Crimean Federal District] (Moscow: Statistika Rossii, 2015).

Sadykova, E.L. *Межцивилизационный диалог в современных международных отношениях: теоретические и практические аспекты* [Intercivilizational Dialogue in Contemporary International Relations: Theoretical and Practical Aspects] (Moscow: Diplomaticheskaya akademiya Ministerstva inostrannȳkh del Rossiĭskoĭ Federatsii, 2014).

Sakwa, Richard (ed.). *Chechnya: From Past to Future* (London: Anthem Press, 2005).

Saparov, Arsène. *From Conflict to Autonomy in the Caucasus: The Soviet Union and the Making of Abkhazia, South Ossetia and Nagorno-Karabakh* (Abingdon: Routledge, 2015).

Sasse, Gwendolyn. *The Crimea Question: Identity, Transition, and Conflict* (Cambridge, MA: Harvard University Press, 2007).

Schabas, William A. *Genocide in International Law: The Crime of Crimes* (Cambridge: Cambridge University Press, 2000).

Schmitt, Carl. *Völkerrechtliche Großraumordnung mit Interventionsverbot für raumfremde Mächte. Ein Beitrag zum Reichsbegriff* (Berlin: Rechtsverlag, 1941).

Schmöckel, Mathias. *Die Großraumtheorie: ein Beitrag zur Geschichte der Völkerrechtswissenschaft im Dritten Reich, insbesondere der Kriegszeit* (Berlin: Duncker & Humblot, 1994).

Shamba, T.M. and Neproshin, A.Yu. *Абхазия. Правовые основы государственности и суверенитета* [Abkhazia. Legal Basis for Statehood and Sovereignty] (Moscow: Izd-vo RGTEU, 2004).

Shaheen, Samad. *The Communist (Bolshevik) Theory of National Self-determination: Its Historical Evolution up to the October Revolution* (The Hague: van Hoeve, 1956).

Schweisfurth, Theodor. *Sozialistisches Völkerrecht? Darstellung-Analyse-Wertung der sowjetmarxistischen Theorie vom Völkerrecht 'neuen Typs'* (Berlin: Springer, 1979).

Simpson, Gerry J. *Great Powers and Outlaw States: Unequal Sovereigns in the International Legal Order* (Cambridge: Cambridge University Press, 2004).

Smith, Anthony D. *Nationalism: Theory, Ideology, History* (Cambridge: Polity Press, 2nd edn, 2010).

Solchanyk, Roman. *Ukraine and Russia: The Post-Soviet Transition* (Lanham, MD: Rowman & Littlefield, 2000).

Speranskaya, L.V. *Принцип самоопределения наций в международном праве* [The Principle of Self-determination of Nations in International Law] (Moscow: Gos. Izd. yurid. lit., 1961).

Starushenko, G.B. *Принцип самоопределения народов и наций во внешней политике советского государства* [The Principle of Self-determination of Peoples and Nations in the Foreign Policy of the Soviet States] (Moscow: Izdatel'stvo Instituta mezhdunarodnȳkh otnosheniĭ, 1960).

Starushenko, G.B. *The Principle of National Self-determination in Soviet Foreign Policy* (Moscow: Foreign Languages Publishing House, 1964).

Starushenko, G.B. *Africa Makes a Choice. The Development of Socialist-Oriented States* (Moscow: Novosti Press Agency Publishing House, 1975).

State Committee of the USSR on Statistics. *Национальный Состав Населения СССР, по данным Всесоюзной Переписи Населения 1989 г.* [The National Composition of the Population of the USSR According to the All-Union Population Census of 1989] (Moscow: Finansȳ i statistika, 1991).

Stavrianos, Letfen Stavros. *The Epic of Man* (Englewood Cliffs, NJ: Prentice-Hall, 1971).

Summers, James. *Peoples and International Law* (Leiden: Brill Nijhoff, 2nd edn, 2014).

Suny, Ronald Grigor. *The Making of the Georgian Nation* (Stanford, CA: Hoover Institution Press, 1988).

Talmon, Stefan. *Die kollektive Nichtanerkennung illegaler Staaten: Grundlagen und Rechtsfolgen einer internationalen koordinierten Sanktion, dargestellt am Beispiel der Türkischen Republik Nord-Zypern* (Tübingen: Mohr Siebeck, 2006).

Tishkov, Valeri. *Ethnicity, Nationalism and Conflict in and after the Soviet Union: The Mind Aflame* (London: Sage, 1997).

Toal, Gerard. *Near Abroad: Putin, the West and the Contest over Ukraine and the Caucasus* (Oxford: Oxford University Press, 2017).

Tomuschat, Christian (ed.). *Modern Law of Self-determination* (Dordrecht: Nijhoff, 1993).

Transnistrian State Statistics Service. *Статистический ежегодник 2017* [Statistical Yearbook 2017] (Tiraspol: Transnistrian State Statistics Service, 2017).

Tunkin, G.I. *Основы современного международного права: Учебное пособие* [Fundamentals of Modern International Law: Tutorial] (Moscow: Vȳsshaya partiĭnaya shkola, 1956).

Tunkin, G.I. *Вопросы теории международного права* [Questions on the Theory of International Law] (Moscow: Gosyurizdat, 1962).

Tunkin, G.I. [Grigorij Ivanovič Tunkin] (Klaus Wolf transl.). *Das Völkerrecht der Gegenwart: Theorie und Praxis* [The International Law of the Present: Theory and Practice] (Berlin: Staatsverlag der DDR, 1963).

Tunkin, G.I. [Grigoriei I. Tunkin] (Centre de Recherches sur L'U.R.S.S. et les Pays de l'est transl.). *Droit international public: problèmes théoriques* (Paris: Pedone, 1965).

Tunkin, G.I. *Теория международного права* [Theory of International Law] (Moscow: Mezhdunarodnȳe otnosheniya, 2nd edn, 1970).

Tunkin, G.I. *Право и сила в международной системе* [Law and Force in the International System] (Moscow: Mezhdunarodnȳe otnosheniya, 1983).

Tunkin, G.I. [Grigorij Ivanovič Tunkin] (Elmar Rauch transl.). *Recht und Gewalt im internationalen System* (Berlin: Duncker & Humblot, 1986).

Tunkin, G.I. (William E. Butler transl.). *Theory of International Law* (London: Wildy, Simmonds and Hill Publishing, 2nd edn, 2003).

Ushakov, N.A. *Суверенитет в современном международном праве* [Sovereignty in Contemporary International Law] (Moscow: Mezhdunarodnȳe otnosheniya, 1963).

Vaksberg, Arkady. *Stalin's Prosecutor: The Life of Andrei Vyshinsky* (New York, NY: Grove Weidenfeld, 1991).

Verdross, Alfred [А. Фердросс] (F.A. Kublitskii and R.L. Narȳshkina transl.). *Международное право* [International Law] (Moscow: Izdatel'stvo inostrannoĭ literaturȳ, 1959).

Verdross, Alfred and Simma, Bruno. *Universelles Völkerrecht: Theorie und Praxis* (Berlin: Duncker & Humblot, 3rd edn, 1984.

Vylegzhanin, A.N. (ed.). *Международное право* [International Law] (Moscow: Yuraĭt, 2010).

Vylegzhanin, A.N. (ed.). *Международное право* [International Law], 2 vols (Moscow: Yuraĭt, 3rd edn, 2016).

Vylegzhanin, A.N. and Zilanoc, V.K. (eds). (William E. Butler transl.), *Spitsbergen: Legal Regime of Adjacent Marine Areas* (Utrecht: Eleven International Publishing, 2007).

Waal, Thomas de. *Black Garden: Armenia and Azerbaijan Through Peace and War* (New York, NY: New York University Press, 2nd edn, 2013).

Wambaugh, Sarah. *Plebiscites Since the World War* (Washington, D.C.: Washington Carnegie Endowment of Peace, 1933).

McWhinney, Edward, Ross, Douglas, Vereshchetin,Vladlen, and Tunkin, Grigory (eds). *From Coexistence to Cooperation: International Law and Organization in the Post-Cold War Era* (Dordrecht: Martinus Nijhoff, 1991).

Wilson, Andrew. *The Ukrainians: Unexpected Nation* (New Haven, CT: Yale University Press, 4th edn, 2015).

Wood, Tony, *Chechnya: The Case for Independence* (London: Verso, 2007).

Yasuaki, Onuma. *A Transcivilizational Perspective on International Law: Questioning Prevalent Cognitive Frameworks in the Emerging Multi-polar and Multi-civilizational World of the Twenty-first Century* (Leiden: Nijhoff, 2010).

Zimnenko, B.L. *International Law and the Russian Legal System* (Utrecht: Eleven International Publishing, 2007).

Zinner, Paul E. (ed.). *Documents on American Foreign Relations 1956* (New York, NY: Harper & Brothers 1957).

Zorkin, V.D. (ed.). *Комментарий к Конституции Российской Федерации* [Commentary on the Constitution of the Russian Federation] (Moscow: Eksmo, 3rd edn, 2013).

Articles and Chapters in Edited Books

Abashidze, A.Kh. 'Концепция «гегемония» в современном международном праве' [The Concept of 'Hegemony' in International Law], *Vestnik Diplomaticheskiĭ Akademii MID Rossii. Mezhdunarodnoe pravo* 2013, 166–79.

Ahrens, Cherylyn Brandt. 'Chechnya and the Right of Self-determination', *Columbia Journal of Transnational Law* 42 (2004), 575–615.

Alexidze, Levan. 'Kosovo and South Ossetia: Similar or Different? Consequences for International Law', *Baltic Yearbook of International Law* 12 (2012), 75–102.

Atrokhov, Wendy Turnoff. 'The Khasavyurt Accords: Maintaining the Rule of Law and Legitimacy of Democracy in the Russian Federation Amidst Chechen Crisis', *Cornell International Law Journal* 32 (1999), 367–92.

Aréchaga, Jimenéz de. 'International Law in the Past Third of a Century', *Recueil des Cours de l'Académie de la Haye en ligne* 159 (1978), 1–344.

Avdokushkin, A.V. and Mayurov, V.G. 'Право наций на самоопределение следует конкретизировать' [The Right of Nations to Self-determination Should be Concretised], *Moskovskiĭ zhurnal mezhdunarodnogo prava* 35 (1999), no. 3, 20–2.

Barseghov, Yu.G. 'Вопрос о правовом статусе и правовых основаниях приобретения титулов на исторические воды в современном международном морском праве' [The Issue of the Legal Status and Legal Foundations for Acquisition of Titles to Historic Waters in Modern Law of the Sea], *Sovetskiĭ ezhegodnik mezhdunarodnogo prava* 1987, 201–22.

Bauer, Otto. 'Das Personalitätsprinzip', in Karl Renner (ed.), *Öste/rreichs Erneuerung: Politisch-programmatische Aufsätze*, vol. 2 (Vienna: Brand, 1916), 160–4.

Bastid, Suzanne. 'The Special Significance of the Helsinki Final Act', in Thomas Buergenthal (ed.), *Human Rights, International Law and the Helsinki Accord* (Montclair: Allanheld, Osmun & Co., 1979), 11–19.

Becker Lorca, Arnulf. 'International Law in Latin America or Latin American International Law? Rise, Fall, and Retrieval of a Tradition of Legal Thinking and Political Imagination', *Harvard International Law Journal* 47 (2006), 283–305.

Bennigsen-Broxup, Marie. 'Tatarstan and the Tatars', in Graham Smith (ed.), *The Nationalities Question in the Post-Soviet States* (London: Longman, 2nd edn, 1996), 75–93.

Bilfinger, Carl. 'Vollendete Tatsache und Völkerrecht—eine Studie', *Zeitschrift für ausländisches öffentliches Recht und Völkerrecht* 15 (1953/1954), 453–81.

Bilková, Veronika. 'The Use of Force by the Russian Federation in Crimea', *Zeitschrift für ausländisches öffentliches Recht und Völkerrecht* 75 (2015), 27–50.

Blay, Samuel. 'Self-determination Versus Territorial Integrity in Decolonization', *New York University Journal of International Law and Politics* 18 (1985–1986), 441–72.

Bogush, Gleb. 'Book Review Notes: The Illusive Nature of "Russian International Law"', *Russian Law Journal* 3 (2015), no. 4, 165–9.

Bordyuzha, Nikolai. 'The Collective Security Treaty Organization: A Brief Overview', in Institute for Peace Research and Security Policy at the University of Hamburg (ed.), *OSCE Yearbook 2010: Yearbook on the Organization for Security and Co-operation in Europe (OSCE)* (Baden-Baden: Nomos, 2011), 339–50.

Borgen, Christopher J. 'Thawing a Frozen Conflict: Legal Aspects of the Separatist Crisis in Moldova. A Report from the Association of the Bar of the City of New York', *St. John's University School of Law Legal Studies Research Paper #06-0045* (2006).

Borgen, Christopher J. 'Imagining Sovereignty, Managing Secession: The Legal Geography of Eurasia's "Frozen Conflicts"', *Oregon Review of International Law* 9 (2007), 477–534.

Borgen, Christopher J. 'Whose Public, Whose Order? Imperium, Region, and Normative Friction', *Yale Journal of International Law* 32 (2007), 331–74.

Borgen, Christopher J. 'Law, Rhetoric, Strategy: Russia and Self-determination Before and After Crimea', *International Law Studies* 91 (2015), 216–80.

Bourdieu, Pierre. 'The Force of Law: Toward a Sociology of the Juridical Field', *Hastings Law Journal* 38 (1987), 805–53.

Bournoutian, George. 'The Ethnic Composition and the Socio-Economic Condition of Eastern Armenia in the First Half of the Nineteenth Century', in Ronald Grigor Suny (ed.), *Transcaucasia, Nationalism and Social Change: Essays in the History of Armenia, Azerbaijan, and Georgia* (Ann Arbor, MI: University of Michigan Press, 1996), 69–86.

Bowring, Bill. 'The Crimean Autonomy: Innovation or Anomaly?', in Marc Weller and Stefan Wolff (eds), *Autonomy, Self-governance and Conflict Resolution: Innovative Approaches to Institutional Design in Divided Societies* (London: Routledge, 2005), 75–97.

Bowring, Bill. 'Positivism versus Self-determination: the Contradictions of Soviet International Law', in Susan Marks (ed.), *International Law on the Left: Re-examining Marxist Legacies* (Cambridge: Cambridge University Press, 2008), 133–68.

Bowring, Bill. 'Marx, Lenin and Pashukanis on Self-determination: Response to Robert Knox', *Historical Materialism* 19 (2011), no. 2, 113–27.

Bowring, Bill. 'Transnistria', in Christian Walter, Antje von Ungern-Sternberg, and Kavus Abushov (eds), *Self-determination and Secession in International Law* (Oxford: Oxford University Press, 2014), 157–74.

Bowring, Bill. 'Review of Books: Russian Approaches to International Law', *British Yearbook of International Law* 85 (2015), 189–93.

Bowring, Bill. 'The Soviets and the Right to Self-determination of the Colonized: Contradictions of Soviet Diplomacy and Foreign Policy in the Era of Decolonization', in Jochen von Bernstorff and Philipp Dann (eds), *The Battle for International Law in the Decolonization Era* (Oxford: Oxford University Press, 2019), 404–25.

Bracht, Hans Werner. 'Das Selbstbestimmungsrecht der Völker in der sowjetischen Völkerrechtslehre', in Boris Meissner (ed.), *Das Selbstbestimmungsrecht der Völker in Osteuropa und China* (Cologne: Verlag Wissenschaft und Politik, 1968), 9–20.

Bracht, Hans Werner. 'Rechtscharakter und Rang des Selbstbestimmungsrechts nach sowjetischer Völkerrechtslehre', in Heinz Kloss (ed.), *Beiträge zu einem System des Selbstbestimmungsrechts* (Vienna: Braumüller, 1970), 29–34.

Breig, Burkhard and von Gall, Caroline. 'Der Vertrag über die Eurasische Wirtschaftsunion', *Jahrbuch für Ostrecht* 56 (2015), 49–63.

Buchanan, Allen. 'Theories of Secession', *Philosophy and Public Affairs* 26 (1997), no. 1, 30–61.

Buchanan, Allen. 'The International Institutional Dimension of Secession', in Percy B. Lehning (ed.), *Theories of Secession* (London: Routledge, 1998), 227–56.

Buchanan, Allen. 'The Quebec Secession Issue: Democracy, Minority Rights, and the Rule of Law', in Allen Buchanan and Stephen Macedo (eds), *Secession and Self-determination* (New York, NY: New York University Press, 2003), 238–71.

Burke, John J.A. and Panina-Burke, Svetlana. 'Eastern and Southern Ukraine's Right to Secede and Join the Russian Federation', *Russian Law Journal* 3 (2015), no. 1, 33–57.

Butler, William E. 'Anglo-American Research on Soviet Approaches to Public International Law', in William E. Butler (ed.), *International Law in Comparative Perspective* (Alphen aan den Rijn: Sijthoff & Noordhoff, 1980), 169–90.

Butler, William E. 'International Law and the Comparative Method', in William E. Butler (ed.), *International Law in Comparative Perspective* (Alphen aan den Rijn: Sijthoff & Noordhoff, 1980), 25–40.

Butler, William E. 'Russian International Lawyers in Emigration', *Journal of the History of International Law* 3 (2001), 235–41.

Butler, William E. 'The Learned Writings of Professor G. I. Tunkin', *Journal of the History of International Law* 4 (2002), 394–424.

Carrère d'Encausse, Hélène. 'Unité prolétarienne et diversité nationale: Lénine et la théorie de l'autodétermination', *Revue française de science politique* 21 (1971), 221–55.

Cassese, Antonio. 'The Self-determination of Peoples', in Louis Henkin (ed.), *The International Bill of Rights: The Covenant on Civil and Political Rights* (New York, NY: Columbia University Press, 1981), 92–113.

Castellino, Joshua. 'Peoples, Indigenous Peoples, and Minorities', in Christian Walter, Antje von Ungern-Sternberg, and Kavus Abushov (eds), *Self-determination and Secession in International Law* (Oxford: Oxford University Press, 2014), 27–44.

Chatham, Robert. 'Defense of Nationals Abroad: The Legitimacy of Russia's Invasion of Georgia', *Florida Journal of International Law* 23 (2011), 75–102.

Chen, Lung-Chu. 'Self-determination as a Human Right', in W. Michael Reisman and Burns H. Weston (eds), *Toward World Order and Human Dignity* (New York, NY: Free Press, 1976), 198–261.

Chernev, Borislav. 'The Brest-Litovsk Moment: Self-determination Discourse in Eastern Europe before Wilsonianism', *Diplomacy & Statecraft* 22 (2011), 369–87.

Chernichenko, S.V. 'Принцип самоопределения (современная интерпретация)' [The Principle of Self-determination (Modern Interpretation)], *Moskovskiĭ zhurnal mezhdunarodnogo prava* (1996), no. 4, 9–21.

Chernichenko, Stanislav and Kotliar, Vladimir. 'Ongoing Global Legal Debate on Self-determination and Secession', in Julie Dahlitz (ed.), *Secession and International Law: Conflict Avoidance—Regional Appraisals* (The Hague: T.M.C. Asser Press, 2003), 75–88.

Chimni, Bhupinder. 'An Outline of a Marxist Course on Public International Law', *Leiden Journal of International Law* 17 (2004), 1–30.

Christakis, Theodore. 'Self-determination, Territorial Integrity and *Fait Accompli* in the Case of Crimea', *Zeitschrift für ausländisches öffentliches Recht und Völkerrecht* 75 (2015), 75–100.

Coppieters, Bruno and Emerson, Michael. 'Conflict Resolution for Moldova and Transdniestria Through Federalisation?', *CEPS Policy Brief*, no. 25 (August 2002), 10–22.

Coppieters, Bruno. 'The Georgian-Abkhaz Conflict', in Bruno Coppieters, Michael Emerson, Michel Huysseune, Tamara Kovziridze, Gergana Noutcheva, Nathalie Tocci, and Marius Vahl (eds), *Europeanization and Conflict Resolution: Case Studies from the European Periphery* (Gent: Academia Press, 2004), 191–232.

Corten, Olivier. 'Are There Gaps in the International Law of Secession?', in Marcelo Kohen (ed.), *Secession: International Law Perspectives* (Cambridge: Cambridge University Press, 2006), 231–54.

Corten, Olivier. 'Territorial Integrity Narrowly Interpreted: Reasserting the Classical Inter-State Paradigm of International Law', *Leiden Journal of International Law* 24 (2011), 87–94.

Crawford, James. 'State Practice and International Law in Relation to Secession', *British Yearbook of International Law* 69 (1999), 85–117.

Crawford, James. 'The Right of Self-determination in International Law: Its Development and Future', in Philip Alston (ed.), *Peoples' Rights* (Oxford: Oxford University Press, 2001), 7–67.

Danilenko, Gennady M. 'The New Russian Constitution and International Law', *American Journal of International Law* 88 (1994), 451–70.

Devyatkov, Andrey. 'Russian Policy Toward Transnistria: Between Multilateralism and Marginalization', *Problems of Post-Communism* 59 (2012), 53–62.

Dinstein, Yoram. 'Collective Human Rights and Minorities', *International and Comparative Law Quarterly* 25 (1976), 102–20.

Douhan, Alena. 'CIS, CSTO and the United Nations: Could an Active Regional System of Collective Security Be Established?', *Baltic Yearbook of International Law* 12 (2012), 131–55.

Draganova, Diana. 'Chechnya's Right of Secession under Russian Constitutional Law', *Chinese Journal of International Law* 3 (2004), 571–89.

Dzidzoev, V.D. 'Национальный суверенитет и право нации на самоопределение (на примере Абхазии и Южной Осетии)' [National Sovereignty and the Right of Nations to Self-determination (e.g. of Abkhazia and South Ossetia], *Severo-Kavkazskiĭ yuridicheskiĭ vestnik* (2016), no. 4, 18–30.

Ermacora, Felix. 'Die Selbstbestimmung im Lichte der UN-Deklaration betreffend die völkerrechtlichen Grundsätze über die freundschaftlichen Beziehungen und die Zusammenarbeit zwischen den Staaten entsprechend der Charta', *Internationales Recht und Diplomatie* (1972), 55–67.

Evers, Frank. 'Damaged Prospects/Damaged Dialogue in Ukraine and Crimea: The Current Situation in Ukraine and Future Co-operation with the OSCE', in Institute for Peace Research and Security Policy at the University of Hamburg (ed.), *OSCE Yearbook 2010: Yearbook on the Organization for Security and Cooperation in Europe (OSCE)* (Baden-Baden: Nomos, 2012), 221–43.

Evgenev, V.V. 'Правосубъектность, суверенитет и невмешательство в международном праве' [Legal Personality, Sovereignty and Non-interference in International Law], *Sovetskoe gosudarstvo i pravo* 17 (1955), no. 2, 75–84.

Evgenev, V.V. [W.W, Jewgenjew] (I. Leuschner transl.). 'Rechtssubjektivität, Souveränität, und Nichteinmischung im Völkerrecht', *Rechtswissenschaftlicher Informationsdienst* 4 (1955), MN 567–77.

Farhutdinov, I.Z. 'Евразийская интеграция и испытание украинской государственности в системе международного права' [Eurasian Integration and Test of Ukrainian Statehood in International Law], *Evraziĭskiĭ yuridicheskiĭ zhurnal* 79 (2014), 15–20

Filippov, A. 'Суверенитет как политический выбор' [Sovereignty as Political Choice], in N. Garadzha (ed.), *Суверенитет. Сборник* [Sovereignty. Compilation] (Moscow: Evropa, 2006), 173–200.

Franchini, Daniel and Antonios Tzanakopoulos. 'The Kosovo Crisis—1999', in Tom Ruys and Olivier Corten (eds), *The Use of Force in International Law: A Case-based Approach* (Oxford: Oxford University Press, 2018), 594–622.

Gaeta, Paola. 'The Armed Conflict in Chechnya before the Russian Constitutional Court', *European Journal of International Law* 7 (1996), 563–70.

Gall, Caroline von. 'Ist die Krim wirklich russisch? Russische Juristen diskutieren über die Rechtmäßigkeit der Aufnahme der Krim', *Russland-Analysen* 295 (2015), 2–7.

Gammer, Moshe. '"Proconsul of the Caucasus": A Re-examination of Yermolov', *Social Evolution & History* 2 (2003), 177–94.

Gazzini, Tarcisio. 'Considerations on the Conflict in Chechnya', *Human Rights Law Journal* 17 (1996), 93–105.

Geistlinger, Michael. 'Art 4', in Bernd Wieser (ed.), *Handbuch der russischen Verfassung* (Vienna: Verlag Österreich, 2014).

Gerrits, Andre W.M. and Bader, Max. 'Russian Patronage over Abkhazia and South Ossetia: Implications for Conflict Resolution', *East European Politics* 32 (2016), 297–313.

Ginsburgs, George. '"Wars of National Liberation" and the Modern Law of Nations—The Soviet Thesis', *Law and Contemporary Problems* 29 (1964), 910–42.

Glazer, Stephen G. 'The Brezhnev Doctrine', *International Lawyer* 5 (1971), 169–79.

Grant, Thomas D. 'United States Practice Relating to the Baltic States, 1940–2000', *Baltic Yearbook of International Law* 1 (2001), 23–110.

Grant, Thomas D. 'Annexation of Crimea', *American Journal of International Law* 109 (2015), 68–95.

Gray, Christine. 'The Conflict in Georgia—2008', in Tom Ruys and Olivier Corten (eds), *The Use of Force in International Law: A Case-based Approach* (Oxford: Oxford University Press, 2018), 712–28.

Grote, Rainer. 'The Russian Federation: Introductory Note', in Rüdiger Wolfrum, Rainer Grote, and Erika de Wet (eds), *Constitutions of the Countries of the World*, vol. 15 (Oxford: Oxford University Press, 2014), 3–45.

Grote, Rainer. 'The Ukraine: Introductory Note', in Rüdiger Wolfrum, Rainer Grote, and Charles M. Fombad (eds), *Constitutions of the Countries of the World*, vol. 15 (Oxford: Oxford University Press, 2015), 3–11.

Grzybowski, Kasimierz. *Soviet Public International Law, Doctrines and Diplomatic Practice* (Leiden: Sijthoff, 1970).
Hafeez, Malik. 'Tatarstan's Treaty with Russia: Autonomy or Independence?', *Journal of South Asian and Middle Eastern Studies* 18 (1994), no. 2, 1–36.
Hafkin, Gregory. 'The Russo-Georgian War of 2008: Developing the Law of Unauthorized Humanitarian Intervention after Kosovo', *Boston University International Law Journal* 28 (2010), 219–39.
Hafner, Gerhard. 'The Intervention in Czechoslovakia–1968', in Tom Ruys and Olivier Corten (eds), *The Use of Force in International Law: A Case-based Approach* (Oxford: Oxford University Press, 2018), 143–57.
Hannum, Hurst. 'Self-determination in the Post-colonial Era', in Donald Clark and Robert Williamson (eds), *Self-determination: International Perspectives* (New York, NY: Palgrave, 1996), 12–44.
Hanqin, Xue. 'Chinese Contemporary Perspectives on International Law: History, Culture and International Law', *Recueil des Cours de l'Académie de la Haye en ligne* 355 (2012), 41–234.
Hazard, John. 'Cleansing Soviet International Law of Anti-Marxist Theories', *American Journal of International Law* 32 (1938), 244–52.
Head, Michael. 'Rise and Fall of a Soviet Jurist: Evgeny Pashukanis and Stalinism', *Canadian Journal of Law and Jurisprudence* 17 (2004), 269–94.
Heintze, Hans-Joachim. 'Völkerrecht und Sezession—Ist die Annexion der Krim eine zulässige Wiedergutmachung sowjetischen Unrechts?', *Journal of International Law of Peace and Armed Conflict* 27 (2014), 129–38.
Higgins, Rosalyn. 'Self-determination and Secession', in Julie Dahlitz (ed.), *Secession and International Law: Conflict Avoidance—Regional Appraisals* (The Hague: T.M.C. Asser Press 2003), 21–38.
Peter Hilpold. 'Ukraine, Crimea and New International Law: Balancing International Law with Arguments Drawn From History', *Chinese Journal of International Law* 14 (2015), 237–70.
Hofmeister, Hannes. 'Don't Mess with Moscow—Legal Aspects of the 2008 Caucasus Conflict', *San Diego International Law Journal* 12 (2010/2011), 147–73.
Illarionov, Andrei. 'The Russian Leadership's Preparation for War, 1999–2008', in Svante E. Cornell and S. Frederick Starr (eds), *The Guns of August* 2008: *Russia's War in Georgia* (Armonk, NY: M.E. Sharpe, 2009), 49–84.
Ishakov D.M., Sagitova, L.V., and Izmailov, I.L. 'The Tatar National Movement of the 1980s–90s', *Anthropology & Archaeology of Eurasia* 43 (2004), no. 3, 11–44.
Issaeva, Maria. 'Conference Review Notes: The Case of Crimea in the Light of International Law: Its Nature and Implications', *Russian Law Journal* 3 (2015), no. 3, 158–67.
Issaeva, Maria. 'Quarter of a Century on from the Soviet Era: Reflections on Russian Doctrinal Responses to the Annexation of Crimea', *Russian Law Journal* 5 (2017), no. 3, 86–112.
Jouannet, Emmanuelle. 'French and American Perspectives on International Law: Legal Cultures and International Law', *Maine Law Review* 58 (2006), 291–336.
Kahn, Jeffrey. 'The Parade of Sovereignties: Establishing the Vocabulary of the New Russian Federalism', *Post-Soviet Affairs* 16 (2000), no. 1, 58–89.
Kapustin, Anatoly. 'Crimea's Self-determination in the Light of Contemporary International Law', *Zeitschrift für ausländisches öffentliches Recht und Völkerrecht* 75 (2015), 101–18.
Khlestov, O.N. 'Российская доктрина международного права' [Russian Doctrine of International Law], *Evraziĭskiĭ yuridicheskiĭ zhurnal* 58 (2013), no. 3, 19–22.

King, Jeff and Hobbins, A.J. 'Hammarskjöld and Human Rights: the Deflation of the UN Human Rights Programme 1953–1961', *Journal of the History of International Law* 5 (2003), 337–86.

Kikot, V.A. 'Проблемы самоопределения. Право и приказ' [Problems of Self-determination. Right and Order], in N.A. Kravchenko (ed.), *Правовые аспекты чеченского кризиса: Материалы семинара* [Legal Aspects of the Chechen Crisis: Workshop Materials] (Moscow: Memorial, 1995), 40–7.

Klein, Eckart. 'Nationale Befreiungskämpfe und Dekolonialisierungspolitik der Vereinten Nationen: Zu einigen völkerrechtlichen Tendenzen', *Zeitschrift für ausländisches öffentliches Recht und Völkerrecht* 36 (1976), 618–53.

Kohen, Marcelo. 'Introduction', in Marcelo Kohen (ed.), *Secession: International Law Perspectives* (Cambridge: Cambridge University Press, 2006), 1–20.

Kokott, Juliane. 'The Development of the Human Rights Situation in Kosovo 1989–1999', in Christian Tomuschat (ed.), *Kosovo and the International Community: A Legal Assessment* (The Hague: Kluwer Law International, 2002), 1–35.

Korbut, L.V. 'Аналитический обзор работы 56-го Ежегодного Собрания Российской Ассоциации международного права 26–28 июня 2013 г.' [Analytical Review of the Work of the 56th Annual Meeting of the Russian Association of International Law, 26–28 June 2013], *Rossiĭskiĭ ezhegodnik mezhdunarodnogo prava* (2013), 408–35.

Korovin, E.A. [Eugene Korovin]. 'Soviet Treaties in International Law', *American Journal of International Law* 22 (1928), 753–63.

Korovin, E.A. 'Пролетарский интернационализм и международное право' [Proletarian Internationalism and International Law], *Sovetskiĭ ezhegodnik mezhdunarodnogo prava* (1958), 50–69.

Koskenniemi, Martti. 'National Self-determination Today: Problems of Legal Theory and Practice', *International and Comparative Law Quarterly* 43 (1994), 241–69.

Kramer, Mark. 'The Perils of Counterinsurgency: Russia's War in Chechnya', *International Security* 29 (2004/2005), no. 3, 5–62.

Kramer, Mark. 'The Prague Spring and the Soviet Invasion in Historical Perspective', in Günter Bischof, Stefan Karner, and Peter Ruggenthaler (eds), *The Prague Spring and the Warsaw Pact Invasion of Czechoslovakia in 1968* (Lanham, MD: Lexington Books, 2010), 35–58.

Krichikova, E S. '"Круглый стол" в МГИМО-У по Севастополю' [Round Table at MGIMO on Sevastopol], *Moskovskiĭ zhurnal mezhdunarodnogo prava* 27 (1997), no. 3, 136–41.

Krüger, Heiko. 'Nagorno-Karabakh', in Christian Walter, Antje von Ungern-Sternberg, and Kavus Abushov (eds), *Self-determination and Secession in International Law* (Oxford: Oxford University Press, 2014), 214–32.

Khrushchev, Nikita S. 'On Peaceful Coexistence', *Foreign Affairs* 38 (1959), no. 1, 1–18.

Kuznetsov, V.I. 'Октябрь и международное право' [October and International Law], *Mezhdunarodnaya zhizn'* (1997), nos 11–12.

Kvacheva, P.I. and Petrova, S.V. 'Политико-правовой статус непризнанного государства в современном мире: историко-правовой аспект (на примере Республики Абхазия) [Political and Legal Status of an Unrecognized State in the Modern World: Historical and Legal Aspect (on the Example of the Republic of Abkhazia], *Vestnik Permskogo universiteta. Yuridicheskie nauki* 35 (2017), 56–65.

Landauer, Carl. 'Regionalism, Geography, and the International Legal Imagination', *Chicago Journal of International Law* 11 (2010–2011), 557–95.

Lavrov, S.V. 'Внешняя политика России и новое качество геополитической ситуации' [Russian Foreign Policy and New Quality of the Geopolitical Situation], *Diplomaticheskiĭ vestnik* 4 (2008), 7–14.

Lefeber René and Raič, David. 'Frontiers of International Law, Part One: The Chechen People', *Leiden Journal of International Law* 9 (1996), 1–6.

Lemercier-Quelquejay, Chantal. 'The Tatars of the Crimea: A Retrospective Summary', *Central Asian Review* 16 (1968), 15–25.

Lenin, V.I. 'Draft Platform of the 4th Congress of the Social Democrats of the Latvian Area' (1913), in *Lenin Collected Works*, vol. 19 (Moscow: Progress Publishers, 1977), 110–18.

Lenin, V.I. 'Cultural-National Autonomy' (1913), in *Lenin Collected Works*, vol. 19 (Moscow: Progress Publishers, 1977), 503–7.

Lenin, V.I. 'The Cadets and "The Right of Nations to Self-determination"' (1913), in *Lenin Collected Works*, vol. 19 (Moscow: Progress Publishers, 1977), 525–7.

Lenin, V.I. 'National-Liberalism and the Right of Nations to Self-determination' (1913), in *Lenin Collected Works*, vol. 20 (Moscow: Progress Publishers, 1972), 56–8.

Lenin, V.I. 'The Right of Nations to Self-determination' (1914), in *Lenin Collected Works*, vol. 20 (Moscow: Progress Publishers, 1972), 393–454.

Lenin, V.I. 'The Revolutionary Proletariat and the Right of Nations to Self-determination' (1915), in *Lenin Collected Works*, vol. 21 (Moscow: Progress Publishers, 1974), 407–14.

Lenin, V.I. 'Decree on Peace' (1917), in *Lenin Collected Works*, vol. 26 (Moscow: Progress Publishers, 1964), 249–53.

Lenin, V.I. 'Report on the Party Programme (19 March 1919)', in *Lenin Collected Works*, vol. 29 (Moscow: Progress Publishers, 1974), 141–225.

Lenin, V.I. 'Preliminary Draft Theses on the National and the Colonial Questions for the Second Congress of the Communist International' (1920), in *Lenin Collected Works*, vol. 31 (Moscow: Progress Publishers, 1966), 144–51.

Levin, D.B. 'Принцип самоопределения наций в международном праве' [The Principle of Self-determination of Nations in International Law], *Sovetskiĭ ezhegodnik mezhdunarodnogo prava* (1962/1963), 25–45.

Lieblich, Eliav. 'The Soviet Intervention in Hungary–1956', in Tom Ruys and Olivier Corten (eds), *The Use of Force in International Law: A Case-based Approach* (Oxford: Oxford University Press, 2018), 48–66.

Littlefield, Scott. 'Citizenship, Identity and Foreign Policy: The Contradictions and Consequences of Russia's Passport Distribution in the Separatist Regions of Georgia', *Europe-Asia Studies* 61 (2009), 1461–82.

Luchterhandt, Otto. 'Das Recht Berg-Karabaghs auf staatliche Unabhängigkeit aus völkerrechtlicher Sicht', *Archiv des Völkerrechts* 31 (1993), 30–81.

Luchterhandt, Otto. 'Der Anschluss der Krim aus völkerrechtlicher Sicht', *Archiv des Völkerrechts* 52 (2014), 137–74.

Luchterhandt, Otto. 'Die Krim-Krise von 2014. Staats- und völkerrechtliche Aspekte', *Osteuropa* 64 (2014), no. 5–6, 61–86.

Luchterhandt, Otto. 'Transnistrien vor und nach dem Regimewechsel in Kiew und Russlands Krim-Annexion', *Osteuropa-Recht* 62 (2016), 4–29.

Luchterhandt, Otto. 'Gegen das Völkerrecht. Die Eskalation des Konflikts am Asowschen Meer', *Osteuropa* 69 (2019), no. 1–2, 3–21.

Lukyanova, Elena. 'On the Rule of Law in the Context of Russian Foreign Policy', *Russian Law Journal* 3 (2015), no. 2, 10–36.

McCorquodale, Robert. 'Self-determination: A Human Rights Approach', *International Law and Comparative Law Quarterly* 43 (1994), 857–85.

McDougal, Myres S. and Lasswell, Harold D. 'The Identification and Appraisal of Diverse Systems of Public Order', *American Journal of International Law* 53 (1959), 1–29.

MacFarlane, Neil. 'Frozen Conflicts in the Former Soviet Union—The Case of Georgia/South Ossetia', in Institute for Peace Research and Security Policy at the University of

Hamburg (ed.), *OSCE Yearbook 2008: Yearbook on the Organization for Security and Co-operation in Europe (OSCE)* (Baden-Baden: Nomos, 2008), 23–33.

McWhinney, Edward. 'The "New Thinking" in Soviet International Law: Soviet Doctrines and Practice in the Post-Tunkin Era', *Canadian Yearbook of International Law* (1990), 309–37.

Makhotina, Ekaterina. 'Keine Experimente. Russlands Geschichtspolitik und die Revolution', *Osteuropa* 67 (2017), no. 6–8, 211–30.

Mälksoo, Lauri. 'The Science of International Law and the Concept of Politics. The Arguments and Lives of the International Law Professors at the University of Dorpat/Yur'ev/Tartu 1855–1985', *British Yearbook of International Law* 75 (2005), 383–501.

Mälksoo, Lauri. 'The History of International Theory in Russia: A Civilizational Dialogue with Europe', *European Journal of International Law* 19 (2008), 211–32.

Mälksoo, Lauri. 'International Law in Russian Textbook: What's in the Doctrinal Pluralism?', *Göttingen Journal of International Law* 1 (2009), 279–90.

Mälksoo, Lauri. 'Contemporary Russian Perspectives on Non-State Actors: Fear of the Loss of State Sovereignty', in Jean d'Aspremont (ed.), *Participants in the International Legal System: Multiple Perspectives on Non-state Actors in International Law* (London: Routledge, 2011), 126–38.

Mälksoo, Lauri. 'F.F. Martens and His Time. When Russia Was an Integral Part of the European Tradition of International Law', *European Journal of International Law* 25 (2014), 811–29.

Mälksoo, Lauri. 'International Legal Theory in Russia: A Civilizational Perspective, or Can Individuals be Subjects of International Law?', in Anne Orford and Florian Hoffmann (eds), *The Oxford Handbook of the Theory of International Law* (Oxford: Oxford University Press, 2016), 257–75.

Mälksoo, Lauri. 'The Soviet Approach to the Right of Peoples to Self-determination: Russia's Farewell to *jus publicum europaeum*', *Journal of the History of International Law* 19 (2017), 200–18.

Mälksoo, Lauri. 'Case Law in Russian Approaches to International Law', in Anthea Roberts, Paul B. Stephan, and Pierre-Hugues Verdier (eds), *Comparative International Law* (New York, NY: Oxford University Press, 2018), 337–52.

Mälksoo, Lauri. 'The Annexation of Crimea and Balance of Power in International Law', *European Journal of International Law* 30 (2019), 303–19.

Mamlyuk, Boris N. 'Book Review', *Review of Central and East European Law* 35 (2010), 111–15.

Mamlyuk, Boris N. 'The Ukraine Crisis, Cold War II, and International Law', *German Law Journal* 16 (2015), 479–522.

Mamlyuk, Boris N. and Ugo Mattei. 'Comparative International Law', *Brookings Journal of International Law* 36 (2011), 385–452.

Marchuk, Iryna. 'Application of the International Convention for the Suppression of the Financing of Terrorism and of the International Convention on the Elimination of All Forms of Racial Discrimination (Ukraine v Russia)', *Melbourne Journal of International Law* 18 (2017), 436–59.

Marochkin, Sergei. 'Contemporary Approaches of the Russian Doctrine in International Law', *Baltic Yearbook of International Law* 12 (2012), 29–56.

Marusin, I.S. 'О соотношении принципа нерушимости границ и права народов на самоопределение' [On the Relationship between the Principle of Inviolability of Borders and the Right of Peoples to Self-determination], *Pravovedenie* 2014, no. 1, 109–19.

Marxsen, Christian, Peters, Anne, and Hartwig, Matthias. 'Symposium: "The Incorporation of Crimea by the Russian Federation in the Light of International Law"', *Zeitschrift für ausländisches öffentliches Recht und Völkerrecht* 75 (2015), 1–5.

Mégret, Frédéric. 'The Right to Self-determination. Earned, Not Inherent', in Fernando R. Téson (ed.), *The Theory of Self-determination* (Cambridge: Cambridge University Press, 2016), 45–69.

Meissner, Boris. 'Die interparteilichen Beziehungen im Ostblock und das Prinzip des "proletarisch-sozialistischen Internationalismus"', *Internationales Recht und Diplomatie* (1961), 147–64.

Meissner, Boris. 'Die Völkerrechtswissenschaft im zaristischen und bolschewistischen Russland', *Internationales Recht und Diplomatie* (1963), 63–9.

Meissner, Boris. 'Das Wesen und der Geltungsbereich des Völkerrechts', in Reinhart Maurach and Boris Meissner (eds), *Völkerrecht in Ost und West* (Stuttgart: Kohlhammer, 1967), 9–38.

Meissner, Boris. 'Lenin und das Selbstbestimmungsrecht der Völker', *Osteuropa* 20 (1970), 245–61.

Meissner, Boris. 'Die Grundsätze der „friedlichen Koexistenz" als Elemente eines gesamteuropäischen Sicherheitssystems', in Boris Meissner and Alexander Uschakow (eds), *Probleme der Konferenz über Sicherheit und Zusammenarbeit in Europa* (Berlin: Berlin Verlag, 1975), 45–66.

Meissner, Boris. 'Der Souveränitätsgedanke in der sowjetischen Völkerrechtslehre', in Eduard Kröker and Theodor Veiter (eds), *Rechtspositivismus, Menschenrechte und Souveränitätslehre in verschiedenen Rechtskreisen* (Vienna: Braumüller, 1976), 110–29.

Meissner, Boris. 'Der sowjetische Nationsbegriff und seine politische und rechtliche Bedeutung', in Boris Meissner and Jens Hacker (eds), *Die Nation in östlicher Sicht* (Berlin: Duncker & Humblot, 1977), 7–39.

Meissner, Boris. 'Die Entwicklungstendenzen in der sowjetischen außenpolitischen Theorie und Völkerrechtslehre 1962 bis 1973', in Boris Meissner, Dietrich Frenzke, and Erika Chilecki (eds), *Sowjetunion und Völkerrecht 1962–1973. Bibliographie und Analyse* (Cologne: Verlag Wissenschaft und Politik, 1977), 9–58.

Meissner, Boris. 'Entwicklungen und Stand der deutschen Ostrechtsforschung und ihre Stellung in der internationalen Ostwissenschaft', in Boris Meissner, Herwig Roggemann, Friedrich-Christian Schroeder, and Klaus Westen (eds), *Grundsatzfragen der Ostrechtsforschung* (Tübingen: Erdmann, 1980), 103–6.

Meissner, Boris. 'The Occupation of the Baltic States from a Present-Day Perspective', in Tālavs Jundzis (ed.), *The Baltic States at Historical Crossroads: Political, Economic, and Legal Problems and Oppurtinities in the Context of International Cooperation at the Beginning of the 21st Century* (Riga: Academy of Sciences of Latvia, 2001), 437–51.

Merezhko, Oleksandr. 'Crimea's Annexation in the Light of International Law: A Critique of Russia's Legal Argumentation', *Kyiv-Mohyla Law and Politics Journal* 2 (2016), 37–89.

Milano, Enrico. 'The Conferral of Citizenship *en masse* by Kin-States: Creeping Annexation or Responsibility to Protect?', in Francesco Palermo and Natalie Sabanadze (eds), *National Minorities in Inter-Sate Relations* (Leiden: Martinus Nijhoff, 2011), 145–66.

Milano, Enrico. The Non-Recognition of Russia's Annexation of Crimea: Three Different Legal Approaches and One Unanswered Question', *Questions of International Law* 1 (2014), 35–55.

Milovanovic, Dragan. 'Introduction', in Evgeny Pashukanis, *The General Theory of Law & Marxism* (New Brunswick, NJ: Transaction Publishers, 2002), vii–xxvi.

Minasyan, N.M. 'Ленинское учение самоопределении наций и международное право' [Lenin's Doctrine of Self-determination of Nations and International Law], *Sovetskiĭ ezhegodnik mezhdunarodnogo prava* (1970), 29–42.

Mirzaev, F.S. 'Принцип uti possidetis в современном международном праве и его применение на постсоветском пространстве: Теория и практика' [The Principle of Uti Possidetis in Modern International Law and its Application in the Post-Soviet Space], *Pravo i politika* (2004), no. 6, 43–53.

Moiseev, A.A. 'Критика концепции относительного государственного суверенитета' [Criticism of the Concept of Relative State Sovereignty], *Moskovskiĭ zhurnal mezhdunarodnogo prava* 67 (2007), no. 3, 16–32.

Moiseev, A.A. 'Косовский прецедент и система международного права' [The Kosovo Precedent and the System of International Law], *Mezhdunarodnaya zhizn'* (2008), no. 5, 79–89.

Moiseev, A.A. 'О некоторых международно-правовых позициях по крымскому вопросу' [On Some International Law Positions on the Crimean Issue], *Mezhdunarodnaya zhizn'* (2014), no. 5, 53–65.

Movchan, A.P. 'The Human Rights Problem in Present-Day International Law', in Grigory Tunkin (ed.), *Contemporary International Law* (Moscow: Progress Publishers, 1969), 233–50.

Müllerson, Rein. 'The Continuity and Succession of States, by Reference to the Former USSR and Yugoslavia', *International and Comparative Law Quarterly* 42 (1993), 473–93.

Müllerson, Rein. 'Then and Now, Here and There', in Julie Dahlitz (ed.), *Secession and International Law: Conflict Avoidance—Regional Appraisals* (The Hague: T.M.C. Asser Press, 2003), 125–65.

Müllerson, Rein. 'Precedents in the Mountains: On the Parallels and Uniqueness of the Cases of Kosovo, South Ossetia and Abkhazia', *Chinese Journal of International Law* 8 (2009), 2–15.

Müllerson, Rein. 'Ukraine: Victim of Geopolitics', *Chinese Journal of International Law* 13 (2014), 133–45, 139.

Müllerson, Rein. 'One Man's Separatist—Another Man's Independentist: Self-determination Claims from Scotland to Ukraine', in Peter Hilpold (ed.), *Autonomie und Selbstbestimmung in Europa und im internationalen Vergleich* (Zurich: Nomos, 2016), 68–83.

Müllerson, R.A. and Vereshchetin, V.S. 'Новое мышление и международное право' [New Thinking in International Law], *Sovetskoe gosudarstvo i pravo* 50 (1988), no. 3, 3–9.

Müllerson, R.A. and Vereshchetin, V.S. 'Примат международного права в мировой политике' [Primacy of International Law in World Politics], *Sovetskoe gosudarstvo i pravo* 51 (1989), no. 7, 3–11.

Müllerson, R.A. and Vereshchetin, V.S. 'The Primacy of International Law in World Politics', in Anthony Carty and Gennady Danilenko (eds), *Perestroika and International Law: Current Anglo-Soviet Approaches to International Law* (Edinburgh: Edinburgh University Press, 1990), 6–14.

Neukirch, Claus. 'From Confidence Building to Conflict Settlement in Moldova?', in Institute for Peace Research and Security Policy at the University of Hamburg (ed.), *OSCE Yearbook 2011: Yearbook on the Organization for Security and Co-operation in Europe (OSCE)* (Baden-Baden: Nomos, 2012), 137–50.

Nikravesh, Babak. 'Quebec and Tatarstan in International Law', *The Fletcher Forum of World Affairs* 23 (1999), 227–58.

Nolte, Georg and Janina Barkholdt. 'The Soviet Intervention in Afghanistan–1970–80', in Tom Ruys and Olivier Corten (eds), *The Use of Force in International Law: A Case-based Approach* (Oxford: Oxford University Press, 2018), 297–305.

Nußberger, Angelika. 'Rechts- und Verfassungskultur in der Russischen Föderation', *Jahrbuch des öffentlichen Rechts* 54 (2006), 35–55.

Nußberger, Angelika. 'Völkerrecht im Kaukasus—Postsowjetische Konflikte in Russland und in Georgien', *Europäische Grundrechte-Zeitschrift* 35 (2008), 457–66.

Nußberger, Angelika. 'Entwicklung der Verfassungsrechtsprechung in Russland', in Angelika Nußberger, Carmen Schmidt, and Tamara Morščakova, *Verfassungsrechtsprechung in der Russischen Föderation: Dokumentation und Analyse der Entscheidungen des Russischen Verfassungsgerichts 1991–2007* (Kehl: N.P. Engel Verlag, 2009), 43–82.

Nußberger, Angelika. 'The War between Russia and Georgia—Consequences and Unresolved Questions', *Göttingen Journal of International Law* 1 (2009), 341–64.

Nußberger, Angelika. 'Supranationales Recht jenseits des Ural—Zur Diskussion über die Übertragung von Hoheitsrechten im Rahmen der Zollunion zwischen Russland, Kasachstan und Weißrussland', *Osteuropa-Recht* 56 (2010), 113–21.

Nußberger, Angelika. 'Völkerrechtliche Bezüge', in Angelika Nußberger (ed.), *Einführung in das russische Recht* (Munich: Beck, 2010), 60–5.

Nußberger, Angelika. 'Lauri Mälksoo. Russian Approaches to International Law', *European Journal of International Law* 26 (2015), 790–3.

Nußberger, Angelika and Yuri Safoklov. 'Art 15', in Bernd Wieser (ed.), *Handbuch der russischen Verfassung* (Vienna: Verlag Österreich, 2014).

Nußberger, Angelika. 'Präambel', in Bernd Wieser (ed.), *Handbuch der russischen Verfassung* (Vienna: Verlag Österreich, 2014).

Nystén-Haarala, Soili. 'Does the Russian Constitution Justify an Offence against Chechnya?', *Humanitäres Völkerrecht* 1995, no. 2, 104–7.

O'Connell, Mary Ellen. 'The Crisis in Ukraine–2014', in Tom Ruys and Olivier Corten (eds), *The Use of Force in International Law: A Case-based Approach* (Oxford: Oxford University Press, 2018), 855–72.

O'Loughlin, John, Toal, Gerald, and Kolosov, Vladimir. 'Who Identifies with the "Russian World"? Geopolitical Attitudes in Southeastern Ukraine, Crimea, Abkhazia, South Ossetia, and Transnistria', *Eurasian Geography and Economics* 57 (2016), 745–78.

Oeter, Stefan. 'Self-determination', in Bruno Simma, Daniel Erasmus-Khan, Georg Nolte, and Andreas Paulus (eds), *The Charter of the United Nations: A Commentary*, vol. 1 (Oxford: Oxford University Press, 3rd edn, 2012).

Okawa, Phoebe. 'The International Court of Justice and the Georgia/Russia Dispute', *Human Rights Law Review* 11 (2011), 739–57.

Papp, Daniel. 'National Liberation during Détente: the Soviet Outlook', *International Journal* 32 (1976–1977), 82–99.

Pashukanis, E.B. 'Международное право' [International Law], in *Энциклопедия государства и права* [Encyclopedia of State and Law], vol. 2 (Moscow: Izd. Kommunisticheskoĭ Akademii, 1926), 868–74.

Peters, Anne. 'Die Zukunft der Völkerrechtswissenschaft: Wider den epistemischen Nationalismus', *Zeitschrift für ausländisches öffentliches Recht und Völkerrecht* 67 (2007), 721–76.

Peters, Anne. 'Extraterritorial Naturalization: Between the Human Right to Nationality, State Sovereignty and Fair Principles of Jurisdiction', *German Yearbook of International Law* 53 (2010), 623–725.

Peters, Anne. 'Das Völkerrecht der Gebietsreferenden. Das Beispiel der Ukraine 1991–2014', *Osteuropa* 64 (2014), no. 5–6, 101–33.

Peters, Anne. 'The Principle of *Uti Possidetis Juris*: How Relevant is it for Issues of Secession?', in Christian Walter, Antje von Ungern-Sternberg, and Kavus Abushov (eds), *Self-determination and Secession in International Law* (Oxford: Oxford University Press, 2014), 95–137.

Peters, Anne. 'The Crimean Vote of March 2014 as an Abuse of the Institution of the Territorial Referendum', in Christian Calliess (ed.), *Staat und Mensch im Kontext des Völker- und Europarechts: Liber Amicorum für Torsten Stein* (Baden-Baden: Nomos Verlag, 2015), 255–80.

Petro, Nicolai. 'The Legal Case for Russian Intervention in Georgia', *Fordham International Law Journal* 32 (2009), 1524–49.

Petrukhin, I.L. 'Правовая оценка военного конфликта в Чечне' [Legal Assessment of the Military Conflict in Chechnya], in N.A. Kravchenko (ed.), *Правовые аспекты чеченского кризиса: Материалы семинара* [Legal Aspects of the Chechen Crisis: Workshop Materials] (Moscow: Memorial, 1995).

Pokhlebkin, V.V. 'К вопросу о геополитическом и международно-правовом положении Крыма' [On the Question of the Geopolitical and International Legal Position of Crimea], *Moskovskiĭ zhurnal mezhdunarodnogo prava* 1996, no. 2, 165–81.

Pomerance, Michla. 'The United States and Self-determination: Perspectives on the Wilsonian Concept', *American Journal of International Law* 70 (1976), 1–27.

Pritzkow, Sebastian. 'Kontinuität and Diskontinuität: Sowjetisches und modernes Völkerrechtsdenken im Vergleich', *Osteuropa-Recht* 54 (2008), 397–406.

Pritzkow, Sebastian. 'Dokumentation zur Integration der Krim in die Russische Föderation', *Osteuropa-Recht* 60 (2014), 426–36.

Pronin, Anatoly. 'Republic of Crimea: A Two-Day State', *Russian Law Journal* 3 (2015), no. 1, 133–42.

Radan, Peter. 'Post-Secession International Borders: A Critical Analysis of the Opinions of the Badinter Commission', *Melbourne University Law Review* 3 (2000), 50–76.

Ramundo, Bernard A. 'Czechoslovakia and the Law of Peaceful Coexistence: Legal Characterization in the Soviet National Interest', *Stanford Law Review* 22 (1970), 963–78.

Randelzhofer, Albrecht and Dörr, Oliver. 'Art. 2(4)', in Bruno Simma, Daniel-Erasmus Khan, Georg Nolte, and Andreas Paulus (eds), *The Charter of the United Nations: A Commentary*, vol. 1 (Oxford: Oxford University Press, 3rd edn, 2012).

Ratner, Steven R. 'Drawing a Better Line: *Uti Possidetis* and the Borders of New States', *American Journal of International Law* 90 (1996), 590–624.

Reshetov, Yu.A. 'Право на самоопределение и отделение' [The Right to Self-determination and Secession], *Moskovskiĭ zhurnal mezhdunarodnogo prava* 1994, no. 1, 3–20.

Reshetov, Yu.A. 'К вопросу о "Мягком праве"' [On the Question of 'Soft Law'], *Moskovskiĭ zhurnal mezhdunarodnogo prava* 34 (1999), no. 2, 26–31.

Roberts, Anthea. 'Crimea and the South China Sea: Connections and Disconnects among Chinese, Russian, and Western International Lawyers', in Anthea Roberts, Paul B. Stephan, and Pierre-Hugues Verdier (eds), *Comparative International Law* (Oxford: Oxford University Press, 2018), 111–39.

Rogozhin, S.L. 'Международное право как диалог и столкновение цивилизаций' [International Law as a Dialogue and a Clash of Civilizations], *Moskovskiĭ zhurnal mezhdunarodnogo prava* 47 (2002), no. 3, 16–30.

Rokhlin, Lev. 'Спецоперация или коммерческая афера?' [A Special Operation or a Commercial Deal?], *Nezavisimoe voennoe obozrenie* (1997), no. 13.

Rosenstock, Robert. 'The Declaration of Principles of International Law Concerning Friendly Relations: A Survey', *American Journal of International Law* 65 (1971), 713–35.

Ross, David. 'Beyond the Soviet Invasion: Afghanistan and the Concept of Self-determination', *University of Toronto Faculty of Law Review* 48 (1990), 92–116.

Rostow, Nicholas. 'Law and the Use of Force by States: The Brezhnev Doctrine', *Yale Journal of International Law* 7 (1981), 209–43.

Salo, Juha. 'Self-determination: An Overview of History and Present State with Emphasis on the CSCE Process', *Finnish Yearbook of International Law* 2 (1991), 268–342.

Sanakoev, Sh. 'Пролетарский интернационализм—основа взаимоотношений стран социализма' [Proletarian Internationalism—The Basis for the Relations between Socialist States], *Mezhdunarodnaya zhizn'* (1958), no. 7, 30–43.

Sauer, Heiko and Wagner, Niklas. 'Der Tschetschenien-Konflikt und das Völkerrecht. Tschetscheniens Sezession, Russlands Militärinterventionen und die Reaktionen der Staatengemeinschaft auf dem Prüfstand des internationalen Rechts', *Archiv des Völkerrechts* 45 (2007), 55–83.

Sayapin, Sergey. 'The United Nations General Assembly Resolution 68/262 in the Context of General International Law', *European Politics and Law Discourse* 2 (2015), 19–30.

Schachter, Oscar. 'The Invisible College of International Lawyers', *Northwestern University Law Review* 72 (1977–1978), 217–26.

Schachter, Oscar. 'Micronationalism and Secession', in Ulrich Beyerlin, Michael Bothe, Rainer Hofmann, and Ernst-Ulrich Petersmann (eds), *Recht zwischen Umbruch und Bewahrung: Völkerrecht, Europarecht, Staatsrecht (Festschrift für Rudolf Bernhardt)* (Berlin: Springer, 1995), 179–86.

Schamiloglu, Uli. 'The Formation of a Tatar Historical Consciousness: Şihabäddin Märcani and the Image of the Golden Horde', *Central Asian Survey* 9 (1990), 39–49.

Schmidt, Carmen. 'Das russische Verfassungsgericht zum Beitritt der Krim und Sewastopol—das Urteil vom 19. März 2014', *Osteuropa-Recht* 60 (2014), 254–5.

Schröder, Dieter. 'Die Idee der kollektiven Regionalintervention. Rechtsvergleichende Betrachtungen zur Breschnew-Doktrin', *Recht in Ost und West* 13 (1969), 203–10.

Schroeder, Friedrich-Christian. 'Die Rechtmäßigkeit des Krieges nach westlicher und sowjetischer Völkerrechtsauffassung', in Reinhart Maurach and Boris Meissner (eds), *Völkerrecht in Ost und West* (Stuttgart: Kohlhammer, 1967), 178–218.

Schwebel, Stephen M. 'The Brezhnev Doctrine Repealed and Peaceful Co-Existence Enacted', *American Journal of International Law* 66 (1971), 816–19.

Schweisfurth, Theodor. 'Vom Einheitsstaat (UdSSR) zum Staatenbund (GUS)', *Zeitschrift für ausländisches öffentliches Recht und Völkerrecht* 52 (1992), 541–702.

Senn, Alfred. 'What Happened in Lithuania in 1940?', *Lithuanian Foreign Policy Review* 6 (2000), 179–95.

Shaw, Malcolm N. and Fournet, Caroline. 'Article 62', in Olivier Corten and Pierre Klein (eds), *The Vienna Conventions on the Law of Treaties*, vol. 2 (Oxford: Oxford University Press, 2011), 1411–36.

Shlapentokh, Dmitry. 'Dugin Eurasianism: A Window on the Minds of the Russian Elite or an Intellectual Ploy?', *Studies in East European Thought* 59 (2007), 215–36.

Shumilov, V.M. 'Взгляд на историю международных отношений и международного права в контексте цивилизационного подхода' [A Look at the History of International Relations and International Law in the Context of the Civilizational Approach], *Moskovskiĭ zhurnal mezhdunarodnogo prava* 95 (2014), no. 3, 46–64.

Shurshalov, V.M. 'International Law in Relations among Socialist Countries', in Grigory Tunkin (ed.), *Contemporary International Law* (Moscow: Progress Publishers, 1969), 59–76.

Socher, Johannes. 'Lenin, (Just) Wars of National Liberation, and the Soviet Doctrine on the Use of Force', *Journal of the History of International Law* 19 (2017), 219–45.

Socher, Johannes. 'Farewell to the European Constitutional Tradition: The 2020 Russian Constitutional Amendments', *Zeitschrift für ausländisches öffentliches Recht und Völkerrecht* 80 (2020), 615–48.

Socor, Vladimir. 'Federalization Experiment in Moldova', *Russia and Eurasia Review* 1 (2002), no. 4.

Sommermann, Karl-Peter (Jeremy Gaines transl.). 'The Right of Resistance: Approaches in Legal Philosophy', in Peter Weibel (ed.), *Global Activism: Art and Conflict in the 21st Century* (Cambridge, MA: MIT Press, 2014), 119–28.

Speranskaya, L.V. *Принцип самоопределения наций в международном праве* [The Principle of Self-determination of Nations in International Law] (Moscow: Gos. Izd. yurid. lit., 1961).

Stalin, I.V. 'Marxism and the National Question' (1913), in *Stalin Collected Works*, vol. 2 (Moscow: Foreign Languages Publishing House, 1953), 300–81.

Stalin, I.V. 'Joint Plenum of the Central Committee and Central Control Commission of the C.P.S.U.(B.): The International Situation and the Defence of the U.S.S.R' (1927), in *Stalin Collected Works*, vol. 10 (Moscow: Foreign Language Publishing House, 1954), 1–62.

Starushenko, Gleb. 'Abolition of Colonialism and International Law', in Grigory Tunkin (ed.), *Contemporary International Law* (Moscow: Progress Publishers, 1969), 77–96.

Stöber, Silvia. 'The Failure of the OSCE Mission to Georgia—What Remains?', in Institute for Peace Research and Security Policy at the University of Hamburg (ed.), *OSCE Yearbook 2010: Yearbook on the Organization for Security and Co-operation in Europe* (Baden-Baden: Nomos, 2011), 203–20.

Šuković, Olga. 'Principle of Equal Rights and Self-determination of Peoples', in Milan Šahović (ed.), *Principles of International Law concerning Friendly Relations and Co-operation* (Belgrade: Institute for International Politics and Economics, 1972), 323–73.

Summers, James. 'Kosovo', in Christian Walter, Antje von Ungern-Sternberg, and Kavus Abushov (eds), *Self-determination and Secession in International Law* (Oxford: Oxford University Press, 2014), 235–54.

Suslov, Mikhail D. '"Crimea is Ours!" Russian Popular Geopolitics in the New Media Age', *Eurasian Geography and Economics* 55 (2014), 588–609.

Talmon, Stefan. 'The Duty Not to 'Recognize as Lawful' a Situation Created by the Illegal Use of Force or Other Serious Breaches of a Jus Cogens Obligation: An Obligation without Real Substance?', in Christian Tomuschat and Jean-Marc Thouvenin (eds), *The Fundamental Rules of the International Legal Order: Jus Cogens and Obligations Erga Omnes* (Leiden: Nijhoff, 2006), 99–126.

Tancredi, Antonello. 'A Normative "Due Process" in the Creation of States Through Secession', in Marcelo Kohen (ed.), *Secession: International Law Perspectives* (Cambridge: Cambridge University Press, 2006), 171–207.

Tancredi, Antonello. 'The Russian Annexation of the Crimea: Questions Relating to the Use of Force', *Questions of International Law* 1 (2014), 16–23.

Tappe, Trent. 'Chechnya and the State of Self-determination in a Breakaway Region of the former Soviet Union: Evaluating the Legitimacy of Secessionist Claims', *Colombia Journal of Transnational Law* 34 (1996), 255–95.

Teague, Elizabeth. 'Russia and Tatarstan Sign Power-sharing Treaty', *Radio Free Europe/Radio Liberty Research Report* 3 (1994), 19–27.

Teper, Yuri. 'Official Russian Identity Discourse in Light of the Annexation of Crimea: National or Imperial?', *Post-Soviet Affairs* 32 (2016), 378–96.

Tkatova, Rima. 'Russian Spirits, Soviet Heritage and Western Temptation: "Un-'Peaceful-Coexistence'" in Russia's International Doctrine and Practice', *Baltic Yearbook of International Law* 12 (2012), 1–28.

Tolkachev, K.B. '"Крымский вопрос" и современное право: к дискуссии о легитимности референдума' ['The Crimean Question' and Contemporary Law: On the Discussion on the Legitimacy of the Referendum], *Evraziiskii yuridicheskii zhurnal* 72 (2014), 90–2.

Tolstykh, V.L. 'Воссоединение Крыма с Россией: правовые квалификации' [The Reunification of Crimea with Russia: Legal Qualifications], *Evraziiskii yuridicheskii zhurnal* 72 (2014), 40–6.

Tolstykh, V.L. 'Reunification of Crimea with Russia: A Russian Perspective', *Chinese Journal of International Law* 13 (2014), 879–86.

Tolstykh, V.L. 'Три идеи самоопределения в международном праве' [Three Ideas of Self-determination in International Law], *Evraziiskii yuridicheskii zhurnal* 76 (2014), 65–72.

Tolstykh, V.L. 'Three Ideas of Self-determination in International Law and the Reunification of Crimea with Russia', *Zeitschrift für ausländisches öffentliches Recht und Völkerrecht* 75 (2015), 119–39.

Tolstykh, V.L. 'Revisiting the Principle of Self-determination', in Władysław Czapliński, Sławomir Dębski, Rafał Tarnogórski, and Karolina Wierczyńska (eds), *The Case of Crimea's Annexation under International Law* (Warsaw: Scholar Publishing House, 2017), 99–108.

Tolstykh, V.L. 'Book Review Notes: Difficult Search for Truth', *Russian Law Journal* 6 (2018), no. 4, 154–65.

Tolstykh, V.L. 'Марксизм, Октябрьская революция и правоведение' [Marxism, October Revolution and Jurisprudence], *Rossiiskii yuridicheskii zhurnal* 118 (2018), no. 1, 9–20.

Toman, Jiri. 'La conception soviétique des guerres de libération nationale', in Antonio Cassese (ed.), *Current Problems of International Law* (Milan: Giuffrè, 1975), 355–75.

Tomsinov, V.A. 'Международное право с точки зрения воссоединения Крыма с Россией' [International Law from the from the Point of View of the Reunification of Crimea with Russia], *Zakonodatel'stvo* 2014, no. 7, 11–26.

Tomuschat, Christian. 'Self-determination in a Post-colonial World', in Christian Tomuschat (ed.), *Modern Law of Self-determination* (Dordrecht: Nijhoff, 1993), 1–20.

Tomuschat, Christian. 'International Law: Ensuring the Survival of Mankind on the Eve of a New Century', *Recueil des Cours de l'Académie de la Haye en ligne* 281 (1999), 9–438.

Tomuschat, Christian. 'Secession and Self-determination', in Marcelo Kohen (ed.), *Secession: International Law Perspectives* (Cambridge: Cambridge University Press, 2006), 1–45.

Tretter, Hannes. 'Human Rights in the Concluding Document of the Vienna Follow-up Meeting of the Conference on Security and Co-operation in Europe of January 15, 1989: An Introduction', *Human Rights Law Journal* 10 (1989), 257–69.

Tunkin, G.I. 'Co-existence and International Law', *Recueil des Cours de l'Académie de la Haye en ligne* 95 (1958), 1–81.

Tunkin, G.I. 'Новый тип международных отношений и международное право' [New Type of International Relations and International Law], *Sovetskoe gosudarstvo i pravo* 21 (1959), no. 1, 81–94.

Tunkin, G.I. (Peter Rossbacher and Dietrich Frenzke transl.). 'Grundlagen des modernen Völkerrechts', in: Institut für Internationales Recht an der Universität Kiel (ed.), *Drei sowjetische Beiträge zur Völkerrechtslehre* (Hamburg: Hansischer Gildenverlag, 1969), 1–57.

Tunkin, G.I. 'Ленинские принципы равноправия и самоопределения народов и современное международное право' [Lenin's Principles of Equal Rights and Self-determination of Peoples and Contemporary International Law], *Vestnik Moskovskogo universiteta. Pravo* 2 (1970), 62–71.

Tuzmukhamedov, B.R. 'Упреждающее применение силы: возможные критерии допустимости' [Pre-emptive Use of Force: Possible Criteria for Admissibility], *Rossiĭskiĭ ezhegodnik mezhdunarodnogo prava* (2005), 36–55.

Tuzmukhamedov, B.R. 'Legislative Regulation of Trans-boundary Use of Armed Force: Russian Case Study', *Baltic Yearbook of International Law* 12 (2012), 57–74.

Uibopuu, Henn-Jüri. 'Art. 76', in Martin Fincke (ed.), *Handbuch der Sowjetverfassung*, vol. 2 (Berlin: Duncker & Humblot, 1983).

Uibopuu, Henn-Jüri. 'Kopernikanische Wende in der sowjetischen Völkerrechtstheorie', *Recht in Ost und West* 32 (1988), 242–5.

Usenko, E.T. 'Основные международно-правовые принципы сотрудничества социалистических государств' [Basic International Legal Principles of Co-operation of Socialist States], *Sovetskoe gosudarstvo i pravo* 23 (1961), no. 3, 16–29.

Usenko, E.T. (I. Brehme transl.). 'Die völkerrechtlichen Grundprinzipien der Zusammenarbeit der sozialistischen Staaten', *Sowjetwissenschaft. Gesellschaftswissenschaftliche Beiträge* 14 (1961), no. 7, 749–65.

Usenko, E.T. 'Международное право в отношениях между социалистическими государствами' [International Law in Relations Between Socialist States], in N.T. Blatova (ed.), *Международное право* [International Law] (Moscow: Yuridicheskaya literatura, 1987), 184–215.

Ushakov, Nikolay. 'International Law and Sovereignty', in Grigory Tunkin (ed.), *Contemporary International Law* (Moscow: Progress Publishers, 1969), 97–117.

Vagts, Detlev. 'Hegemonic International Law', *American Journal of International Law* 95 (2001), 843–8.

Vahl, Marius and Emerson, Michael. 'Moldova and the Transnistrian Conflict', in Bruno Coppieters, Michael Emerson, Michel Huysseune, Tamara Kovziridze, Gergana Noutcheva, Nathalie Tocci, and Marius Vahl (eds), *Europeanization and Conflict Resolution: Case Studies from the European Periphery* (Gent: Academia Press, 2004), 149–90.

Velyaminov, G.M. 'Соотношение принципов самоопределения народов и территориальной целостности, а также проблемы признания' [The Ratio of the Principles of Self-determination of Peoples and Territorial Integrity, as Well as the Problems of Recognition], *Gosudarstvo i pravo* (2010), no. 10, 101–4.

Velyaminov, G.M. 'Воссоединение Крыма с Россией: правовой ракурс' [The Reunification of Crimea with Russia: Legal Perspective], *Gosudarstvo i pravo* (2014), no. 9, 12–18.

Velyaminov, G.M. (Alexander Trunk transl.). 'Wiedervereinigung der Krim mit Russland—eine Skizze aus russischer Sicht', *Kieler Ostrechts-Notizen* 18/19 (2014/2015), no. 1/2, 10–14.

Vidmar, Jure. 'The Annexation of Crimea and the Boundaries of the Will of the People', *German Law Journal* 3 (2015), 365–83.

Vitzthum, Wolfgang Graf. 'Russland und das Völkerrecht', *Archiv des Völkerrechts* 65 (2016), 239–60.

Voronin, E.R., Kulebyakin, V.N., and Nikolaev, A.V. 'Государственный переворот в Киеве в феврале 2014 г.: международно-правовые оценки и последствия' [The Coup d'État in Kyiv in February 2014: International Law Context and Consequences], *Moskovskiĭ zhurnal mezhdunarodnogo prava* 97 (2015), no. 1, 11–28.

Vylegzhanin, A.N. and Sokolova, E.L. 'Приобретательская давность в международном праве' [Prescription in International Law], *Moskovskiĭ zhurnal mezhdunarodnogo prava* 94 (2014), no. 2, 37–58.

Vyshinsky, A.Y. 'Тезисы по международному праву' [Theses on International Law], *Sovetskoe gosudarstvo* 7 (1938), no. 5, 119–22.

Vyshinsky, A.Y. 'Международное право и международная организация' [International Law and International Organisation], *Sovetskoe gosudarstvo i pravo* 10 (1948), no. 1, 1–24.

Vyshinsky, A.Y. 'О некоторых вопросах теории государства и права' [On Some Questions of the Theory of State and Law], *Sovetskoe gosudarstvo i pravo* 10 (1948), no. 6, 1–17.

Walter, Christian. 'Postscript: Self-determination, Secession, and the Crimean Crisis 2014', in Christian Walter, Antje von Ungern-Sternberg, and Kavus Abushov (eds), *Self-determination and Secession in International Law* (Oxford: Oxford University Press, 2014), 293–312.

Waters, Christopher. 'Rule of Law in the Secessionist States', in Christopher Waters (ed.), *The State of Law in the South Caucasus* (London: Palgrave Macmillan, 2005), 59–80.

Waters, Christopher. 'South Ossetia', in Christian Walter, Antje von Ungern-Sternberg, and Kavus Abushov (eds), *Self-determination and Secession in International Law* (Oxford: Oxford University Press, 2014), 175–90.

Whelan, Anthony. 'Self-determination and Decolonization: Foundations for the Future', *Irish Studies in International Affairs* 3, no. 4 (1992), 25–52.

Whelan, Anthony. 'Wilsonian Self-determination and Versailles Settlement', *International & Comparative Law Quarterly* 43 (1994), 99–115.

Williams, Brian Glyn. 'Hidden Ethnocide in the Soviet Muslim Borderlands: The Ethnic Cleansing of the Crimean Tatars', *Journal of Genocide Research* 4 (2002), 357–73.

Wright, Quincy. 'Intervention, 1956', *American Journal of International Law* 51 (1957), 257–76.

Wydra, Doris. 'The Crimean Conundrum: The Tug of War Between Russia and Ukraine on the Questions of Autonomy and Self-determination', *International Journal on Minority and Group Rights* 10 (2003), 111–30.

Zadorozhnii, Oleksandr. 'To Justify against all Odds: The Annexation of Crimea in 2014 and the Russian Legal Scholarship', *Polish Yearbook of International Law* 35 (2015), 139–70.

Ziemele, Ineta. 'The Role of State Continuity and Human Rights in Matters of Nationality of the Baltic States', in Tālavs Jundzis (ed.), *The Baltic States at Historical Crossroads: Political, Economic, and Legal Problems and Oppurtinities in the Context of International Cooperation at the Beginning of the 21st Century* (Riga: Academy of Sciences of Latvia, 2001), 248–71.

Zokhrabyan, R.P. 'Принцип равноправия и самоопределения народов: эволюция содержания в системе принципов международного права' [The Principle of Equality and Self-determination of Peoples: Evolution of the Content in the System of Principles of International Law], *Vestnik Moskovskogo universiteta. Pravo* (2009), no. 2, 61–73.

Zokhrabyan, R.P. 'Формы реализации права народов на самоопределение в международном праве и доктрине' [Forms of Realisation of the Right to Self-determination in International Law and Doctrine], *Vestnik Moskovskogo universiteta. Pravo* (2010), no. 2, 75–85.

Multimedia Resources

American Society of International Law. '2014 Annual Meeting Videos: Is International Law Effective? The Case of Russia and Ukraine', Washington, D.C., 9 April 2014, https://www.asil.org/resources/2014-annual-meeting-videos.

Center for Polish-Russian Dialogue and Understanding. 'Conferences and Seminars: The Case of Crimea in the Light of International Law: Its Nature and Implications', Warsaw, 19–20 March 2015, http://cprdip.pl/en,events,conferences_and_seminars,61,the_case_of_crimea_in_the_light_of_international_law_its_nature_and_implications.html.

Diplomatic Academy of the Russian Ministry of Foreign Affairs. 'Круглый стол на тему: «Международно-правовые аспекты присоединения Крыма к России»' [Round Table: International Legal Aspects of the Integration of Crimea into Russia], 10 April 2014, https://www.youtube.com/watch?v=4k620BZKyto.

Diplomatic Academy of the Russian Ministry of Foreign Affairs. 'Лекция Черниченко: Нерешенные проблемы международного права' [Chernichenko Lecture: Unresolved Problems of International Law], 14 November 2014, https://www.youtube.com/watch?v=T7ohudXoXU8.

Kapustin, Anatoly. 'В поисках системного понимания международного права: взгляд из России' [A Systemic Understanding of International Law: The Russian Perspective], UN Office of Legal Affairs, Audiovisual Library of International Law, 2017, http://legal.un.org/avl/ls/Kapustin_IL_video_1.html.

Kondrashov, Andrei. 'Crimea: Path to the Homeland', 2015, https://www.youtube.com/watch?v=3Mw4Y9jRwCQ.

Index

For the benefit of digital users, indexed terms that span two pages (e.g., 52–53) may, on occasion, appear on only one of those pages.